Zhong Guan Village

NING KEN

Translated by
James Trapp

ACA

Published by
ACA Publishing Ltd.
University House
11-13 Lower Grosvenor Place
London SW1W 0EX, UK
Tel: +44 (0)20 3289 3885
E-mail: info@alaincharlesasia.com
Web: www.alaincharlesasia.com

Beijing Office
Tel: +86 (0)10 8472 1250

Author: Ning Ken
Translator: James Trapp

Published by ACA Publishing Ltd arrangement with
China Translation & Publishing House

Chinese language copyright © 中关村笔记 *(Zhong Guan Cun Bi Ji)* 2017, Ning Ken

English translation text © 2022 ACA Publishing Ltd, London, UK

ALL RIGHTS RESERVED. NO PART OF THIS PUBLICATION MAY BE REPRODUCED IN MATERIAL FORM, BY ANY MEANS, WHETHER GRAPHIC, ELECTRONIC, MECHANICAL OR OTHER, INCLUDING PHOTOCOPYING OR INFORMATION STORAGE, IN WHOLE OR IN PART, AND MAY NOT BE USED TO PREPARE OTHER PUBLICATIONS WITHOUT WRITTEN PERMISSION FROM THE PUBLISHER.

The greatest care has been taken to ensure accuracy but the publisher can accept no responsibility for errors or omissions, or for any liability occasioned by relying on its content.

Hardback ISBN: 978-1-83890-020-5
Paperback ISBN: 978-1-83890-532-3
eBook ISBN: 978-1-83890-533-0

A catalogue record for *Zhong Guan Village: Tales from the Heart of China's Silicon Valley* is available from the National Bibliographic Service of the British Library.

CONTENTS

Foreword	v
PART ONE	1
1. FENG KANG'S PLAN (1)	2
Diary Note 1: A Silent Cornerstone	20
2. FIRST MAN	24
Diary Note 2: Serendipity	44
3. THE PULL OF THE FUTURE	47
Diary Note 3: Time	71
4. TILTING AT WINDMILLS	73
Diary Note 4: Volcano	81
PART TWO	83
1. LENOVO CHINA (1)	84
Diary Note 5: History	104
PART THREE	106
1. FENG KANG'S PLAN (2)	107
Diary Note 6: The Feng Kang School	126
2. MS—2401	128
Diary Note 7: A Different Kind of Generational Knowledge	142
3. THOUSAND YEARS	145
Diary Note 8: The Thousand-Year Installation	185
PART FOUR	187
1. LENOVO CHINA (2)	188
Diary Note 9: All the Shadows	206
2. WANGMA	209
Diary Note 10: The Essence of Chinese Characters	215
3. FENG WUKUAI	218
Diary Note 11: The Spirit of the Lowest Rung	224
PART FIVE	227
1. FENG KANG'S PLAN (3)	228
Diary Note 12: A Bronze Statue Forever Upright	246
PART SIX	248

1. LENOVO CHINA (3)	249
Diary Note 13: MOUNT TAI	269
2. KV300	272
Diary Note 14: Illness and Creativity	280
3. INTERNET	283
Diary Note 15: Shades of Yesteryear	292
PART SEVEN	297
1. LENOVO CHINA (4)	298
Diary Note 16: 'Potential'	307
2. FINGERPRINTS OF ALL CREATION	311
Diary Note 17: New Generation Man	319
3. GARAGE CAFÉ	321
Diary Note 18: ZHONGGUANCUN, BEIJING	344
4. SHARING OR ENJOYING TOGETHER	348
Diary Note 19: Entrepreneurship and Innovation Unstoppable	384
AFTERWORD	387
APPENDIX *CHRONOLOGY OF MAJOR EVENTS IN ZHONGGUANCUN*	389
APPENDIX *INDEX OF PEOPLE*	405
Endnotes	418
About the Author	423
About the Translator	424

FOREWORD

"Why do you want to climb mountains?"

"Because they are there."

This was the famous reply of George Mallory; it is a mountaineer's reply, and its fame resides in the fact that it sounds rather nonsensical and is not really a reply at all. Why do I want to write about Zhong Guan Village (Zhongguancun)? When I come to think about it, my reply now is very similar: because it is there. For many years now, Zhongguancun has been familiar territory to me, but at the same time, unfamiliar. When I don't really think about it, I think it is very familiar, but if I stop to consider, I find it is very strange to me. It is situated in the northwest part of Beijing, and when the weather is fine, especially after a spell of strong winds, and when I look towards it and the uplands beyond, I can actually see the Western Hills. At sunset, with the clouds aflame, the serried ranks of buildings and distant mountains under the magnificent red-tinted sky, and the light reflecting off walls of glass, themselves emitting their own light, have something of a science-fiction-novel quality about them. That is how it looks at a distance and the effect is even more pronounced up close.

It was in 2015 that I first got up close to it and traversed it. Before that, I clearly remember the day when I wrote in the margin of a book, "Leaving my obsession with literature was like going back to university and began on a plane to Mount Wuyi." That was on 21 April 2015, I was on a plane reading a book by Deborah Perry Piscione about Silicon Valley, called *Secrets of Silicon Valley: What Everyone Else Can Learn from the Innovation Capital of the World*. Such a book would never usually have been on my reading list, especially given my preference for modernist fiction. The two things are polar opposites. What do Kafka or Calvino have to do with Silicon Valley? (Actually, in truth, there are some connections). But there, in 2015, I suddenly decided to change. When someone has been at the end of one road for a long time, they look to find enlightenment at the end of another.

For almost twenty years I had been immersed in literature, immersed too deep, and soaked through so my nerves were raw from head to toe. I needed something else, something like Silicon Valley. At the beginning of the 1990s, I moved on from literature and turned from a poet into an advertising man. After five years, I returned to the altar of literature, and wrote an essay called *Death of a Traditional Scholar*. In it I wrote, "Turning away from literature and looking at it from the outside has been hugely beneficial to me." After that, I wrote five full-length novels in a row, and once again became a traditional man of letters.

While I was on the plane, I wrote, "When you enter into a new world, like the world of Silicon Valley, you rediscover the borders of literature; you stand on the other side of the border looking back at it, and it is as if you are looking at your old self." Because the mountain is there, because Zhongguancun is there, I wanted to read a different sort of book, I wanted to read Deborah Perry Piscione's *Secrets of Silicon Valley*. Right at the end of the book, surprisingly there is a mention of Zhongguancun and, although I had started a reading list about the place, I hadn't read it yet. Deborah Perry Piscione makes a comparison between Silicon Valley and Zhongguancun and, of course, she also talks about Israel's hi-tech zone, which she unquestioningly praises, while expressing doubts about Zhongguancun's credentials.

She says, "Reports on the ability of the rising giant of the East to become the new global hub of innovation are conflicted, however... The problem with Zhongguancun, however, is that it has substantial weaknesses. The immigrant talent pool is thin and the quality of life in Beijing is questionable. Chinese company Lenovo – with its headquarters in Zhongguancun, Beijing – is now poised to overtake one of the original Silicon Valley icons, Hewlett-Packard, as the largest PC maker in the world. Regardless, this would be the first time in the past several centuries that a Chinese company has been number one in a global technology sector. At the same time, Apple's fastest growing market for its innovative products is China itself, and Silicon Valley has itself moved on to other areas of dominance in search engines, social media and big data. It would seem that Chinese companies have overtaken the past of Silicon Valley, but not yet its future."

This was different from anything I had read before, two completely different contexts, but it reconfigured me, and I discovered this was what I wanted. Then I also read, "Amongst Silicon Valley entrepreneurs, the middle-aged and late middle-aged outnumber the young". And, even more surprisingly, Piscione goes on to say, "the most exciting entrepreneurs are between 55 and 64 years old." In 2015, I was just 56. In truth, it is often more meaningful to be always questioning than to be sure of everything: you see things more clearly, Zhongguancun's place in the world, for example. Piscione's estimation of Zhongguancun is, in fact, higher than mine. At that time, I didn't yet know that the world was debating whether Zhongguancun was already the new innovation capital of the world, and whether it was already one of the top three world centres for scientific and technological innovation.

All I knew was that Zhongguancun was a part of Beijing that had already hugely changed not just Beijing, but the whole of China too. It was there and, just like a mountain to a mountaineer, it was challenging me. If I wanted to change myself and leave literature, Zhongguancun was perfectly suited to the task. Consequently, and by necessity, first I had to understand Silicon Valley and its companies like Yahoo, Google, Cisco, Apple and Oracle, so I could examine, from an even greater distance, the world of literature and novels and their connection with the real world.

In the middle of that year, I gave an interview to *Fiction Monthly* in which they asked me what book I had read most recently. I replied that I was actually in the process of reading several non-fiction works simultaneously. One of them was Deborah Perry Piscione's *Secrets of Silicon Valley*, another was Ling Zhijun's *China's New Revolution 1980-2006: from Zhongguancun to Chinese Society*, and there was also Wu Xiaobo's *Thirty Years of Agitation*. All of these books were redirecting my attention away from literature.

After I had finished them, I began to frequent Zhongguancun, and when you enter a new world, if the internal workings of that strange world are unfamiliar to you, the external appearance is equally unfamiliar, no matter how many times you go there. Whether I drove or took the Metro, or rode my electric scooter, I gradually became part of Zhongguancun, and Zhongguancun became part of me. I would go past the big brown building of the Physics Institute of the Chinese Academy of Sciences to the Academy of Mathematics and Systems Sciences and the State Key Laboratories where I would admire the bronze statue that had already been erected to the mathematician Feng Kang. There I would listen to Feng Kang's colleagues and students discussing him, talking about events from many years ago. Many of these people were academics; in fact, I had never seen so many academics. In the Fang Zheng Building, I met Wang Xuan's secretary, visited his memorial hall and heard all about his life.

On the 18th floor of the Raycom Infotech Building, I met Liu Chuanzhi; on Creativity Avenue, I met Wu Gansha; in the Garage Coffee Shop, I saw Su Yao; in Numeral Valley I saw Cheng Wei... I met so many people, and whereas a year before I hadn't even set foot in Zhongguancun, now I was going twice a week, or even three times. Zhongguancun's 'internal workings' are its people, every one of them deep wells of time, windows on history and, no matter that they are now youngsters in their 80s, they are like tunnels back through time. Indeed, Liu Chuanzhi, Wang Hongde, Wang Qizhi... all these old folk are treasure houses of time. I completely forgot about fiction and became an archivist and a thinker. Of course, I could always return to fiction and, indeed, could hope for it to be a different kind of return but that is another matter. What I want is for this sketchbook to be a homage to the Grand Historian, Sima Qian; a small and insignificant homage.

[PART 1]
Feng Kang's Plan (1)
冯 康 构 图(一)

Who is Feng Kang?

IT WAS MARCH 1960 in the cold snap of Spring before the snows in the north of China have thawed; one morning, a detachment of PLA soldiers wearing thick, padded winter uniforms, arrived in front of the Chinese Academy of Sciences Institute of Computing Technology on Zhongguancun's South Street. Not long ago, this place was arable land, but now it was the administrative area of the Chinese Academy of Sciences and the stretch of grey-coloured office buildings in the even broader expanse of fields formed a stand-alone futuristic street, with something of the flavour of a 'space city'. Previously, the bulk of the general scientific institutes had been scattered throughout the old city and the Institute of Computing Technology had operated on the fourth floor of the Xiyuan Hotel but in 1958 it became part of the 'space city'. The office building was very new but it didn't look it because of its grey colour; it was very understated and subdued, just like science itself.

The soldiers were not carrying weapons but satchels and briefcases and some of them were wearing glasses under their caps. Even though they were not carrying weapons and had a rather gentle refined air about them, there was something arresting about the sight of this detachment of soldiers. This was a place of science, undemonstrative and quiet, and the arrival of soldiers gave it something of the mysterious air of a base of military operations. If it had been only one or two soldiers, it would just have been a little tremor, not amounting to much, but with seven or eight, a detachment in fact, it was a demonstration of military power.

When the soldiers reached the third floor, they met the equally mysterious Feng Kang. Feng Kang was not a tall man, he was even a little hunched, but his gaze was calm and steady, almost indifferent, as he led the soldiers to the fifth floor. The sentry on the door once again individually inspected the soldiers' passes, photographs and letters of introduction, even more carefully than had been done at the entrance to the building. Feng Kang waited patiently, throwing an occasional glance out of the window. When the formalities were complete, he led the men to his own private office on the fifth floor. This was his office on the fifth floor; he had another on the third floor. The difference with this one was that it was entirely anonymous, with no nameplate, only the serial number 803, and no one knew what that signified. All the rooms on this floor simply had numbers, so there was no way of checking nameplates to find a particular room.

1. FENG KANG'S PLAN (1)

There was nothing distinctive about the interior of the room either, in fact you couldn't even tell what it was used for. This was the office of the top secret 123 Special Duties Unit (more simply known as Unit 123; it was a closely guarded secret as, indeed, was the whole fifth floor). The soldiers stood to attention as if they were back at their base, even more stiffly in fact; none of them sat down, and they stood there forming a semicircle. Feng Kang sat behind his desk, for all the world like a general, and asked things about their life at 'Base 21', like what they got to eat, although he was, in fact, exceeding his authority in doing so. Feng Kang was not a general, he was a mathematician, but in his eyes, they were pretty much the same thing.

He was already in charge of three sections, comprising seven sub-units, to which he had recently added Unit 123, but this remained a stand-alone, and was not incorporated into the hierarchy of the other units. The other seven units were all accommodated in a dozen or so rooms on the third floor. The stand-alone Unit 123 was on the fifth floor, so Feng Kang had two offices, one on each of the two floors. The men from the unit on the fifth floor had free access to the third floor, but other than Feng Kang, no one from the third floor could go freely up to the fifth. While he was in charge, the unit was on the receiving end of no inspections, but Feng Kang himself inspected the guards on sentry duty.

There were three small sub-groups within Unit 123 comprising one for calculations regarding fluid mechanics, one for aerodynamics and one for blast waves. Apart from these, the fifth floor was the computing centre, with two computers - Machines 103 and 104 – occupying two enormous rooms. This was one of the main reasons the fifth floor was so heavily guarded.

In fact, at the time, these were the only two computers in all of China.

Feng Kang took the soldiers to show them the computer rooms and divided the seven of them into three groups: one for guided missiles, one for atomic bombs and one for satellites. These soldiers from Base 21 were no ordinary soldiers and, apart from their uniforms, they were just like the university students recently assigned to the fifth floor. They were all new graduates from the top universities: Peking University, Tsinghua University and the PLA Military Institute of Engineering.

But since they were in uniform and had come from Base 21, they were genuine soldiers with not a thread out of place, their faces clearly marked by nature and weathered by wind and frost; the only oddity was that they all wore glasses. Because of their youth, their faces weren't tanned but were flushed red and glowing. After the departure of the Soviet experts, they had come to China's most exalted hall of mathematics, looking for the help of the mathematicians there. Their backs were ramrod straight, and their movements neat and precise as they threw the occasional reflex salute; they were deeply respectful to every teacher they met, model soldiers in every way. They had come there to work, to study and to accomplish the mission with which they had been entrusted. They were there representing not just themselves but the whole of Base 21.

Base 21 was one of the most mysterious military installations anywhere in the world. It was comparable to America's Area 51, the Soviet Union's Semipalatinsk-21, the UK's Maralinga, and France's Mururoa Atoll. It was under the administration of the Lop Nor Nuclear Testing Station, and was located at Malan, a place not identified on any maps of China at the time. Malan is to be found in Bayingolin Mongol Autonomous Prefecture's Hoxud County, five kilometres south of Wushitala Township. To the north are the foothills of the Tianshan Mountains, to the west is Lake Bosten, and to the east is the Lop Nor Nuclear Testing Site on the edge of the Gobi Desert. The whole thing started two years previously in August 1958 when the Central Military Commission appointed Zhang Yunyu as director of China's nuclear testing unit. In January the next year, Zhang accompanied Fang Yi, Director of the General Armaments Department, and Tang Kai, Director of the Military Engineering Planning Institute, on a flight from Beijing to the Gobi Desert in Xinjiang to conduct an aerial survey of the previously chosen site at Lop Nor and, on their return, to report on the progress of the nuclear site there. Once the Ministry of National Defence ratified the report and informed the Xinjiang military command, 0673 Division established a garrison in Xinjiang. They advanced into and occupied an empty area of land south of Wushitala township in Hoxud County. Although this land was uncultivable, with no vegetation, there were abundant underground springs and its location was eminently suitable: 250 kilometres to the east was the testing site, bordering on the Tianshan Mountains to the north and Lake Bosten 20 kilometres to the west. It was situated at a place in the Gobi Desert where there was a sparse growth of the herb called *malan* grass, and that was how it got its name: Malan. Within two years it had a hospital, a school, a guest house, an office block, dormitories, an assembly hall, a public square, a military social club, a motor vehicle repair shop, a military airfield and the poplars on either side of its arrow-straight roads had grown tall and straight too. This is how the world gained another military site, shrouded in secrecy.

The site was connected to the agreement on new technology for national defence signed between China and the Soviet Union in 1957 in which the Soviets explicitly undertook to provide China with the mathematical models and actual blueprints for an atomic bomb. The following year, China took on the responsibility for setting up in Beijing, the Second Mechanised Industrial Unit for the Production of Nuclear Weapons (Number 2 Mechanised Unit) and the Ninth Research Institute (Number 9 Institute). It was with this background that Base 21 was established. But within two years of this, in 1959, the Soviet Union informed China by letter that they were refusing to provide China with the mathematical models and technological information for the atomic bomb. They subsequently officially informed China that they had decided to withdraw all their atomic experts, and to cease provision of all technical equipment and resources. The full extent of China's impoverishment and backwardness was exposed. Its impoverishment needs no explanation, and its backwardness, in terms of expertise with atomic weaponry, lay in its lack of specialist scientists. With nowhere else to turn, Qian Xuesen recommended Guo Yonghuai to Qian Sanqiang.

Guo Yonghuai stepped up to leadership in this time of crisis and, along with Wang Ganchang and Peng Huanwu, in the teeth of the absence of the Soviet experts, formed China's very own 'troika' of atomic weapons research scientists. It was a pivotal moment and China was extremely fortunate to have these three men. However, none of the three were, in fact, atomic bomb specialists (no more was Feng Kang of the computing centre Room 3). Wang Ganchang was, however, a theoretical nuclear physicist, as was Peng Huanwu, and each had made outstanding achievements in their individual fields. Guo Yonghuai had held successively the posts of deputy director of the Institute of Applied Physics and Computational Mathematics, and deputy director of the Institute of Physics and Engineering. Despite leading work in the fields of mechanics and engineering, when he took on responsibility for the atomic bomb, the institute he headed had neither relevant blueprints nor data.

The Number 9 Institute's *raison d'etre* was as the computing centre for the Chinese Academy of Sciences so, by necessity, it was home to the republic's pre-eminent mathematicians. Where else was there to look since it is always the case that a country's scientific institutions provide the foundations for its development? To be completely accurate, what Number 9 Institute gave the Chinese Academy of Sciences was Room 3 which was tasked with large-scale calculations such as the blast radius of an atomic bomb which, being partly fluid dynamics, applied equally and inseparably to both atomic bombs and guided missiles alike. This was an extraordinary responsibility: even though Unit 123 had been specially selected from seven other units, and even though both of the only two computers in the whole country, Machines 103 and 104, were in the computing centre, none of the mathematicians had any relevant experience where atomic bombs were concerned, particularly their blast radius, and including the related fluid mechanics of guided missiles. What is more, most of the occupants of the centre were youngsters, some even younger than the soldiers who had arrived from Base 21, but even so, Room 3 took on the task under the professional guidance of Feng Kang.

Ao Chao graduated from the Mathematics Department of Peking University in 1958, and had been working at the Computer Centre for no more than two years when he was transferred to work on the heavily-guarded fifth floor, and by the time we are talking about he had already become a section leader in Unit 123. He still remembers now that although most of the people working in the Computer Centre had studied computing, and the centre had one huge room containing both Machine 103 and Machine 104, the computing capacity of these machines was limited to around 1,000 processing units and 1kb. Even after so many years, Ao Chao still remembers the massive size of these computers, and the innumerable punch cards. He says that a cell phone today is 4G and asks what that means in terms of size. He answers himself by saying that it is 4 to the 49th power, which means that the entire computing power of that huge room was only several hundred thousandths of a 4G cell phone. Number 7 Computer Unit, Number 2 Computer Unit and Number 2 Institute were sent a continuous stream of tasks concerning guided missiles, atomic bombs and even satellites. Ao Chao's little unit researched the blast radius of atomic bombs, their destructive power, defensive measures against them, and how to construct buildings that were proof against their blast, all of which were principally a matter of aerodynamics. However, it proved to be an exceptionally difficult task to calculate the blast radius relying solely on the computers they had in that room, and in the end they found themselves unable to make any progress.

Ao Chao's field was mathematical dynamics and although he was a section leader, he had never worked on atomic bombs before. There were other members of the section who had graduated in 1955, three years before Ao Chao, but their field was computing, and they had even less experience of atomic bombs. At that time, Feng Kang was engaged with the universally adopted 'finite element method', had no experience with atomic bombs and, indeed, had given the matter no thought at all. Fortunately, as a mathematician, Feng Kang was like a high-flying bird, the level of his knowledge allowed him to take an overview of several related matters. In his collection of essays called *Birds and Frogs*, the American mathematician and physicist Freeman Dyson wrote: "Some mathematicians are birds, others are frogs. Birds fly high in the air and survey broad vistas of mathematics out to the far horizon. They delight in concepts that unify our thinking and bring together diverse problems from different parts of the landscape. Frogs live in the mud below and see only the flowers that grow nearby. They delight in the details of particular objects, and they solve problems one at a time… Mathematics is rich and beautiful because birds give it broad vision and frogs give it intricate details."

Feng Kang was both a bird and a frog, and was able to consider the challenges of atomic bombs, guided missiles and satellites from a lofty mathematical viewpoint. In his youth, he had graduated from the Department of Physics at the National Central University where he majored jointly in Electronics, Physics and Mathematics. In his early fifties, he did advanced research in the Soviet Union under the great Soviet mathematician Lev Pontryagin. Some people say he was very similar in character to Pontryagin, which is to say that their talent determined that they both were high-minded and direct. Feng Kang was also a gifted linguist, fluent in English, Russian, French, German, Italian and Japanese. This meant that he could read almost anything he liked without the need for translation, so it was as if all the many foreign periodicals at the Academy of Sciences were written in the same language.

So it didn't matter that he started with no knowledge of atomic bombs, since he could read for himself the vast majority of foreign-language resources. Master Feng did his own research amongst the available resources and foreign periodicals, and then organised seminars to study and discuss them. In these seminars, he was like a military general directing the troops under his command. And he did, in truth, have troops to command: the soldiers from Base 21. He divided the various articles and sets of data amongst them, determining who should go off and read what.

This was how China's atomic bomb project was started from scratch. Ao Shao says, "If we hadn't had Master Feng at that time to get to grips with this project, there was no one else who could have done so. As a section leader it was beyond me, as I simply didn't have the knowledge. Master Feng had a broad field of vision because he was not just a mathematician, he understood physics and electronics as well, and he was good with foreign languages, not just one or two, but many. That is why later, during the Cultural Revolution, he was accused of being "a spy for seven foreign nations". There was no one else at the centre at the time who had a similar command of languages. How was it possible to learn so many languages from scratch? The truth is that at that time, this man, who was later to be called "a spy for seven foreign nations" read countless scholarly articles, but he did not necessarily read them in detail from start to finish. Rather he grasped the essence of them, skimming through for the essential points, so that he understood what it was they were saying, where there was something special, where there was something new, and where the innovation lay. Then he would pass all this on to the other members of Unit 123.

At the same time, Feng Kang's job on the 3rd floor was to direct the theoretical research work in Room 3 there in solving the most pressing problems facing the nation and, in addition, producing high quality academic papers on them. Amongst these, his work on *Research into differential methods of calculating numerical values for frictionless supersonic flow and the question of initial values* undoubtedly made significant breakthroughs, both theoretical and practical, and achieved considerable results. It produced a mass of relevant data for the Ministry of National Defence and, in particular, made an important contribution to China's fledgling aviation and space projects. At that time, the problem of calculating numerical values in this area was a widely recognised stumbling block internationally.

Another such problem was calculating the physics of nuclear reactors, and the need to resolve the Boltzmann equation. The difficulty of resolving these problems at that time was enormous, and it was Feng Kang's 'high-flying bird' approach to mathematics and mechanics that allowed him to establish differential equations from the principle of constants in integral calculus. It also enabled him to give specific guidance to Unit 123 in deriving a string of constant formats for resolving the Boltzmann equation, and to find success in practical calculations for the construction of an atomic bomb. He also carried out important research in the field of theoretical analysis and produced reliable data and mathematical models for China's prototype atomic bomb and plans for the first nuclear reactor on a submarine.

Feng Kang was directly responsible for research into the problem of finding a method for accurately calculating the problematic indeterminate constant of blast waves; for leading the problem-solving groups through research into practical computing; for summarising the particular characteristics of all the different methods and their adaptation to given circumstances, including selection of all the relevant parameters, and for taking the preliminary steps in finding ways and means, both practical and theoretical, for resolving all these kinds of problems.

He told his young soldiers, "The problem of blast waves can be looked at as a problem of fluid mechanics, and fluid mechanics can be addressed with partial differentiation equations. Partial differentiation equations are part of the science of mathematical equations. Such equations have hyperbolic form, elliptical form and parabolic form. The most important form where blast waves are concerned is the hyperbolic form, and calculating their final form is a question of mathematics. Computers can solve these problems if they are presented in algebraic form, and if they are not, the computers won't recognise them. Similarly, the differential is on a curve and is reciprocal; that reciprocity lies between the actual speed and the deceleration. If you divide the one into the other, the distance variation becomes the differential, and that can be put into algebraic form. Other than the differential equation method, there are also the physical simulation method and the special average convergence method. The problem with blast waves is that there can be a sudden hiatus. This is why we can use differential equations and differential resolution, as then the hiatus can be comparatively smoothed out. But if the differential is not that accurate, then the necessary precision is not achieved. If the length of the hiatus is short, the period of variability is necessarily also short and there is no problem." Feng Kang explored the general principle of calculating blast waves and all its ramifications in his seminars.

Fifty years later, Ao Chao said, "At that time, when it came to the atomic bomb, of course, we were not discussing actual construction, and the most important thing was to study what was being done in the USSR and the USA. That said, we were also putting great effort into feeling our own way forward. It also has to be said that it took a good many years' work, but from our original standing start, we gradually got closer to their developments, and later still, when we looked at them, we could see that the problems they were discussing were pretty much the same as the problems we were considering. It was not easily accomplished but in the end we were pretty much matching them step for step in the things we were working on."

At three o'clock in the afternoon on 16 October 1964, China exploded its first atomic bomb in the skies above Lop Nor from the remotely situated Base 21 at Malan. The Americans were alarmed, and the Soviets even more so. The Americans had constructed three atomic bombs in 1945, two of which were of the 'implosion model', and one was a 'gun-type' device. The bomb that exploded over Hiroshima was one of the implosion models, and the one over Nagasaki was the 'gun-type' device. The so-called 'implosion model' compressed the majority of its explosive force internally, generating high temperatures and enormous pressure, causing fission in the nuclear material it contained, and releasing a huge amount of nuclear energy. The difficulty with this method came immediately after the explosion when, if the energy was not completely channelled internally, but dissipated in all directions, atomic fission became impossible. Addressing this technological problem, Chinese scientists conducted innumerable theoretical calculations and practical experiments in Zhongguancun and at Base 21, at Jinyintan in Qinghai and at Lop Nor in Xinjiang, using small, medium and large-scale models, working both locally and nationally, and experimenting step by step until finally they succeeded in directing the entire blast internally. This breakthrough coincided with a worldwide crisis focused on technological advance. At the time, the soldiers from the computing centre were actually out at the site of the detonations, and were quite exceptional in seeing their task through from the 5th floor of the computing centre to Base 21 and even on to the Lop Nor testing range. They were fully aware who it was who had played the crucial role, and who it was who had taught them in class after class, explaining everything to them and showing them the way.

Moving forward to 1999, with the New China already established for fifty years, the back-room hero of that time long ago had disappeared into the abyss of time. The nation honoured 23 scientific and technological experts involved in China's production of two bombs, one atomic and one hydrogen, and one satellite. Amongst them, Deng Jiaxian, Yu Min, Wang Ganchang and Guo Yonghuai have long been well known to people. But there has been no mention of Feng Kang. The difference between him and the others was that even back then, he had an international reputation as a mathematician, and his most important success was not in the field of nuclear weapons; he was more comfortable as a back-room hero. Even so, during the award ceremony, the first holder of the post of Secretary to the Central Advisory Commission, Zhang Jingfu, did not forget Feng Kang and, as his immediate superior, was fully cognizant of everything about him. Once, when discussing the outstanding achievement in developing the 'Two Bombs One Satellite', he made particular mention of Feng Kang, calling him "another back-room hero; he made an outstanding contribution to the famous 109C computer that achieved such glorious success in the 'Two Bombs One Satellite' project and his computing methods had enormous impact."

This was only fair. Of course, this story of Feng Kang as a mathematician is far from complete, and although most of the stories about him are now nestling in the folds of history, history never stands still, and people always re-emerge from those folds.

1. FENG KANG'S PLAN (1)

Liujia Gorge

As the mighty Yellow River winds and coils its way eastwards, it makes a big turn back on itself at the Liujia Gorge, and in 1958 the Liujia Gorge Hydro-Electric Station commenced operation there. The reservoir at the Liujia Gorge was designed to have a water storage capacity of 5.7cu km, a figure never approached before. It has a surface area of more than 130sq km, and the dam is 147m high and 840m long. At the base of the dam are the generator buildings under which, in a huge turbine hall, is a row of five massive generator units with an overall generating capacity of 1,225MW. It was the first hydro-electric power generating station in China with a capacity of over 1,000MW. It was engineering on a scale hitherto unknown and presented problems incomprehensible to all but a few.

In the early spring of 1963, the deputy head of the Liujia Gorge Dam Planning Team, Master Engineer Zhu Zhaojun, braved the seemingly endless desert to make his way to Zhongguancun. When he saw the row after row of identical grey slab-like buildings, he felt greatly reassured. Although in the distance he could see a vast expanse of countryside and the place was cut off from the city, it was the very existence of that countryside that gave him a certain feeling of confidence in the nation. In Room Three of the Computer Centre of the Central Academy of Sciences Zhu Zhaojun met the scientists at work there and asked for their help in resolving the problems that had stopped work on the remote Liujia Gorge dam. In his office on the 3rd floor, it was Feng Kang, the man responsible for the high-speed computing projects for developing the atomic bomb, guided missile and satellite, who welcomed this traveller from afar.

When Feng Kang heard what was going on, he fetched Cui Junzhi from Number 3 Section, and gave that young man, later to become an academic himself, the task of coming up with specific solutions to the problems. He was like a general handing out his battle instructions or briefing a secret agent. Zhu Zhaojun explained to Cui Junzhi the 'crown bar method of calculating weight distribution' they were using on the construction site, and Cui Junzhi took detailed diary notes.

After he had seen Master Engineer Zhu Zhaojun off, Cui Junzhi himself braved the sandstorms of the western regions to arrive at Liujia Gorge. The magnificence of the Yellow River at the gorge was a different kind of scene through Cui Junzhi's eyes, and it was with a mathematician's gaze that he carefully surveyed every detail of the site. He realised that the coefficient ratio Zhu Zhaojun's 'crown bar method' produced for the construction of the dam was flawed, and the only thing to do was to abandon the method, go back to square one, and turn to the elimination of principle elements method to seek out and resolve the flawed sets of linear equations caused by 'the crown bar method'.

Although these flaws were easily resolved, when Cui Junzhi carried out stress checks on the computational results, he discovered that the localised stresses were all out of equilibrium. Consequently, Cui Junzhi developed a fundamental distrust of the 'crown bar method' of calculation and went on, with Cai Zhongxiong's assistance, to employ the standardised procedures of the stress function method written about by Huang Hongci and others, to carry out his computations. However, the results of these computations were still unable to restore equilibrium to the localised stresses.

The question of keeping stresses in equilibrium is a major one. It is both practical and theoretical, and causes problems worldwide. At that time they used a thirteen-point differential form of stress function computation to analyse the stresses on the dam, but the main reason they could not achieve satisfactory results was that the whole structure employed a square-grid pattern when, in reality, the borders of the dam could not fit properly into such a pattern. Recognising this point was of vital importance, it was Huang Hongci of the theoretical section in Room 3 of the computing centre who determined that the use of an incremental approach to the inner nodes meant there was no alternative to applying extrapolation and interpolation on the border nodes. The application of this kind of unintegrated, mismatched approach, however, was also the reason that the results of the computations were imperfect. And, quite apart from the method of computation, the limited memory storage of the computers themselves was also one of the major causes of difficulty in completing the calculations.

The Liujia Gorge Hydro-Electric Station was unlike any of the previous small-scale hydro-electric stations, and experience derived from their construction was of no use. At the same time that Cui Junzhi was at his wits' end with the calculations for the Liujia Gorge dam, Feng Kang pointed out to him an article in the computer centre's first annual report, which came as an instant revelation to Cui Junzhi. The article Feng Kang referred to in the report was by Prager and Synge and had appeared in a 1947 edition of the American *Applied Mathematics Quarterly*. Coincidentally, Prager had been Qian Weichang's academic supervisor when he was studying for his doctorate at the University of Toronto in Canada. Feng Kang introduced Synge as someone who had done outstanding work in the fields of applied mathematics and mechanics, and later become a fellow of the British Royal Society. Feng Kang's recommendation at that time had a decisive effect on Huang Hongci, Cui Junzhi and the others, as Feng Kang's thinking in the report on the use of the variational principle in incremental calculation directed the research paths of many young students.

Feng Kang's report had enormous repercussions and following it, a craze erupted amongst the men under Feng Kang's direction in Room 3, for the meticulous study and investigation of the incremental method. The youngsters all borrowed the Central Academy of Sciences Library's copy of a book written in 1960 by the two Americans Forsythe and Warsow, entitled *The Incremental Method of Solving Partial Differential Equations*. There are two chapters in it that deal with the calculation of elliptical equations and talk about the formating of variable increments. Huang Hongci, Cui Junzhi and the other youngsters in Room 3 greedily vied with each other to read this book. As there were no photocopying machines, they made a copy themselves and cut steel mimeograph plates, just as some poets of that period were also doing. In Beijing at that time, the two most active underground literary and artistic salons were the 'Poet X Society' set up by Guo Moruo's son Guo Shiying, and Zhang Langlang's 'Column of the Sun'; they both used steel mimeograph plates to print contemporary foreign poetry. In this connection, there was a kind of contemporary consistency, and mathematics often just like music also has a perfect harmony, a stratified elegance, a geometric aesthetic and an abstract beauty. The two disciplines are interconnected, and the ups and downs and variations of music are just like the serial and discrete forms of geometric variation.

The poet and mathematician Cai Tianxin says in an essay on poetry and mathematics that mathematicians and poets are our world's prophets who see and feel things before the rest of us. But whereas poets are by nature proud and aloof, and people think of them as vain and conceited, mathematicians are seen as refined and exceptional, and are admired from a respectful distance. In fact, Feng Kang's subsequent breakthrough in his research into the 'finite element method' was a product of imagination, exploration and inspiration. It was one man's trail-blazing inspiring others to set out on the road, it was one man opening up the way resulting in everyone else setting their course, seizing the opportunity and pursuing the hunt. So this too was a kind of poetry, not just in its content, but also in the passion with which everyone cut the steel plates and set about printing with them.

At the same time, under Feng Kang's planning and arrangements, several projects involving the atomic bomb and the guided missile reached their final stages. At that time, the 3rd and 5th floors remained separate and Feng Kang provided the link between the two with a certainty of command that allowed the two to run in parallel without conflict. On the one hand he explained the vital importance of the partial differentiation equation to guided missiles, and on the other, he divided the youngsters of the section working on the calculations for the dam into three groups so they could progress systematic research into the subject from three different directions. Of the three sub-groups, one of the deputy leaders of Number 2 Group, Lin Zhongjie, led one in redrawing plans using the stress-function method to make the calculations; another deputy leader of Group 2, Wei Daozheng, led the second sub-group which took equilibrium equations as their starting point, and input the stress-contingency relationships into Lamé's equation to progress their calculations; Cui Junzhi was in this sub-group. The remaining sub-group was under the leadership of Chai Zhongxiong, and also contained Wang Jinxian. They took the variation principle as their starting point and moved straight to using the displacement vector difference quotient instead of the difference vector derivative in their calculations.

These three sub-groups were like the movements of a concerto, or a three-stanza poem. They had regular communications and rehearsals of their progress and reported to their conductor, Feng Kang. And Feng Kang, like the great Herbert von Karajan, conducted the tone and pitch of the whole ensemble. In order to be absolutely certain of the equilibrium of stresses across every part of the internal structure of the dam, Cui Junzhi and the recently recruited Wei Xueling used the integral conservation of difference format derived from Lamé's equation, as so often mentioned by Feng Kang; they adopted an irregular rectangular grid for the interior, with a triangular grid at the edges, thus ensuring that all the nodes occurred in the interior or at the edges of the dam.

In the spring of 1964, actually on the day before the successful detonation of the atomic bomb, dividing the work between them, Cui Junzhi and Wei Xueling came up with a new set of calculations for the dam using the results obtained by employing the integral conservation of difference format. After the most meticulous checking of the stresses, not only did they succeed in achieving fundamental equilibrium at the nodes around the edges of the dam, they also achieved the same for the stresses at every part of the interior. This was of crucial importance, and it was like them producing a practically flawless musical performance. For the first time, Feng Kang indicated his approval to the young fellows in those subgroups, and also to the youngsters on the 5th floor, where all the calculations over the blast wave radius were complete, and all they were waiting for was for the mushroom cloud to rise into the sky.

The construction team at the Liujia Gorge Reservoir were delighted with the results of the calculations, and work now continued there. Cui Junzhi made important corrections to the original computer programmes that he and Wei Xueling had collaborated on, using a standardised data format, and produced the first standard programme for plane stresses – all on Computer Model Number 104 in the computing centre. In the same year, he also created a similar programme for Computer Model Number 119. It was by using these two programmes that he produced the new plan for the Liujia Gorge project. All this time, research continued, with Cui Junzhi and Wang Jinxian working together. They used both the format based on integral conservation of difference and the format based on the principle of variational difference; proceeding in that way they discovered that the difference formats at the edge nodes were identical – indeed they were also identical with those later obtained using the finite element method. Where the difference formats at the internal nodes were concerned, they optimised the data compilation to obtain the best difference format possible at that time. Based on these difference formats, Cui Junzhi, Wang Jinxian and Zhao Jingfang collaborated to produce a computer programme for the standardised analysis of plane stresses to use with Computer Model 109-B. With this, they carried out plane stress analysis on another different type of structural engineering project. By May Day in 1964, after working night and day, barely stopping to eat, they completed their systematic analysis of the calculations for the Liujia Gorge Reservoir. Consequently, under the baton of its conductor, Feng Kang, the first concerto of the Finite Element Method Suite, the Practical Concerto, proved a huge success.

The Finite Element Method

If things had stopped at this point, the value of China's independent success in researching the 'finite element method' and establishing its theoretical basis might have disappeared forever under the reinforced concrete of Liujia Gorge Hydro-Electric Station Dam, and the world might never have heard of Feng Kang. He came to realise that the process for the overall planning of the Liujia Gorge Reservoir was far from straightforward but, relying on his global 'high-flying bird' overview, there were a few elements that could be grouped together for thorough investigation and taken to the next level. But this was something only he could do, just as only a general can take full control of a military campaign.

At this time, Feng Kang worked alone, and he had to do so, just as all great generals also have to occupy the most lonely and remote of positions. Link by link, he slowly fashioned his report. In the course of doing so, he discovered the previously undiscovered, but in the end he still found a method of calculation that already resided in the reinforced concrete, for completely resolving the boundary value problem of the partial differential equation, and also a way of using the variational principle to carry out the calculation of the difference: by dissecting the interpolation, and creating the functional scope for fragmenting the polynomial function, he found the solution to the partial differential equation.

This was what later became the famous finite element method although, at the time, Feng Kang called it 'difference schemes based on the variational principle'. At the time, this discovery shook the world of computational mathematics. In May 1965, the National Computing Conference was held in Harbin and Feng Kang presented a report on these 'difference schemes based on the variational principle'. This report was then published in 1965 in issue 4 of the periodical *Applied Mathematics and Computational Mathematics*, entitled *Difference Formats Based on the Variational Principle*.

This outstanding treatise uses profound mathematical theory, applied to an extraordinarily wide range of circumstances, to prove the convergence and stability of the difference schemes based on the variational principle, and establish a firm framework for the finite element method. It also provides the same method with a reliable theoretical basis for its practical application and meant that Western mathematicians acknowledged that the standard for the finite element method was first established by a Chinese mathematician. But following the Cultural Revolution, this was not talked about for many years until 1981, after Deng Xiaoping's reform and opening up of China to the rest of the world.

In 1981, the French mathematician Jacques-Louis Lions, who was to be both the president of the International Mathematical Union (IMU), and president of the French Academy of Sciences, visited China and expressed the highest respect for Feng Kang and his team's important 1965 discovery of the finite element method. In the same year, Lions told the IMU, "The significance of Feng Kang's finite element method is enormous; independently of the rest of the world, Chinese mathematicians established this method, and this achievement stands in the first rank of world discoveries. Its contribution is shared by the whole of mankind."

In 1982, Feng Kang and Li Wengsi jointly presided over the China-France Finite Element Method Symposium, where Feng Kang and his student Yu Dehao jointly presented their paper *The regular integral equation for ellipse boundary value and its numerical solution*. This was one of the two most important papers presented at the China-France Finite Element Symposium. In the same year, Feng Kang received a special invitation to deliver a 45-minute paper at the International Congress of Mathematicians (ICM) entitled *The finite element method and natural boundary normalisation*. The ICM is an opportunity for mathematicians to exchange, demonstrate and discuss developments in mathematics, to meet up with old friends and make new ones. It is held every four years. The first congress was held in Zurich, Switzerland in 1897, and it has only been interrupted by the two World Wars. It is one of the highest-level scientific conferences held worldwide.

The lowest number of mathematicians that ever attended was 208, and the highest 4,000 but each time the congress invites distinguished mathematicians to deliver 45-minute academic papers away from the main body of the conference. In international mathematics circles, it is considered that in the decades after Feng Kang established his research into the finite element method, with extensive participation by mathematicians from the Czech Republic (as represented by I. Babuska), the US (as represented by J. Douglas and J. Bramble), France (as represented by P. Ciarlet and P. Raviat), Italy (as represented by F. Brezzi) and many other countries, he was ultimately able to confirm the approximation properties and approximation accuracy of the finite element method, its relationship between size and polynomial order, and thereby make a qualitative leap in the overall method. In the course of these studies, distribution theory, Sobolev spaces, the Hilbert space method for partial differential equations and other modern mathematical theories all had important uses. What is beyond question is that the discovery of the finite element method elevated Feng Kang into the worldwide pantheon of mathematical masters.

In 2006, Professor of Mathematics at Oxford University, Nick Trefethen, wrote in his analysis *Numerical Values* a millennial review of the development of computational mathematics and in the list of major achievements, the first section is "263 AD, Gaussian elimination, Liu Hui, Lagrange, Gauss, Jacobi". The ninth section is "1943, finite elimination method,

Courant, Feng Kang, Clough". So, after Liu Hui, the next Chinese name is Feng Kang.

Additionally, according to Dieudonné's *Panorama of Pure Mathematics* and the *Iwanami Sūgaku Jiten* (*The Encyclopaedic Dictionary of Mathematics*), and the comprehensive quantitative analysis of the *Ranking of 20th Century Mathematicians*, there are only seven Chinese (including American overseas Chinese) in the first 200 names. These are Shiing-shen Chern, Hua Luogeng, Feng Kang, Wu Wenjun, Zhou Weiliang, Shing Tung-yau and Xiao Yintang. In 2002, when the quadrennial International Congress of Mathematicians was held in Beijing, the then chairman of the IMU, Jacob Palis, said at the opening ceremony, "The ground-breakers and nurturers of this mighty tree that is Chinese science and mathematics are Shiing-shen Chern, Hua Luogeng and Feng Kang; they also include Gu Chaohao, Wu Wenjun and Liao Shantao. More recently there are also Shing Tung-yau and Tian Gang."

On 17 August 1993, Feng Kang died as a result of a fall in his bathroom. His death shook the international world of mathematics. Professor Peter Lax, the famous US scientist, former scientific adviser to the US president and director of the American Center for Atomic Energy Computational and Applied Mathematics, wrote an article dedicated to the memory of Feng Kang. In it he said, "Feng Kang, China's leading applied mathematician, died suddenly on 17 August, in his 73rd year, after a long and distinguished career that had shown no sign of slowing.

"Feng's early education was in electrical engineering. physics and mathematics, a background that subtly shaped his later interests. He spent the early 1950s at the Steklov Institute in Moscow. Under the influence of Pontryagin, he began by working on problems of topological groups and Lie groups. On his return to China , he was among the first to popularise the theory of distributions.

"In the late 1950s, Feng turned his attention to applied mathematics where his most important contributions lie. Independently of parallel developments in the West, he created a theory of the finite element method. He was instrumental in both the implementation of the method and the creation of its theoretical foundation using estimates in Sobolev spaces. He showed how to combine boundary and domain finite elements effectively, taking advantage of integral relations satisfied by solutions of partial differential equations. In particular, he showed how radiation conditions can be satisfied in this way. He oversaw the application of the method to problems in elasticity as they occur in structural problems of engineering.

"In the late 1980s, Feng proposed and developed so-called symplectic algorithms for solving evolution equations in Hamiltonian form. Combining theoretical analysis and computer experimentation, he showed that such methods over long periods are far superior to standard methods. At the time of his death, he was working on extending this idea to other structures.

"Feng's significance for the scientific development of China cannot be exaggerated. He not only put China on the map of applied and computational mathematics through his own research and that of his students, but he also saw to it that the needed resources were made available. After the collapse of the Cultural Revolution he was ready and able to help the country build again from the ashes of this self-inflicted conflagration. Visitors to China were deeply impressed by his familiarity with new developments everywhere.

"Throughout his life, Feng was fiercely independent, utterly courageous and unwilling to knuckle under to authority. That such a person did survive and thrive shows that even in the darkest days, the authorities were aware of how valuable and irreplaceable he was.

"In Feng's maturity the well-deserved honours were bestowed upon him - membership in the Academia Sinica, the directorship of the Computing Center, the editorship of important journals, and other honours galore.

"By that time his reputation had become international, many remember his small figure at international conferences, his eyes and expressive face radiating energy and intelligence. He will be greatly missed by the mathematical sciences and by his numerous friends."

But, who was Feng Kang? There aren't many people who can answer that now. For a world-renowned mathematician, he was a man of mystery in China and this has left something of a blank for posterity.

Yet, in a very small way, his story is still alive. The award of the Nobel Prize to the Chinese scientist Tu Youyou provoked much general discussion, and in a small corner of the internet, someone posted the question: who was the greater mathematician, Hua Luogeng or Feng Kang? The post went on, "When I read Mr Chen An's article *Who was the greater master, Hua Luogeng or Feng Kang?* I decided to join in, not to take sides but just for the sake of debate. What is innovation? To be quite honest, before this I really hadn't understood what innovation meant, but when I read Master Liao Junlin's essay *Tu Youyou bears witness to the deep-rooted flaws of the Chinese educated classes* I received a very forthright education in the matter. Innovation means creating something out of nothing, it means finding hidden treasure whilst wandering in the wilderness. From this view of innovation, Master Feng Kang's invention of the finite element method and its practical applications has very few rival pieces of work that stand comparison with it at that time. So, does everyone understand what the answer to the question is now? To properly understand science, you have to know what is at its very core; that is the real meaning of innovation and the role it plays."

Someone replied, "Hua Luogeng's followers have spread worldwide and into almost every field of mathematics. One could even say that it is thanks to the efforts of Hua Luogeng and his followers that Chinese mathematical research got off to such an excellent start and delved so deeply into so many fields. In mathematics departments everywhere, many of the distinguished academics are Hua Luogeng's students. Feng Kang was also a man of exceptional talent. He alone was responsible for establishing the finite element method of calculation in the West; in modern times its use has spread across the whole world, and in China it has influenced many different fields. Master Hua Luogeng's mathematics do not have the same breadth of use; in fact, the same can be said of the uses of number theory as a whole and many kinds of complex variable functions. If I had to choose just one mathematical master, I would find I couldn't because the two men are great in different ways, but it is greatness nonetheless."

This is a perfectly fair assessment.

DIARY NOTE 1: A SILENT CORNERSTONE

> The scientists of Zhongguancun have an indissoluble bond with the 'Two Bombs One Satellite' project, but they are mostly unsung heroes, as is Feng Kang. Back then, the Chinese Academy of Sciences took on a string of crucial scientific and technological projects as part of the development of the atomic bomb and guided missile which included theoretical analysis, scientific experiments, action plans, research that extended to every kind of specialised new materials, components, apparatus and equipment. The creation of the satellite, from design to proposal, was all seen to completion by the Chinese Academy of Sciences. In 1999, Zhang Jingfu wrote in an article that the research team from the Chinese Academy of Sciences that worked on the 'Two Bombs One Satellite' project comprised more than 3,000 people, a full two-thirds of all the academy's research personnel. The site of the field

1. FENG KANG'S PLAN (1)

observation of the first atom bomb test importantly was also the responsibility of the academy's Geophysics Institute, Mechanics Institute, Physics Institute, Acoustics Institute, Optical Instrument Institute and other establishments. Along with the Nuclear Test Base Research Institute, they agreed the technical solutions to every one of the 15 measurement systems involved.

The President of the Chinese Academy of Sciences at the time, Zhang Jingfu, wrote in an article in the 6 May 1999 edition of the *People's Daily*, entitled *Let us ensure that history records the memories of the people from the Chinese Academy of Sciences who worked on the 'Two Bombs One Satellite' project*, "The real heroes of the 'Two Bombs One Satellite' project, other than those scientists I have already mentioned who had such a profound influence on me, are also some scientists from different fields of study who also made contributions, some of them of very great importance. There are, for example, Wang Ganchang, the renowned physicist from the Atomic Power Institute, the physicists Peng Huanwu and Zhu Hongyuan, and the mathematicians from the Scientific Institute, Guan Zhaozhi and Feng Kang. Let us ensure history remembers them!" That's right! History should remember them, and Zhongguancun should remember them too. How could a book about Zhongguancun omit them? They were the people who laid the foundations for today's Zhongguancun.

The fundamental concept of Zhongguancun cannot be restricted to its status as a new, high-tech industrial park with a host of celebrity entrepreneurs; quite the opposite, in fact, as today's Zhongguancun should never forget the obscure and forgotten men who are its foundation, a foundation as solid as the strata of rock beneath this Earth. Without this bedrock, Zhongguancun would have found it impossible to become the high-rise forest it is today, the symbol of the success not just of Beijing but of the whole of China. Despite his vital contribution to the atomic bomb project, the great mathematician Feng Kang never considered himself any kind of backroom hero and he didn't even mention it in his own academic CV. Of course, the 'Two Bombs One Satellite' project was only a part of Feng Kang's work, and the most important aspect was his outstanding ability as a mathematician and the way he formed the 'troika' of Chinese mathematicians along with Hua Luogeng and Shiing-shen Chern. The American overseas Chinese mathematician and Fields Medal recipient, Shing-Tung Yau, says, "There are three reasons modern Chinese mathematics has been able to outstrip, or at the very least stay on a par with the West. One is Shiing-shen Chern's work on characteristic class; another is Hua Luogeng's work on the functions of several complex variables; and the third is Feng Kang's work on the finite element method."

If we accept that Feng Kang's dedication to the 'Two Bombs One Satellite' project has remained a secret all this time, and is the 'silent cornerstone' of Zhongguancun, then the same is even more true of the people I interviewed from the Chinese Academy of Sciences Computing Centre: Qin Mengzhao, Shao Yuhua, Zeng Jirong, Liu Yinquan and Ao Chao. Under Feng Kang's direction, they carried out top-secret computations for the atomic bomb, the guided missile and the satellite, whilst at the same time continuing their own personal fields of research. Master Qin Mengzhao collaborated with Feng Gang on 'Symplectic Algorithms of the Hamiltonian System' but, although he was Feng Kang's assistant all along, like the others, he doesn't say very much about it, as though he has acquired the habit of taciturnity, that same taciturnity that defines the bedrock.

But are not the Chinese Academy of Sciences and its scientists also the bedrock of the whole nation?

We must pay our respects to these foundations, recognising that they are both silent and dazzling.

They are the mica in the rock strata.

The First Man

第一人

A New Particle Gives Rise to a New World

1978, PRINCETON, NEW JERSEY.

A Chinese physics delegation visited America. It consisted of four people, amongst whom was the nuclear fission specialist from the Chinese Academy of Sciences Physics Institute, the man who was later to be called 'the founder of Zhongguancun', Chen Chunxian. Like the others in the delegation, for this visit Chen had bought the same style grey Western suit and the same leather shoes and then crossed the vast Pacific Ocean to visit what not long ago in China had been called the 'rotten and licentious' nation of the United States of America. After so many years of enforced seclusion, what was the outside world going to be like? As if part of a century-long cycle, one hundred years later, they were once again becoming the first people to go out and see the world.

The reason for the delegation's visit was to observe the testing of the Princeton Plasma Physics Laboratory's Tokamak Fusion Test Reactor, a type of circular magnetic confinement device. Not only did they want to compare the figures from the Princeton experiment against those from Beijing's Number 6 Tokamak Reactor, they also wanted to inspect the blueprints for the device in advance of the construction of China's Rmb40 million Number 8 Reactor to further explore mankind's nuclear energy capabilities through nuclear fusion. So, despite the cyclical element mentioned above, it is clear that this was a very different affair from a hundred years before.

At the Kurchatov Institute of Atomic Energy in Siberia in 1954, the Soviet Union's father of nuclear energy, Andrei Sakharov, had succeeded in producing plasma containment devices, which were known as Tokamaks. In 1968, a huge breakthrough was made using Tokamak Device T-3 in which the stability of plasma in a circular chamber was achieved at temperatures in excess of 10 million degrees Celsius. The following year, scientists from the Culham Centre for Fusion Energy in the UK conducted tests on the Soviet Union's T-3 device and confirmed the Soviet Union's great breakthrough. This caused a worldwide sensation and, one after the other, every country in the West began to build their own Tokamaks. In 1974, Chen Chunxian and his task force miraculously succeeded in developing China's own Number 6 Tokamak Reactor, breaking the Western developed nations' monopoly on nuclear fusion. It was with this success behind them that they went to visit the United States to observe and learn in a logical and rational way.

2. FIRST MAN

The renowned American Chinese research physicist, Samuel C.C. Ting, met the delegation and once observed, "The results of scientific experiments often go against people's original expectations, throwing up new particles and new worlds." Indeed this is true not only of scientific experiments, but many other things as well: the accidental determines the inevitable, and something apparently entirely unrelated can change the whole aspect of something else. Just like a new particle giving rise to a whole new world, in the course of his visit to America, the thing that made the deepest impression on Chen Chunxian was not the advanced laboratory or the Makalov, but the explosive power of scientific research. He noticed that the first Makalov and the first man-made satellite were both successes of the Soviet Union, but it was America's father of nuclear fusion, Professor H.P. Furth and his research team, who developed their Makalov within a few months, surpassing the Soviet Union, and establishing a Makalov research centre for the Japanese, the Germans and the French. Subsequently, America's space programme also overtook the Russians, not just in launching satellites but in manned space flight and putting a man on the moon, thus surpassing the achievements of Yuri Gagarin. How did America manage this so quickly? In addition, Chen Chunxian also noticed that American research into nuclear fusion was carried out along both military and civilian lines, so that military discoveries also aided the development of civilian nuclear energy and promoted economic advances from the same mutual fountainhead. This greatly aroused Chen's interest and prompted a revelation.

It wasn't long before Chen Chunxian had a second opportunity to visit America, this time as a civilian reporter, giving him greater freedom of action as there was no one hosting him. Without the restrictions an official visit would have imposed, he could go where he liked and look at everything he wanted to see. The American friends he had made on his last visit opened many doors for him, and he felt free and relaxed. He paid closer attention to civilian facilities, visiting more than twenty cities and inspecting dozens of nuclear fusion laboratories. He met with many surprises, and these surprises changed him. For one thing, those laboratories' equipment was all manufactured by small companies, with no more than 100 employees at most and a dozen or so at the fewest.

"How can such small companies manufacture nuclear fusion equipment? In China it would take several thousand people!"

Chen Chunxian asked his friends, and they told him, "These are all new technology companies from America's new technology diffusion zones; the newer one is Boston's Highway 128 and the old one is San Francisco's Silicon Valley. They are home to several thousand new technology companies between them and comprise two different sets of people: in one are professors, engineers and university students who have technical skills and are responsible for production planning, research and development, manufacturing and sales. In the other set are venture capitalists, entrepreneurs, and people from the banking world, who have the money, and are responsible for providing the finances necessary to set up a new company. The magnetic superconductors our laboratory uses are made by the Permanent Magnet Company on Highway 128."

This all came as a great revelation to Chen Chunxian, who felt as though he had been transported into the future. After the closing down of his country and its subsequent opening up, all this was completely new to him. "Professors and university students running businesses?" If the Chinese were ordinary human beings, then the Americans were something else, and if it was the Americans who were the human beings, then the Chinese must be something else: the gulf between them was too great and their ways of thinking were too different for it to be otherwise. Chen Chunxian completely forgot the original reason for his visit, the Makalovs.

Makalovs were the old 'new', Silicon Valley and Highway 128 were the present.

Highway 128 made Chen Chunxian think of Beijing's Second Ring Road, and Zhongguancun had similarities with Silicon Valley in terms of its concentration of talent, but there was a clear difference: they were of different eras. That is to say, there was too great a 'time lapse' between them. Physicists are great thinkers, and their thinking often takes them out of the realm of physics. If China wanted to put itself on the same time footing, then it was Zhongguancun that held the key.

Chen first made a tour of Highway 128 and Silicon Valley. This great Chinese nuclear physicist brought about a nuclear fusion in himself, and just as Samuel C. C. Ting said that a new particle gave birth to a new world, a new thought gave birth to a new Chen Chunxian as his great brain underwent a structural change.

The forest of towering new high-tech company office buildings on either side of Highway 128 were the focus of Chen Chunxian's interest, and he found the Permanent Magnet Company that his friend had mentioned. Thom, the company boss, was a Dutch American, and a professor in the Physics Department of Boston University, so you could say that he and Chen Chunxian were of the same profession. Except that Thom, whilst still a physics professor, had opened the Permanent Magnet

Company to supply the American space agency. Chen Chunxian felt that this put Tom in a different era from him.

"I had the technical know-how and others had the money", Professor Thom told Professor Chen Chunxian. "It's that simple. We put the two together and were able to start production."

"Was it really that simple?" Chen asked disbelievingly.

"Absolutely."

"How many employees do you have?"

"Twenty or so, but our products are used in every nuclear fusion laboratory around the world. When we are particularly busy, we can always recruit extra temporary staff."

The conversation was short and simple, but the seismic effect it had on Chen Chunxian was far from either.

Highway 128 is a semi-circular highway in Boston, constructed before the Second World War. A number of research laboratories belonging to Massachusetts Institute of Technology (MIT) were situated there, and they spawned a few new-technology companies such as the Ion Company, the High Pressure Electricity Company and EG&G. Chen Chunxian absolutely understood that at that time, MIT encouraged its engineering teaching staff to form relationships with the private companies in the area. This not only allowed MIT teaching staff to seek the services of the private companies, but also encouraged them to go and open their own businesses. At the start of the revolution in micro-electronics technology, MIT and the federal government either set up venture capital companies or provided financial aid so that this area quickly grew into a recognised high-tech zone. In the 1960s, America invested $20 billion in its project to put a man on the moon, and in the course of the 'cold war' with the Soviet Union, they also invested many millions in weapons research and development. Although they led the world in the arms race, these massive investments didn't bring America any economic benefits, and it found itself losing the economic war with Japan and other countries around the world. Japanese automobiles, semiconductors, colour televisions and other products were best-sellers around the world, greatly disadvantaging similar American products. In order to reverse this negative position, America promoted Highway 128 and Silicon Valley's technology diffusion zones, and implemented supportive policies affecting taxes, venture capital and stock flotations, thereby encouraging the scientific researchers' companies to spread the new technology, so that the new-technology industries became the new growth node of the American economy.

This episode in history provides a very important viewpoint from which to observe the engine of America's economic development.

Chen Chunxian went back to Silicon Valley. This is situated in the north of California, in the southern part of the San Francisco Bay Area. From early on, it was famous for the design and production of silicon chips, and that is how it got its name. Subsequently other high-tech industries began to flourish, so that now, the name Silicon Valley has become a general reference to all kinds of high-tech industry. Silicon Valley is the foundation of America's electronics industry, and the world's best-known electronics centre. Already more than 1,500 computer companies have chosen it as their favoured location. Its strengths are the way it gets support from all the nearby universities that have strong research capabilities, such as Stanford, Berkeley, the California Institute of Technology and other world-famous institutions, and the way it uses small and medium-sized high-tech companies as its foundation. Moreover, it has Hewlett Packard, Intel, Apple, Cisco, Nvidia, Lucent and other major companies bringing together science, technology and manufacturing all in one place.

In Silicon Valley, Chen Chunxian was fascinated by the small companies formed by professors and university students. Stamford University's former principal Lyman was a visionary scientist, and back then he decided to rent out some plots of land on the campus to staff and students to set up high-tech companies, to encourage them into business and turn what they had learnt at university into productivity and products. There were two students who set up the first high-frequency oscillator in a garage. In another garage, the world's first microcomputer appeared in the hands of a youngster. As byproducts of these technologies, the garages of Silicon Valley later produced two companies famous around the world: Hewlett-Packard and Apple.

Chen Chunxian immediately set about trying to understand why it was that America's nuclear fusion experimentation was so efficient in such a short time. Before this, he had always thought that American experimental technology was very advanced, and the standard of its equipment manufacturing very high, but now he also understood the concepts of Boston's Highway 128, of the San Francisco Bay Area's Silicon Valley, of Stamford University and of technology diffusion zones. Finally, he understood the *Gestalt* system of "creating close ties linking factories, schools and scientific research institutes. The German word *gestalt* has the principal meaning of a coherent whole; that is the organic unity of disparate elements. This special characteristic was used in psychological research to form the *Gestalt* school of psychology, and in technology diffusion zones in the organisation of Highway 128 and Silicon Valley.

Scientists are logical people; logic signifies inevitability, and inevitability signifies action. Science is like this, and does not admit ambiguity.

First Chen Chunxian returned to Zhongguancun and re-examined this place he had previously been so familiar with. If it didn't have American ways, or Highway 128's and Silicon Valley's know-how, Zhongguancun would still be Zhongguancun, and maybe it would remain stuck in a rut; but if Silicon Valley could shine its light on it, then everything would be different. Chen Chunxian saw this previously static Zhongguancun begin to move; at least he saw it moving in his head. This is what interaction, departure and seeing the world do: it is only by seeing other people that you see yourself, recognise yourself and that self is often to be found in the illumination of others.

Not having any interaction is like not having a mirror, and this is just as much true of a nation.

In the reflection of a mirror, you see the differences in yourself, the similarities, the possibilities and the mutual influences.

Isn't this how history progresses?

Birth

There was a certain inevitability about Zhongguancun in the past. In October 1949, when the foundation of the People's Republic of China was being proclaimed at Tiananmen, the Gate of Heavenly Peace, and a huge crowd cheered their approval, Zhongguancun was genuinely still a village in the northwest of Beijing, and a very desolate sight. At that time, it consisted of no more than twenty or so households who farmed for a living, and the village clearly maintained its generational role in guarding its family graves. Its scattered buildings were all constructed next to their tombs. But the movement of history is like the tectonic shifts in the earth itself that can suddenly make the ground shift and bulge. A national review decided that, since Peking University and Tsinghua University were already situated not far to the north, a science city and university city should be built at the lonely spot that was Zhongguancun. With the encouragement of the government, university campuses sprang up, one by one, in the northwest of Beijing. Next to the narrow road, eight colleges swiftly emerged so that, later on, the narrow road came to be called College Road. In the second half of the 1950s, as well as the universities, the first research institute of the Chinese Academy of Sciences was built there; Zhongguancun's 'science city' and 'university city' had become a magnificent sight and were considered one of the world's greatest concentrations of talent and learning.

This was the first seismic shift. Could there be a second one?

Of course, Chen Chunxian's own thinking had not taken him that far; all he had observed was that the degree of concentration of talent in Zhongguancun was very similar to that of Silicon Valley, but the university professors and scientific and technical staff were very set in their ways and were content to remain in their ivory towers, discussing the results of their experiments and who should win which prize. When they achieved significant scientific or technological results, no matter how much money had been spent, or how high the costs had been, they didn't feel it was any part of their remit to consider whether the end product was affordable to the general public. It was all very 'un-*Gestalt*' and there was a very elitist attitude prevailing towards their results.

A new and changed man, Chen Chunxian returned to Zhongguancun as a mover and shaker. The nation was still licking its wounds from the Cultural Revolution; still not recovered from those 10 catastrophic years, and still struggling to free itself from the 'Two Whatevers', namely to uphold whatever policies Chairman Mao decided on and to follow whatever instructions he gave. His eyes full of the desolation after the disaster of the Cultural Revolution, and aware of a hundred things that urgently needed to be done, the new Chen Chunxian, like an alien visiting from a different planet, was already going on at length about Silicon Valley, Highway 128, Hewlett-Packard, Intel and An Wang; he talked about Professor Tomke's Perpetual Magnet Company, and about Steve Jobs and Apple. It was really quite something for him to be talking about Steve Jobs in 1979-1980, as Jobs himself had only signed the agreement setting up his computer company on the 1st April 1976. In April the following year, Jobs exhibited the Apple II computer at America's first computer fair. So Chen Chunxian was talking about Steve Jobs more than thirty years ago, many many years before most Chinese had even heard of him. So how did we get where we are today. In some ways, it all started with Chen Chunxian, and his progressive ideas certainly bear comparison with those pioneers of a hundred years previously. Of course, it is true that most of his colleagues didn't have the same opportunity to go to America and hear things previously unheard of, almost as though they came from another world. Chen

Chunxian said at the time, "We can be like that", but most people thought this was just the talk of a dreamer.

"These are not just dreams," he said. "The pool of talent we have here is just as good as can be found in Silicon Valley, Stamford and Highway 128. All we have to do is change our outlook and we can catch up and overtake them."

It was China's good fortune to have, at this crucial juncture, a pioneer like Chen Chunxian, a one-off who could change history. But at that time, no one believed him.

But what other people believed or not was not important; the important thing was to make key people believe. Such people were essential or history could not have been made. The China Association for Science and Technology, for example, showed a keen understanding of Chen Chunxian's different 'context' and asked him to write a report on his visit to America. On 23 October 1980, in a public lecture attended by several hundred people, Chen Chunxian delivered his report to a mixed audience of the young, the old and the middle-aged.

"I observed that the cutting edge of American science advances very quickly. The reason for the speed of this development lies in the exceptional pace with which new technology is commercialised. Scientists and engineers there have a strong pioneering spirit and are always eager to see their inventions, discoveries and technical know-how turned into commercial products. They go out themselves to borrow the capital and open joint-stock manufacturing companies. What really interests me is that, over there, there are already emerging industries with multi-billion-dollar output values. Many of us have been working in Zhongguancun for more than twenty years and, by comparison, the pool of talent here is no lower than those to be found in Boston and San Francisco; the fundamental quality is also comparable, and I feel that we have reserves that we have not yet touched. In the past, we developed lasers and, to begin with, we kept pace with America but now the gap is growing larger and larger. This is not something we can feel good about. We must change our attitude and make innovations in our processes."

In the course of the lecture, Chen Chunxian revealed a startling piece of news: he was going to set up a 'company' in Zhongguancun just like the ones in Silicon Valley and on Highway 128. Nor was this just idle talk and the irresistible logic of science made his fellow scientists shift into gear. The reason I have put 'company' in inverted commas is because he wanted to open it in the Physics Institute and applied to the authorities several times but always drew a blank in terms of response. On the one hand the brains of the authorities were working along different lines from Chen Chunxian's and they felt that the whole thing was an unrealisable fantasy. On the other hand, although they were swept up in Chen Chunxian's enthusiasm, they felt there was no way they could support the setting up of his company, since how could a research institute possibly run a company? It simply wasn't equipped for it.

Chen Chunxian's only option was to open a company outside the Physics Institute and he sought out the person in charge of the Science and Technology Advisory Department in Beijing, Zhao Qiqiu, to explore the possibilities. When Zhao heard what was going on in America, she was as excited as Chen Chunxian. Her mind buzzing with ideas, Zhao Qiqiu suggested that maybe they should hold back on the company idea for the moment and first write a full paper on the subject since what he had to say was so astonishing. Of course, this presented no problem for Chen Chunxian, who set about writing his report.

Women are both emotional and, at the same time, highly practical. These two factors often make them more efficient administrators than men; that is to say, they are less bound by bureaucracy. Zhao Qiqiu told Chen Chunxian, "Your thinking is very novel but, although I support you, setting up a company is very troublesome; you have to be able to register a barrel-load of capital, find premises for the retail side, the higher authorities have to give their approval to the Department of Industry and Commerce and only then can you get permission. I'm afraid you'll have trouble jumping through all those hoops. If you get blocked at any point, that puts the whole project in jeopardy, and it will take you a year, or half a year at the very least, to get all the necessary permissions."

Zhao Qiqiu understood business better than Chen Chunxian and what she said was no more than the truth.

Chen Chunxian had run into a very intransigent obstacle, one that was a product of the times, but once he had broken through the barrier of the era in general, the more specific barriers were bound also to melt away. Zhao Qiqiu came up with a plan for him: "What you want is not completely impossible. You are director general of the Plasma Physics Association, so you could set up a service department in the association which reports to you. That would be pretty much the same as setting up a company." Chen Chunxian was very grateful to Zhao Qiqiu and felt he could see a glimmer of light, like a crack appearing in a cast-iron plate. It was a crack that had been opened up for him by Zhao Qiqiu's extraordinary vision and administrative abilities.

When Chen Chunxian found his way blocked at that time, he needed a miracle-worker, and Zhao Qiqiu was that contemporary miracle-worker. After he had talked it over with a few like-minded people, Chen Chunxian settled on a name for the service department: the Beijing Plasma Physics Association Service Department for Advanced Technological Development, thus avoiding the word 'company'. Several months after this, when he had received the approval document from the Beijing Science and Technology Advisory Department, he had a circular official seal cut at the Public Security Bureau, opened a bank account, and that's how the 'company' was established. It was just a day like any other and no one knew just what was going to come from it. It was only later that people came more and more to realise that this was the birth of the Zhongguancun Company. The great Argentinian author, Jorge Luis Borges, once made a puzzling but very profound observation, "Often it is those who come after who bring about the biggest changes in those who came before." From this we can understand that it was the strength that Zhongguancun was to develop that allowed Chen Chunxian to make such big changes. Or, to put it another way, if Zhongguancun had not achieved its later rainbow-like grandeur, who would ever have remembered Chen Chunxian? If people now delve into Zhongguancun's history, they will work their way back to the day that Chen Chunxian set up his 'Service Department'.

The Socratic Precedent

The opening expenses for the service department of Rmb200 were provided by the Beijing Science and Technology Advisory Department, and one should not belittle that Rmb200, as its significance was enormous. It represented both approval and permission to proceed; it was both the action of individuals and of a nation, a composite of the two that included Liu Chuncheng, Pan Ying, Li Bing and Geng Xiumin from the Physics Institute of the Chinese Academy of Sciences, Wu Deshun from the Electronics Institute, Cao Yongxian, Wang Dianru and Wang Shijin from the Mechanics Institute, Chen Shoushen from the Electrical Engineering Institute and Luo Chengmo from Tsinghua University. These individual actions by personnel from scientific research institutes and universities had something of the concept of Highway 128 about them; the organisation of the Service Department was conducted entirely along business lines with specialist personnel for financial affairs, external relations, research and product development, marketing and so on.

The Service Department had workspaces in two locations: one was

Chen Chunxian's office and the other was the Physics Institute warehouse. Its initial work relied on the names of the Chinese Academy of Sciences and the Beijing Science and Technology Advisory Department to draw up plans for local Beijing businesses and to resolve technical problems. Its staff all worked in the evenings or at weekends and if they weren't out and about they all sat together working as consultants and problem-solvers, collecting service expenses as relevant to individual cases.

That the Service Department wasn't earning any money, or very little at most, was not a problem as people watched and waited, some even cracking jokes about it, but when they did start to make money, immediately it was 'big money', quickly stirring up the waters of the quiet pond that was Zhongguancun. At first, Chen Chunxian's Physics Institute found this very hard to take, calling everything into question, even getting angry about it, and piling criticism on top of criticism.

In 1981, the staff of the Service Department kept increasing in number, and its professional services extended from consultancy into manufacturing. In the midst of it all, Chen Chunxian made another trip to America, this time bringing back large quantities of microchips which they used to manufacture electronic power source switches for nuclear fusion equipment. These became the Service Department's principal product. That year the Service Department earned more than Rmb30,000 and Chen Chunxian used that money to construct two wood-plank rooms a bit over 30sqm and hung up two name plaques. One read 'Beijing Plasma Physics Association Advanced Technological Service Department', and the other 'Beijing Plasma Physics Scholarly Review Editing Office'. He also began to hold electronics training classes as another professional service provided by the Service Department; Chen Chunxian and Li Bing took on the responsibility of training youngsters waiting for job assignments, giving classes in computing and electronics. These electronics classes were of enormous importance to the subsequent runaway success of Zhongguancun and nurtured the talents of a host of gifted students. Later on, people praised Zhongguancun's Electronics Street as the equivalent of the Whampoa Military College of earlier times.

The teachers of these classes were recruited from Tsinghua University, Peking University, Beihang University and other such establishments. In order to get the best teachers, the pay Chen Chunxian offered was Rmb6 per hour when, at that time, the national fixed pay for subsidiary teaching was Rmb1.5 per hour.

A problem arose: some people reckoned that as the most important staff of the Service Department came from the Physics Institute and were drawing a salary from it, selling their products back to the institute was profiteering from public funds. Also that in selling the electronic power source switches the Service Department produced to other work units, they were working as competitors against the interests of their employers at the Physics Institute for private gain. This was all regarded as a 'culpable offence' in that Chen Chunxian was taking on too much responsibility and not acting in accordance with national regulations. Moreover, their teaching fees were excessive, also going against national guidelines. At the same time, the story also went round that Chen Chunxian was drawing a monthly allowance of Rmb15. His salary differential was Rmb7.5 so this was equivalent to him advancing himself two levels up the pay scale. These were all seen as problems within the Service Department, and their accounts needed to be audited.

In this time of difficulty, the miracle-worker Zhao Qiqiu came to the Service Department as lead manager and Chen Chunxian told her about the recent work they had done there. She was delighted to learn that the Department had progressed from teaching external classes and providing consultancy services to manufacturing specialist electrical switches and developing new projects with the same external scientific research institutes. At the same time, she was extremely angry about the accusations of profiteering, the fight over commercial enterprise at the Physics Institute and the excessive tuition fees. She gave Chen Chunxian her unequivocal support. Chen Chunxian said that scientific exploration could only take place in an atmosphere of academic freedom. If the Service Department was going to be able to bring about reform and open up to the outside world, and to carry out true scientific exploration, then they had to break free of the old ways of scientific research. Zhao Qiqiu was greatly moved by this and told Chen Chunxian to keep calm and not lose his temper as there was always going to be resistance to revolutionary change. The Service Department was doing nothing wrong, and all they had to do was explain things clearly to the relevant parties and they would be understood. Chen Chunxian made a resolution: the Service Department would not touch any of the national funds allocated to the nuclear fusion project, they would pay a monthly wage of Rmb7-15 to all comrades working in the Service Department to stop others accusing him of drawing a double salary. If the staff of the Personnel Department had borrowed pliers, screwdrivers, testing equipment and so on from the Physics Institute, these things would all be accurately recorded in the Service Department's accounts.

Zhao Qiqiu warned him that from now on, the Service Department could no longer compete with any of the other institutes of the Chinese Academy of Sciences for professional services, would have to get any other work unit's permission to use their equipment, and pay the going rate for its use. "When you started out, you had no financial experience in managing the Service Department's affairs, and perhaps some of the entries in your accounts were not sufficiently clear. If you get the city Science and Technology Advisory Department to look them over first, then no-one will be able to get one over on you. Chen Chunxian agreed to this procedure and not long after, when the Science and Technology Advisory Department audited all of the Service Department's accounts, they found no financial irregularities in any of the more than 20 entries for income and the more than 350 entries for expenditure. After the Spring Festival of 1982, Sun Hong, the chairman of the Science and Technology Advisory Department, and Zhao Qiqiu sought out the relevant parties to discuss the question of the Service Department, and told them of the afore-mentioned findings.

Putting her cards on the table, Zhao Qiqiu said, "The Service Department staff all receive a monthly wage of Rmb7-15. There is no problem with this; the more they work, the more they earn. This is a powerful tool for breaking the tradition of equal pay for unequal effort. As for the question of Service Department staff using Physics Institute equipment, that is not a fundamental problem. You can't drive forward a revolution without going through a few red lights; revolution is all about breaking the old rules."

Chen Chunxian was delighted, but the authorities did not share this attitude. With pressure from above mounting on the Science and Technology Advisory Department, they told Zhao Qiqiu, "The Service Department's accounts have to be audited by the Physics Institute, and not only that, the results of that audit have to be passed on to the Chinese Academy of Sciences. The senior staff of the Service Department all come from the Physics Institute, and when we inspected the accounts for Number 1 Research Unit, for which Chen Chunxian is responsible, we found quite a few problems, all relating to the Service Department."

The authorities had their say, tucked their hands in their sleeves and left. From then on, when reports were made to the relevant department of the Chinese Academy of Sciences, there was no way of recording in the Service Department's sales ledger any of Chen Chunxian's research projects that they claimed had used state assets. In addition, there were several tens of thousands of Rmb in state funding that had been moved into the Service Department's individual account, that needed to be fully investigated. On top of all this, Chen Chunxian was publicly criticised at the General Congress of the Physics Institute where it was said that his Service Bureau was not transplanting and nurturing the ideas of Silicon Valley in China, nor disseminating new technology, but was a purely commercial enterprise, taking the knowledge that resulted from decades of national research and acting as the middleman in selling them off. The fact that the Service Department paid a monthly wage simply encouraged the research staff to neglect their mainstream jobs and was corroding the integrity of their research teams with dishonest practices.

When they heard this, a number of the staff at the Service Department began to regret having moved there because it was quite obvious that after this there were almost certainly going to be problems with any pay rises, performance reviews and housing allocations. That very evening someone turned up at Chen Chunxian's home, laid down the wages he had earned from the Service Department and turned and left without a word. There was nothing Chen Chunxian could say.

Zhao Qiqiu came up with a theory of her own about all this: if Chen Chunxian got on with his official job, and only provided consultancy services in his spare time, that would be approved. Additionally, the Service Department was a subordinate organisation officially approved by the Science and Technology Advisory Department, so the only actual obligation was for its accounts to be inspected by the Advisory Department.

If both sides continued to consider that Chen Chunxian was in charge of the Service Department and part of the Physics Institute, then it was quite in order for the Physics Institute to inspect the accounts. Normally so elegant and refined, Zhao Qiqiu couldn't restrain her fury, and shouted, "Why should the Physics Institute inspect the Service Department's accounts? I think they just want to break you and the Service Department. What are you thinking of?"

In May, a work team from the Physics Institute established a presence in the Service Department, and on that day, the Service Department, normally such a busy scene with people coming and going all the time, was quiet, as no one dared show their face. Only Chen Chunxian stood at the entrance, openly and magnanimously welcoming the newcomers. Someone holding a batch of 'IOUs' asked him, "What was the basis for issuing these?"

Chen Chunxian replied, "According to the rules of the China Science and Technology Advisory Department and the National Science and Technology Commission, if it is not affecting the requirements of their official job, scientific and technical personnel can use their spare time to carry out scientific and technical consultancy work, and can draw a monthly wage of around RMB15 for it."

When he heard this, the man held out his hand to Chen Chunxian and said, "Show me the documentation on this from the China Science and Technology Advisory Department and the National Science and Technology Commission."

Everyone there knew that this was a deliberate attempt to put Chen Chunxian on the spot as, at the time, all departmental documentation was classified as confidential, and Chen Chunxian couldn't possibly have it. Completely unexpectedly, however, Chen Chunxian nonchalantly produced a photocopy of the draft of a speech given by Vice-Premier Fang Yi, saying, "You will find the relevant rules in Vice-Premier Fang Yi's speech."

Having read the speech, the leader of the work team argued, "This is just a speech by one of our leaders, not an official document. Besides, scientific and technical staff are intellectual workers, how can you separate their work time from their free time? How can you differentiate between their official and extracurricular work?" Despite Chen Chunxian's opposition, the auditors photocopied all the written accounts and sent people to Beijing and anywhere else to investigate any work units that had any connection with the Service Department in order to track down questions about Chen Chunxian's finances. The Physics Institute held face-to-face interviews with everyone who drew a wage at the Service Department. The leader of the work group opened the meeting by saying, "The most important action in this year's national development programme is to crack down on serious financial crime. The Physics Institute has already identified Chen Chunxian as the object of an in-depth investigation, and anyone who has worked for the Service Department must step forward voluntarily to explain themselves. From now on, all members of staff at the Physics Institute must seek the approval of the leadership for any work done for the Service Department, irrespective of whether it is undertaken during their official working hours or in their spare time.

When the meeting broke up, no one dared walk out with Chen Chunxian, as they were afraid the association would be bad for them. It wasn't long after the end of the Cultural Revolution, and it remained fresh in people's minds; the universal mentality was one of lingering fear. The Physics Institute was rife with daily gossip and rumours about the Service Department: Chen Chunxian has been identified as a major player in an important criminal financial gang; the Service Department accounts are all in double Dutch; they are padded accounts; no one can read them; the accounts consist entirely of IOUs; Chen Chunxian has been knowingly paying himself a salary two levels above his actual pay grade. One evening, beside himself with anger, one of the key members of the Service Department staff went to Chen Chunxian's home and said to him, "The boss wants to file a case against us in court. It will be a death blow to us. If he's going to play dirty with us, then he needs to know we can do the same and cause him considerable harm. I know that this fellow was vice-chairman of the Revolutionary Committee. After Chairman Mao's death, several of the top brass on the Revolutionary Committee wrote to Jiang Qing pledging allegiance. I saw the letter at the time when I was in a government work group. We could use that letter to warn him off us. What do you think?"

But Chen Chunxian was still Chen Chunxian, and even in such threatening circumstances, he still did not think this was a proper way to act. He said to his colleague, "Even if you have proof of this letter, we should look at this dispassionately, and not play him at his own game." Even after being bad-mouthed so many times, and despite the fact he was in a bad temper, Chen Chunxian never even considered using such underhand methods to pay someone back. Every day when he got home, he would close his eyes and silently contemplate whether he would be disciplined as a result of the court case, be sent for re-education through hard labour or be sent to prison. On occasion, the spectres of defeat and death came to mind. .

Chinese culture emphasises the spirit of benevolence(仁 ren). At the core of benevolence are the ways of loyalty and forgiveness. Even if you do not show benevolence that does not permit one to act unjustly, and this principle is embodied in the ways of honesty and forgiveness (if you don't harm me, I won't harm you, but if you do harm me, I will harm you, is a way of thinking that only appeared later). Ancient Greece had a principle similar to the Chinese 'benevolence'. The philosopher Socrates advocated atheism and freedom of speech. He was accused of disrespecting the Athenian political system and had a case brought against him by three citizens. The jury voted twice, the first time to decide innocence or guilt, and the second time to decide the punishment. Socrates was sentenced to suicide by poison. His family and disciples all urged him to flee the country. His disciple, Crito, told him they had already put together some money to help him escape and some of his admirers were all set to receive him and his family.

Socrates was not willing to go along with this plan. According to his way of seeing things, once the law had made a ruling, it had to be followed. Even if the judgment was mistaken, any attempt to evade the law was equally mistaken. He had no right to avoid punishment. He said, "Suppose I make plans to escape, the law of Athens could ask me, 'Socrates, what are you thinking of doing? Are you going to act to break our laws and harm our country? If a city state has already made public a legal judgement but has no deterrent legislation, and a private individual can cancel or break it at will, do you think that city state could survive and not be overthrown?' In my case, the country has passed a mistaken judgment falsely accusing me, but how can I actually consider breaking the law?"

So Socrates did not flee, and right up to the point he took the poison, he even kept discussing philosophy with his disciples. He was still talking when the executioner told him that the poison required him to walk around for it to take effect. In 1789, Jacques-Louis David painted the famous 'Death of Socrates', depicting the scene as Socrates took the poison: in a gloomy prison cell he is sitting solemnly on his bed, his family and disciples standing on either side. The cell door is half open and a ray of sunlight is slanting in through the gap. Socrates is placed in the centre of the scene, his body looking thin and weak from his ordeal but he has his left hand raised vigorously high in the air, as he continues to expound to his disciples his views and opinions, while his right hand is calmly extended, taking the cup of poison from the hand of one of them...

It doesn't matter whether Chen Chunxian knew this story or not, he had his own principles for living. Although he could have escaped his misfortune, he wouldn't let his colleagues (disciples) help him to do so. Although it wouldn't have been difficult for him to do it, in fact, it would have been very simple, just as science is sometimes very simple, that simplicity itself is actually very complex.

Many of the intellectuals in Zhongguancun secretly followed what was happening to Chen Chunxian with great interest. If this forest giant of the Service Department did not fall, they would be able to emerge from their scientific research establishments. If, however, the giant tree was felled by 'manageritis', Chen Chunxian and the others in the Service Department would not come to a good end. It would probably be many years before anyone had any thoughts about opening a company again.

To relieve his low mood, Chen Chunxian went every evening to the Service Department office to sit by himself, long into the night. The Service Department had essentially been broken up, and only Ji Shiying and a couple of other key members remained; the others had scattered in all directions, as if they expected him to be taken away one day soon. Chen Chunxian had his principles but he was not Socrates. He was preparing to surrender, never to pick the burden up again. He still held fast to the bottom line of what made him who he was but his faith in what he had learned from Silicon Valley began to waver.

One evening, Chen Chunxian was alone as usual in the Service Department, when he suddenly saw Zhao Qiqiu pacing to and fro outside the doors. He immediately went out to greet her and they clasped hands. Zhao Qiqiu looked at Chen Chunxian and said, "I heard the news that you are going to be prosecuted, and it made me very sad. I didn't think I would be very welcome if I went looking for you at the case review, so I thought the best thing I could do was come to the Service Department and wait. But you mustn't get too agitated that things have progressed to this stage." Zhao Qiqiu's eyes were filled with tears when she finished speaking.

Long Haul

Zhao Qiqiu's sighs at this time attracted the attention of her husband Zhou Hongshu. After he had heard his wife out, he frowned at how serious the thing was, a crucial matter of the success or failure of progress and reform. He told his wife that he wanted to write an 'Internal Summary of General Trends' and give it to the central authorities to hear what they had to say.

The same year, Zhou Hongshu took on the role of deputy head of the Beijing branch of the Xinhua News Agency; he was very tuned in to the government and had a very clear understanding of the current reformist trend. The newspaper article that had shaken the country that year, entitled *The Beijing Municipal Committee makes redress for the Tiananmen Incident* was researched by Zhou Hongshu from the mass of documents of relevant meetings in Beijing he had attended. This is not a reference to the Tiananmen incident of 1989 that the West is so familiar with. It refers to a protest in Tiananmen Square on 5 April 1976, the day of the Qingming grave-sweeping festival which was a day of national mourning. The protests were triggered by the removal of memorials in the square to Zhou Enlai, who had died earlier in the year. People from all walks of life brought their own tributes to Zhou, and the square was ordered cleared by the central authorities, essentially the Gang of Four, at that time. The incident gave the authorities an excuse to arrest Deng Xiaoping, who was accused of organising the protests.

Things took a turn for the better in the early morning of 25 January

1983 at No. 88 Building in Zhongguancun, the Chinese Academy of Sciences dormitory building where Feng Kang, Chen Jingrun, Yang Le and Zhang Guanghou all lived. The corridors of the building were as full of noise and bustle as always when, that morning, the stalwart member of the Service Department, Ji Shiying, was shocked awake by an urgent knocking on his door. A voice from outside shouted, "Quick! Turn on the radio and listen to the Beijing news and newspaper round-up!"

China National Radio was broadcasting an important report which confirmed a new direction for Chen Chunxian's Service Department to explore. By the time Ji Shiying came rushing out, the broadcast was already over. At the time, no one knew the reason for the report, but history was later to show that in that instant, the luck of Zhongguancun had changed. It turned out that a reporter in Zhou Hongshu's circle, Pan Shantang, had twice interviewed Chen Chunxian, personally reviewed and corrected the transcript, given it the title *Research scientist Chen Chunxian sees the first results of his experiment in disseminating technology*. He then sent it to the Xinhua News Agency's *Concise Report on National Trends* which was a confidential internal document. It was a digest of all the interviews on any subject conducted by the reporters of the Xinhua News Agency. The articles in it were concise and up-to-date, and the whole thing was passed up for the Central Party Committee and the State Council to read. The article Pan Shantang had written was one thousand five hundred characters long and gave an account of the significance and performance record of Chen Chunxian's Service Department; it also highlighted the scientific and technical achievements of the Zhongguancun district and the wealth of its talent. The majority of these developments were stalled at the theoretical, sample or exhibit stage, only able to demonstrate their financial potential, rather than speeding into production to reap the economic benefits.

This wasn't any ordinary report, it was a confidential consultation document for committee members at the very heart of the Chinese Communist Party government, published in the 52nd edition of the Xinhua News Agency's confidential digest of news. Effectively the eyes, ears and mouthpiece of the party, compiling this digest was a very important responsibility for the reporters of the Xinhua News Agency as its content touched on areas of uncertainty and reports not suitable for public dissemination: things that were still in progress and of a sensitive nature, important matters that were only at the proposal stage and so on. The digest had a set format, modelled on the *Concise Report on National Trends*: it was printed on 16-*kai* paper, roughly equivalent to A4 size, and the content had to be brief and concise as the word count was limited to two thousand characters or less. At that time, only around a hundred people in the whole of China had the seniority required to read it. This exclusive top-level readership ensured the exceptional effectiveness of this confidential report, in particular in the clear conclusions at the end: "Despite the successes of Chen Chunxian's scientific research, and his experiments in the dissemination of new technology, he has met with opposition from some members of the leadership of this department, particularly from certain individuals from the Physics Institute of the Academy of Sciences, who consider that Chen Chunxian and the others are engaging in dishonest practices and neglecting their proper work, and who have put obstacles in the way of this project. This has laid a heavy intellectual burden on those carrying out these experiments and severely compromised their enthusiasm for continuing this work."

The confidential digest was published on 6 January 1983, and on 7 January, in the *Concise Report on National Trends* Vice-President of the State Council, Fang Yi commented on the report on Chen Chunxian, "Comrade Chen Chunxian's work methods are entirely correct and deserve to be encouraged." Fang Yi telephoned the Academy of Sciences asking them to stop the investigation into Chen Chunxian. He also invited Chen to his office for a two-hour-long conversation.

The next day, 8 January, the then member of the Central Committee of the CPC, and clerk to the Secretariat, Hu Qili also commented, "Comrade Chen Chunxian has taken the lead in this phase of opening-up innovation, opening up a new path along which, on the one hand we can expedite the development of science and technology into productivity, and on the other, can open up a new channel for workers in the field of science and technology to contribute to the Four Modernisations, namely, the goals first set by Deng Xiaoping to modernise agriculture, industry, defence and science. A few members of the scientific and technological community may initially profit from this, breaking the tradition of the iron rice bowl and the iron cooking pot so, of course, we must also investigate necessary methods of management and formulate new policies. The China Science and Technology Advisory Department must give its energetic support to this matter. Whatever the decision, please ensure that it is ratified by Comrade Hu Yaobang."

On the same day, General Secretary of the CPC, Hu Yaobang also commented, "Let the Science and Technology Leadership Sub-Committee research and draw up policy on this." These were the policy-makers of China in the 1980s and it is little wonder that they drew the admiration of later generations. And so it was that, just as history itself braves the wind and the waves, Chen Chunxian's Service Department was able to continue with the support of the high-ups, and became the boundary stone marking the dawning of a great new age. The scientists and professors of Zhongguancun no longer watched and waited but put their abilities on full display and became part of history.

DIARY NOTE 2: SERENDIPITY

Although history doesn't admit what-ifs, it is impossible not to consider how things might have been if it weren't for Chen Chunxian; that is to say if Chen Chunxian hadn't visited America in 1978, would Zhongguancun ever have turned into what it is today? Of course, you can say "cometh the hour, cometh the man", and if there hadn't been a Chen Chunxian, there would have been a Wang Chunxian or a Li Chunxian. There is nothing new about this thought; it is the viewpoint of historical determinism which discards the idea of serendipity, but however genuine it may outwardly seem, in fact it is divorced from reality. Sometimes we must believe that one man has the power to change history, be it for good or ill. Yet even the fortunate times can often equally cause people to sigh and bemoan them. In 1978, when most Chinese were still caught up in the shackles of the 'Two Whatevers' of the Cultural Revolution, Chen Chunxian, to the great good fortune of Zhongguancun, was walking around Silicon Valley; for it was then that he indulged his fantasies by thinking that Zhongguancun could pursue the same path as Silicon Valley, and that scientists and professors could simultaneously run companies and, as individuals, could turn science and technology into productivity. He took note of the research that was going on in Zhongguancun and recognised that it already represented a concentration rivalled by few places in the world, let alone what it might become in ten years or so. It is hard to believe it was not serendipity that the Chen Chunxian of that time found himself marching to a different tune from the majority of his fellow countrymen who were still constrained by the 'Two Whatevers'. There were other people at the time who went abroad as he did, so why did no one else like Chen Chunxian appear on the scene? And why was there no one else who acted with the same honourable single-mindedness. It was serendipity and we have no choice but to admit its value.

Zhongguancun at that time, like the rest of China, was a monolith of revolutionary slogans, and Chen Chunxian was alone in pushing against that monolith. Looking back at the context of those times, the difficulty of the task was enough to make a man despair, yet it is often in the depths of one man's despair that history advances. Someone later said, "One little step from Chen Chunxian was a giant stride for science and technology in China", and they were not wrong.

By way of summary, Ling Zhijun, the author of *China's New Revolution* sees Zhongguancun as a microcosm of China's reform and opening up, opining, "In the last twenty years of the 20th century, this country broke free of its psychological shackles and allowed itself to become the great manufacturing workshop of the world. In the first ten years of the 21st century it longs to seize the sunny uplands of new technology in order to turn China the workshop into China the creator. The reason China can change the world is that it knows how to change itself."

This change all stems from Chen Chunxian and, properly considered, his significance is enormous. In the depths of difficulty and despair, he remained true to himself, just as Socrates did. "Do not do to others what you would not have done to yourself". This was a principle from ancient philosophy that Chen Chunxian took with him into science and technology. In his determination to remain true to himself, he was in every way the equal of the monolith he pushed against with such difficulty, and the two complemented each other.

The Pull of the Future

未来的引力

Free-fall

In 2015, Wu Gansha resigned as director of Intel Labs China and, in a major news event for the New Year in business circles, took up the post of CEO at UISEE Technology. In fact, while he was still director of Intel Labs but in the process of resigning, his thoughts were already on UISEE. He spent every day on a continuous round of interviews, meeting venture capitalists, hoping to be able to set up the first round of finance before the end of the year. Intel had five large research labs around the world and, as director of Intel China Labs, Wu Gansha was the direct equal of the director of Intel itself. He had an annual salary of several million yuan but he had no hesitation in resigning.

UISEE Technology (Beijing) Co Ltd's temporary first location was an office in the Hailong Building in Zhongguancun. It was plain and sparsely furnished with just a long office desk and a sofa. Its small size and emptiness made the globe on the desk look rather incongruous. Recently, Wu Gansha has just moved into the high-tech incubator that is Zhizao Street in Zhongguancun, hatching place of dreams. The company specialises in smart cars and driverless vehicles.

As Beijingers say, that's more than enough for one dream.

We can't even cope with vehicles with drivers, and now we're going to have driverless vehicles too?

For many people, driverless vehicles are unimaginable, beyond even their wildest dreams. Why should you want a driverless vehicle? Isn't our addiction to ordinary cars bad enough already? Isn't this all too fast? Isn't it going too far? Besides, will they actually work? Our cities already have so many cars, how can we have driverless vehicles as well. Intel is a huge name which everyone knows, so to abandon a post as laboratory director and chief engineer, and dream of making driverless vehicles is surely the dream of someone not from this planet.

Some people's lives turn them into superhumans, extra-terrestrials, and you have no idea how their minds work.

That's how ordinary people see things.

Wu Gansha graduated from the computing department of Fudan University in 2000, and while he was there, he was one of the 10 fortunate recipients of an Intel scholarship. After he graduated, he joined Intel and stayed there for 16 years. When he first joined, he worked on user interfaces and, in his second year, met with his first great opportunity: he chose to change teams and join the core technology team. After this switch, Wu

Gansha and his teammates had the support of the technical teams in America and gradually began to set up their own projects and carry out original research. After another three years, he became a project manager, then a departmental manager, then technical director and finally chief engineer.

Being chief engineer for Intel's worldwide research and development set-up is second only to being an academic; it carries very high status and requires at least four different abilities: the first is professional influence, the second is technical ability, then strategic leadership and finally team leadership. All of Intel's research departments are dedicated to servicing product needs and business development so, by consensus, professional influence is the most important quality that needs to be demonstrated. On that count, Wu Gansha could not be faulted. He had solved technical problems in many different programming tools, shown innovation in parallel computer programming tools and successfully transferred these skills from the research laboratory into production departments, thereby transforming Intel's product base.

Technical leadership means that any results achieved must be accepted as industry leaders. In his innovations in the parallel programming environment CT Array Building Blocks, Wu Ganfa resolved the future difficulties of developing programmes to meet the needs of Terabyte-scale computing, making it much easier for programmers to handle huge volumes of data. It also rendered it unnecessary to rewrite today's code, so it would be immediately usable by the processors of the future. To display strategic leadership you have to be able to predict future trends, decide the importance of every different kind of technology, and take the initiative in judging the potential of different problems.

It was the above-mentioned qualities that not only made Wu Gansha chief engineer, but also propelled him to the chairmanship of Intel Labs China. At Intel, he had already reached both a personal and professional peak. This was an exceptionally firm and substantial peak, a dazzling peak that to many people's eyes was like a high, unclimbable, snow-covered mountain whereas, in fact, it was just one of five such snowy peaks. But Wu Gansha chose to leap down from this peak and in one stride found himself in a single computer sales office in the Hailong Building, fiddling with a globe on an office desk, dreaming of driverless cars.

Even as he was in this kind of pioneering 'free-fall', Wu Gansha considered himself conservative and non-arty, a typical rational, hard-working

Capricorn personality. But when someone in a dream says they are wide awake and completely rational, that should give people cause for alarm, "He can't understand what he's doing but he may succeed". That was the judgement of the people around him. Certainly, wrapped up in his dream and unswervingly confident as he was, Wu Gansha seemed as though he could see something that was undeniably and undoubtedly going to be a success in the next 10 to 20 years. He was so calm and unconcerned, condensing the essence of his whole experience from youth to middle age and his 16-year career at Intel, that it gave him something of the air of an automaton.

Of course, despite Wu Gansha's trance-like calm, Rome was not built in a day. But, in any case, he was at least quite right in calling himself conservative and hyper-rational. So was there any rapid progress? There are plenty of youngsters, and creative youngsters at that, just as there are dreams that catch them up and sweep them along. But Wu Gansha took 16 years and although he was not yet 40, his hair was already turning grey. However, it was that greying hair that made this 'free-fall' of his certain and not open to doubt.

In his 16 years at Intel, Wu Gansha conceived at least three different entrepreneurial ventures. The first was during the great wave of changes in the internet in 2001; at that time, he hadn't been at Intel for very long, and feeling that this was the tidal surge of the times, he wanted to ride it and set up on his own. But after due consideration, he abandoned the project. The second was the eve of the rise of the mobile internet, when the department that Wu Gansha headed developed a better product than Android (at that time Android hadn't yet been bought by Google), but the executive department at Intel halted the project and sold off their mobile phone project. What is more, they sold it in January 2007, at the critical time before Steve Jobs launched the iPhone. Something else also happened before the sale; Jobs asked for Intel's help in making the microchips for the iPhone but, in a high-handed way, the CEO of Intel refused. At the time, the company was rather contemptuous of cell phones, immersing itself in computer chips, and really not expecting the advent of the mobile internet era. Once again, Wu Gansha thought of leaving Intel and setting up on his own but, once again, he hesitated and the moment was lost.

The more a company matures and grows, the more it may misread the times, because what the management of the time look at are the trends that exist 'now', and they don't have a clear vision of the revolutionary products of the next era, or don't even see them at all. It is just as Gödel's theorem says: you cannot have both completeness and consistency. Gödel believed that logic dictates that self-consistency cannot be complete in itself; it must have boundaries and limits, and what is outside those boundaries is the equivalent of a black hole to it. By extension or rather, as Wu Gansha saw it, the management of any given era relies on the logic of the self-consistency of success, the era of the PC for example, but that era has its boundaries, and the mobile internet appeared beyond those boundaries. It was bound to go unnoticed by those invested in the success of the PC. Intel was unaware of the revolutionary nature of the mobile internet, to the extent that, on the eve of its launch, Intel had its back turned, cutting itself off from the dawn of the new era.

This made a very deep impression on Wu Gansha and the ice in his heart increased by another layer.

The third occasion was 2013; the mobile internet was continuing to flourish, the BAT triumvirate comprising Baidu, Alibaba and Tencent was now commanding popular attention, and everyone was well aware that, with the addition of the big data from Taobao, Tencent and Baidu, the mobile internet was bringing about earth-shaking changes. Keeping his eye on the moment, he saw the opportunities the mobile internet brought for online education, and once again thought of setting up on his own. But, just at that time, he was appointed director of Intel Labs China and once again he hesitated. He used a particularly vivid simile to illustrate his situation: he said it was like queuing to check in at the airport when the queue is exceptionally long. Just as you finally get halfway to the front, suddenly another counter opens next to you, and everyone behind you scurries over to that one. This is what the youngsters have been doing over the last few years, but should you do it too? Should you change queues or not? Would you be able to change back again? In the end, he didn't make the move but he envied the youngsters who rushed over from behind to end up in front of him.

Although he was unable to set up on his own, as director of Intel Labs China Wu Gansha was determined to keep pace with modern advances and brought about a revolution in its former ways of working that more than somewhat mirrored his own character. The first thing was to change the institution's slow pace and slow ways of working with the mobile internet, and master better ways of internet working. The second was to consolidate Intel's position in China and adapt to the growing number of foreign companies' research laboratories that wanted to increase their presence in more places around China to be part of the new trails Chinese society was blazing and to be at the centre of economic development; for example, in terms of China's industrial revolution and digital economy, he wanted to integrate Intel Labs China more closely with the path of the nation's development but the problems lay not just in the presence of American research laboratories in China but also in their employment of native Chinese talent. The third thing was that he hoped to change what was formerly primarily a support service research organisation into one that had a leadership role. The systems and communications of the old-style research had left Intel at the back of the marketplace, and that had to be changed.

In 2014, under Wu Gansha's leadership, Intel's research laboratories were manufacturing a number of things, whereas American research laboratories in America were not. Intel Labs China could call itself a world leader in, for example, the fields of artificial intelligence and robotics. Before this, the fields that Intel had been concerned with, such as cloud computing, the internet, big data and wearable computers, were comparatively old fields but for Intel, artificial intelligence was something completely new.

As Wu Gansha saw it, the information technology revolution was a cyclical phenomenon. In the 20th century, the 20 years from 1950 to 1970 represented the development of the architecture of computers; 1970 to 1990 represented the PC era of digitalisation; 1990 to 2010 was the connected era of 'networkification'. These were all 20-year periods. The 20 years from 2010 to 2030 will represent the dominance of 'smartification'. In the past, if you got it wrong, you got it wrong but now you can't afford to make another mistake. But Wu Gansha's changes were not without opposition, some of which he himself could not overcome. For example, he could not turn Intel Labs China into an internet company, nor could he switch out three-quarters of the workforce.

Shangri-La Thinking

In the autumn of 2014, under the star-studded sky of Shangri-La, Wu Gansha was reading the American author Mark Malone's book *The Intel Trinity*. Shangri-La was formerly called Zhongdian County but was renamed on 17 December 2001 and upgraded into a county-level city on 16 December 2014 as Xianggelila/Shangri-La after the fictional land of Shangri-La in the 1933 James Hilton novel *Lost Horizon*, in an effort to promote tourism in the area. That autumn Wu Gansha was taking a three-month extended vacation (it was the norm at Intel that you could take a three-month break after working there for seven years), and, as autumn is the most beautiful season, Wu Gansha had brought his wife and children to Shangri-La to stay in the very stylish Songtsam Retreat. It was not cheap at Rmb2,000 a night but, for someone with a headful of dreams, someone who ceaselessly travelled the world in search of the unusual, Songtsam was undoubtedly a paradise. The pillars and beams of the wooden architecture were grand and imposing, in the corner of the room was a copper, Tibetan-style fireplace and on the wall beside the dining table hung an enormous *thangka*. In both the room and its courtyard, you could discern the three hundred years of history of the Sumseling Monastery and then there were also the silent, spectacular mountain ranges, not to mention the star-studded sky above them. From time to time, Wu Gansha would open the wooden doors onto the sun deck and overhead he had the Shangri-La night, cool, clear and moonlit, with the occasional passing cloud.

The publishers of the Chinese edition of *The Intel Trinity*, Cheers Publishing in Beijing, had at first thought of asking Wu Gansha to translate the work. Wu Gansha really wanted to do it but he didn't have the time so, in the end, it was done by one of his colleagues. He did, however, agree to write a foreword once the translation was completed. He had brought a digital copy of the manuscript with him to read under the stars. There was something about it that made him feel that under a starry night sky was the right place to be reading this kind of book, so he did so, there in Shangri-La, with part of him on vacation, part of him reading attentively and part of him writing the foreword. When his family were asleep, he would often go out into the courtyard, look up at the night sky and sigh deeply.

It is often the case that when people find themselves in a particularly magical place, they find their thinking changes and they can step outside themselves and look at themselves, at the future and at the past. Originally, Wu Gansha only thought of writing two or three thousand characters but he ended up writing 16,000 all in one go. In fact, it wasn't just a foreword, it was a revelation of his innermost thinking. With the galaxy of stars as a backdrop, he saw the whole early history of Intel flash past his eyes and a face gradually revealed itself to him, softly murmuring in the language of the stars. The early years of Intel became a summons to a magical quest to be bravely assumed for the future, with no fear of the risks, of mistakes or of defeats. Once sure of himself, he should double down on his wager, lick his wounds and get back on his feet after defeat; once back on his feet, he should only seek to strengthen his position. On the other hand, if he was to stay the same as he was then, cautious, dependable, painstaking, moving step by step from promotion to promotion but always locked in an internal struggle with himself, then he could retire from Intel in 10 years' time. But in those 10 years, like some kind of figure from mythology, he could see himself clearly, with everything fixed, everything predicted, everything in its right order. Was that really to be imagined? Having the Grim Reaper standing watching you at the end of 10 years and blindly following his ordained programme?

When it comes down to it, should people seek certainty or seek the unpredictable? In fact, he already had his answer to that: if, at this juncture, the state of all the atoms in the universe was fixed and predictable, then you could infer the state of any given moment in the past and any given moment in the future; that was the world according to Newtonian theory. Einstein had developed that theory but it still remained a determinist one. But, Wu Gansha thought to himself, today's world is not fixed in that way, today's world is based on probability. Schrödinger's Cat bore witness to that: is the cat in the box alive or dead? The truth is it can be both at the same time, and it is only when the box is opened that one can be sure of which state it is in. By opening the box, you have a 50% chance of killing the cat. In fact, this is also Heidinger's uncertainty principle, which is to say: your actions themselves can change the subject of your observations.

Newtonian mechanics are a kind of determinism, or a determinist world view. Whatever size an impetus is, it has the same size result; whatever you did in the past or are capable of now, that is all you can do. This is the Newtonian way of seeing things. But, in truth, the world is governed by Merton's Law[1]: one person, a leader say, must first fix on a future and, once they have the courage and conviction to bring about that future, that courage and conviction can itself have an influence on their actions today. That influence is not fixed, it is based on probability, not the Newtonian certainty of cause and effect. Newton clearly saw death as the inevitable end but Merton offers another possibility, like Schrödinger's Cat: it depends what it is you are seeking. For the 16 years Wu Gansha was director of Intel Labs China, the world was in a constant state of flux. Cloud computing, the Internet of Things, big data, internet banking, VR/AR... wave after wave of technology had surged past him... None of these new phenomena had been certain at their outset, Wu Gansha thought to himself, but what had he actually achieved by responding to their uncertainty with his determinist approach at Intel? What had he lost? As he looked at the host of unfamiliar stars of the Shangri-La night, thoughts swirled around his brain, as numerous as those stars. He had two principal hobbies, playing football and reading. Every year he intensively read about 20 books and extensively read about a hundred on science, mathematics, philosophy and history. He read a lot and thought a lot... he thought even more when he looked at the night sky and once again he had been drawn back to the night sky of Shangri-La.

The book *The Intel Trinity* talked about how Robert Noyce, Gordon Moore and Andy Grove had founded the Intel saga and at the end, the author, Mark Malone, says to them, "If you remain the same as you were 40 years ago, daring to take risks and not afraid of making mistakes, the world will still be yours, but if you become cautious and prudent, you will lose out."

Wu Gansha went back into his room and hastily scribbled down his foreword. He was no longer just any old Intel employee and, stung by Malone's words, his Capricorn star sign began to flare and twinkle in the sky. He was already almost 40 years old: was this an age of self-confidence or an age of crisis. The 'smart' age had arrived and that opened a new window. Did he want to go over to it or did he want to stay in the same queue. What was he queuing for? Where did he want to go?

When he was little, Wu Gansha lived in a small township on the north bank of the Yangtze and the distinctive building of that township was a small bell tower. Early on, when the industrialist Zhang Jian built a big cotton mill there, the little bell tower stood within sight of the township and it was now more than a hundred years old. The township was, in fact, named after the cotton mill. When he thought back, Wu Gansha's first impression of the township was of industrialisation, and the symbols of that industrialisation were the cotton mill and the bell tower. Another memory was of the simplicity of nature and how, every summer holiday he always wanted to go back to his grandma and grandpa in the countryside, and listen to his grandma telling stories in the still, sunny summer evenings. Later on, every year he would take the ferry which chugged down river for several hours to reach Shanghai. He would disembark at Shiliupu from where he could see the city with its myriad tall buildings. Industry, the country and the big city were compartmentalised for him when he was little, so now, did his contrasting free-thinking and conservatism have something to do with this compartmentalisation?

In the Shangri-La night, Wu Gansha's inner thoughts and the night sky became one. Ideas were whirling round his head but, as he looked at the night sky, those ideas were stilled; he thought this was because of the faint stirrings of an excitement which had been set in motion the night before. In truth the excitement was 90% full of confidence but there was still 10% that made him uncomfortable. Yes, uncomfortable, but that was just another kind of excitement. But, even though his mind was 90% made up, he did not make his move immediately after he left Shangri-La.

That was Wu Gansha for you: even with his thinking that well advanced and matured, he still did not make his move.

It went against his nature and it went against his profoundly held rationale of only acting right at the last moment.

The Summer Palace

The fuse was lit after Wu Gansha's return from Shangri-La when he took part in an eight-month Intel top-level executive training programme. Intel's dozen or so Chinese executives all gathered together for a course led by a world-famous training company, where the attendees were all top-level experts. The interesting thing was that, after the course had been completed, more than half of the participants left Intel and, extraordinarily, one of them was Wu Gansha. It wasn't that the training course was a bad one, it was that it was too good: it had awoken the latent energy of the participants' innermost thoughts, causing a massive explosion. In particular, there was one instructor, whose lecture had made the deepest possible impression. It was entitled: "To lead is to design a future that is unpredictable and which no one would bet on." In a sense, this was where even such a big company as Intel lost out. Wu Gansha couldn't sleep a wink that night and he thought of that night in Shangri-La when he wrote the foreword to Malone's book. What the instructor had said and what he had thought were identical, and it all pointed to one thing: starting up something with an uncertain future was where the true value of life lay; success and failure were two sides of the same coin.

People always have an existing path to set off down and for Wu Gansha the direction was towards intelligent robots. This was also a project that he had started at Intel but there was a bottleneck that had to be negotiated: it seemed that artificial intelligence can always surpass humans in a given specialist field, such as playing Go, but an intelligent robot must not only match humans at playing Go, it must also be able to communicate naturally with them and help them in everyday life, for instance, with cooking and with folding and ironing clothes; but this demands a high degree of dexterity from the robot. In the field of artificial intelligence robotics, there is a thing called 'Moravec's Paradox': counterintuitively, specific high-level human intelligence requires very little computational capability, but autonomic sensorimotor skills and intuition require a very great deal. It is easy to get a computer to play chess but to get a computer to feel and act even like a very young child, is extremely difficult and requires computation that even now is barely achievable. It was only when Wu Gansha chanced to meet Deep Glint's CTO, Zhao Yong, that he suddenly saw the light. Once again he became caught up in a way of thinking founded on Newtonian mechanics but it wasn't Newtonian thinking. He realised that old habits die hard and he still hadn't escaped from his own. He was still thinking step by step: you did this previously, now you can do that and your next step is this. Progressing in this way means that your future is always dependent on your past. But revolutionary thinking is seeing the future at a stroke and then experiencing for yourself what that future is like. Then you project that future back to the present, see what you have to do now, see where you are now, then call on the influence of the future.

Wu Gansha and Deep Glint's Zhao Yong met in 2013. They were fellow alumni of Fudan University but hadn't previously encountered each other. They did, however, have a mutual friend who brought them together at a dinner party. After Zhao Yong graduated, he left Shanghai for America to study at Brown University. He obtained a PhD in computer engineering and in 2010 took up a post at Google HQ's research institute as a senior researcher. He was the designer of the image processing architecture in Google's Android operating system and he was a core member of the research team that worked on the early stages of Google Glass. He was also responsible for the design of the cloud computing architecture of Google's future high-performance image processing and analysis.

Zhao Yong left Google in April 2013 to become the combined creator and founder of Deep Glint, relying on his technical experience accumulated over a decade in the field of computer vision. He led a technical team in successfully developing the Deep Glint Unmanned Security Monitoring System. This system could implement accurate human recognition, tracking, movement and posture detection and analysis (including violent motion, falls and other kinds of movement), and human movement trajectory detection and analysis (including stopping, traversing and hesitating in human searches). In a traditional security surveillance centre, a public security officer has to monitor well over a hundred street views and, if something unusual happens, the likelihood of that officer noticing it is very low; moreover, after the actual occurrence, the burden is on manpower to trawl through the data on a huge number of discs looking for clues. This is a massive task, extremely time-consuming, very inefficient, and Deep Glint's product very neatly cleared this business bottleneck and struck a nerve in the industry. Zhao Yong's explanation of Deep Glint was: a computer vision company that provided a complete programme to resolve the question of computer vision. It encompassed giving the user visual analysis, including the results of dynamic analysis of, for example, people, vehicles and surroundings. It can thereby be of service to users of all professions and businesses. The range of businesses includes security, professional standards testing, consumer behaviour analysis, smart vehicles and even smart cities. Not long in the future, it will be offering visual analysis products for universal use.

In June 2015, Wu Gansha went to visit Zhao Yong at Deep Glint. Deep Glint was a little eccentric as it was located in a traditional courtyard house at the Summer Palace and Zhao Yong lived in a small building opposite. He never left the courtyard; he started work when he got up and went to sleep when he was tired, rather like an automaton in the repetitiveness of his actions. At the beginning of the year, Zhao Yong had spent Chinese New Year in America, staying with an old classmate. Because of the time difference, on the first day he woke up at five o'clock in the morning and went and sat in the back garden. There were some fruit trees in the garden with oranges growing on them. He picked one, peeled and ate it. It was very sweet and, even better, it had no pips. He ate five of them, one after the other. He had a small courtyard, wore a t-shirt all day, ate oranges straight from the tree, took his children to the library or to swimming lessons in the morning... Zhao Yong was living the dream and he had it all there in California. But later on, he realised that in the course of a whole year, he had only been into the garden a few times, the ground was thick with fallen leaves and they were beginning to rot. Why had he not lived the life of his dreams in that small courtyard? What had he been doing? It turned out it was the same old story: *plus ça change, plus ça reste la meme chose*; the more things change, the more they remain the same. He had turned the little building in the courtyard into his laboratory, the living room was adorned with lots of spy cams and a whole load of computers, and it was in that little living room that Zhao Yong built the first prototype of Deep Glint. He was a workaholic and his life was as simple as some kind of robot. He had no connection with the landscape around him but he couldn't leave it. He might not even see it but he had to be in it. This was quite similar to Wu Gansha: he didn't go out into the psychedelic beauty of Shangri-La but he had formed an incurable liking for the place. He didn't want to see any stars except the stars of Shangri-La. Indeed, where else was there to see them? What is more, it had to be on the high plateau, even though he had no interest in the plateau itself.

At the Summer Palace, in a pavilion with a magnificent view in the rear courtyard of the courtyard house next to the river, Wu Gansha and Zhao Yong talked for a long time without even noticing their surroundings. From the point of view of the Summer Palace, they were like extra-terrestrials or, if they weren't that, then it was the Summer Palace that was the product of some alien civilisation. They wanted to change the world, including China, of course, and they wanted to change the world from China. They were like two hobbits or perhaps even more ancient folk from the *Shan Hai Jing (The Classic of Mountains and Seas)*, certainly bearing no resemblance to contemporary folk. In his conversation, Wu Gansha did not fail to ask why it was Deep Glint had set up office at the Summer Palace although, in fact, that topic of conversation actually led them away from the place. As always, there was a dramatic, cinematic element to what Zhao Yong did and, not without some pride, he explained to Wu Gansha how things had come about. Deep Glint's first office had been in an ordinary house on College Road but when the work force grew to 14 or 15, they thought about moving. Serendipitously, Zhao Yong and the CEO, He Bofei, were simultaneously excited to find this small courtyard house by the river behind the Summer Palace. They kept it secret and only after they had fitted it out as an office did they plan a spring outing on which they would be taking all the staff there as if discovering it by chance. Only then would they announce that the company would be moving there. But Zhao Yong could not contain himself and one day when He Bofei was away from the office, he opened up a satellite map, switched off the road names and told his colleagues, "Our new office is in a part of Beijing that has greenery and water."

The staff looked at the map and worked out it was showing the Summer Palace. Zhao Yong slid his hands across the screen, enlarging the map, then enlarging some more and some more again. When the staff saw where the map was showing, they were ecstatic. "But I shouldn't have let this slip," Zhao Yong told Wu Gansha. "So I begged the staff not to tell He Bofei and to pretend they knew nothing. But they couldn't contain themselves either and went running over there at the weekend, taking lots of photographs. Later on we came here on our spring outing, held a barbecue and, at the agreed moment, He Bofei solemnly made the great announcement and all the staff pretended to be so surprised and delighted you could have knocked them down with a feather."

The two men chatted away very happily, moving back into their 'land of legend' personae.

Zhao Yong time and time again used the word: privilege.

3. THE PULL OF THE FUTURE

"We are living in a particularly fine era. All the many things I longed to do in the future when I was studying, I am now doing at Deep Glint. The things that I planned decades ago have happened in 10 years, yet we are still at the frontier, pushing it further forward. When I consider this, I feel that it is a privilege. Take 3D computer vision for example: when I was studying, I chose that field but my teachers didn't really understand it. I wrote my graduation thesis on it and today Deep Glint is still pursuing it. If we are successful, I will feel extraordinarily proud. This technology itself is like a child and since I chose it, I am responsible for nurturing it to adulthood."

Wu Gansha agreed that they had a kind of privilege, if not even a mission. People of every era have their own feeling of being on a mission and may all feel they are special, privileged in fact. Their specialness comes from their position at the frontier, a place where Wu Gansha had already found himself several times. But each time it had only been a brief stay and he had let the opportunity slip. This was another such occasion and a particularly clear-cut one, now, in the age of smart technology.

Zhao Yong said, "These people of today are so out of the ordinary that it is far easier to get a good programmer to write a programme that strikes at the heart of a problem than it is to get him to talk to a girl. The truth is, some of the things we are making today will certainly make people exclaim: 'That's just abnormal!' But it's an abnormality born out of technology!"

Zhao Yong asked Wu Gansha, "If there wasn't this kind of 'abnormality' then we wouldn't exist either, so don't you feel that history is born out of the abnormal? We, and in that I include our staff, often work from dawn to dusk. For them the work itself is their reward and the reward becomes the work. Looking at it like that, I think we are still just hanging onto the hind leg of the realm of science fiction. Some of those science fiction writers were alive a hundred years before us and even Hollywood beats us by 30 to 50 years. As things stand now, I feel I am just four or five years ahead of the majority of our contemporaries."

"Maybe a little more," Wu Gansha replied.

"The science fiction writers may be all worked up and ahead of themselves but for us there is nothing for it but to move calmly through the gears, changing the future into the present."

"That's right," Wu Gansha said. "We are changing the present, programme by programme."

What was it they were talking about, there in the imperial wooded parkland of the Summer Palace?

They were certainly two of a kind, like a kind of interstellar association that also encompassed everything there is in a human friendship. Deliberately, Wu Gansha did not reveal any of his own plans, just wanting to understand about Zhao Yong's company. He was used to keeping a low profile and maintaining a certain reserve, very unlike Zhao Yong's directness.

But although the two of them were certainly kindred spirits, it only went so far: Zhao Yong was fully aware why the other had come and kept himself astonishingly under control, and didn't talk about the real substance of the visit. He was very talkative on some topics but made sure to keep his acuity hidden.

They are both extremely intelligent. There were certain key subjects they didn't need to discuss immediately, since everything they did talk about was essentially related to them, and the rest would come naturally.

Zhao Yong returned the visit, going to see Wu Gansha in his office at Intel Labs China. This was inevitable. There were no parks and woodlands this time, nor was there any need for them. Everything was straightforward and direct: they would collaborate to create a new company.

Last time it was the Summer Palace, this time it was in the science-fiction setting of Intel Labs China's office space in Block A of the Raycom Infotech Park. Three months later, in September 2015, Zhao Yong used computer vision to give a thorough explanation of smart cars and driverless vehicles, and he even gave Wu Gansha some demo models. At the end of October, Wu Gansha came to a decision: he would carry forward the work on smart vehicles in the post of CEO of UISEE Technology. More often than not, this is how things go: when they are complicated, they are extremely complicated, and when they are simple, they are extremely simple.

Is there anything simpler than the natural course of events?

Driverless Vehicles

Many of the staff at Intel Labs China wanted to work with Wu Gansha, no matter how, and even though he had been at Intel for 16 years, his departure had to be considered something of an act of rebellion. When Wu Gansha left Intel taking a number of people with him, it couldn't help but remind people of the first chapter of the first part of *The Intel Trinity*, entitled *Departures: the Eight Rebels*. While he was in Shangri-La, Wu Gansha wrote in the foreword to the first part: "One morning in September 1957, the 'eight rebels' left Shockley Semiconductor as a group, unconsciously beginning the unrolling of the magnificent scroll that was the development of Silicon Valley. Within 12 years of this, a host of 'elves' began to feed the growing surge in the semiconductor industry not just of Silicon Valley, but of the whole world."

When Wu Gansha led that group of staff away from Intel, of course, it was not the same as the 'Eight Rebels', although there was some similarity in that it was only by leaving that they could create history – "the mission of a leader is to design an indeterminate future, a future that no one would bet on." This was indeed Intel's former tradition, and perhaps it was only by them leaving Intel that Intel could reinvent itself. "If you remain the same as you were 40 years ago, daring to take risks and not afraid of making mistakes, the world will still be yours, but if you become cautious and prudent, you will lose out."

When all is said and done, Wu Gansha was not like this, and he told the staff who wanted to follow him, "Brothers, I am very grateful that you want to come with me, but I still have to speak to (Intel) HR and give them a chance to persuade you to stay. They might offer you a 50% raise! If you want to stay on those terms, I will quite understand as you are certainly worth it. If they do offer you this package but you still want to leave, I will welcome you with open arms."

The vast majority of them did still go with him, as they were all willing to bet on the future.

"His team absorbed exceptional talent in a way that is seldom seen," is the opinion of Kai-Fu Lee. "He had computing experts from university, the top experts in computer vision, including members of Google's machine learning team. Then, of course, there was Wu Gansha himself and the specialist semiconductor team he led. Wu Gansha was an exceptional leader who was able to bring together and lead this disparate group of people, and that speaks for itself."

Wu Gansha was no beginner at "management". From the time he started as director of Intel Labs China, he began to experiment with all sorts of different management innovations, such as bottom-up management, delayering, Amazon's 'two pizza' rule, business innovation and the dual framework main business model. These were all cutting-edge systems.

Deep Glint was the most important and influential stockholder, and one day, Zhao Yong went as far as to solemnly issue a Deep Glint press release that set the internet alight: "Deep Glint has joined with the director of Intel Labs China, Wu Gansha, Jiang Yan, the man in charge of the team that won the National Smart Car Future Challenge Competition and others to form a company together specialising in the field of driverless vehicles – UISEE Technology. What UISEE Technology aims to do is to detremine the case once and for all for automobile manufacturers with a fully developed driverless car which, on the one hand, will not discriminate between travellers but allow everyone, even disabled people, to be in control of their journey. On the other hand, we aim to reduce the number of traffic incidents and fatalities, promote road usage, guarantee the prerequisite safety for any journey undertaken and ensure its maximum efficiency."

Apart from Zhao Yong and Wu Gansha, the other founder of UISEE Technology was Jiang Yan who was responsible for driving technology. Previously, he had been a professor at Beijing Institute of Technology School of Mechanics and Vehicles, held a PhD from Beijing University of Aeronautics and Astronautics and had been a doctoral research student at the University of Illinois at Urbana-Champaign; his field of research was the design of the infrastructure of automatic driving systems. Up to this date, Jiang Yan had already competed six times in the Smart Car Challenge Competition; in 2013 he won the China Smart Car Champions Challenge Competition, and after that victory, he moved from the competition track to Beijing's Third Ring Road, and began research into how automatic vehicles could actually drive in a real environment. In his longest trip, he spent two hours on the Third Ring Road, and the automatic car covered 48km. There were major traffic jams, with the cars at a standstill, and before this he had really never dared think that a driverless car could actually work in such heavy traffic conditions.

At the meeting for Zhao Yong's press release, Jiang Yan talked about his test drive on the Third Ring Road, announcing that the test was not complete after just a single day; the test drive itself was experimental. One of the key things about driverless cars is that if you fix on one aspect, and decide everything in relation to that, you will never actually succeed, so what you must do is to be sure of everything your vehicle can do and everything it can't do, and factor in the public's degree of acceptance. "What we are doing here is not intended to allow everyone to experience a perfect, flawless system, but to allow the people who are doing the work to discover where the problems lie," Jiang Yan said. "But if, after they discover a problem, they come to see the danger isn't as great as they expected, then that can be considered an even better result. So our test is firstly open in nature and secondly open-ended so, just like 1.0 or 2.0 upgrade releases, we can carry out continuous iterations."

Even though he was top of the class, number one in the China Smart

Car Challenge Championship and had test driven the Third Ring Road, when Zhao Yong first found Jiang Yan and invited him to join him in setting up UISEE to develop the driverless vehicle industry, he declined as he thought it simply couldn't be done. But when Zhao Yong also approached Wu Gansha, Jiang Yan decided to leave the university to join them. Without the team from Intel, he thought there was no chance of a viable product, and the whole thing was still just a research project; without the possibility of commercial production, and without integrated capability, it remained just a curiosity. But with Wu Gansha on board, it was a completely different matter and Zhao Yong had found the right man.

The relationship between the three men was a very interesting one, and they very much gave the impression of a 'Holy Trinity'. History sometimes repeats itself like this, sometimes even in different countries, which is a distinctive feature of globalisation. They were the optimum combination for driverless vehicles in China, the Three Musketeers, and they were a cutting-edge force in the rest of the world too.

Undoubtedly, they were faced with an enormous challenge.

Whatever that challenge was, that was what defined them: the greater the challenge, the greater their success.

Whether it is a driverless vehicle or an automatic vehicle, they are both essentially a vehicle with a super computer onboard; they are the product of big data, composite super robots with artificial intelligence; they need powerful video and radar guidance data; they need real-time processing, analysis, harmonisation and decision-making. Currently, across the world from America to China to Europe, the major players in traditional microchip production and traditional car manufacturing are launching themselves into research and development into smart cars and driverless vehicles. Driverless vehicles have become a 'must have' in the eyes of the big commercial players. Companies vying for supremacy include Google, Baidu, Tesla, Mercedes, BMW and Mobileye. Amongst these, even the one with the lowest market capitalisation, the Israeli company, Mobileye, has US$8 billion. But with the marketplace in its infancy, whether it is UISEE, Google, Baidu, Tesla or Mobileye, none of them can be seen to be attempting any kind of coordination with their rivals. Moreover, barely 10 years ago, who would have thought that the Chinese car industry could have the opportunity to stand on the same starting line as equivalent companies across Europe and America? The guiding light of China's Holy Trinity, Wu Gansha, reckoned the way driverless vehicles were a test for the capabilities of artificial intelligence, microchips and big data analysis, at the highest level, meant that the gap between China and the rest of the world was not very great. In the practical uses for artificial intelligence, where there is zero time lag across the world, we are effectively in step with the top-flight countries such as America, and out in front of Europe and Japan. From that point of view, Wu Gansha said, "We have an excellent differentiated competitive pathway, and may even find ourselves able to overtake on the inside. Additionally, China has its own unique testing environment in which to solve problems that are even more difficult than in Europe and America, so we are even more able to develop the skills of our research workers. This is why I am very optimistic." UISEE Technology's ultimate goal is to be the brain behind automatically driven cars and vehicles, and in that respect it is the same as Intel.

Of course, no competitor should be undersestimated. Take Google, for example. At present, Google has the best driverless car. It uses Vision 2.0 – this finds solutions in radar and laser, high precision GPS and a high precision inertial navigation system. The whole package costs Rmb2 million. On the other hand, UISEE chose to use Vision 1.0 plus formidable computing and artificial intelligence. Why? Wu Gansha says, very rationally, "Affordability is what wins in the marketplace. UISEE Technology aims to keep its product under US$2,000 to US$3,000. Google is making 'eyes' but we are investing even more heavily in making a 'brain'. That's what a computer is, a brain. I have used Vision 1.0 which has a webcam, millimetre wave radar, commercial-grade GPS and a commercial-grade inertial navigation system. But my car is more intelligent and has a more powerful computer. When you compare 'eyes' with a 'brain', it is the 'brain' (computer) that will get cheaper and cheaper as time goes on."

This strategy has a lot to do with Wu Gansha's many years at Intel and his profound understanding of Moore's Law. Moore's Law is named after one of the founders of Intel: Gordon Moore. Its general proposition is that the purchasing power of US$1 in terms of computer capability will more than double every 18-24 months, and it illustrates the speed of progress in information technology. Although Intel's Moore's Law has persisted for more than half a century, it is not a physical or natural law, it is a commitment from one company to the digital society – it is human effort that allows it to be met.

Wu Gansha says, "In my many years at Intel, I came more and more to realise that this thing we call a computer must always be looking to the future: within one or two years your computer can halve in price and double in computing capacity. This is what you must stake your money on, because it is the future that will reward you."

Taking Mobileye as his model, Wu Gansha made his attitude clear from the start: he skipped right over driver assistance, did not use ADAS (Advanced Driver Assistance System), and went straight to automatic vehicles. Mobileye, which introduced ADAS to the world, as well as making driver assistance, also targeted automatic vehicles. As Wu Gansha put it, "We often say that the people who discover something are the last ones to see that it is outdated. By dint both of their 'genes' and their ideology, they suffer from path dependence, and cannot simultaneously achieve both consistency and completeness. Just look at Intel and its manufacture of PCs; it has been the last to recognise that PCs have had their time."

Wu Gansha's 16 years at Intel had taken him to the top of his profession.

"Mobileye has a quasi-religious belief in visual perception, and from 1999 right up to the present, has taken the potential of traditional vision algorithms as far as they can go. The next step upwards will have to rely on deep learning, but it is unwilling just to discard its traditional algorithms – there is not much space left on the Mobileye microchip for deep learning. This is the historical baggage it carries. We don't have any historical baggage so we can use whatever works best for us. Quite simply, with deep learning we can leapfrog a dozen or more years of development. Both our own low-cost lidar (laser-based radar), standard radar and a vision system are all usable, and all have their merits and their drawbacks," Wu Gansha says, impartially. "A computer vision system has the best resolution for the physical world, it has texture and colour but, in bad light conditions or dense fog, it can't see anything. Lidar can achieve exceptionally accurate modelling of its surroundings but it doesn't work in rain or snow. Standard radar has a long range, and its speed and distance measurements are both extremely accurate, but there are some materials, such as wood, which it penetrates rather than reflects from... it is a combination of things that provides the best results. Of course, we have researched deeply into this and, given the rising computing costs and the fact that ADAS is not really our thing in the first place, we haven't wasted time on it and its beep alarm. To tell the truth, the way I see it, if I encounter difficulties while driving, neither me desperately slapping myself to stay alert nor some alarm beeping at me is actually of any use. We have gone straight to automatic vehicles where you let the car do the driving."

Wu Gansha also says about UISEE Technology's core competitiveness: "Where AI's powers of perception and recognition are concerned, we are unwilling to pass on the responsibilities to others. That is number one.

Number two is the exploration of the fundamentals of the automatic car, and one of UISEE's key personnel, Jiang Yan, was the 2013 Smart Car Future Challenge Champion; he is also the first person in the country, in open conditions, to use our low-cost sensory methods to take a driverless car at an average speed of 80kph for more than 10,000 km around the Third Ring Road. In the past, the competition was like exam-oriented education, all you had to do was stick to the letter of the rules to be quickest to the finish line, no matter how crookedly the car drove. But if you want to be truly commercially viable, there are three vital considerations: number one, an outside observer can't tell it is a computer driving the car. Number two, a passenger in the car must not be able feel that it is computer driven – this is particularly difficult, and we joke about it saying that the main reason a husband and wife quarrel is because one thinks the other is going the wrong way; certainly I myself go 'crazy' if I'm in the passenger seat when my wife is driving! Number three, if you are sitting in the driving seat, facing the front as if you were actually driving, it is entirely natural to feel as if that is what you are actually doing. Taking these three considerations together, we believe that China stands alone in this field!"

Wu Gansha is a low-key kind of person, and when he makes this kind of boast, he is still so matter-of-fact about it, it sends a shiver through people who hear him. His words may not be razor-edged, but they have a steely quality to them so that, when he is at the podium in some discussion forum or other, when he speaks, you can hear a pin drop.

In 2008, Bill Gates ridiculed the automobile industry at a computing convention saying that if General Motors (GM) were to progress at full throttle, as the computer industry did, we would be driving US$25 cars that do a thousand miles to the gallon. Deep in crisis as it was, GM was quick to retort that if cars were like computers, they would "crash" twice a day for no good reason, and when the reset button fails you have no choice but to re-install; finally, before the safety airbag deploys, there would be a dialogue box deciding your fate on your thought processes in answering the question "Are you sure?". Bill Gates' view derives from current trends and consumer demands, and the automobile industry's stance draws on its opponents' weaknesses. Who will win? At the time, my money was on Gates. Eight years later, things have not yet turned out quite as anticipated. COMDEX is on the decline as an event and CES has suddenly emerged with great vigour, with automobiles occupying a full third of the exhibition space. Does that mean Bill Gates has won, or the standard automobile has won? Is it the computer that has won, or the automobile? The fossil fuel industry has a stranglehold on the electric car.

But all is not over yet. In fact, the first electric car was produced in 1890 and the first automobile battery replacement service appeared in 1910, but these innovations lost out to the ferocious onslaught of the late-comer, the internal combustion engine (ICE). A hundred years have passed in a flash, and nowadays we hold that the electric car began its revival in the 1990s. Now the roles are reversed with the ICE vehicle defending its position and relying on support from its patron, the fossil fuel industry, to throttle the growth of the electric car. After 10 years, the first star in the electric car firmament, Fisker, collapsed, as did the plan by Better Place to revive the battery-exchange business model. When karma provided another opportunity for an electric revival, Tesla rose like a phoenix from the ashes; but Tesla has already moved on from the original concept of a car and now has much more of the computer about it.

Wu Gansha Says

As a car's electronics and software comprise more than half of its manufacturing costs, and the battery half of those; and if, as in the case of the much-trumpeted Apple Car, it has the Apple logo; and as it hides a super-computer in its trunk that gives it the capabilities of an automatic car; and since its development has been through the open-source community at Local Motors, can you really still link it to a traditional automobile?

Wu Gansha remains unruffled by all this, a steely glint in his eyes, and says, as if looking towards an endless future:

"This time, GM's closest competitor is not an isolated lone revival; what has come shouting and yelling upon us is a whole new era. Close up, the new energy-source automobiles and car sharing seem to be the storm that is battering the shores of the traditional car industry; but from a distance, you can see that, as the great wave swells, internet connectivity, smart ability and the self-driving car are also bursting onto the market. In 2008, Bill Gates could not accurately have predicted everything that has developed over the following eight years, but the world he is at home in is a future-facing one. Moore's Law is a prediction of the future, a self-fulfilling future, and it is the man who can master these trends who will be able to follow a path of exponential growth to a victorious future. To predict the future, you have to invent it. Why does a believer in the law of exponential growth have nothing to fear from traditional power? Because of the formula that says: even if you have enjoyed outstanding success in the past period x, in the next period, someone can simply come along later and overthrow everything you achieved in period x. In this day and age, linear growth is a quick way to ruin. Speed of innovation is not enough in itself, it must always be accelerating. You mustn't waste time over the past, because the past always gives way in face of the future. It is never too late to leap into the exponential maelstrom: the peak may be passed, there are no tickets for the boat, great mountains threaten to crush you, the imperfections of the past are laid bare, but none of this matters. Victory will be yours in x+1.

The great technological revolution and the great economic cycle had been resonating for 60 years when, after the end of the 2008 financial crisis, a new 60-year cycle began. The information technology revolution forms a 20-year mini-cycle, and after a period of structuring from 1950-1970, a period of digitalisation from 1970-1990, and a period of 'netification' from 1990-2010, one great stride takes us into the 20 years of 'smartification', a root and branch change where artificial intelligence and automation take centre stage.

The most important factor is the once-in-a-century coming together of three elements: an epoch-making transformation is dragging open the heavy curtain that has been constraining it, and the ropes pulling on it are the information stream given impetus by the internet of things and big data; the new power source stream being brought about by new-energy vehicles (NEVs); and the way the world's traffic flow has mastered a never-before-seen form of kinetic energy through comprehensive study of the elements involved. Just as Wu Xiaobo said in his *Thirty Years of Surge*: "As that era approaches, all living things grow in profusion, dust and dawn rise together, the Yellow River and the Yangtze River converge in a great flood plain, nameless hills thrust up into towering peaks, and heaven and earth simultaneously draw apart." For many people, this favourable confluence of events may be a once in a lifetime event, and may even exceed Bill Gates' original imaginings. At UISEE Technology, all of our staff members are throwing themselves headlong into this momentous surge for no other reason than that they are heeding the summons of the times.

Why is it called UISEE (驭势科技 *yushi keji* meaning Driving Trends Technology)? We want to foretell the future and we want to drive (驭 *yu*) the trends (势 *shi*) of the future. We have engraved our mission into the letters of our English name, UISEE: 'U' stands for Utilisation of Time: liberating brain, hands and feet; giving the people setting out on the journey mental and physical freedom, adding a billion hours of useful time per day (if you transfer that into productivity, that makes products worth US$1 quadrillion); 'I' stands for Indiscrimination, enabling everyone, including the aged, children and disabled, to drive themselves about; 'S' is for Safety: reducing traffic accidents by more than 90%, equivalent to saving a million lives and US$1 trillion; 'E' is for Efficiency: the optimisation of traffic in terms of both time and space will reduce the number of vehicles in cities by 80%, and traffic flow will improve four times; parking spaces will be freed up (equivalent to about 15% to 20% of useful city space) and the immediate demands of all traffic will be met without traffic jams; 'E' is also for Environmentally Friendly: increased environmental protection will reduce CO_2 emissions and air pollution by 15%. UISEE is pronounced 'you see' because you can see the future our mission envisages. In Chinese 驭势 *yushi*, 'driving the trend', and in English, 'you see the future'. The value we stand for is to give drivers more safety and comfort, but in 10 years' time, we will be focused on travellers enjoying at least 10 times their current levels of convenience and value for money.

I have a dream: to free the capital city from its capital city traffic jams, to allow people to travel without having to worry about it; that should take 10 years. Today, Beijing has close to six million vehicles, the majority of them privately owned and, in the wings, there are a further million people in the lottery for one of the 60,000 license plates released every year. The number of cars just keeps increasing and parking becomes more and more difficult. With two parking spaces for every car, it is hardly surprising that 15% to 20% of city land is given over to parking; the restrictions on use by licence plate just make people buy more cars, the roads become more and more jammed, exhaust emissions cause smog, the accident rate keeps rising and the whole thing becomes a vicious circle. Why does everyone want a private car? For the reason everyone knows perfectly well: Beijing has 70,000 taxis, on top of which there are the 'guerrilla' cabs of Didi and Uber but, even so, there aren't enough to provide prompt service when needed by so many people. So, consider this scenario for a moment:

In 10 years' time, Beijing will have only one million private cars, but two million taxis. Using big data for the dispatch algorithms, they can provide on-demand service for 10 million passengers, with the taxi already waiting outside when you leave home. Someone might object that it is too expensive to take taxis everywhere, but they should know that the fare will be only a tenth of what it is now. Why? A taxi today has a profitable life cycle of five years; 10% of the fare goes on repayments and maintenance,

30% goes to the taxi franchise, 30% goes on petrol and the final 30% represents the driver's income. In 10 years' time, there will be no franchise charge, the cost per kilometre of the new energy source will be lower than that of conventional fuel, and the cost of the car itself will be even lower. Someone might also object that electric cars are really expensive. But that is not true of these taxis; the majority of them are one-seater or two-seaters, so they only need low-capacity batteries. If there are charging posts, underground charging points and battery exchanges all over the city, and if big data algorithms can guarantee that the battery has enough charge for the next person's trip, then it will always be possible to recharge in time. If the car itself is cheaper, there is no franchise charge and the cost of the energy source is lower, then the biggest proportion of the money will be the driver's income. But then, as you will already have guessed, these taxis are driverless cars! So where today you might have to spend Rmb50, in 10 years' time you will only need Rmb5. The three rivers of traffic stream, information stream and energy stream will converge into one great tsunami, redefining all aspects of the transport of both people and things, guaranteeing a nirvana-like rebirth in which the service industry will find an explosive new launch pad. These driverless taxis will be a third operating space on top of home and the office: they will be mobile business premises, mobile cinemas, mobile offices and mobile Starbucks.

"Someone might ask, will it only take 10 years?" Wu Gansha spoke to his workers with rare passion. "Just think back 10 years: the iPhone hadn't yet appeared, there was no sign of the mobile internet, the iPad didn't exist yet and the PC ruled the roost. In those 10 years, even the most extreme of prophets would never have predicted that the mobile internet would make such a radical change to the world. King for 40 years, the PC turns away, frustrated and disappointed, leaving just the drawn-out view of its retreating figure; the iPad has followed the complete course from rising sun in the east to setting sun in the west; smart phones have united every corner of the earth but are already showing signs of fatigue. The flywheels of time turn quicker and quicker; the gap between the future and the present, when compared to the gap between the past and the present, is smaller than you think, much smaller. Human life is short, so should we let it just pass as nothing special or embrace UISEE's future? If in the future there comes a day like the one in the film *Interstellar*, and we have the opportunity to send a Morse-code message from the fifth dimension back to our present selves and our children, I hope it would be like the words of the song *Welcome to the Future*:

3. THE PULL OF THE FUTURE

Fly...
Dreaming...
We ride the wings of time
To our future we will fly
Higher and higher now
Our love takes us higher now

DIARY NOTE 3: TIME

If Feng Kang represents the scientific foundations of Zhongguancun in the 1950s and 1960s, and Chen Chunxian represents the new trend at the end of the 1970s, what does Wu Gansha represent? I would say time. The thing to note is how quickly time passed and how enormous the changes were. I am not talking so much about Feng Kang's 1950s and 1960s, but certainly if we take 1978 in Chen Chunxian's period as the starting point then, 35 years later, Wu Gansha's Zhongguancun had been turned completely on its head; it was a completely different era and you might even say it was now on a completely different planet. Wu Gansha was in step with this new world or, you might even say, one step ahead. When Wu Gansha studied the heavens in Shangri-La, he was studying the future; he was thinking about driverless vehicles and, at the Summer Palace, in Zhao Yong's charmingly located high-tech company, two high-tech experts found themselves discussing time and the future, like two hobbits, or two characters from the classical text, *Shan Hai Jing*, talking about 3D computer vision, about privilege, about responsibility and about the city of the future – a city that no one could yet see. Except the difference was that, with the aid of 3D computer vision, they themselves could actually see the city of 10 or 30 years in the future. They were living ahead of their times or, you might say, they were living in the fairy tale of the future. Was their Zhongguancun and the Zhongguancun of 1978 the same place? Yes and no. But at the very least, we have to recognise that Wu Gansha has transcended the Zhongguancun of 1978 into a Zhongguancun where a whole new generation of people have broken through.

Tilting at Windmills

站风车

"I HAVE DECIDED to leave the Computing Institute from tomorrow, and the best thing would be for management to agree to my formal departure. If that's no good then you should second me. If that's no good, then you should transfer me. If that's no good, I will resign. If you won't accept my resignation, then you should sack me!" This was the famous 'five ways of leaving' forcefully delivered by Wang Hongde in 1983 at the Chinese Academy of Sciences Computing Institute's first conference. Its formulation was rather reminiscent of the verse forms of the contemporary Misty Poets Movement who reacted against the restrictions on art during the Cultural Revolution, so named because their work was officially denounced as obscure, misty or hazy poetry. It was rather like reading a manifesto ; it was also rather like reading Bei Dao's famous contemporary poem *The Answer*:

"I tell you, World
I... do... not... believe... in... you
If you have a thousand challengers at your feet
Then take me as the thousand and first."

They are undoubtedly of the same period, but that is not to say poetry is the same as science.

When Wang Hongde finished speaking, he walked out of the conference room, leaving everyone open-mouthed and dumbstruck in his wake. But they could see from behind, in the way he walked, how his inner tension was being outwardly manifested.

In particular it was his final words which had something of the flavour of the line from Jing Ke's poem *Song of the Yi River*: "How the wind shrills and howls; how cold is the water of the Yi River!"

But you don't get three feet of ice from one cold day or, to put it another way, Rome wasn't built in a day. Although upper management approved Chen Chunxian's ways, down at the lowest level, in breaking out of the shackles of old conventions, middle management was still very rigid and monolithic, and liable just to squash people.

"My family background is not good, and within a year of entering the Academy of Sciences, I was labelled a 'rightist' and subsequently attacked as 'an anti-revolutionary working in his own interests not the government's'. This went on incessantly until 1978. During that seemingly endless time, I had intense feelings of repression and humiliation, and suffered indescribable pain and vexation. I love the party and I love my country. My enthusiasm for the project has never flagged but there has simply been no chance to develop it." These were Wang Hongde's heartfelt words, not the least complex but, nonetheless, the same as the heartfelt wishes of the age. In the olden days, people were repressed, humiliated and harmed, but in this new era, hope has emerged, and light, shining down from the zenith, is releasing the long-suppressed thoughts of those below.

From Wang Hongde's point of view, his specific light appeared in the winter of 1979.

That winter was particularly cold and a bitter wind was blowing as Wang Hongde made his way into the Re-educated Youths' Club of the Chinese Academy of Sciences' Computing Institute. He saw the youngsters, all returned from far-flung places, warming themselves round the stove. Their hands were covered in gaping cracks caused by the cold where blood had spurted out from the hard labour they had been doing. But they stood there, apparently unconcerned in the icy wind, because the pain in their hands was nothing compared to the pain in their hearts. After their return to the city, employment for the re-educated youths had become a big social problem at the time. In the Chinese Academy of Sciences, a place already brimming with talent and achievement, these children of professors and specialists had to rely on physical labour, shovelling sand, cleaning and that kind of thing, to earn a meagre income.

It was hard on these youngsters, and Wang Hongde's heart bled for them. But he had a sudden inspiration: could he lead a team formed out of the youngsters of the Re-educated Youths Club to produce the equipment he had planned for the computer system in the computer room in the Computing Institute's own factory? Not only would this have the potential to promote the use of technology, it could also improve the lives of the re-educated youths; and later on, when their skills had matured, they could organise the installation of computer systems in computer rooms all over China.

In 1979, Wang Hongde was in charge of the team installing the electrical air-conditioning in the Computing Institute's Number 4 research room, and undertook a study of the environmental conditions in computer rooms. At that time, computer room equipment technology was a blank page in China, and Wang Hongde invested his whole department's energy into research on the subject. Wang Hongde had suffered great privations in his life, and his 26 years at the Chinese College of Sciences had been spent struggling against adversity; however much 'fighting skill' he had, he had had no opportunity to deploy it. But the fragrance of flowers growing inside a wall can be smelled outside it, and the level of his expertise began to be recognised by a wider audience. As an expert in computer room technology, Wang Hongde was already famous in industry circles. At the time, the Tianjin Computer Company, the Tianjin Electrical Equipment Factory, the Tianjin Wireless Number 5 Factory, Number 7 Factory, Number 11 Factory and so on, all asked Wang Hongde to act as a consultant. This gave Wang Hongde even more confidence that computers were on a rising tide and there was huge potential in the field of computer room technology. One evening, after he finished work, he once again braved the icy wind to go over to the Re-educated Youths Club, found the director amongst all the bustle, and talked over his idea. He told the director, "I can act as your consultant, draw up a plan for you, arrange for the re-educated youths to install the products…"

Before Wang Hongde could even finish, the director was nodding his head continuously.

Grasping Wang Hongde by the hand he said, "We will do whatever you say! I will be guided by you. The club really wants to find a way out for these youngsters who are all the children of intellectuals from the various scientific institutions, and finding manual labour for them is not a long-term strategy. Finding them work in the fields of science and technology is more than we could have dreamed of." And that is, indeed, how things turned out. The re-educated youths who had returned to the city were ecstatic when they heard, knowing that this was a turning point in their lives. Wang Hongde was like an angel sent from heaven. They were going to study technology and make their living from it.

This increased Wang Hongde's workload, and he spent his evenings and weekends drawing up plans. He often worked until three o'clock in the morning and sometimes straight through until dawn. At the same time, he was training, lecturing and leading the re-educated youths forward, hand in hand. As a consequence, very soon, all kinds of computer room equipment were being put into production. Naturally, sales were not a problem as Wang Hongde's contacts and reputation in the industry were the best of guarantees. So it turned out that through his introductions, large-scale computer work units all wanted to buy the equipment produced by the re-educated youths and to get them to install it. As the youths' work capacity expanded, Wang Hongde and the director discussed establishing a formal computer room equipment product installation team. What started out as the tiny Re-educated Youth Club suddenly took off; the youngsters themselves raised their level of technical expertise and, most importantly, saw their wages rise accordingly, so their original monthly salary of Rmb50 went up to Rmb90, which was even more than their parents earned after working at the Computing Institute for many years.

That year, the re-educated youths earned more than Rmb600,000, which was an astounding, not to say miraculous, sum for those times. Wang Hongde's support for the re-educated youths to engage in technological services, in the service society, caused a sensation in the news. As always with things like this, different people had different viewpoints and different conventions. Rmb600,000 was an enormous profit, and at first it alarmed the Department of Trade and Industry which suspected illegal activity. The end of year accounts were inspected very closely and the Re-educated Youth Club was the focus of detailed investigation by the Chinese Academy of Sciences. Wang Hongde himself was suspected of financial irregularities.

When the news reached the Discipline Inspection Committee of the Academy, they treated it as a major economic crime. They sought out Wang Hongde, wanting him to explain the circumstances of this 'economic crime', and to write a self-criticism. The Trade and Industry Bureau considered that he was running an illegal operation and engaging in unlicensed business activity. Tearfully, Wang Hongde told the bureau personnel, "The new production plans I drew up were all filling a yawning national need: if we didn't plan our own production, then we would have had to buy in foreign goods. I was supplying what the country needed but didn't have, and as for finding employment for the re-educated youths, what crime did I commit there?" To his amazement, the bureau personnel looked at each other in consternation and simply let him go. However, the Academy Discipline Inspection Committee detained him and the investigation into him took a year and a half. But Wang Hongde retained his self-confidence; he handed over his monthly consultancy fee of Rmb30 as his only admitted 'defective behaviour'. This surrendering of meagre income was relatively common behaviour among the revolutionaries of Zhongguancun at that time and among other businessmen as well. More often than not, it was not a product of their innate virtue, but of necessity in order to fend off unwarranted inspections, examinations and accusations. Random inspections at the drop of a hat were the common way of doing things in those times.

For no good reason, except that first impressions are the strongest, the investigation fuelled by an assumption of guilt proved too much for Wang Hongde. While he was still a young man, he was labelled a 'rightist' just because of a scrap of childish verse and he could never hold his head high at the Computing Institute again. He had joined the Communist Youth

League at the age of 21 and at 22 his name was expunged from the records. When the academy held its first conference, by force of habit, he put on his army cap, pulled the brim down low and hid himself in a corner. But even after the end of the Cultural Revolution, old behaviour kept resurfacing and, right up until 1979, he continued to be denounced as a 'counter-revolutionary'. Who could possibly have thought that even now it would be accusations of 'economic irregularities' that would be thrown at him. He was 46 now: was this how life was always going to be for him? Fortunately, the long-drawn-out investigation eventually cleared his name of all guilt. His far-sightedness and instinct for nipping trouble in the bud saved him, as his return of his consultancy fees illustrated. But, for many years to come, this whole affair completely destroyed his trust in his work unit and in the higher authorities, as he felt that this great institution, to which he had given 28 years of his life, had proved completely unreliable.

"Moreover," Wang Hongde mused, "working in a closed research system like that, so far removed from the practicalities of manufacturing, leads to a lazy and repetitive way of living. With a single project being divided into so many pieces, and each person just doing their own little bit, there isn't enough to satisfy anyone. It really was a case of wanting to do one thing but not being able to, and wanting to stop doing something else but not being able to give it up. I developed a plan to set up the kind of computer room company that the country was lacking, and to make it a large-scale project. Even if it killed me, I would have no regrets."

Wang Hongde was already entering into middle age at this point, with no time to waste, and he had decided to burn his bridges and go for broke.

He was not, however, an impulsive man, and in the summer of 1980, when acting as consultant to the Tianjin Specialist Electrical Equipment Factory, he suggested that they invite to Tianjin a certain Dr Rossi who was CEO of an Italian company specialising in the manufacturing of computer room equipment, with the aim of introducing new technology and collaborating in the production planning of computer rooms, flooring, low-airflow air-conditioning and other such equipment. The original idea was for a one-off exchange of technology but one thing Dr Rossi said shook Wang Hongde to the core. Dr Rossi's company, HIROSS, started with just three people and US$350. Seventeen years later it had grown into a large international computer room manufacturing company. If the business over the inspection of the Re-educated Youth Club accounts had made Wang Hongde begin to think about retreating, this real-life example came as a revelation.

First off, he went to talk to the Haidian District Association to make the preparatory moves for affiliating with them and then he registered a company through them. Everything was in place: he was ready both psychologically and in practice to take on the system single-handed, just like Don Quixote couching his lance and challenging the establishment. The scene was set for the opening act: "I decided to leave the Computing Institute the very next day and the best thing would be for the management to formally let me go. If not, they could second me. If not that, they could transfer me. If not that, I would resign. If they wouldn't accept my resignation, they should sack me!"

At the time, many people saw Wang Hongde as Don Quixote, or even King Quixote. For one thing, at that time there was one system for the whole country: everyone belonged to their work unit and to their country; resigning was tantamount to saying you were stopping being Chinese, which was unthinkable. Besides, the research staff of those temples of science were the gilded elite, members of an envied profession, so at the time, the majority of those who left research institutes, universities and colleges to found companies stayed within the civil service or were on unpaid leave when they took the plunge. Some people called this "keeping one foot in each camp": when they moved one foot into a new camp, they kept the other one very firmly anchored in the old one. This allowed them to keep some kind of mental equilibrium and gave them the option to continue to advance if things were going well or to retrench if income unexpectedly fell. In the early 1980s, this was not an uncommon situation. But Wang Hongde was different: he was the first person in the history of Zhongguancun to resign from a national institution. That is to say, Wang Hongde's choice was not a rational one, and in the eyes of many it was even quite comical, especially the bit where he said "you can sack me". But was his attitude and way of expressing it comical or quixotic? For one man to set himself against such a huge opponent, especially so "arrogantly", was completely out of all proportion. And yes, the out-of-proportion is always laughable.

But Wang Hongde was not Don Quixote, or not completely, at least, and the part of him that was, was perfect for the time.

Wang Hongde came into this world naked, and 'naked' was how he left the academy. But 'naked' as he was, the amazing thing was that, after searching for so long amongst so many, he had found his own turning point. After going through the proper formalities at the Bureau of Industry and Commerce, he set up the Jinghai (Beijing Shanghai) Computer Services Company. He no longer had senior administrators to order him about, and was responsible for his own decisions and his own development. Wang Hongde didn't have a penny to his name when he registered his company, so he borrowed Rmb10,000 from the Re-educated Youth Club, opened a bank account, and after four days repaid the loan in full.

One of the four co-founders of Stone (Sitong), Wang Jizhi, son of Wang Li, later wrote in an article entitled *The Heroic Four Companies of the Early Days of Zhongguancun*: "At Baishiqiao, Wang Hongde consulted the Beijing Library's land acquisition registry, and put up several single-storey buildings without even a chair to sit on at the outset. All they had were several wooden trunks; they covered the tops with newspaper to serve as drawing boards, and began to draw up plans." The four companies referenced here were: Stone, Santec, Jinghai and ScienceSea.

Wang Jizhi had an apartment in Shuangyushu where he often held dance parties, at which Wang Hongde, who was an enthusiast, often had a dance or two. He was as defenceless as a newborn babe with his newly founded company, and his fellow party-goers often broke out in a cold sweat worrying about their Don Quixote.

"There's no need! No one need worry about me!" Wang Hongde knew what he was doing.

The first project Wang Hongde's company took on after it was established was to rebuild Peking University's Honeywell computer system. The project was supported by a loan from the United Nations' World Bank, and Honeywell was a big American computer systems company with worldwide influence. The project was already out to tender before the Jinghai Company was set up, and in competition for it were the Chinese Academy of Sciences Computer Services Company, China Computers and other major players. But the project leader at Peking University said, "We were not interested in brand names and we gave the project to Wang Hongde's Jinghai Company because he had so many years' experience at the Computing Institute and is the acknowledged expert in computer room planning. We trusted him." After they took on the project, Wang Hongde and his men, who were the master engineers who had left the Institute with him, were so happy they could hardly sleep. Four days later, when the down payment had been received, Wang Hongde immediately also asked the Re-educated Youth Club for a loan.

But almost as soon as the work on the Peking University computer system was under way, they encountered a problem. When they were installing the outside cooling system, the construction workers discovered that there was a huge quagmire outside the university's main building, so deep it was like a bottomless pit. Some people suspected it might be one of Beijing's so-called 'eyes of the oceans', with some even mentioning that when Liu Bowen built Beijing, he discovered several of these 'eyes' which connected with the ocean. One of them was blocked up at Yuquanshan, another at Baita on the Beihai, and the third at Beixinqiao. It is said that the Beixinqiao 'eye of the ocean' has been disturbed twice. Once was when the Japanese occupied Beijing when it was hauled up for one or two kilometres on a great iron chain they found there, so you could see the gurgling currents of mud surging upwards, faintly hear the sea winds and catch a slight fishy smell. The Japanese panicked and quickly let the chain drop back down. The second time was during the Red Guards' Destroy the Four Olds Campaign when, not being superstitious, they once again hauled up the great iron chain, with the same result as the Japanese. They were equally terrified when they heard the great rumbling noises, and immediately let go of the chain. These two stories were known by all the re-educated youths in Beijing, and Wang Hongde's construction team were mostly re-educated youths.

The head of the construction team made a report of the situation to Wang Hongde, including mentioning the 'eye of the oceans'. Wang Hongde leaped on his bicycle and hurried over. 'Eye' or no 'eye' he jumped straight down to find out what was going on. The water and mud in the quagmire were pitch black and they stank to high heaven. It was clearly an old pond, no telling how old, but what was it doing there? Maybe it really was an 'ocean eye'. Wang Hongde was in a state of great agitation when there was a sudden popping noise in his ears and he found he couldn't hear a thing. It was as though there was a great thick wall pressing up against his ears. A sudden excess of internal heat had turned him deaf. Even though he couldn't hear his own voice, he gave a great shout of "Fill it in!". Then he was hurried off to Number 301 Army Hospital to investigate the cause of his sudden deafness.

It was indeed a sudden excess of internal heat, overriding all kinds of nervous response and inducing temporary deafness.

Certainly, Wang Hongde was overwrought, as Jinghai's opening foray into the business world might have been ruined on the first day by this ancient pond. How could he stand it? Was his long-cherished dream of being his own boss going to come to an abrupt end? How could he be so unlucky as to run into such a thing as one of these legendary 'eyes of the oceans'? The position of the computer was already fixed, and the air conditioning couldn't be moved either. There was no way of working round it and Wang Hongde had no alternative plan nor any technical solution. All he could do was go back to basics and fill the pond in with cartload after cartload of sand. But it seemed to have an ever-ravenous, unappeasable belly, so no matter what they threw in there nor how much sand and stone they tipped in, it all just disappeared. Thirty tonnes of sand, 50 tonnes of sand, 70 tonnes of sand... Wang Hongde was like the foolish old man who moved mountains[1], digging out a mountain of sand and rock every day. He didn't believe it was an 'eye of the oceans', but whether he believed it or not, like the bird Jingwei[2], he had to fill it in, and it was driving him mad. If he wasn't able to fill it in, he probably really would have gone mad, and he was indeed beginning to show the early symptoms. He reckoned this was like the 'quagmire' of his life: it had started with all the 'anti-rightism' and took him right up to this real-life quagmire. He had to fill it in and if he couldn't, he would use his own body – he would dive headlong into it, and when he reached the bottom, he would swim through to the ocean.

Then, just as in the legend, Wang Hongde moved the gods with his efforts, and as they reached the hundredth tonne of sand, the quagmire levelled out to be as motionless as Wang Hongde's numbed heart. They then inserted steel reinforcing bars, poured concrete and when it dried, the whole area was as strong and sturdy as could be. Wang Hongde was a changed man, a man cast in his own chosen mould.

Several months later, although the project had run over its allotted time – how could it not have? – it was finally completed. Either through the bird Jingwei's persistence or Don Quixote's determination (it doesn't matter which), nothing was left undone. The Americans who had previously inspected the site were amazed by the project and gave it a big thumbs-up, saying that the computer room Wang Hongde had constructed was 'A1'. The principal of Peking University invited the leaders of the engineering team to a banquet in honour of the Jinghai Company. Although the project had gone way over budget, the company cleared their first profit, and Wang Hongde completely recovered his hearing, so his dancing wasn't interfered with. The Peking University engineering project was no ordinary project, and with one shake of the leg at Wang Jizhi's dance party, to the tune of the hornpipe, all Wang Hongde's former worries melted away.

DIARY NOTE 4: VOLCANO

What can one feel emanating from Wang Hongde? Something like a suppressed volcanic explosion. If Chen Chunxian was a logical, intellectual heaven-sent physicist, Wang Hongde came from the earth, a deep place in the earth, a deep ancient place like those spoken of in ancient verse. If the age were to be depicted in a painting, it might show three hands: one coming down from the sky, one reaching up from the earth, the one beckoning to the other. It would be painted in a surreal, cubist style, with the third hand being the hand of poetry: it is a graceful feminine hand, or maybe the hand of Bei Dao[3], and the three hands are reaching out to grasp the heart of the age.

Some people stand out in the geometry of an age, and the longer ago it is, the more they stand out. Wang Hongde's deafness and filling in of the 'eye of the oceans' are imbued with a kind of heavenly symbolism, something almost mythological, and all three hands have the character of creation. Yes, that's it! Looking back now, wasn't that time truly an age of creation?

In the spring of 1987, I was working at a local newspaper when I interviewed Wang Hongde. I was 27 at the time, so young, and Wang Hongde was not yet 40, so still young himself in generational terms. I arrived at the Jinghai offices on Electronics Street, that same Jinghai Company that was one of the four stellar companies of Zhongguancun, and met with the fast-talking Wang Hongde. In truth, his voice was a little old-sounding, rather hoarse, and somewhat out of kilter with the fire in his eyes and his rapid speech; or perhaps it was like the juxtaposed tension in a painting. Thirty years later, we were chatting on WeChat; we had had no contact, written or spoken, in the intervening years, and the distance between Zhongguancun and myself, and vice versa, had grown greater and greater. The book I was writing about Zhongguancun had brought me back there, and taken me back 30 years. Wang Jizhi had given me Wang Hongde's WeChat address, and the instant we connected online, it was as if we had only met yesterday. It was the same hoarse voice and the same four stellar companies. The only thing that was hard to process was the circumstances: Wang Hongde was in hospital, and lying on the operating table.

I was able to go and visit him, and it was like visiting the spirit of the age.

[PART 2]
Lenovo China (1)
联想中国(一)

Overture

"LETTING OTHERS CONTRACT THE COMPUTING INSTITUTE is certainly not a feather in my cap; it is like me going out touting on the street. But at least it is me, the institute director, doing the contracting and it means I don't have to sack anyone. If it takes me opening a street-side bicycle repair shop, so be it; I have fifteen hundred people to look after."

In the summer of 1985, Zeng Maochao, the director of the Chinese Academy of Sciences Computing Institute submitted a report to his superiors which contained the above words, smacking of suppressed anger. The report was very solemn and stirring, revealing the pressure he was under; it read like a last cry for help on the edge of a precipice. They were such progressive and urgent times, you could see their leading edge even from the safety of the middle. It was particularly hot that summer, and Beijing was assailed by wave after wave of blistering temperatures; but it was another kind of heat that pervaded Zeng Maochao's report: the heat of a revolution in the organisation of science and technology. Several days before, one of the leading members of the Science and Technology Commission had called a big meeting at which were announced a number of concrete steps towards swingeing reform. A number of very vociferous heads of companies were present at the time, and the chairman of the meeting turned to them smiling, and asked, "Do any of you dare take on the contract to run the Computing Institute?" They replied, quite directly, that they certainly had the capability to do so, but if they did, they would dismiss 90% of the staff. This question and answer infuriated Zeng Maochao, who said, "I will not sack a single person. If it takes me opening a street-side bicycle repair shop, so be it; I have fifteen hundred people to look after."

Zhongguancun was growing by leaps and bounds at this time. The four outstanding companies, Stone, Santec, Jinghai and ScienceSea, for example, were creating great waves both at the academy and in China as a whole. Scientific research institutes were no longer ivory towers, as science and technology were quickly turning to productivity and production. Simply put, the days of "wait for the project, do the project and submit the project" were in the past; the country was allocating fewer funds to scientific research institutes, and some were even having to fend for themselves. Specifically in relation to Zeng Maochao's Computing Institute, there was news that their public funding was going to be cut by 20% that year, and in five years' time it would be gone completely. If this was true, then quite apart from any scientific research, the institute's fifteen hundred staff would have trouble even putting rice in their bowls.

No one had dreamed that the revolution would be so radical. For the great majority of people on the spot that day it was extremely serious; despite the boiling weather, a shiver went through their hearts. As they looked at each other they saw a kind of chilly numbness combined with an inability to comprehend what was going on. So violent was the tide of the times that many people couldn't negotiate the change. After the 10-year calamity that was the Cultural Revolution, a calamity for the whole population, it was very difficult to get to the root cause of it and set things back to rights. What people most wanted was to wrest back the losses of those 10 years, to hurry back to their laboratories, to go back to the past, to before the Cultural Revolution, to get back to proper research and bravely scale the peaks of scientific knowledge. With the smashing of the Gang of Four, the chaos was brought to an end but, just as they had struggled back into the light, when the Big Dipper had turned and the stars had moved, had another stormy sky appeared? A sky in which those four great companies towered over them? After only a few years, Zhongguancun was no longer the Zhongguancun of the ivory towers. A returning overseas Chinese observer arriving at Zhongguancun was confronted with this scene: on the main street the first thing that greeted his eye was the steel-clad Stone building, its wooden frame covered in a steel skin; downstairs it sold electronic components, and upstairs sat Shen Guojun and Wang Anshi. Next came the name plates of Santec, then Jinghai and ScienceSea. The old overseas Chinese thought the scene fresh and new, but for the majority of the scientific and technical staff in Zhongguancun, there was nothing fresh and new about it: they saw change happening every day to the extent that they didn't want to look at it full-face, but just glance sidelong so they were looking without really seeing.

In truth, the situation was very grim; you got nowhere if you were not able to change, and in the case of the Computing Institute, first the research projects from the Ministry of Defence dried up, then government funding was substantially reduced and the one thousand technical staff and five hundred workers were left idle with no work to do. This left them deeply worried. Additionally, looking at the institute's warehouse, the once awe-inspiring mainframe computers, which they had manufactured one by one and in which were coalesced the knowledge, blood, sweat and time of more than a thousand people, now had only the awards and accolades they had once been awarded; they had never been mass produced, let alone been considered from the viewpoint of economic efficiency. Zeng

Maochao, the institute's director, felt doubly pained. Changes had to be made because there was nowhere to go without changing, but the question was, how to change? Contract out the Institute's work? Like a farming village working to fixed quota outputs? They were a scientific institute, not a farming village.

Zeng Maochao's report came into the hands of Zhou Guangzhao, a scientist, deputy director of the Academy of Sciences and an expert administrator. At the start of the 1980s he had gone to study abroad, first in America then in Europe. After learning about the ways of the outside world, he returned to China to direct the country's scientific and technical revolution.

The overall situation in China had to change, there was no doubt about that. To begin with, Zhou Guangzhao focused on the major problems, respecting the principle of the golden ratio: no more than 20% of research personnel should concentrate on fundamental theoretical research, while the vast majority should be working on research that could be put to practical use. What he meant by 'practical' was turning the results of research into products to be launched onto the open market. After reading Zeng's report, Zhou Guangzhao summoned him, and told him that he still had a use for his researchers and technical staff, and there was no need to take seriously the talk of contracting out the institute. This set Zhou and all his staff's minds at ease. But at the same time, Zhou told Zeng Maochao that he had to change, that he couldn't just sit and wait, but had to find outlets for the results of their research and turn them into products for which there was mass demand.

Zeng Maochao didn't argue with any of this but accepted it all. In fact, as it turned out, he was pretty much prepared for it. Nor did he have any argument with making the massive change of turning Zhongguancun's research into productivity, but he did want to be steady and cautious about it: how could a scientist not have at least some reservations about such a thing, and how could he not be a little cautious? Zeng Maochao laughed mischievously then, making a show of being very earnest, informed the refined and scholarly Deputy Director Zhou Guangzhao that, by way of meeting the current circumstances, his institute had already set up a company in November the previous year. This was a 'surprise' he had set up in advance, and the founder of the company was the institute's own Liu Chuanzhi. Zhou Guangzhao was delighted and ordered Zeng Maochao to tell Liu Chuanzhi to come and see him. Zeng Maochao was a little agitated at this prospect because Liu Chuanzhi's company was only recently established, and the marketplace was being rather stuffy about it.

It had been swindled out of more than half of the start-up capital of Rmb200,000 the institute had provided, and it was in a tight spot with no obvious way out.

With his heart in his boots but putting a brave face on it, Liu Chuanzhi went to see Zhou Guangzhao and made a solemn promise.

High water

Twenty years later: 9:10am, Wednesday, 8 December 2004.

A historic moment, originally set for 9:00am but delayed by 10 minutes when the elegant, smiling figure of Liu Chuanzhi, already chairman of the board of Lenovo, appeared at the Beijing Continental Grand Hotel in front of all manner of honoured guests and reporters from every imaginable agency. A veritable barrage of cameras was pointed at Liu as he stood in the spotlight. All the guests and reporters knew very well the history he was going to make, a history they were going to be witness to. Apologetically but good-humouredly, Liu Chuanzhi addressed the phalanx of microphones and camera lenses, "Generally speaking, a baby with a large head makes for a difficult birth, so I apologise for being a little late this morning." His voice was clear and well modulated, giving the occasion something of the air of the kind of political moment with which history is littered, and with which people are all too familiar. But this wasn't a political moment and, because of that, there was something strange and unfamiliar about it.

It may not have been a political moment, but it was an iconic moment for globalisation, with a significance that transcended politics. Liu Chuanzhi announced, "The Lenovo Group has paid a total of US$1.25 billion for IBM's worldwide PC business. IBM's deputy chairman Steven Ward will be the new CEO of the Lenovo Group, and Yang Yuanqing will be Chairman of the Board." The room exploded with applause, and shouts and whistles of approval. When Liu Chuanzhi further announced that the purchase included the whole of IBM's global business in both PCs and laptops, including research and development and procurement, the applause and whistling rose in wave after wave.

Several hours before, at 5:00am on 8 November, negotiations were still in progress. This was just like many negotiations throughout history which are always only resolved at the last minute. After the conclusion of two all-night trans-Atlantic conference calls between Lenovo Group Vice-President Song Qiao and IBM Deputy Chairman Steven Ward, there was a long sigh of relief as Lenovo Group's chief financial officer put his signature to the purchase agreement.

On the same day, Microsoft Chairman Bill Gates was also visiting China, but 8 December was a day on which even the richest person in the world was eclipsed. This time, the spotlight was not on him, and the eyes of the world were on the Beijing Grand Continental Hotel.

It was a day that changed China and changed the worldwide structure of the PC industry.

The first edition of the German newspaper the *Frankfurter Allgemeine Zeitung* reported, "As Big Blue becomes Big Red, IBM's 200,000 employees' new boss is called Lenovo. If, until now, Lenovo has been a second-tier company and brand name, after its purchase of IBM, no one will be able to call it that any more."

By purchasing IBM's worldwide PC business, Lenovo's strength leapt forward in three ways: firstly, its brand image received a tremendous boost; secondly, the scope of the company was immediately enlarged; thirdly, it acquired an even larger purchasing base and online market. Previously, in the Chinese marketplace, although Lenovo aspired to be seen as the largest computer manufacturer, it had no unique core competitiveness. From the point of view of cost control it couldn't rival Dell which had espoused direct marketing at its outset, and from the point of view of technical innovation, it was a long way behind the deliberately unconventional Apple. So, when IBM, the grandfather of the PC, announced it was withdrawing from the market, it was an unmissable opportunity for Lenovo. By integrating IBM's PC business, it could greatly shorten its internationalisation process and leap straight to the number three spot in the world.

Reuters News Agency's former China current affairs manager, Doug Young, followed Lenovo's merger and acquisition trail for 10 years and articulated the West's most pragmatic viewpoint. In 2015, he wrote in an article entitled *Ten years after purchasing IBM computers, can Lenovo keep up the good work?*: "World PC industry leaders, Lenovo, are very gratified by the performance of the IBM PC business that they purchased 10 years ago. This milestone purchase has helped Lenovo develop into a PC business at the peak of the industry. When this sale was announced in 2005, I was suspicious of it, but my view has become more optimistic since then. Ten years ago, when Lenovo announced it was spending US$1.25 billion on buying IBM's famous PC business division, I and many others predicted that it could send Lenovo tumbling, because it had no experience in running a large-scale international company like that."

Doug Young's doubts were not without some foundation, because he had seen other Asian companies attempting something similar, and all had failed dismally. Among these failures were when the Taiwan company BenQ and the mainland company TCL purchased the cell phone divisions of Siemens and Alcatel respectively, both sales taking place at about the same time. Doug Young went on to write, "Lenovo's purchase of IBM's PC business did not go well to start with, and for several years afterwards, in order to establish itself as an international PC company as well as a brand name on the Chinese market, Lenovo had to undergo a very significant restructuring process. But once that was over, Lenovo's performance was outstanding and it went on to make a series of other purchases, entering markets as far afield as Brazil, Germany and Japan. As someone who had followed Lenovo's development over more than a decade, I began to feel genuine respect for the company, as one of the most successful Chinese companies on the world stage."

Doug Young particularly admired one aspect of Lenovo: in general, the top-level management of companies that have been purchased leave within one or two years as they are replaced by senior executives from the new owners; but this has not been the case with Lenovo. Today, 10 years after the purchase, there are at least two of IBM's senior executives working for Lenovo in North Carolina, which proves that Lenovo has all the appeal of a genuine international company. These two men are Thomas Looney, who joined IBM in 1974, and is now CEO of Lenovo America; and Peter Hortensius, who had already been at IBM for 17 years before joining Lenovo. Today he is Lenovo's CTO. Hortensius has said, "I have great respect for Lenovo's current CEO, Yang Yuanqing. His most admirable quality is that he runs the company very much in the Western style but comes off very well in any market in the world he enters."

Doug Young's opinion is considerably respected in the West and Liu Chuanzhi too can increasingly be considered a world business leader. America's *Fortune* magazine rankings of the top 500 companies in the world, the Fortune 500, listed Lenovo for the first time in 2008. In 2013, when the BBC interviewed Liu Chuanzhi, the interviewer complimented him saying, "You have a deep understanding of both business and world affairs", and invited Liu Chuanzhi to help Western businesses to come up with ideas for how to consolidate their worldwide influence.

Liu Chuanzhi told that foreign correspondent, "Most American and European business leaders came into business after studying for MBAs and, as CEOs, their main sources of knowledge are what they learned at college and their own experiences. They are like cooks for whom the most important thing is to follow the recipe book. For them, that recipe book is, as I just mentioned, what they learned at college. So, when a situation changes, they do not always know how to respond. When Chinese businessmen set up a business, they are self-driven and are faced with situations in constant flux. It is more as though we are the ones writing the recipe book. Each side has something to learn from the other."

By 2013 China was already the biggest manufacturing nation in the world; from New York to Cairo and from London to Buenos Aires, seemingly in every corner of the world, you could find goods manufactured in China, from computers, televisions and cranes to clothes, shoes, hats, toys and other things too numerous to list. With this background, which admittedly is part of a strategy of state support, the more important thing to note is that a Chinese entrepreneur has finally made it on to the international stage. Lenovo's purchase of IBM not only created a world-class Chinese business, it also created a world-class business leader.

Ballad

In 1985 or 1986, Liu Chuanzhi attended his first IBM agents' meeting at the Great Wall Hotel. The hotel in Liangmaqiao had not been open very long and the majority of those attending the meeting were official institutions; Lenovo, however, was a privately-owned company that had been running for less than two years and for it to have agent status was something to be very proud of. Liu Chuanzhi remembers that at the time he didn't even own any decent clothes, and was wearing his father's woollen overcoat. He had gone most of the way to the meeting by bus, but when he got close to the Great Wall Hotel, he got off the bus and hailed a taxi for the sake of appearances. He had expected there to be people meeting delegates at the hotel door, but it turned out that there weren't, and he regretted taking the taxi. When he got to the meeting room, he took off his overcoat, under which he was also wearing his father's clothes: a coffee-coloured suit and tie from his father's youth. He looked like something from the 1930s not the 1980s, rather like the Bund in Shanghai. There was a refreshments table in the meeting room, and as it was Liu Chuanzhi's first time at a meeting like this, and the first time he had seen a help-yourself buffet, he couldn't help but start stuffing himself. Recalling this so many years later, he still thinks those snacks were delicious – some of them he had never even seen before – and he certainly never imagined then that one day he might buy IBM, let alone become the boss of an international company like that. He also remembers that although IBM had a Chinese working environment, it really wasn't adapted to the Chinese way of doing business. When Liu Chuanzhi handed his Chinese business card to the IBM executives, they were very haughty and arrogant, making him think to himself: you're acting for their profit, you're the one helping them, but they make you feel as though you are coming to them cap in hand.

But a big company is a big company, and something to be respected, and it's not bad at all if you can act as their agent in however small a way. There was no gainsaying Liu Chuanzhi's respect, not to say deep reverence for, IBM's strength but, at the same time, nor did he underrate himself. Every time he felt their arrogance it just increased his own resolve, his determination, and something he couldn't yet put a name to.

Liu Chuanzhi was born in Jiangsu in 1944. As a young child he moved to Beijing when his father, who worked for the People's Bank of China, was transferred there. He went to a primary school in Dazhiqiao Lane (*hutong*). Dazhiqiao is situated on Xuanwumenwai Avenue and at its west end were five army drill grounds. Before the Qing Dynasty it hadn't actually been a lane but a small creek that linked up with the other creek that flowed south from Xuanwumen. Where the two creeks met, there was a small bridge. In 1895 Dazhiqiao was the site of the 'Gongche Shangshu Incident'[1] when Kang Youwei[2] supervised the drafting of the famous '10,000-word petition' at the Songyun Shrine there. In 1966, Liu Chuanzhi graduated from Xidian University which had also been called the People's Liberation Army (PLA) Institute of Telecommunication Engineering before changing its name again to the Northwest Institute of Telecommunication Engineering. There are two major army institutes in China, one is Harbin University and the other is Xidian. After graduating he took up a post in Number 4 Building of Number 10 Institute of the China National Defence Scientific Work Committee. During the 10-year catastrophe of the Cultural Revolution, Liu Chuanzhi effectively abandoned research but, fortunately for him, he had some reading and study behind him, and was able to write something in support of the rally in Tiananmen Square in what is known as the Tiananmen Incident. The Chinese Academy of Science's Workshop 109 produced four stone steles mourning the death of Zhou Enlai on which were written "May there be a catching of witches and an exorcising of demons". This caused quite a stir. Afterwards, the academy pronounced that this was a counter-revolutionary act, and they went to arrest the men of Workshop 109. They also appointed a task force with a remit to investigate, expose and arrest, and to explain how savage and counter-revolutionary the steles were. The Computing Institute also formed a task force intending to make arrests. The black cloud of the Gang of Four loomed over the city, and the city wanted to disperse it. It was in those circumstances that, cunningly using his left hand, Liu Chuanzhi wrote a letter on behalf of the men of Workshop 109, which said: "I firmly believe that, when capturing witches and exorcising devils, one should not be afraid of being seized by devils". It was signed "The Revolutionary Masses" and was something of a cause celèbre at the time. Although this movement can't really compare to the 'Gongche Shangshu Incident', and they are two completely different things, there is a kind of visceral relationship between them. In 1983, Liu Chuanzhi transferred from the Computing Institute to the academy's cadre office. There he spotted men from the Security Bureau and knew that the case against him was still ongoing, but they hadn't cracked it yet. That letter of his had been posted in an anonymous letter box on Baishiqiao Road, and he had written it using his left hand, so there were several factors hampering any identification. Courage, care and attention to detail – was it possible to say the courage came first or was it the care and attention to detail that gave him the courage? With Liu Chuanzhi, it was already difficult to tell them apart. But what else was there in addition to those qualities?

Undoubtedly, Liu Chuanzhi was a man capable of wielding power, and no matter what was going on at the time, he could do what he believed was right without a second glance, whilst still remaining prudent in his decision-making. He was also the kind of man who dared to make decisions and stand by them. There were two reasons he transferred to the cadre office. One was for himself: he could see the problems at the Computing Institute, that the results of their research were always put on the back burner where they were of no practical use, which was absurd but he was not in a position to do anything about it. The other reason was simply being in the cadre office itself: he was, on the surface, a talented man, likeable and eloquent, and destined for high office. He was quite clear in his head about these two reasons, but what also became clearer and clearer to him was that high office was not where he wanted to go; times were changing, and he could see quite distinctly where power lay: it was in Chen Chunxian leaving the academy; and in the way the four great new companies of Zhongguancun were breaking the system, manifesting a new energy. This bottom-up energy was every bit as good as top-down energy, and it represented great power, undoubtedly fraught with danger, but great power nonetheless.

. . .

There was another reason too. It was a time of great poverty and deprivation, and of unimaginable shortages. When people are deprived of dignity and see even the slightest chance of changing things, they seize it. Take accommodation, for example: Liu Chuanzhi was a technician at the Chinese Academy of Sciences and in a normal marketplace, he would be a high-status individual – naturally a high-status job confers high status on the person who holds it. But at that time, he was actually living in a bicycle shed; he couldn't even afford a basic *tongzilou*[3]. The bicycle shed was built against the west wall of the Computing Institute; it was two metres high and three metres across. It had a corrugated asbestos-sheeting roof and a concrete floor. At the end of the Cultural Revolution, with a thousand things to do, and everyone looking forward to a peaceful life, no housing had been built for a very long time, and accommodation was in short supply. A good number of people at the Computing Institute, Liu Chuanzhi amongst them, had been casting covetous glances at the bicycle shed, and eventually they broke into it. They divided the shed up into a square lattice pattern and used a daub of mud, grass and dried reeds to fill in any gaps and cracks; they cut square holes in the western outer wall to serve as windows and cut an opening in another wall and fitted a door frame. In a very short time, that bicycle-shed housing development had taken proper shape: it had a long narrow alleyway running through it which the residents jokingly called Zhongguancun's Dongjiaomin Alley. The real Dongjiaomin Alley is just off Tiananmen Square and was the Legation Quarter in the old days; it was a popular gathering point, with something of a foreign atmosphere, so these modern technicians certainly knew how to make fun of themselves. This kind of self-mockery didn't just belong to the city's alleys and back streets, it was found in the establishment compounds and research institutes too. Very few other places can match Beijing for its shared citywide temperament and personality. The reason for Beijing's common taste for self-mockery is worthy of study. It may well have something to do with the city's great disparity in circumstances, but this is not something for discussion here and if you are interested, you will have to do your own research.

Liu Chuanzhi moved into 'Dongjiaomin Alley' in 1971, and he and his wife papered it all round with newspaper and lined the ceiling with bamboo mats. Since the work unit didn't allocate housing, this became their home, like birds building a nest, and that was where they bore and raised their children. The room was 12sqm, but they managed to make it up to 16sqm by hanging some oilcloth down from the end of the sloping asbestos sheeting of the roof. So, there was the family; with the addition of the father-in-law and the mother-in-law, for most of their time there, there were seven people living in 16sqm: how was that possible? Well, they were scientists and technicians, weren't they! They found ingenious, scientific ways round it. Liu Chuanzhi's wife, Gong Guoxing, also worked at the Computing Institute; they had been fellow students at university, had gone through the Cultural Revolution together, and cadre school[4], and had joined the Chinese Academy of Sciences' Computing Institute together. The institute had four main areas of specialisation: one was main processing units, the equivalent of today's CPU (Central Processing Unit); one was building memory units. These memory units worked by passing a current through magnetic cores: one core conducted electricity and another didn't, and these effectively became the switches 1 and 0, on and off. Gong Guoxing worked in the room that produced these and where eventually they stored the commands on a disc. What I was initially talking about was internal storage, but these discs were external storage, and these were what the room Liu Chuanzhi worked in was making. The two of them could genuinely be called a husband-and-wife team. It wasn't just in their work unit that they displayed their intelligence and ingenuity; they had many other opportunities for collaboration. Their home was one of these: space was very limited, so their furniture was all collapsible: chairs, tables, benches, even the sofa. During the day, everything was opened out with a flourish and put in its proper place but at night it was all collapsed down to its constituent parts.

Take the bed, for example: it took the form of a sturdy sofa in three sections. You pulled one out to make it wider, and then pulled the sofa-back down so it formed a single flat area, thus turning the whole thing into a bed that could sleep three. The whole thing could also be hoisted up to the height of a proper bed. Everything was like that, facilitating a multitude of changes and flexibility, all extraordinarily neat, so the room was like a high-tech workshop, just like the Computing Institute itself. Usually, it was his wife who had the ideas and Liu Chuanzhi who put them into practice, which was pretty much the same as the way they worked at the institute. Or, to put it in the vernacular, the boss did the talking and the underling did the leg work. So when his wife came up with the plan, Liu's first question was, where is the wood coming from? And once the wood was 'borrowed' or found, they still needed a carpenter, and more challenging still, a set of wheels to transport the stuff. As a last resort, Liu Chuanzhi sought out his fellow demobilised soldiers and the people he had played football with, and lo and behold, it all turned out very neatly.

That motley crew of chance acquaintances were just the people to put into practice the 'boss and underling' principle.

As time went on, the family home became more and more refined, half automated and half manually operated; whatever they did seemed to make that 16sqm more spacious, but there was a problem. Liu Chuanzhi felt that Gong Guoxing had a fault (even Gong herself admitted it was a fault): every so often she wanted to change where everything was in the room, and Liu Chuanzhi had to make it happen. With spare time on her hands, she wanted to find things for Liu to do; so when she got bored and annoyed with the way the furniture was arranged, she came up with a completely new layout. The main reason his wife was so fussy and fastidious was because she got other people to do the actual work and did nothing herself. When Liu Chuanzhi discussed with her his idea of setting up his own company, she immediately agreed with him. She didn't think very much of the cadre office, but even if she had, she didn't think that Liu Chuanzhi was senior management material. His ideas were on too grand a scale for him ever to be a manager. Besides, his research at the institute wasn't going anywhere, most of the results were being put on the back burner; other than some merit awards, he hadn't seen any benefit from them. If the whole institute was going nowhere, where was there for him to go? He might as well stay at home moving the furniture around for her and hatch some new plans. "We shouldn't put all our eggs in one basket," Gong Guoxing said, and Liu Chuanzhi decided that his wife was being very wise about this. If he let himself be guided by her, the results would definitely be advantageous. He reckoned that it should be his wife who stayed at the institute and he should break away. Then, if it didn't work out, they had a backstop, and if it did, it would bring the family new hope.

Of course, you can't just blame the times you are living in, you have your life to live too. Some things in life, such as making plans, are just as important as historical trends, and have more growth potential too. A lot of great principles are only developed after the event, and people who are truly living their lives don't root themselves in principle, they root themselves in living, in dealing with concrete issues so the tree of life remains forever green. These two pragmatic minds, seasoned by life, and embodying their own kind of philosophy, no matter how illustrious Liu Chuanzhi was later to become, can trace the roots of their pragmatism and resolution to the solid foundations of their life back then.

In addition, most of the companies in Zhongguancun back then were selling computers, and many of them, like Wang Hongde's Jinghai Company, came out of the Computing Institute. And although ScienceSea was pioneered by Chen Qingzhen, the main money-making force behind it was Xu Yunsheng, who also was a product of the institute. In the constant flow of people resigning to go into the commercial world, the majority were educated at vocational secondary schools. They had nothing to lose, carried no baggage with them, and had considerable practical skills, more than enough than were needed for building computers. They began earning money as soon as they left, making many times more than they earned at the institute. And, in all honesty, it was how much you could earn that really mattered. Even if your level of education wasn't very high, and you were only a graduate from a vocational secondary school, that was fine as long as you were earning good money. What difference did your academic level make if you were an undergraduate, a research student or a research associate? Did you dare abandon your current research work to go out and make money? No, you didn't! These may seem like subtle differentiations, but in truth they were what really mattered in making your way in life; it was making money that was the motivation for these vocational school graduates to go out and hustle. The institute's director, Zeng Maochao, understood that it would be better to have a company under the control of the institute than to see all his staff leaving to go to outside businesses. It would not only be moving with the tide of the times, it would also be a popular move that had a stabilising effect on the team. Stuck in the cadre office, Liu Chuanzhi had the same idea, and the two men hit it off together immediately.

Zeng Maochao rather admired Liu Chuanzhi's competence and popularity at the institute. In fact, not long after the demise of the Gang of Four, Liu was already displaying some rather different talents. At that time, scientific and technical staff were allowed to supplement their income in their spare time through private enterprise, as so-called 'Sunday engineers'. There was a magazine called *Outside the Eight Hours*, the implication being that your time was your own outside working hours. This would have been impossible while the Gang of Four were in control, when everything belonged to the state, even your spare time, so the magazine was especially welcome. This was, in fact, a pivotal moment in the process of restoring order out of chaos, a time when the lives of the masses began to return to normal and individuals were allowed to have their own individual space. Liu Chuanzhi was at the head of the trend as he began to push his products. In the past, the magnetic memory tape his workroom made was all handed over to the authorities, but now he could offer it to other work units. Most of the money he made this way went to the institute, but he was able to give a bit to his colleagues in the workroom and keep a bit for himself. His standard of living began to improve. Most of the business was brought in by Liu Chuanzhi himself; it was something none of the others could do, and his ability to make outside contacts was greatly admired. Of course, this also brought him certain influence, and he also attracted people's admiration for the way he handled the inevitable conflicts of interest that profit attracts. Profit is the most difficult thing to get the balance right with, as it is entrenched deep in human nature, and Liu's innate skill in handling it was obvious to everyone. His wife, Gong Guoxing, could see how his ambition was already being stifled. In fact, he was always on the lookout for a way to make his mark, for a way out. He thought of transferring to the patent office, but Zeng Maochao was unwilling to part with him. However, the cadre office also had its eye on Liu Chuanzhi, and although Zeng wanted to stop the move, he didn't dare do so.

"The problem is, now you're in the cadre office, how can you come back here to run the company? Are they just going to let you go? The cadre office is there to look after cadres, and I don't dare challenge them!" That was Zeng Maochao speaking. Liu Chuanzhi just smiled and said that he knew a way. All Zeng had to do was go to the cadre office and ask, and they would be sure to let him go. Zeng was incredulous; he didn't know what kind of cunning plan Liu had, nor could he imagine what it might be. Nevertheless, he tentatively suggested to the office that he wanted Liu Chuanzhi, and presto! he was released. Zeng Maochao asked him what magic arts he had used, but Liu Chuanzhi just smiled again and said, "It's a secret!"

Transferring people between offices was a very complicated matter in those days, and Zeng Maochao had had no idea what means Liu Chuanzhi had to make the cadre office let the tiger return to the mountain. With grave reservations, he had gone ahead and submitted a request. By this time, Liu Chuanzhi had been thinking in advance about who it would be best to set the company up with and who would be in charge, that is to say, as CEO. So he began to sound out institute personnel. Liu Chuanzhi didn't consider it would be proper for him to transfer back from the cadre office and take charge, especially as it was the institute's company, and he had already left there once. So he came up with a name: Wang Shuhe. Wang Shuhe could be CEO, and he and Zhang Zuxiang would be deputy chairmen. The three of them working together would be the most advantageous and the most appropriate arrangement. You can't make yourself the focus when setting up a company; however suitable you are, it may not be appropriate to the circumstances. You have to be open-minded and give way where necessary. Wang Shuhe was department head of the science and technology section of the institute, and a man Liu Chuanzhi had great respect for. Moreover, by making a department head CEO of the company, the company itself would gain a certain status. This was a crucial element. (Eight months after the company was established, Wang Shuhe suddenly resigned. This was a severe blow to the company and to Liu Chuanzhi. The company went through a very difficult period when the direction it should take was very uncertain. However, objectively speaking, his departure also gave Liu Chuanzhi an opening, but that is something to be addressed later on.)

Liu Chuanzhi spent a long time talking Wang Shuhe round as, at that time, it was no easy matter to persuade someone to leave a senior post. Wang vacillated, raising minor objections, but the real consideration was whether he really wanted to leave the work he was doing and abandon his senior position. In the end, Liu Chuanzhi persuaded him. Next came Zhang Zuxiang who was deputy head of the institute's Number 8 Workroom. He was a computer specialist, though, and since it was the Computing Institute's company, there was no shortage of computer specialists; moreover the institute's specialists were indeed the nation's specialists. At the time there was another company in Zhongguancun that wanted to entice Zhang Zuxiang away, and Liu Chuanzhi caught him just in time. The first time Liu went to talk to Zhang about the company, he pulled a pack of Daqianmen cigarettes out of his pocket. Normally, they all smoked Haihe or some such brand that cost around 20 cents a pack, but Daqianmen cost 34 cents, so bringing them out immediately signalled that he meant business.

Once the team sheet was drawn up, it was time to recruit the troops, and although the four big companies of Zhongguancun had already created quite a stir, provoking an itch that demanded to be scratched, a lot of the people who proclaimed their eagerness to break away from the institute were really quite scared to do so. The effect of Liu Chuanzhi luring Wang Shuhe and Zhang Zuxiang away, plus one deputy department head and one deputy workroom chief, was considerable, and this was undoubtedly part of his strategy. He continued to use his gift of the gab and his network of connections in an intensive campaign of persuasion and mobilisation so that, by the end of 1984, he had assembled a team of a dozen or more institute personnel. Institute Director Zeng Maochao generously gave him Rmb200,000 start-up money, and the company was formally opened. Although I say 'formally opened', there was no great beating of drums and ringing of bells, nor any ceremony; all it meant was that the company was allowed, free of charge, to use a small bungalow that had been the institute janitor's office. Many years later, on the day of the IBM purchase at the Beijing Grand Continental Hotel, when he faced the flashbulbs of the world's media, Liu Chuanzhi remembered that bungalow as though it were some kind of weird hallucination. Although that was how it seemed later on, at the time it was no hallucination, nor was it any longer the vacant institute janitor's bungalow, empty and full of dust. The company held its first general meeting there amidst the dust, and the first item on the agenda was to bring in desks and chairs, and give the place a good clean. After a burst of frantic activity, everyone sat down on three benches; no one, not even the director and assistant directors, had proper desks yet, just those three benches.

The second item on the agenda was to decide what the company was actually going to do. Since they were a science and technology company, that was, of course, their focus, but they had to recognise that the Rmb200,000 start-up money couldn't immediately be used for scientific and technical development. The top priority was to earn some money as, if they didn't, that start-up money would quickly disappear on basic running expenses; and if the company disbanded, it would not be an easy matter for everyone just to go back to the institute. Although there was an agreement that if the worst did happen, they could return, as the institute was guaranteeing them their posts, everyone felt that "a good horse doesn't go back to pasture where it has already grazed" and that they had burned their boats in leaving, and really couldn't go back.

There was a lively discussion with everyone talking at once as they pooled their collective wisdom, and although they did not know precisely what they were going to do, they were clear on one point: they would do whatever they had to do to earn some money. When they had some money, some capital, they could discuss it again. So that was how the company proceeded at that time, but the times themselves imposed a condition on their ability to earn money. Thanks to so many years of a government-controlled economy, the whole of the 1980s was a time of economic shortage: raw materials were scarce, the consumer economy was not yet developed; many daily necessities were unobtainable even if you had money and if it didn't need a ration book, it needed a ticket. Under these conditions, anyone who could make something could earn a few cents. Selling steel was a way to make big money, but did anyone have any contacts? What about small consumer goods? They were safe but didn't make much profit. Electronic watches, then? Or roller skates? They were all the rage. Sweatpants, I've heard they're a hot item. I've got it: there's a real shortage of refrigerators and colour televisions. Has anyone got a contact? Everyone was offering their opinion, but it all came down to the same thing. Liu Chuanzhi was in the same boat as the rest of them; he wasn't a magician, and he couldn't buck the trend of the times. He sent out the members of the Re-educated Youth Club to scout around all over, looking for a commercial opportunity.

Hard work and enthusiasm eventually paid off and, after a thorough search, they finally discovered that far off in Jiangxi Province there was a woman who worked for the Women's League who had a consignment of colour televisions she wanted to sell.

So, there was their chance to make some money. Everyone was overjoyed: there's nothing that delights a person more than the thought of making some money. Of course, according to Liu Chuanzhi's meticulous and painstaking way of doing things, it was vital for them not to show their hand, and time and again he had to remind his staff that they must inspect the merchandise first before handing over any money. A junior member of staff was sent off to Jiangxi with the management's instructions, and he was delighted with his inspection of the televisions. Yes, indeed, he absolutely saw them with his own eyes, and he rushed to transfer the funds before anyone else could get in ahead of him. As soon as the money was transferred, the consignment of colour televisions mysteriously disappeared. The woman supposedly from the Jiangxi Women's League was a professional con artist and the consignment of televisions the man had inspected were a blind, just like the fake tanks that the allied forces in World War Two got Hollywood to make to fool Hitler. Rmb140,000 of the Rmb200,000 start-up money disappeared, just like that, leaving only Rmb60,000. This was a bitter blow to receive right at the start of things and, because it was so bitter, it stirred something nameless in Liu Chuanzhi, something firm and unyielding. This was something that had been missing in Liu Chuanzhi in the past. The rage suddenly cleared from his brain; he realised that all his past experience had been in public office, only in the Academy of Sciences, in fact. In that closed environment, he was considered careful and experienced, but now he had left, on the outside, he was far from either. Previously, he had been swimming in a swimming pool, but now he was in the open ocean; previously he had been able to use butterfly and free-style, but now he was reduced to breaststroke. Breaststroke is not very pretty or impressive, but it is a long-distance stroke. In amongst the wind and the waves, only if his breaststroke was as firm and reliable as he was himself, could it last the distance, and only then could he be sure of not being swallowed up by the waves.

Liu Chuanzhi had often thought about the ocean, and although he had very seldom actually been to the seaside, that was enough for him to make sure he kept a firm eye on himself from then on.

The sudden reduction of Rmb200,000 to Rmb60,000 gave Liu Chuanzhi something else as well, and that was a kind of resolution. Since he had already lost everything except his trousers, he really didn't have much more to lose. In order to plug the gap in the finances, at a stroke, Liu Chuanzhi personally led his work force in the transformation into small consumer goods middlemen and set up a stall selling electronic watches and sweatshirts at the gates of the Computing Institute. Of course, this was a very demeaning situation for him: how could he hold his head up, going running back home to beg for food after losing all his money on the outside? But Liu Chuanzhi set his face and got on with it. "I may have lost everything, but I haven't given up!" That was Liu Chuanzhi's new-found resolution. Selling electronic watches didn't make much money, but it represented a kind of manifesto commitment: from now on, I'm not going to lose any more, I'm only going to win; little by little, I'm going to win. Moreover, in the final analysis, what he was doing was showing strength and determination and there is nothing shameful in making your way through blood, sweat and sheer hard work.

There may be something wrong in being as firm and unyielding as that, but even that wrong has great rectitude about it.

At that time, the pioneers of the four great companies of Zhongguancun, people like Santec's Jin Yanjing, Jinghai's Wang Hongde and Science-Sea's Chen Qingzhen, were all already the trend-setters of Zhongguancun, with output values in the tens of millions, and Liu Chuanzhi was selling electronic watches. No one knew who Liu Chuanzhi was or, if they had heard of him, all they knew was that he had lost a lot of money and was now selling watches.

Six of the eleven staff in the company were smokers and, since their wages were pretty low, they couldn't afford good cigarettes. They found it particularly shaming that they didn't have any decent cigarettes to offer any guests or clients who visited the company. Using company money to buy cigarettes to offer clients wasn't a proper thing to do, nor was there any natural way of producing them and offering them if you did. You couldn't just take them out of a desk drawer, because that didn't fit the conventions of offering a smoke. Offering a smoke is a personal thing, a way of showing you are equals and a way of establishing a relationship. If you take the cigarettes out of a drawer, what does that look like? It looks like you're making it a business transaction, doesn't it! How about buying some with company money so each person can have two packs of cigarettes in their pockets, one their own and one the company's? The three men on the management team talked it over this way and that. It was a detail that couldn't be overlooked, as it was an everyday occurrence.

"Stop smoking then!" Liu Chuanzhi said. "Starting today, I'm giving up!" And that's what he did.

Liu Chuanzhi threw his cigarette end on the floor and stamped it out. He never smoked again. Wang Shuhe and Zhang Zuxiang hesitated for a moment, then stamped their butts out too. They threw the rest of their cigarettes out of the window. People joked about this, saying, "If a man can give up smoking, what else can't he do?" There is some truth in that, and you might even say it was a kind of symbolic exorcism.

Zeng Maochao didn't call Wang Shuhe, Liu Chuanzhi and Zhang Zuxiang to account over their responsibilities, and this laissez-faire attitude of a general toward his elite troops proved somewhat detrimental and caused some concern. But Zeng Maochao persisted in his attitude that they were indeed elite troops and should be treated as such. If they were selling electronic watches, let them sell electronic watches to begin with: it was a kind of baptism of fire, putting them into mortal combat so they would fight for their survival; what didn't kill them would make them stronger.

That was just what happened and the elite troops took their chance. The Chinese Academy of Sciences bought in five hundred IBM computers and were preparing to allocate them to their different research institutes. When they heard this, Liu Chuanzhi and the later-to-be-famous Li Qin besieged the academy's facilities office. They were certainly no watch salesmen now, any more than elite troops are peasants. They were much more sensitive to matters to do with computers than with electronic watches, and there was an air of almost superhuman sharpness and excitement about them, like generals hearing the news of battle. Every day, they ran around lobbying, and arguing, talking until they were blue in the face, tenacious as bulldogs and utterly determined to win. There was nothing on earth that was going to stop them getting their hands on those five hundred IBM computers.

To be precise, what they got was the monopoly on initial inspection, training and repairs for the computers. They also received a 1% hardware back-up contingency allowance from the facilities office and the contract to hold classes in each of the research institutes, after which the computers would be released to those institutes; after the handover, they would also be responsible for any repairs that were necessary. Five hundred computers filled two whole buildings, and the yard space was too small and narrow to lay them all out in a row for inspection. The only thing they could do was to give one building entirely over to inspections and move everybody and everything into the other office. Once they had inspected one batch of computers, they packed them up and sent them out to the different institutes. Then they inspected another batch. Wang Shuhe, Liu Chuanzhi and Zhang Zuxiang took the lead, pedalling the flat-bed trikes laden with computers with all their might, while the female staff pushed them from behind. Their sweat fell like rain, trip after trip. Just like the Red Army going through the hardest part of the Long March, this was Lenovo's 'time of climbing the mountains and crossing the grasslands'.

Maybe it was Zhongguancun's 'time of climbing the mountains and crossing the grasslands' too. Unlike Silicon Valley, Zhongguancun, at least in its early stages, didn't have much of a hand in technological innovation, but concentrated on business and commerce. Transport was very simple, and the most important vehicle was the flat-bed trike. If America is a country that runs on automobile wheels, in the early 1980s, China was a country that ran on the wheels of bicycles and flat-bed trikes, with the latter the commonest freight vehicle. Particularly in the south part of Beijing and Tianqiao, trikes, particularly Xuannan brand, were the emblem of the common people and their daily haunts. Who could have thought that Zhongguancun in the 1980s would become another Tianqiao, with scientists professors and master engineers pedalling trikes all over the place? It wasn't clear at the time whether this represented progress or a step backwards. The nearby 'Swindlers' Street' was certainly a more quarrelsome place, but there was no doubt that the trikes left a negative impression. But they were extremely convenient: they only took one man to operate, they were agile and adaptable, weren't subject to traffic regulations, and in a straw poll of which delivery drivers were the gutsiest, pretty well everyone said the flat-bed trike. The trike is the most satisfying vehicle, the one closest to man in character, especially to the Chinese character. However you look at it, the trike has made a heroic contribution to China's resurgence and re-establishment, so much so that many modern-day BMW and Mercedes drivers still have the trike habit, and there's nothing they can do about it.

Many years later, the Computing Institute's Hu Xilan has not forgotten the scene he glimpsed out of his office window that day: the Lenovo trikes shuttling back and forth and a team of twenty or so people moving a great pile of computers into the yard; and the sight of Liu Chuanzhi and Li Qin, those two men who would later be the movers and shakers of Zhongguancun, slaving away under the scorching sun, manhandling almost two thousand huge packing cases with their sweat falling like rain so their clothes were wet through; they ended up stripped to the waist just like the pedicab drivers of Tianqiao. Hu Xilan was Zeng Maochao's wife, and also a researcher at the Computing Institute but the most remarkable thing was that not long after seeing this touching 'Tianqiao tableau', she had no hesitation in joining Liu Chuanzhi's team

In the end, they received a bigger fee than they had agreed. Even so, when the project was over, after deducting 3% project costs, they were left with less than 1% of the cost of five hundred IBM computers. But what mattered was that their great efforts, particularly the manual labour, won them respect. Not only could they sell electronic watches, they could also work just as hard as any Beijing labourer with a flatbed trike. They were even more expert at installing computers, giving technical training, and maintaining and debugging the machines. If that isn't an elite force, what is? Because of the exceptional service, the academy increased the original 1% service fee to 7%, so the 'Chinese Academy of Sciences Computer Technology Institute's New Technical Development Company', the forebear of Lenovo, earned Rmb700,000 in 1985. This was Lenovo's first pot of gold, and it brought to an end their period of selling electronic watches. The cloud that hung over them following the 'Great Colour Television Scam' was lifted, and they were finally able to turn their knowledge and practical technical skills into profit. They had climbed the mountains and crossed the grasslands, and their story now took a new direction.

DIARY NOTE 5: HISTORY

There are two people whose lives run as a linking thread through this book: one is Feng Kang and the other, Liu Chuanzhi. The choice of these two itself illustrates my view of Zhongguancun. They naturally formed the foundations and the headquarters, mutually supportive: the deeper the foundations, the higher they could build their office blocks, and from the top of those office blocks they could look down and see how deep the foundations were. At that time, when technical staff longed to take the plunge and go into business, what hindered and buffeted them was the scientific establishment, not the science itself. The idea behind Zhongguancun was not just high-tech industry and entrepreneurs, although that is what people immediately think of when you mention it now. Zhongguancun had a hundred years of education behind it; it had behind it Tsinghua University, Peking University, Beihang University, Beijing Institute of Technology, more than thirty major universities and more than two hundred national-level research institutes, engineering centres and national laboratories. If you think Zhongguancun is just about high-tech industry and entrepreneurs, then you are doing it a giant disservice.

Right up to now, Lenovo has continued with the Chinese Academy of Sciences having a 30% stake in the company. This admittedly isn't completely in accordance with Zhou Guangzhao's pronouncement back then that "no more than 20% of research personnel should be working on underlying science so the majority can pursue practical research and turn the fruits of that research into marketable products." However, as far as the recognition of the theoretical difference between underlying science and profitable production goes, it seems symbolically quite fitting. Every time Director Zhou Guangzhao is mentioned, the expression on the face of Liu Chuanzhi, that titan of industry, takes on a kind of dreamy, timeless quality, coloured with spontaneous respect. He strongly emphasises how useful Zhou Guangzhao and the academy were to Lenovo as, without Zhou's 'golden revolution' back then, and the academy's continuing generous and enlightened support, there would be no Lenovo. "I don't want any spotlight on me as an individual, I want it on the academy and Director Zhou, and now, 30 years on, the time is right."

Interviewing Liu Chuanzhi is like confronting the complete history of Zhongguancun, totally impartial, full of reason and intelligence, gentle, clear, unassuming and profound. It is hard to imagine him, stripped to the waist, dripping with sweat at the effort of pedalling a flatbed trike; hard to imagine him labouring like a Tianqiao pedicab driver in his heroic efforts to establish Zhongguancun. The surreal story of China often manifests itself in the way a man was at a certain time, so different from how he is now, that it seems like a different person. Yet it undoubtedly is the same man.

Equally, it is still Zhongguancun, but a world away from how it was then.

[PART 3]
Feng Kang's Plan (2)
冯康构图(二)

Feng Kang's disciples: Shang Zaijiu

1

IN FENG KANG'S LATER YEARS, he was like an ageing stallion that still imagined galloping across the plains. He devoted his efforts to research into innovations in methods of calculation in Hamiltonian geometry. He had a good number of his followers working in this field, one of whom was the director of the Chinese Academy of Sciences Mathematics Institute, Shang Zaijiu.

In 1988, the 25-year-old Shang Zaijiu was admitted onto Feng Kang's doctoral programme. He still clearly remembers the day he started his studies and how one of the directors of the Computer Research Department of the Academy of Sciences took him to Feng Kang's home for a visit. It was a cloudless, sunny afternoon, and sunlight flooded the apartment in Zhongguancun. Although it wasn't a traditional *hutong* scene, there were pigeons circling in the sky, making a great whistling, whooshing noise that carried clear and resonant through the air. They made their way to Feng Kang's home from what is now the China Software Park – in the organisational reform of 1988, the original Computer Centre consisting of four different mathematical research institutes was consolidated into the Mathematics and Systems Scientific Research Institute.

In 1988, business saturated the atmosphere, and everywhere on university campuses people were discussing business ventures; the whole population was pre-occupied with the marketplace, and very few people were able to settle down to serious study.

At the time, Feng Kang was living on the fourth floor of Block 809 in the Huangzhuang District. This was the institute director's block, only recently completed, and it was considered the best of the buildings owned by the Chinese Academy of Sciences. Mr Wu Wenjun lived on the second floor and Yang Le lived in the corresponding apartment in the block opposite. Shang Zaijiu had never met Feng Kang before, but in the course of his Master's studies, he had read a book edited by Shiing-Shen Chern called *The Outlook for 21st Century Chinese Mathematics*. It listed many important future directions of study, amongst which Feng Kang presided over computational mathematics. Of course, Feng Kang was a man of great renown and the leading figure in the discipline of computational mathematics so, having been accepted onto his doctoral programme, Shang Zaijiu was very nervous about going to visit him. But once he actually met him, Shang Zaijiu's excited nervousness disappeared completely as he was immediately drawn to the internal energy that radiated from Feng Kang himself. He simply forgot to be nervous.

Physically, Feng Kang was a small man, but his internal energy was remarkable. He was very animated as he sat, bright-eyed, on a sofa; his voice was clear and direct. It was very different from when he was just chatting idly, passing the time of day; his cadence and modulation were very impressive, and his aura was imposing. Even just a few words from him were inspiring, and any normal person would be drawn to him on first meeting. More than an hour's conversation passed like a dream for Shang Zaijiu. This four-room apartment was the great master's home, the great master's temple hall. This was also the first time Shang Zaijiu had seen a four-room apartment and he felt that this must be the right environment for mathematics: the man and his surroundings were as one, just as in a temple. Feng Kang asked Shang Zaijiu about what books he had read and who his professors had been at university. In fact, Feng Kang already knew that Shang had taken the topology course taught by Professor Chen Jie of the University of Inner Mongolia. Chen Jie had previously been a lecturer at Peking University and, before the Liberation, after he graduated from Sichuan University, he worked at the Central Research Institute, following Shiing-Shen Chern in his research. In 1957, Peking University offered support to the University of Inner Mongolia and Chen Jie went there as a senior figure in the history of the university. Chen Jie had once said that Feng Kang's finite-element method was a very rigorous system of theoretical mathematics and an extraordinary achievement. Feng Kang was delighted when Shang Zaijiu mentioned this.

Feng Gang told him what he would be doing on the doctorate programme, mentioning especially symplectic geometric algorithms. In fact, back in the 1970s, before academics had their new 'freedom', he had already begun studying the question of mechanical systems computation: the field of dynamics which, over time, mathematicians have come to describe through differential equations, is effectively a method to be used for long-term computation in this kind of research. The finite-element method of that time offered a complete set of computational methods for the question of equilibrium in, for example, calculating the stresses on the ox-hide skin of a drum, or the deformation of the curvature of a board at the point of equilibrium, and so on: this was essentially the question of typical equilibrium. Under normal circumstances, the finite-element method can give pretty satisfactory results in predicting the precise range of equilibrium. However, as Feng Kang told Shang Zaijiu, there was currently no reliable set of computational methods for the dynamics of things with inherently conservative characteristics, which included many important aspects such as wave motion, and the current understanding of the dynamics of the long-term progression of celestial bodies. If the calculations were only over the relatively short-term, current computational methods were adequate, but if they were required for a longer period, most of those methods were of no use. So it was of particular importance to research the question of long-term progression in this kind of conservative dynamics.

Feng Kang plunged into this research and investigation, pondering over how to resolve the computational methods for these kinds of questions. In 1984, at the Double Differential Conference (that is *The International Symposium on Differential Geometry and Differential Equations* first proposed by Shiing-Shen Chern), Feng Kang first made public the Hamiltonian system for calculation in symplectic geometry, which was the result of many years of thought and research on his part. Feng Kang considered that symplectic algorithms were only the first stage, but still of vital importance and with a huge potential for future development. Feng Kang spoke concisely and with great weight, leaving little room for doubt and this was a great morale boost for Shang Zaijiu: he could see clearly the direction he must take, and he was eager to get going. He recalls: "Mr Feng Kang had this great ability to swiftly rouse you to action; he possessed great clarity and exceptional charisma."

2

So this was how Shang Zaijiu's life as a doctoral student began; Feng Kang really liked this young man from the grasslands of Inner Mongolia whose face bore the marks of having endured great hardships. Feng Kang regarded him as a piece of unpolished jade, a rare piece of raw material. With great care, he laid out for him the direction he should take: starting from the Lyapunov Stability Theory he moved on to the structural stability of mechanical systems and the famous KAM theorem, which was the theory of the use of phase space in an integrable Hamiltonian system, proposed and completed by the famous mathematicians Kolmogorov, Arnold and Moser (hence the name KAM). Its most recent context was that of the stability of the solar system, and it also had important applications in many aspects of physics and mechanics. Feng Kang wanted to prove the stability of symplectic algorithms and believed that research into this should be done within the framework of the KAM theorem. At this time, he had already done a lot of work from the aspect of the structure of symplectic algorithms and computational testing; numerical value tests had shown that on the question of using a Hamiltonian system in calculating motive force, symplectic algorithms had a demonstrably overwhelming advantage over the traditional non-symplectic algorithms. Amongst all this, one of the most important questions was: is there a rigorous and coherent theory to definitively prove this advantage?

From the point of view of computational mathematics, the stability and convergence of computational methods, and the stability and convergence of algorithms were two fundamental questions. Feng Kang and his students discussed them thus: if you draw a curved line, it is in essence a circle, so the fundamental property of a circle is that it is a closed curved line that does not bisect itself; the stability of an algorithm resides in the results of its numerical calculation being roughly circular and as represented by computer graphics it is indeed more or less a circle; the bare minimum requirement is that it does not deviate very far from a circular course. Convergence is fundamentally connected to the accuracy of an algorithm and all compatible algorithms (those that satisfy the minimum requirements of accuracy) are convergent. Feng Kang said that convergence and stability were intimately connected and that stable algorithms were all convergent; however, not all convergent algorithms were stable, and that was the nature of the connection between the two states. Feng Kang decided the direction of Shang Zaijiu's research and specified the topic, "You must prove the stability of symplectic algorithms; that is to be the subject of your doctoral thesis." There were no doubts there about how the master was leading his disciple.

Feng Kang led his pupil in the initial step, reminding him which framework to use in establishing the stability of symplectic algorithms: the KAM theorem. So he already had the theoretical backdrop for his thesis. It was all rather reminiscent of the most attractive feature of the old traditional stories of heroes and knights errant: in a fortuitous encounter, a magical volume of mental cultivation and martial training is bestowed. Feng Kang passed on a complete 'fundamental mental attitude' and also gave Shang Zaijiu some material, most of which he had personally photocopied at the library and a lot of which was in Russian. He even went as far as to draw up a schedule of work for Shang which required him to talk through the whole project with Feng before the New Year.

Shang Zaijiu threw himself into the material that his master had given him as though it was, indeed, a rare manual of martial arts. In the course of doing so, he discovered that some of the articles in Russian by Vladimir Arnold were very difficult to understand: the leaps in thinking they made were so great, and they included many even more difficult aspects of celestial mechanics. Shang wanted to concentrate his efforts on clarifying for himself the KAM theorem and understanding its proof, so he decided not to concern himself for the time being with the practical applications of the theorem in areas such as celestial mechanics. One day, he went to see Feng Kang to tell him there was too much content in the material for him to assimilate all at once, and he asked if there was anything a little less dense. Only a few days later, Feng Kang gave him a synopsis which had been written by some Italian experts in the field of celestial mechanics, of discoveries made within the last five years. Where Arnold's material had been written in 1963, the Italians had come up with a clear and succinct proof of the KAM theorem, the thinking behind which was still that of Kolmogorov but expressed in a way a post-graduate student could understand. Shang Zaijiu finished reading the whole of it within two months. Throughout this time, Shang continued to attend at least one seminar a week. To begin with, he did not understand symplectic geometric algorithms but a senior student called Wang Daoliu talked about them cogently in the seminars.

In December, less than two months after Shang Zaijiu began attending the course of seminars, Feng Kang asked him how his studies were going, and Shang said he had completed them and thought he was in a position to talk them through. Feng Kang immediately arranged for him to lead a seminar on the KAM theorem. Shang Zaijiu led the seminar four or five times, each time talking for at least two hours. The proof of the KAM theorem was very long, and Feng Kang told Shang to take it slowly and go into great detail, as he listened with great care to each step of the proof. The seminars were held on the fifth floor of the old Computing Institute, which was also the place where, years before, Feng Kang had led the computational work on the atomic bomb, the guided missile and the satellite. At the end of the final session, Feng Kang was delighted and, although he seldom complimented anyone, on that occasion he complimented Shang Zaijiu.

Feng Kang came to a final decision: "We will fix the topic of your doctoral dissertation as this: *On KAM Theorem for Symplectic Algorithms for Hamiltonian Systems*.

With the topic decided, Shang Zaijiu pursued this direction of study even more meticulously, even more doggedly and even more precisely whilst, at the same time, delving more widely into related literature. Just before the end of 1990, Shang Zaijiu produced his completed thesis on the KAM theorem. It was an extraordinary achievement.

Of course, he met with all kinds of problems during this period but very seldom did he go to see Feng Kang. If he did hit a snag, he would first telephone Feng to make an appointment, and only then go and see him. Feng would listen attentively and patiently to his student's problem, and in the course of Shang's account, he would sometimes suddenly interrupt saying, "Just wait a moment", and would run into his library to find a particular book: "If you read this section of this book, it might help you." Often, when Shang Zaijiu read the relevant volume, he would find densely packed hand-written notes in the margins going into meticulous detail. In some books there would be important places where the author was not sufficiently detailed in his explanations, and Feng Kang had supplemented them with painstaking detail. All of this was of enormous help to Shang's thesis, and almost all the real problems he met were resolved in this way.

Feng Kang's leadership of his disciples was both holistic (although along a defined path) and detailed. When Shang Zaijiu was starting his proof of the KAM theorem for symplectic algorithms, he originally thought first to use Kolmogorov to fix his thinking on angular frequency, but after trying it for a while found he wasn't making any headway, so he changed to using Arnold's method. But Arnold's essays were very difficult to follow and there was a lack of rigour in some of the Apollonian estimates which were too crude to be of use to him, so he had to make his own meticulous estimates. Although he couldn't deny the overall usefulness of the Apollonian method, he found the process quite hard to fathom. When he discussed this problem arising from Arnold's work with Feng Kang, Feng Kang explained that the way he saw it, an author often reflects his own thought patterns in the process of his deliberations, so a complicated process reflects complicated thought patterns, and a negative process can cast a pall over his thought processes. Later, Feng Kang gave his student another 'magical manual': it was a book jointly written in 1967 by Arnold and a French mathematician, André Avez, entitled, *Ergodic Problems of Classical Mechanics*, first published in French but later translated into English. On this occasion, Feng Kang didn't give Shang the whole book, but just the section that related to his student's problem. The relevant section was an appendix. The book had many appendices; Shang Zaijiu recalls there being more than thirty, and what Feng Kang gave him was a photocopy of appendices 32-34. There were lots of annotations in the margins where

1. FENG KANG'S PLAN (2)

Feng Kang had supplemented the shortcomings of Arnold's proof. Shang Zaijiu has kept that material right up to the present day.

"This was the form his leadership took," Shang Zaijiu later recalled. "Extremely specific, and he didn't let you grope about from first beginnings but, as these were always things that he had already read himself, paths he had already trodden, he left behind him many precious experiences from his explorations which one could pick up and use. I admired him enormously for it. Just think, he had read all these things, but he still claimed he hadn't understood them. What did he mean by that? He meant he wasn't the one who had done the research. Of course, he understood them completely. This is very important because later on, when I had my own doctoral students, I used the same method. Sometimes it was successful but, more often than not, it wasn't because I was at a level of expertise far below Feng Kang's, nor had I read nearly as many books. Master Feng was first and foremost a computational mathematician, and there were some books that were out of his specialised field, but he read them meticulously, nonetheless. Nowadays, many of us researchers do not take such pains over reading material that is outside our particular field, and use the time in a more focused fashion. Feng Kang was not like that; his thinking was very broad in range but very detailed at the same time."

So this was the manner in which Shang Zaijiu's doctoral thesis was written, the thesis that proved the KAM theorem for symplectic algorithms for Hamiltonian systems. Feng Kang was delighted to see a long-cherished project realised by one of his students. He recommended that his student should take his thesis to the International Theoretical Physics Centre in Italy to join a discussion forum. Because the thesis was so long, Feng Kang told Shang Zaijiu to write a synopsis, and to get help putting it into English. Shang put a lot of knowledge and skill into writing that synopsis, making many corrections, and only when he was himself completely happy with it, did he give it to Feng Kang to read. The first time Feng read it through from beginning to end, Shang was sitting beside him. When Feng had finished and said that it would do, Shang Zaijiu was delighted. Then Feng Kang picked up his pen and began to make corrections, saying that in one place this word might be better, then suggesting that that sentence might be changed thus. First, he corrected words, then he corrected sentences. When he had corrected sentences, he revised whole paragraphs, so that after several goes through, it was no longer the same text. Shang Zaijiu's small amount of complacency and self-satisfaction disappeared but his admiration for his teacher only increased.

3

Just after New Year 1991, Shang Zaijiu began to consider where he would go after receiving his doctorate, and he also began to think about settling down and getting married. He reckoned he would get married after graduating and, as his girlfriend lived in Inner Mongolia, he thought he would bring his new wife down to join him. At that time, work transfers were very difficult but he had heard that once he had his doctorate it would be easier to arrange a transfer for a family member. One day, Shang hurried over to Feng Kang's home to discuss this matter in preparation for after he graduated. But Feng Kang had already submitted a report to his superiors about Shang, requesting that he should stay on to work at the Computer Centre. Feng made a telephone call to Shao Yuhua, the head of the personnel department at the Computer Centre, asking whether family members of new doctoral graduates could apply for work transfers. Shao Yuhua confirmed that such a transfer was certainly permissible but that there was a waiting list and it would take at least two years. Feng Kang asked if there was any way of speeding up the process and Department Head Shao gave him a detailed description of the people ahead of Shang Zaijiu in the queue.

There was nothing for it but for Feng Kang to ask Shang if he could wait two years. Shang Zaijiu said that he would rather take up a post-doctoral position elsewhere so he could get a transfer for his wife immediately. Feng Kang didn't agree at once but one day he suddenly asked Shang to stay behind after a seminar to discuss the matter of his post-doctoral position. He said, "How about this? You go and have a look around for yourself to see where they are recruiting for post-doctoral positions. Shang Zaijiu didn't have any personal contacts and what he didn't understand at the time was that, in saying what he did, firstly Feng Kang was agreeing to Shang's way of thinking and, secondly, he was preparing to give Shang a recommendation but he wanted Shang to go out and try for himself first.

In his attempts, Shang Zaijiu ran into a brick wall every time. One day, Feng Kang summoned Shang to his home and told him that he had already written a letter for him which he put in an envelope saying, "Give this letter to Professor Xu Shuxian, director of the research department at the Institute of Mathematics; I have already telephoned Academician Yang Le, who told me it was alright to give it to Professor Xu." The envelope wasn't sealed and when Shang Zaijiu read the letter, he was speechless with emotion, and when he thought about the trouble his master had gone to, his eyes reddened with tears. The letter was a page and a half long, all hand-written. There were a lot of applicants for post-doctoral posts at the Institute of Mathematics that year, all of them very capable, but only four were selected: two from Peking University, one from Zhejiang University and Shang Zaijiu. One of the two from Peking University was Liu Peidong who went on to be director of the Mathematics Department at Peking University, and another was a student of Master Ding Tongren, who went to America in the second year after he received his doctorate. At that time, Shang Zaijiu's thesis hadn't yet been published, indeed it wasn't yet even fully collated, and in those circumstances he couldn't possibly have got the post-doctoral position without Feng Kang's recommendation.

Shang Zaijiu got married in Inner Mongolia in September 1991 and when he returned to Beijing in October, he reported for duty at the Institute of Mathematics Centre for Post-Doctoral Studies. The Institute allocated him a small 15sqm house and that's where he set up home. Nearby was a place which is now the Chinese Academy of Sciences Library and Information Centre, but then it was just an open space on which there was a row of small buildings, one of which was the Xinhua Bookshop. Shang Zaijiu's little house was to the north of the bookshop and from time to time he would go in on his way past to browse through the books. One day he bumped into Feng Kang there. Feng was leafing through a thick volume open in front of him. It was a hardcover book and didn't look like a mathematics text. The mathematics books in the shop were not that classy and Shang Zaijiu's impression was that it was *A Mirror for the Wise Ruler*[1] or some such work. Shang greeted his master warmly and the two men began chatting. Feng Kang was rather surprised to find his student living in the area and was so curious about it that he even actually asked Shang if he would show him his house.

The two men, teacher and pupil, walked across the open space to Shang Zaijiu's 15sqm house where Shang made his master a cup of tea and the two of them sat down to talk some more. It was autumn and the weather was not cold; in fact, the sun was warm and everything was very calm and peaceful. Shang poured Feng Kang his tea and Feng gulped it all down. Shang added some more water to the cup and Feng again drank it all down. Shang poured again and Feng said there was no need, he'd had enough. But he still drained the cup down to the last drop. Most people don't drink the cup dry like that but Feng Kang did, just leaving the tea leaves in the bottom of the cup.

Feng Kang normally always wore a Mao suit and a blue cap, like a worker, or a worker cadre or technician. By that time, Western-style suits were already popular, or safari jackets, and women's clothing was even more varied, including strappy summer dresses and gym pants; but no matter how times had changed, Feng Kang didn't change with them and his attire remained stuck in the 1970s.

Even though his accommodation had changed, it didn't really seem to have had any effect on him.

Shang Zaijiu remembers quite clearly that you went in through the front door into the lounge which was actually divided into two parts: the south side was Feng Kang's study proper and the north was a dining room. You went through the dining room to the bedroom and bathroom. Seminars were usually held in the study and there was a sliding door between it and the dining room. This could be locked shut but it was usually open, whether there was a seminar being held or not. The whole apartment ran north to south and Feng Kang's study was in the southeast. In the centre of the study, next to the south-facing window, there was a circle of sofas. There was another part of the room on the other side of the sofas, so the room was effectively divided in two, and Feng Kang had an office desk on this other side. On the desk there was a computer and a printer on which Feng would occasionally print out documents to give his students during the seminars. In effect, this was his office. On the other side of the sofas was where the seminars were held and there was a blackboard in the northeast corner for Feng to write things on. There was a small door next to the blackboard which led to Feng Kang's small second study and no students ever went in there. There was a little storeroom also in the northeast corner, and when Shang Zaijiu was writing his thesis and went to ask his master something, Feng Kang would often either go into his small study to find something, or he would rummage around in the storeroom, and come out brandishing some relevant book or document to give to his student. So that was how his home was set up.

Shang Zaijiu didn't often catch a glimpse of Feng Kang's wife but what he did see suggested she was both young and pretty, quite tall and capable-looking, and very characterful. It was usually she who opened the front door when there was a seminar being held but, after a nod of the head, she would go back into her room.

Occasionally, Feng Kang had no choice but to wear a western-style suit, which made him look completely different. These occasions were normally international gatherings of some sort when Feng Kang gave the impression of having travelled through time to appear fully-fledged where he belonged, amongst the master mathematicians of the world. He seemed like a totally different person from that other man who wore a blue Mao suit, but all those international assemblies actually did was to display Feng Kang's inner character to an even greater extent.

In 1992, Feng Kang chaired a very important international meeting with a lot of VIP guests who included world-famous mathematicians, professors and administrators, all of them impressive characters, poised and elegant. Feng Kang was bursting with energy; he held their attention with just a few sentences and after that you could hear a pin drop in the hall. He didn't need an interpreter but spoke directly in English, his voice clear and magnetic, and full of humour. The solemn and respectful atmosphere suddenly became charged with laughter. This was the occasion of the welcome banquet, held in the ancient and beautiful surroundings of the Oriole Listening Hall of the Summer Palace, and Feng Kang's speech was both dignified and humorous, captivating the whole elegant, distinguished assembly. If he had been the everyday Feng Kang, clad in Mao suit and blue cap, he would inevitably have brought a flavour of the flawed and destructive times of the Cultural Revolution, so he had transformed himself for the occasion and, inside and out, was brimming with the new glamour of internationalism.

Even though in the 1970s, Feng Kang was never subject to 're-education through labour', he still faced the same historical problems as anyone else, and for him to start studying the question of dynamics in the closed-down period of the 1970s was testament to the way a scientist can transcend time. All great people have this transcendental quality, and no matter whether the times they are in are normal or shut-down, they are able to rise above them. Even now, in the 21st century, when research into the fields of mechanics and mathematics are so rumbustious and lively, his work remains at the cutting edge of world mathematics and physics.

Shang Zaijiu's participation in this research was one of the backbones of its success. Even now his contribution to the international field of symplectic algorithms in Hamiltonian systems, including the geometric algorithms for mechanical systems he developed from that foundation, are still important directions of research in the field of numerical integration. After finite element analysis, *Geometric Symplectic Algorithms for Hamiltonian Systems* is Feng Kang's second great achievement. In 1997, it received first prize in the National Natural Sciences Awards, and Shang Zaijiu was one of the contributors to it.

4

But, thinking back on it, Shang Zaijiu remembers that when he was studying for his doctorate, Feng Kang never told him in detail why he had chosen geometric symplectic algorithms in Hamiltonian systems as his field of research; it just seemed to evolve over time as the scenery of the future became clearer and clearer. Just as the scenery unfurls itself at the end of a mountain track and many more tracks appear – too many tracks, but even so, you can already make out which one is yours. As Feng Kang progressed, behind him and to his left and right were the disciples of the 'Feng Kang School'. Within the Hamiltonian systems, were not their numerical orbits an everlasting cycle of constant reciprocal motion? It was Shang Zaijiu who proved this proposition. That was one track. The successful use of passive systems in creating volume-preserving algorithms: this was a question that, not long after, Feng Kang began to raise continually in his seminars. This was another untrodden track which Shang Zaijiu embarked upon, and in the winter of the year after he took up his post-doctoral post at the Institute of Mathematics, he resolved it.

When Feng Kang dedicated himself to this question, Shang was also configuring and researching it. Many times, Feng Kang stressed in his seminars: on the one hand, symplectic algorithms have a set of configurations for generating function but, in terms of volume-preserving systems, that generational function was not to be found. This was one difficulty. The second one, Feng Kang recognised from the aspect of symplectic geometry: volume-preserving mapping could give an object any kind of curvature, but inverse mapping could not do the same. This was the famous Gromov Rigidity Theorem. This suggests that if all you need to preserve of a camel is its volume, then that camel can pass through any narrowness of pipe, as long as the pipe is long enough, but if the constraint is that you have to comply with symplectic structure, then the camel will not necessarily be able to pass through. However small the radius of the camel, if the radius of the eye of a needle is smaller, then the camel will not be able to pass through it. This is known as the rigidity of symplectic structure and this was the direction from which Feng Kang approached the problem. The third difficulty was this: there are limitless rational functions to generate symplectic algorithms but there are no rational functions to generate volume-preserving algorithms.

Feng Kang raised these issues so many times that Shang Zaijiu naturally found himself pondering deeply over them. Shang was very assured about undertaking research with his master and had no doubts. All the problems his master raised were important problems and really everyone should follow his example: if the master said a problem was important, no one should question it. Even at that stage he knew quite clearly that all of those problems were at the cutting edge of world research and there were foreign mathematicians also working on them but none of them had leaders of the exceptional quality of Feng Kang.

Later on, there was a New Zealand professor called Robert Maclachlan who was a leader in this field, researching at a very high level. But it was only in 1993 that he raised the question of the structure of volume-preserving algorithms, whereas Feng Kang had already been talking about it in 1990. Also, in 1993, the Fields Research Institute in Canada conducted an exercise, organised by the famous mathematician Jerrold E. Marsden, who was also the director of the Fields Institute. Maclachlan and the American James Scovel from the Los Alamos National Laboratory co-wrote a summary report on the exercise enumerating several problems, amongst which was the structuring of volume-preserving algorithms. This report appeared in 1996 but this was the same problem that Feng Kang had raised in 1990 and resolved in 1992.

One day in 1990, Feng Kang summoned Shang Zaijiu and Shang's young student Ge Zhong to his home. They sat on the sofa under the south window with Feng Kang in the middle. Feng Kang took his notebook, wrote down a whole load of notes and then explained what was in them to his two students, filling their ears with exhortations (this notebook of Feng Kang's is exhibited in the exhibition hall of the Institute of Mathematics, preserving his memory for posterity). Feng Kang explained to his two students the background to the problem of the structure of volume-preserving algorithms, its origins, its mathematical principles, the results obtained so far, his own thinking and the difficulties he had encountered. He gave them a few specific examples, all of which involved the problem of three-dimensional working. At the end he said, "Go back and think about this; you can take this notebook with you. Ge Zhong took the notebook away with him and when he had finished reading it, he handed it on to Shang Zaijiu.

After Shang Zaijiu got home that day, he stayed there for a whole week without going out of the door. He could feel how important this issue was: it was a problem his master had been racking his brains over, and one which his master had explained very clearly; it was the matter of three dimensions that had made the deepest impression. He manipulated the problem every which way, and for several days could see no way forward. He never stopped thinking about it though. Sometimes, when he was watching television, although his eyes were on the screen, his brain was still turning the problem over and over. His wife sometimes asked what he was doing watching television, when he had all his research going on. But mathematicians have a particular characteristic and, although it may be rather exaggerated in the story of Chen Jingrun riding into the telephone pole, there is certainly some point to it. "Because a man can't just keep staring fixedly at something as he calculates, he must always be thinking, and when he is thinking he sometimes needs to readjust his thought patterns," Shang Zaijiu says. "Take television, for example: my eyes may be fixed on the screen but my brain is thinking about something completely different. Besides, there may be something I see on the television that sparks an unexpected association."

Indeed, this is actually what happened. Shang Zaijiu was watching television when a thought suddenly came into his head. He took the three-dimensional passive vector field he was stuck on, and broke it down into several units, each of which roughly corresponded to a Hamiltonian vector field. In this way, he could rewrite the passive system as two superimposed Hamiltonian systems. These two systems were not coupled, nor did they share the same symplectic space; but with each system in its own symplectic space, you could then structure a symplectic algorithm, and each symplectic algorithm was a volume-preserving algorithm in three-dimensional space. That was how the solution came about on that particular day.

Shang Zaijiu was delighted and immediately began his calculations, which turned out perfectly from beginning to end, in three dimensions. If they worked out in three dimensions, then they could quite naturally be applied to any number of dimensions. If N was a number of degrees of freedom greater than three dimensions, then you had N-1 uncoupled Hamiltonian systems and each Hamiltonian vector field could be calculated from a pre-determined passive vector field. The problem was solved!

Shang Zaijiu was so overjoyed, he ran straight over to the Computer Centre's big building in the Software Park Internet Centre to find Feng Kang. It was the opening day of the China Japan Computational Mathematics Conference, and the conference hadn't yet broken up when he arrived, so he waited outside. Feng Kang was at the back of all the people as they came out at the end of the conference, so Shang Zaijiu bounded in to stand in front of him and tell him that he had worked out the structuring of volume-preserving symplectic algorithms.

At first, Feng Kang was a little sceptical, but soon his eyes lit up and his doubts vanished.

He really had no reason to doubt his student, he could see the success in his eyes. At that moment, Shang Zaijiu gave Feng Kang the notebook with his calculations to look at, which Feng did on the spot. He was delighted with what he saw, and he kept nodding as he looked at Shang Zaijiu and explained to his student the primary reasoning, making everything clear at a stroke. The fact is, many things are as fragile as a sheet of window paper, and this is true of science and mathematics, and even literature: that is to say, they are what is commonly called 'the narrow gate'[2]. Feng Kang had understood immediately, as this was a problem he had been researching for a very long time, and there was just this one element that remained unsolved. He was very moved and very happy. He told Shang Zaijiu, "Go back and write out in minute detail all your deductions and the final specification!"

Of course! Shang Zaijiu hadn't written out the final specifications and the formula, so he urgently hurried off to do so. Perhaps this might be called a 'generational difference', as his delight had meant he didn't give everything his full care and attention. Feng Kang still had people to greet, as there were a lot of honoured guests at the conference, so master and student were separated for a short while. But what are a few minutes in the face of such an important problem! Such a sophisticated problem! Such a cutting-edge problem!

Feng Kang was 71 that year.

When Shang Zaijiu finished writing out his deductions, the specifications and the final formula, he gave them to Feng Kang. In that week's seminar, the little blackboard was full of characters and formulae demonstrating Shang Zaijiu's results and presenting them in meticulous detail.

Feng Kang encouraged his student to take that one step further beyond this pinnacle of enlightenment, and that is indeed what happened. The 'Feng Kang School' had quite a few successes in the field of Hamiltonian geometric algorithms; two of them were Shang Zaijiu's and one was Ge Zhong's. The latter showed that non-linear circumstances do not exist in an energy-preserving symplectic format. Tang Yifa also had one success showing that there are no symplectic algorithms in a multi-step method. This multi-step method was a very important advantage for tracking computations, so this had many practical applications. All this time, the seminars were continuing, and Feng Kang kept returning to this question, until Tang Yifa finally made a huge breakthrough: he proved that, in the multi-step method there was only one essentially single-step symplectic algorithm, and no others.

Another important result was Feng Kang's own. He proposed a theory for formal vector fields and formal phase flow fields and, in the same space of time, he also formally proposed the concept of geometric algorithms for dynamic systems. Originally, Hamiltonian algorithms, volume-preserving algorithms and also the contact algorithms that he himself completed, were all algorithms focused on how the structures of particular systems maintained that structure. It was based on the success of the above structure-preserving algorithms, that he had the overall idea for his geometric algorithms for dynamic systems. In the seminars during this period, Feng Kang mostly talked about this concept, including his theory for formal vector fields and formal phase flow fields. It was at this time that the First National 'Climbing' Programme Projects were launched in 1992, and Feng Kang's particular projects were centred on methods and theories for large-scale science and engineering computing; first among these were his geometric algorithms for dynamic systems. This was the earliest international formulation but later on, in 1996, the Spanish mathematician Professor J. M. Sanz-Serna proposed his theory of geometric numerical integration. So, this currently fashionable internationally recognised name, actually arrived on the scene at least four years after Feng Kang.

In Feng Kang's geometric algorithm for dynamic systems there is a theory for formal vector fields and formal phase flow fields. Currently there is a very fashionable and well-known term called 'Backward Error Analysis Theory'. "Master Feng Kang died a long time ago, and latterly there have been a lot of western scholars taking the lead in this field. But a lot of the fundamental work for it was done by Master Feng's task force and the Chinese school of thought," Shang Zaijiu says. "Our task force finished a lot of the work a long time ago but the papers were only published much later, many of them in the form of conference papers. Our work was very much ahead of its time, especially in the work we did between 1991 and 1993. At that time there were only two original fields of work: the backward error analyses of the Runge-Kutta methods and the targeted systems (where energy functions were kinetic and potential energy combined) were a foreign construct. In the early days, the credit goes to the Swiss mathematician Lasagni, the Spaniard, Sanz-Serna and the Russian, Sulis; latterly, the credit lies with the Japanese, Yoshida. But the backward error analysis of systems in general all stemmed from Feng Kang's work. It is fair to say that at the beginning of the 1990s, Feng Kang's seminars were on the international front line in this field."

1. FENG KANG'S PLAN (2)

5

In the three years of Shang Zaijiu's doctoral studies, and the two years after he took up his post-doctoral position, he didn't miss a single one of Feng Kang's seminars during those five years, and while Feng Kang was alive, he had no feeling of being special; he felt calm in himself and intensely proud because he could see clearly the direction Feng Kang was headed and knew that it was at the cutting edge of world mathematics. All of Feng's disciples were the same: they followed their master in his dramatic progress and, as they surveyed the world, they were very clear about their place in it. But then Feng Kang died unexpectedly and, at a stroke, Shang Zaijiu and his colleagues from the seminars were in decline, without their prop and even without a direction.

"Even after so many years, I am still desolate," Shang Zaijiu says.

"I think of him on so many occasions. Every detail of my time with him is still crystal clear even now, 20 years later, and I often dream of him."

"I neglected so many things in that time."

A mathematician's eyes are usually very serene, and even at this time they were still the same. There is nothing more moving than that serenity in these circumstances, and it was a serenity that defies description. Of course, it also defies any attempt to quantify it, as it seems that mathematicians have their own unique set of emotions.

Before Feng Kang's death, Shang Zaijiu and his students went on a trip with his master. Shang Zaijiu recalls that time like a lucid dream. In June 1993, Feng Kang went to teach at Xi'an Jiaotong University, and Shang went with him as his assistant. On the train to Xi'an, Feng Kang asked Shang whether he had been to Xi'an before and, without waiting for the answer, began to talk about past events. Feng had been to Xi'an himself many years before but, on that occasion, he fled before he had even left the station. It was during the Cultural Revolution, Shang Zaijiu recounted, and Feng was shut up in a 'bullpen'[3] in Beijing. Terrified, he managed to escape but only ran into an even more terrifying situation, so Feng Kang told his student. He had escaped from the 'bullpen' on the spur of the moment and, because of that, had no idea where he was going to go. It was just a kind of mad dash. He ran to Xizhimen, where he saw a train arriving. Without a thought as to where it might be going, he leapt onto it. Very soon, the train departed and then stopped at a station in the middle of the night. Feng Kang got off to see where he was and discovered that he was at Hohhot station in Inner Mongolia. He sat in the station trying to work out where to go but couldn't come up with any clear idea. In the end, he decided to head south. He still had no idea where to head, when another train came into the station from the west. Not caring where it was going, he jumped on it, thinking that was the only place he could be safe, because he was in danger every second he stayed in the station. The train had either come from Lanzhou or was going to Lanzhou, he didn't know which, and it was only after he got on it that he realised it was heading in the direction of Shanxi. After a 'violent struggle'[4] at Fenglingdu, he left the train and boarded another one at random. Finally he arrived in Xi'an. He could see the city walls but he didn't leave the station. He wandered blindly around China, never leaving the stations he disembarked at, until finally he arrived at Suzhou, which was his hometown, and that was where he stopped. He hid out there for a week. Once, as he was standing in front of Suzhou Middle School, staring blankly around him, he remembered going to school there many, many years ago, and recalled past events. He must have revisited the place many times before, one day, someone seized him by the back of his collar, and he heard whoever it was shout, "We've been looking for you for a long time!" He was sent back to Beijing under escort, and he actually thanked his captor because otherwise he had been getting ready to kill himself. He had been put on the wanted list after his escape from the 'bullpen' in Beijing, so there were people on the look-out for him, although he didn't know it at the time. He had good reason to be grateful to the young man from the Red Guards who had arrested him because he had as good as saved his life.

Feng Kang told his student this for the first time as they headed west on the train. When Feng Kang had finished his teaching, he left Xi'an, but Shang Zaijiu stayed on for a week to look after the follow-up to Feng's classes. He returned to Beijing on 12 July, and that evening went to see Feng Kang at his home. Feng was getting ready for the International Congress of Young Chinese Mathematicians to be held in the Fragrant Hills in August and was very busy. He greatly valued the international congress; it received a lot of written contributions, and even at the advanced age of 70, he personally read every one. Working round the clock, he chose who would be allowed to address the conference. Shang Zaijiu vividly remembers Master Feng's great respect for a student of Chen-Ning Yang called Deng Yuefan. He said that Deng's submission was outstanding: its subject was the problem of the computation of C60 fullerene, and it had a very promising future. He also said that most of the flower of young computational mathematicians would be at the International Congress of Young Chinese Mathematicians.

"Looking at it now, that was certainly true. Most of the outstanding

Chinese computational mathematicians who are now in their fifties, were at that conference. It was a genuinely distinguished occasion, of a kind that I'm afraid hasn't been repeated for many years. I too attended it." Shang Zaijiu remembers that he stayed at Feng Kang's home until very late, and as well as discussing the preparations for the congress and giving an account of the examinations of the students on the summer vacation course at Xi'an's Jiaotong University, they also touched on work on the project on which Shang was collaborating with his master; it was already completed and needed to be written up, so they discussed the specifics of how that was to be done. It was already one in the morning by the time Shang left. He recalls that, just as he was about to go, Feng Kang also mentioned that the famous American mathematician and academic, Peter Lax, had recommended him as a foreign fellow of the American Academy of Sciences, and also that he had been invited to give a paper at the International Finite Element Conference. These were very important and cheering matters, and Feng Kang had seldom appeared so happy.

That was the last time Shang Zaijiu saw his master.

After Shang Zaijiu left Feng Kang's home in the early hours of 13 July, he stayed closeted at home, not going out of his front door for several days as he sat preparing to write his paper and the report for the Fragrant Hills Congress. Suddenly, around noon one day, one of his students rang him from Changsha to tell him that Feng Kang was seriously ill in hospital. Shang Zaijiu went pale with alarm as the news came as a complete surprise to him. He rushed over to Peking University Third Hospital where Feng was in a deep coma. He had fallen over in the shower and started bleeding from his head. Shang stayed at the hospital all through the night, along with Yu Dehao and Wang Deliu. The three of them waited until dawn without Feng Kang regaining consciousness.

Feng Kang was in hospital for a week, during which he came round once or twice, but only fleetingly. "We were completely at a loss when Master Feng died. We were still very young and not yet established. We lost our core when he died. The seminar group was without its mainstay, and without its leader and strategist. In terms of computational mathematics, it was a great loss not just for China but for the whole world.

The memory is still very vivid to Shang Zaijiu.

And there is still a profound and meaningful serenity in his gaze.

DIARY NOTE 6: THE FENG KANG SCHOOL

Theory, experimentation and calculation are already established as the three most important stages of a modern scientist's activities. Only in the second half of the 20th century did calculation in particular develop into one of the most important elements in scientific progress. Not only is Feng Kang the undisputed founder, pioneer and incubator of Chinese computational mathematics, and not only did he give the world the finite element method, the natural boundary element method and the Hamiltonian geometric algorithm method, he also brought to maturity a huge number of computational mathematicians. This cohort of scholars with Feng Kang at its core, are collectively known as the 'Feng Kang School' and are the focus of world mathematics. From the 'Feng Kang School' one can highlight at least the following few famous names: Huang Hongci, Shi Zhongci, Cui Junzhi, Lin Qun, Yuan Yaxiang, Qin Mengzhao, Zhang Guanquan, Wang Lieheng, Yu Dehao, Shang Zaijiu, Wang Daoliu, Ge Zhong, Tang Yifa, Zhu Youlan and Gui Wenzhuang. Even without considering their individual contributions to the world of computational mathematics, within their number there are five academicians, and numerous directors and assistant directors of mathematical institutes. Such a school is a rare thing, not just in China, but in the whole world.

MS—2401

Yokohama

1986, Yokohama. Wang Jizhi took a telephone call informing him his father, Wang Li, was critically ill. The call didn't come from his family but from his domestic company office. His father had always been in excellent health and, despite his age, he had seldom been ill. So, up until that telephone call informed him that his father was in hospital, Wang Jizhi had had no real concerns about him. But now, the call made him completely forget about his work.

"Your father's illness is very serious… that is to say… he may not last until you get back to China."

Perhaps he was already… Wang Jizhi didn't dare finish the thought and he broke out in a cold sweat.

The call came from his company chairman whose attitude was very clear: if necessary, he could interrupt his work and come back to China to see his father one last time. Wang Jizhi knew full well that his chairman was implying that it would cause the company a considerable loss and, in fact, he really couldn't abandon his task.

Wang Jizhi didn't immediately say what he was going to do, and sat in silence for a moment, before hanging up the phone.

Outside the window, the cherry blossom was out, and although there was nothing ostentatious about the Yokohama night scene, there was a dreamlike quality to it. He had been up to his ears in work ever since he arrived in Japan, and hadn't had time to go anywhere else, but he dreamed of just once visiting the Sankeien Garden with his father. The garden is a famous spot for viewing the cherry blossom by night and is situated on a hill near Yamanote. High up on the hill there is a three-tiered pagoda in the style of the Chinese Northern and Southern Dynasties, and every year, in the cherry-blossom season, hordes of people go there to enjoy the delightful way the blossom and the ancient building complement each other. The best time to view them is at night, when the blossom closes up under the gentle lamplight, turning the park into a kind of dreamland. Indeed, a dreamland was all the Sankeien Garden was for Wang Jizhi, because it was only in his dreams that he had seen it. Despite the urgent nature of his work, Wang had really hoped to be able to go there with his father to see the fabled nighttime cherry blossom, especially as Lu Xun mentions "the cherry blossom of Ueno" in one of his essays. Wang's father was a linguist who deeply admired the beginning of that particular essay of Lu Xun, highlighting its fine linguistic structure.

A Different Mountain

Wang Jizhi was a professor at Peking University, the fourth son of the great linguist Wang Li. Although his was a very academic family, Wang Jizhi had not followed in his father's footsteps but, at the age of 16, had passed the exams to study at Peking University's Department of Mathematics and Mechanics, as the youngest student in the cohort. Because of the diversity of his timetable, he had not stayed in the family home on the campus, but had moved into a communal dormitory block, living on the 28th floor. His room faced north and by opening the window, he could see his family home in the Yannanyuan Building. At that time, the Yannanyuan Building could be called a crouching tiger and a hidden dragon, as Feng Youlan, Ma Yinchu, Lin Geng and other great masters were gathered there, and the younger teachers had a saying that "after 30 years of struggle, you get to live in the Yannanyuan".

Wang Jizhi was born in 1941. At the age of four, when he should have gone to kindergarten, he said he didn't want to "muck in" with children of his own age so his mother, who was a primary school teacher, had no choice but to take him with her to attend year-one classes at her primary school. A year later, after he had completed year one, he took the year-two entry examinations, even though he was only five, and the difficulty of the exam questions exceeded the understanding of a five-year-old. There were rules for the examination and if a candidate didn't know how to write a particular character, they had to draw a circle on the squared paper instead. Wang Jizhi conscientiously drew a circle in every square on the paper. Wang Li was watching through the window and saw his extraordinary son earnestly answering all the questions. He thought his son must be doing really well, little knowing that he was drawing circles in every square. Not only did Wang Li not tell his son off, he actually rather admired his resourcefulness and calm. Of course, he didn't offer him any encouragement, as one shouldn't really encourage the offbeat, but nor did he tell him off, deciding the best thing was to let well alone. This awareness of how best to behave is only found in fathers like Wang Li, and every time he remembered the occasion, Wang Jizhi felt how fortunate he was. Who can say that drawing those circles wasn't the beginning of Wang Jizhi's life-long obsession?

Because Wang Li was so busy, he was seldom involved in his son's education and his most important contribution was teaching by example.

In fact, Wang Jizhi's memories of his father are fairly abstract: a fixed rear view of him hunched over his desk working away. In the evenings, the lights in the study of the little building at 60 Yannanyuan would be on until who knew what hour; from morning to night, when people were asleep and people were awake, they were always glowing away and it seemed as though his father never slept. When he was little, Wang Jizhi found this quite extraordinary and mystical. In the lamplight, the books his father wrote grew into a small mountain. Year on year, they piled up like a cliff face, although there was a brief interruption during the 10 years of the Cultural Revolution. *Chinese Linguistics*, *A Study of the Metrical Rules of Chinese Poetry*, *Classical Chinese*... the seemingly endless project on the Chinese language was slowly completed in that rear view of his father. None of this, however, seems to have had anything to do with Wang Jizhi's desertion to mathematics – and what a gulf there is between linguistics and mathematics. But did it have anything to do with drawing circles? A circle is the symbol for zero, but zero is not just a question for mathematics; it is, in fact, the ultimate question of all questions.

Who can say that there is not another picture to be seen in the attraction of opposites?

The fact that his father was already a lofty figure is another aspect.

It is particularly interesting that this other aspect comes round in a great circle to connect with his father, and to connect with linguistics and literary studies; could it be that, by necessity and by pre-destiny, Wang Jizhi should mirror his father from a different lofty perch?

A Different Route

In 1963, now graduated from the mathematics department of Peking University, Wang Jizhi was allocated to the Psychology Institute of the Chinese Academy of Sciences. In linking psychology with mathematics, this seems like a very unusual allocation; or was it intended as a nudge towards a new direction in life? To turn from pure mathematics to the humanities? Inexplicable things always have a metaphorical meaning. Although he was not yet fully through the gates of psychology, the unprecedented move had begun. During the Cultural Revolution, psychology was criticised as a 'pseudo-science' and, for this reason, the Institute of Psychology was categorised as a work unit in need of the 'three corrections': struggle, criticism and liberation. In 1969, the Chinese Academy of Sciences decided to send all the staff of the Institute of

Psychology, apart from the elderly and infirm, to the May 7th Cadre School[1]. In one fell swoop, the 28-year-old Wang Jizhi found himself dumped down in the Academy's Cadre School in Qianjiang County, Hubei. It was only in February 1971 that he returned to Beijing and was allocated to the metallurgical instrument factory on Peking University's campus in Beijing's Fengtai District. At this point, the complete change of direction and profession from mathematics to psychology was completely inconceivable, as the latter was in no way considered a legitimate specialisation: it was nothing, a zero, and Wang Jizhi was back to when he was a little boy drawing circles.

Putting aside what is 'conceivable' or not, it was by chance that the course of Wang Jizhi's life brought him in contact with the metallurgical world. Although the instrument factory was quite small, the departmental system of the Department of Metallurgy was extensive and, as an intellectual and a university graduate, Wang had the opportunity to rise through that system. It was only because of this lucky chance that he was later able to make his great discovery. If there had been no Cultural Revolution, Wang Jizhi might have stayed with psychology and become another anonymous psychologist. The Cultural Revolution made him alter his direction, like a river changes its course, and took him from the May 7th Cadre School to the instrument factory to the Department of Metallurgy, and finally to the Institute of Automation and Computer R&D. With mathematics as his major, sooner or later, he was going to come into contact with computers, and when he did, it was inevitable that the sensibilities passed on from his father would direct him to the field of Chinese characters.

What is particularly interesting is that back in 1957 when Wang Jizhi was taking his university entrance exams, his father, Wang Li, didn't agree with him studying mathematics. Nor, of course, did he want him to go into linguistics and, instead, he told him to study computing. Wang Jizhi stuck with his own choice of mathematics but many years later, when he changed course to work with computers, his father's hopes and the course of his own life miraculously converged. What is interesting about this is that, although fate had a great hand in it, it is still entirely rational and falls within the compass of normal human life.

In the course of the years he spent at the Institute of Automation, Wang Jizhi had access to a lot of information about technological advances in computing from abroad. Starting in 1976, he was fortunate enough to spend three years working on a very important national project as a member of the team researching the computer control system for the

Wuhan Iron and Steel hot steel rolling press. It was in those three years that his knowledge of computers and his technical abilities advanced most quickly and, in particular, he deepened his knowledge and understanding of large-scale industrial real-time control operating systems. It wasn't long before Wang was sent to Shanghai to make preparations for the second phase of the Baosteel engineering project, where he entered into year-long negotiations for the introduction of new technology with computer experts from many different countries. During that time, almost every day, he was making contacts with master engineers from all over the world, at a time when computer technology overseas was very advanced. For Wang Jizhi, his contact with those foreign engineers was as useful as if he were attending a series of lectures by them. All these contacts were made using English, so it wasn't just Wang's computing knowledge that rose to another level, it was his English as well. Although his father was a master linguist, whose book *Classical Chinese* was universally used in classical Chinese teaching across the country – every science or humanities student in China knows Wang Li's *Classical Chinese* – he still paid close attention to the completely unrelated field of computing, and showed great interest in his son's work.

Return

In 1979, when Wang Jizhi became the lead for a small team in the institute's practical computing research team, China had just started importing micro-computers, and his team was considering buying one. There was a kind of unstoppable inevitability about it as Wang moved, step by step, into the very nucleus of human life; it was an inevitability that stemmed partly from his father, partly from his education and partly from some indefinable driving force. Through the introduction of one of his colleagues, he met a Macau Chinese called Kuang Zhenkun, who owned a company called DATAMAX. When DATAMAX computers first appeared, IBM PCs did not exist. The machine Kuang Zhenkun showed Wang was the DATAMAX 8000 which used WordStar as its word processing software, Calculstar for number processing and dBase II as its database software. This micro-computer which incorporated WordStar word processing and MailMerge capabilities, opened Wang Jizhi's eyes to new horizons.

Soon, Wang Jizhi was using a DATAMAX 8000 as the main processor with a TeleVideo monitor, to which he added an Itochu printer, to form a comparatively inexpensive micro-computer system. Because it was a system he had assembled, he had to make the relevant device drivers and, as he began to read the operating manual for the printer, he suddenly discovered that the print head consisted of eight needles, the movements of each of which was controlled by software commands, so it was classified as a dot matrix printer. The Chinese character printers in use in China at the time could only print lower case English letters, namely, a, b, c, d, and so on. Evidently, however, this kind of dot matrix printer was much more flexible in what it could do and, theoretically speaking at least, it could use its dot matrix function to print any kind of pattern or script.

Was the discovery of this principle, which is historically credited to Wang Jizhi, down to mathematics? Down to his father? Down to computing? Down to an innate sensitivity to characters? It has to be said that it was down to all of them, equally. But if Wang Jizhi hadn't had that innate feeling for language and characters, would he have had the insight to make that discovery? Wang Jizhi was exceptionally excited and he could feel the blood coursing through his veins. He worked through the night writing a computer programme for the printer based on the principle that "it could use its dot matrix function to print any kind of pattern or script". Using it he printed out on a sheet of paper the seven characters: 冶金部自动化所 (Institute of Automation Metallurgy Department). This was unprecedented, a seismic shift for the Chinese language, something never seen before.

Wang Jizhi was beside himself with excitement at his success: if he could print seven characters, that meant he could, in principle, print any character. It meant that getting computers to process Chinese characters was no longer a dim and distant prospect.

He told his father about what he had done.

He still remembers his father's expression: solemn and dignified.

As solemn and dignified as an ancient bronze vessel.

There was a gleam in his eye like the reflection from that ancient bronze vessel: it was the gleam that emanated from the flame of Chinese characters, Chinese language and Chinese civilisation. It was the flame of a thousand years.

It was miraculous: against all odds, his father's intuition had proved correct.

Of course, printing seven characters only solved the problem in principle. This computer system had to be able to use Chinese characters to process every kind of application, and then there were a whole series of practical problems to be solved. Firstly, there needed to be a word bank of

Chinese characters before the printer could truly be said to be able to print Chinese characters. But where to find such a word bank? He would have to build it himself.

Wang Jizhi used a different method from his father to research Chinese characters.

But similarity of method was not something Wang Li expected.

Wang Jizhi brought in a Go set from home and laid the plastic-sheet board out on his desk. He got all the members of his small team to gather round and help: one of them used the pieces to lay out characters in dot matrix form, another encoded the character forms using the hexadecimal system and yet another entered the data into the computer. Using this novel method to carry out the digitalisation process was rather like using a horse and cart to pull a locomotive as it was labour-intensive and hard work. They worked continuously for more than a month and ended up with a 16 x 16 dot matrix word bank that included all the 'Category A' *Guo Biao*[2] Chinese characters.

This was all beyond the capability of Wang Li, the author of *Classical Chinese*, to understand.

Nor did he need to understand, as he had already completed his own life's work.

But it wasn't enough to have a word bank of characters; the crucial thing was to find out how to input a whole article in Chinese characters into the computer. They needed a Chinese character input method. At that time the 'Category A' *Guo Biao* characters were arranged in *Hanyu Pinyin*[3] sequence, and if you looked at it in terms of workload, the easiest task would be to develop a *pinyin* input method, so Wang Jizhi began to create just such a method. There were no difficulties, and it wasn't long before he had a simple practical *pinyin* input method. But there are many homophones in Chinese characters, and if you used *pinyin* to input them you had to solve the problem of choosing the right character. This meant that you had to have the different potential characters visible when you input the *pinyin*. You had to be able to see them, that was the crucial thing. That required a terminal and it required a screen, which meant a standard computer or a standard PC.

But at that time all terminals and screens were formatted for English letters and were fundamentally unable to display Chinese characters; in general, they could actually only display 80 x 24 formatted English letters. The core of human life is fashioned one link at a time, and each link represents challenge and innovation, and each is forged by genius. Once Wang Jizhi had started his journey of creation and invention, he couldn't stop.

This is especially the case if you know that your destination is correct, for then, everything leading up to it must perforce be soluble; the logic of the thing itself makes it unstoppable. Wang Jizhi was propelled by this logic; he was himself, yet he was out of himself, and finally the day arrived when he came up with a method: if he used a single character M as a dot matrix then, using a square of 16 x 16 M's as his starting point on the screen, he could create a Chinese character. Proceeding this way, although the screen could only display four very large Chinese characters, it was still a basic and somewhat primitive way of solving the problem of inputting Chinese characters. If there had been someone else in Wang Jizhi's position, they might have found a better way of solving it, but there was no one else. From any point of view, Wang Jizhi was in the absolute vanguard of the story of Chinese characters.

In solving this set of problems, Wang Jizhi had already completed the first stage of a system for the input and output of Chinese characters. The first practical use he put it to was in filling in the official report for the Finance Department of the Institute of Automation: he input the financial data in Chinese into the computer using dBase II, then printed out the report in Chinese for the very first time.

This was an astonishing achievement that was significant in so many ways. It signified Chinese characters crossing a chasm of thousands of years into digitalisation: the five thousand years that separated Wang Li from Wang Jizhi. Who could say of Wang Jizhi that he wasn't following in his father's footsteps? And who could deny that Wang Jizhi had brought a new meaning to the word 'linguist'? Chinese civilisation had made an amazing transition into modern civilisation, and what is more, was going to make the transition into the future. This is the only time in history an ancient civilisation has made the transition into modernity seamlessly, without a break, as a civilisation that is still developing. When the Nobel laureate poet Pablo Neruda came to China in the 1970s, he expressed his feeling as follows when he saw the Great Wall, "So many civilisations have disappeared, but you still survive". But suppose it had been impossible to digitalise Chinese characters; suppose they could only be turned into *pinyin*, could only be Latinised? That would have been a huge chasm blocking the further development of Chinese-character culture, and who knows what would have been the significance of such a barrier? But now, father and son clasped hands across the chasm, or rather they embraced across it, so this great civilisation was both complete in itself and reinventing itself. That is the good fortune of this civilisation and it is hard not to see it as fate showing its approval. Of course, Wang Jizhi wasn't alone in doing the work on digitalising Chinese characters, but his embrace with his father across that chasm is the most significant aspect. What is even more significant is that his father nurtured Wang Jizhi not just in body, but also in the mysteries of the mind.

Living up to the ardent expectations of the year

An era has many forks in the road and people take about as many wrong turns as right ones; or it may be that sometimes at certain points they go wrong more often than they go right. It is the same for a nation and for an individual. But for Wang Jizhi in particular, and at this pivotal moment in particular, every step Wang took was miraculously correct.

Just as Wang Jizhi succeeded in developing a digitalised Chinese input and output system, generational changes were taking place all around him. In Zhongguancun, Chen Chunxian was setting up China's Silicon Valley research institute; the establishment of Wang Hongde's JingHai Company was also catching people's eye and Stone was about to be founded. A whole bunch of people came to the seashore of the age, but they didn't linger there. Without a second thought, they left dry land and headed off into the distance. With his Chinese input-output system, Wang Jizhi suddenly found himself on the seashore, with the possibility of leaving dry land, but he hesitated. Going to sea is not easy when you are used to dry land. As you stand on the shoreline, you feel that the land is incomparably strong and steady, and the sea is full of uncertainty and danger.

So, would he be able to set up a company within the framework of the Metallurgy Department of the Institute of Automation? Would he be able to carry out a trial reform within the organisation? Wang Jizhi discussed this idea with the management but the 'land mass' blocked him, and no matter how much he continued to struggle, there was no way through. Sometimes there is no alternative but to put to sea and, besides, he felt he might have some skill in the water; he had seen other people swimming and felt there was nothing impossible about it, so he began to consider setting up his own company and how he might raise the necessary capital. It was then that the Stone Company opened a door for him. He remembers the date exactly: 16 June 1984. Stone had registered its establishment in Zhongguancun, and in September the same year it began its retail sales operation. In June-July, Wang Jizhi joined the company as chief engineer, and became one of Stone's most important employees in its initial stages.

2. MS-2401

In November, Wang Jizhi formally resigned from the Metallurgy Department of the Institute of Automation.

At that time, every work unit, no matter how small, belonged to the country: the unit represented the country, and the people in it were people of the country. Resigning meant severing your connection with the country and that the country would no longer look after you. This was not just a question of survival; it was a question of mentality and of spirit. Resigning was like a child being weaned, and although Wang Zhiji was perfectly determined, his head still found it difficult to adjust to, and he didn't know how his family would feel about it; his mother, for example, and more particularly, his father. His father was a national figure, so would he be opposed to his son 'resigning from the country'? To his surprise, his father not only did not oppose it, he was actually very open-minded about it. He talked a lot about his view of the work unit/country and the fact was he had long-held ideas from his youth about 'the individual'. It was also true that Wang Jizhi had lived all his life in the consciousness of the work unit/country and any sense of it that he had was that of a 'minor'. But now he was beginning to have some of the fears of a grown-up.

His father wrote a *qilü*[4] for him, rather like a 'coming of age ceremony':

To live up to the ardent expectations of the year,
  Use the Zhou Classic to measure your fields.
  Frosty hooves fear not the distance of the journey,
  Computers turn their happy gaze on the new technology.
  How can you only seek a living for yourself?
  You must also work on behalf of the people.
  I hope my son will exert himself to even loftier ambitions,
  Not just be content with wearing gaudy clothes to amuse his ageing father.

That last line was something Wang Jizhi had not considered. His father could see even further than him, not just into the future but into the past as well, because he was a man of experience, a man of history. For a long time, his father had not been a 'work-unit man', he had been his own man. Wang Jizhi took his father's calligraphy to the Rongbaozhai art gallery in Liulichang to have it properly mounted, then hung it on the wall back home. From then on, it became his personal maxim for living.

At the beginning of 1985, Stone imported a Model 1570 colour printer from the Japanese company Itochu. To ensure the survival of the company,

Wang Jizhi temporarily put aside the still incomplete development of his Chinese-character terminal and led a small team in making Chinese programming cards for the Itochu printer. Compared to starting work on the Chinese character terminal, the work was much easier and was quickly completed. While they were doing that, Stone realised that the majority of work units that were buying computers were also taking a matching printer to print off contracts, reports and other such documents. At the time, a computer system like that cost close to Rmb50,000, so the profit margin is obvious. In the light of the prevailing market conditions, if Stone could produce a machine priced at around Rmb10,000 that could print characters and edit documents, they could make themselves competitive against the products of state-owned brands on the market, and realise a substantial profit.

MS-2400

The time was right and Stone began to consider developing a Chinese-character processor. Having resigned from the work-unit environment, as an individual, Wang Jizhi was like a fish diving back into water, and he began his own journey. Since Japan was a country that also used Chinese characters, there were already all sorts of Chinese-character processors for sale on the Japanese market. Could he find one with good capabilities at a decent price there, and turn its Japanese Kanji (Chinese-character) word bank into a Chinese word bank; change its Japanese input method into a Chinese one, without changing the editing function? Would this be a way of speeding up the launch of Stone's Chinese-character processor as a marketable product. But Wang Jizhi discovered that although the thinking behind this was good, he couldn't actually carry out any practical experiments because the Japanese processors were all geared to thermal transfer printing, which required high specification paper and room temperature control. Additionally, the colour ribbons were very expensive and they couldn't print on waxed stencil paper. This didn't match the current Chinese requirements for printing.

The Stone Company decided to get help from Japanese industry and restart development of equipment tailored to the particular requirements of the Chinese market, which meant a printer engine that used impact printer heads. This was entirely consistent with Wang Jizhi's work on Chinese input and his research proved to be a timely union of market demand with specific Chinese requirements. Moreover, he was able to develop equipment over which there were individual intellectual property rights and this had very favourable implications for the long-term independent development of the company. In the end, the Japanese company ALPS, which had been chosen by Stone and Mitsui, settled on a method of joint development: at Stone's end, Wang Jizhi would be responsible for the overall project design while ALPS would be responsible for the printer engine, the liquid crystal display screen, the hardware design and the BIOS interface. Stone would provide the software design and manufacture the final product.

Stone's small development team consisted of only four people, with Wang Jizhi in charge of planning. He was simultaneously responsible for the development of both the Chinese-character processor software and the *pinyin* input method. Work started in August 1985 and Wang's thinking was this: since Wordstar was capable of English alphabet editing, with that base it should certainly also be capable of Chinese character editing. In order to more closely meet Chinese market demands, Wang Jizhi began to plan the product from its target audience's point of view. He settled on junior high school as the educational benchmark for the product and ensured that the instructions on the screen, the characters used in the commands for the processor and the printer, and also in the instruction manual, were as easy to understand as possible, and avoided technical computer jargon. Although Wang Jizhi had never studied consumer psychology, his work history at the Institute of Psychology had given him a theoretical understanding of the basics of psychology so, with hindsight, we can see that Wang Jizhi's development planning for MS-2400 already had some flavour of the consumer psychology maxim 'always proceed from the consumer's point of view'. In fact, from a modern point of view, a lot of his work would already be considered outside the remit of an engineer and much more in the realm of marketing, and this was a major factor in the extraordinary success of Stone's printer within a day of it hitting the market.

Another thing particularly worthy of note is that in China at that time, the majority of people were not accustomed to Chinese-character computer processing, so to simplify and facilitate publicity and eliminate their natural fear of computers, as a former 'psychology student' Wang Jizhi decided to call the new product a Chinese electric typewriter with the product name Stone MS-2400. The M stood for Mitsui, the S for Stone; 24 was the number of needles in the printer, and 00 showed that it was first generation. In order to completely meet the demands of the Chinese market, Wang refused the suggestions of some Stone personnel that they put a foreign-language superscript on the housing or give it a foreign logo.

In March 1986, Wang Jizhi took his team to ALPS in Japan to carry out the final debugging. He planned that they should stay in Japan for three weeks, working seven days a week, 16 hours a day, without a break, so that they could get the work done as quickly as possible in the limited time available to them. Three weeks passed very quickly but the equipment wasn't completely debugged. If he went home at this point to see his father, the work would have been interrupted and all the effort, resources and time put in up to that point would effectively have been wasted. Moreover, if they didn't complete the debugging this time, the next time... well, he didn't know how long they would have to wait. But then, if he didn't go back...

I hope my son will exert himself to even loftier ambitions

Wang Jizhi phoned home and asked his mother to decide whether he should come home or not. If his mother told him he should, he would leave immediately. He put the call through with the utmost gravity, his heart pounding, as he prayed to heaven to bless and protect his father. If it did so, then he could stay on and complete his crucial task. His mother answered the call and, by god's blessing, his father was still alive and in the hospital. Wang Jizhi heaved a long sigh of relief... to tell the truth, he had already been thinking about the funeral. Wang Jizhi had a sudden premonition that there would be no point in him going home. Of course, his father's condition was very serious; when he fell ill, the first symptom was a fever and everyone thought it must be the flu; no one anticipated how serious it would get after he went into hospital: it was leukaemia, and the deterioration was very rapid.

"I know that your work in Japan is very important. If it can't do without you, then you shouldn't come home; your younger brother and sister are here in Beijing," his mother said.

Putting work first was a Wang family tradition. From when he was little Wang Jizhi could remember that his parents did not lightly ask for time off work just because they weren't feeling well and persisted in going to work despite minor illnesses. When Wang himself was at primary school and middle school, whether it was a stomach ache or some other form of discomfort, his mother always urged him to do his best to go to classes. So, following this ruthless doctrine, for Wang Jizhi to stay on working in Japan was both the necessary and the natural choice. Still with the deepest concern for his father, he worked day and night with his team and finally completed the debugging.

The Stone MS-2400 Chinese-character electric typewriter was born and in no time at all it was reeling out page after page of Chinese documents; the busy bee buzzing that came from its print head was the best sound in the whole world. Wang Jizhi was the expert who developed China's first Chinese-character electric typewriter. After the first year of production of the MS-2400, they had sold more than 7,000 units which gave them a turnover of more than Rmb70 million. This was a result unmatched by anyone else in Zhongguancun. When it came to finalising the next year's production, they updated the product to the even more refined MS-2401 with the addition of a floppy disc drive which removed any limit on the length of document it could print. Even more importantly, the MS-2401 incorporated a new liquid crystal display screen, giving it very much the feeling of a PC. Whereas the LCD screen of the preceding MS-2400 gave two rows with a total of twenty Chinese characters, the MS-2401 could display five rows of forty characters each. At the time PCs usually used 5-inch floppy disc drives and 3.5-inch discs were only just emerging. Wang Jizhi decided that the MS-2401 would use these smaller discs. Looking back, his forward-thinking decision proved to be absolutely the right one.

Additionally, the MS-2401 used Fang Song, Kai and Hei fonts – in fact it had four in all – and it also raised the capacity specification of the character storage Mask ROM. The MS-2401 was a mature product and one of the Japanese engineers who worked with Wang Jizhi assessed him thus: "We Japanese are very good at making products but we lack innovation. You Chinese have that innovative ability." The Mitsui Company said this, "The MS-2401's technology not only matches Japanese products, it surpasses them." The MS series Chinese-character processors played a critical role in the history of the development of Stone; they were the decisive product for the company as they were one of the earliest independently-owned brands in the field of 1980s and 1990s Chinese office automation. From the day it first hit the market, this product sold consistently for more than 10 years. By the end of 1996, cumulative sales of the MS-series Chinese-character English alphabet processors reached over 300,000 units with a cumulative turnover in excess of Rmb3 billion. It meant that in the IT world of the 1980s, China had its own brand.

On 12 April, as the MS-2400 Chinese-character printer was reeling out page after page of documents, and the bee-like buzzing was resounding merrily, solemn in the midst of all the joy, Wang Jizhi returned to Beijing.

He didn't go home from the airport but headed straight for the Beijing Friendship Hospital where his father had been admitted. His eyes were misty with tears; the great linguistic scholar of the age, Wang Li, had unexpectedly regained consciousness and he was grasping the hand of his son who had returned from so far away. His gaze was earnest and reserved: it was his father's gaze, but not entirely. It was also the gaze of prose, the gaze of language, the gaze of a Shang Dynasty oracle bone and of a bronze ritual vessel. Although he was already incapable of finishing complete sentences, he was still able to speak and his voice was abnormally clear. It was that clarity that was supporting the father as he waited for his son's arrival: life was not extinguished, and the fire still burned. Before he left the country, Wang Jizhi had explained to his father the theory behind the work on the Chinese-character processor, but his father hadn't understood at all, and couldn't work it out. Wang had wanted to bring in a computer to demonstrate to his father to help explain but, for one thing, work got too demanding and, for another, the product was about to be launched onto the market and wouldn't it be better to wait until it was out there and explain it all then? Who was to know that by the time the device was fully developed, his father was already in the very last stage of his life? Wang Jizhi spent ages explaining the theory but, of course, his father didn't understand, and just smiled.

And with a smile, as though it was the smile of civilisation, his father left this world.

After 13 days, on the second anniversary of the founding of Stone, the Stone MS-2400 Chinese-character printer was formally launched. It made Chinese-character input-output a reality in the age of the micro-computer and, at a stroke, it cured the aphasia of the Chinese people in the printer age. On that day, in the room full of distinguished guests who had come to offer their congratulations, the sound of clapping and commendation seemed as if it would never stop. As he watched the scene, what Wang Jizhi thought of was his father's smile.

Even though he didn't understand, he still smiled. That's right! His father's smile was not just one of gratification. Even now, many years later, Wang Jizhi still recalls his father's smile.

DIARY NOTE 7: A DIFFERENT KIND OF GENERATIONAL KNOWLEDGE

> Wang Li was a professor of Chinese linguistics and Wang Jizhi implemented Chinese-character printing. What is the connection between the

two? I planned to establish an intrinsic connection. But when I told Wang Jizhi this, he was rather startled and alarmed. He had never thought there was any connection between his father's linguistic studies and his own research into printers. In Wang Jizhi's home in Taiyanggong on Beijing's 3rd Ring Road, the sun was shining in through a French window that took up a whole wall. It was the calm after a storm, there was no smog, and the sunshine was as bright as it is at the seaside, so Wang's alarm seemed at odds with the brightness. Even so, I carried on: "When Master Wang Li first suggested that you study computing, you went to study mathematics but in the end you came back to computing and, moreover, used computing to advance civilisation. Can you really tell me there is no kind of connection?" When I finished speaking, a sombre mood descended on that extraordinarily bright sunshine. It came from Wang Jizhi's intense gaze. He didn't disagree with me, nor did he agree, but I could see he was pondering deeply or rather than say pondering, it might be better to say he was trawling through his memories.

"Surely you must see that your research represented a different kind of generational knowledge? Certainly different from the norm, but doesn't its complexity just make it more meaningful?" Master Wang Jizhi was listening carefully; he almost seemed to be listening with his eyes, in which I fancied I could almost see the image of his father. "There may be something in what you say," he told me at last. When I was about to leave, he led me to one end of the living room to see the poem Wang Li had given him. I looked at the calligraphy mounted in an already yellowing vertical scroll. He gave me a copy of Wang Li's recently reprinted *A Study of the Metrical Rules of Chinese Poetry*. It was a slim volume but it carried the weight of history in it.

Wang Jizhi solemnly signed it for me.

Thousand Years

千年之约

Return

WHEN WANG XUAN BOARDED THE TRAIN, the admission letter from Peking University in his pocket, and left Shanghai, speeding towards Beijing, it was impossible to imagine that, seven years later, he would be a mere ghost of himself, at death's door, being carried back to Shanghai. The person carrying him was a fellow student at Peking University, and when they reached Wang's home, he couldn't help heaving a long sigh of relief, delighted to have reached their destination without mishap. He even made sure not to stay too long at the Wang family home, as if he was afraid that if he did, something else might happen. He just exchanged a few words and hurried away.

Wang's mother wept at the sight of her son's emaciated frame and at his laboured breathing. How could this be her son of seven years ago? That elegant and graceful young man? Wang Xuan's eyes were filled with tears for the first time, too, as he looked at his mother, but he couldn't speak even a single word. He had never wept back in Beijing, no matter how much pain he was in, but had just lain there numb and apathetic.

Seven years before, Wang Xuan passed the entrance exams for the mathematics department, which that year had accepted 200 candidates who represented the cream of young mathematicians from all over the country. The youngest of them, Ma Xiwen, was 15 years old. Wang Xuan was 17, which was still younger than the average. Four years later, on the back of his outstanding results, he returned to his alma mater as a teaching assistant in the department of radio engineering.

In the winter of 1960, as in so many other places, food in the dining hall of Peking University was in very short supply, to the extent that even staples like *mantou* (steamed bread) and rice were missing from the evening meal. Like everyone else, Wang Xuan's dinner consisted of three bowls of thin congee and a side dish of yellow bean paste. Two years previously, he had been part of the project to debug Peking University's 'Red Flag Computer'. The computer had been designed by Professor Zhang Shilong, and after he had fixed the main design principles and the thinking behind them, the professor boldly handed over responsibility for the overall design to his favourite pupil, Wang Xuan. The design work wasn't easy and the debugging was even more challenging. Wang Xuan would often get up in the middle of the night to go and take over in the computer room, working on the debugging straight through until lunchtime the next day when he would stagger over to the dining hall to eat. In the middle of lunch one day, he suddenly noticed that the blue overalls he was wearing had turned iron grey, but he didn't give it a second thought. His head was completely filled with the Red Flag Computer. Just before he had gone into the dining hall, he had suddenly thought of some data for the debugging process and, in case he should forget it, he pulled out a pen to write it on the palm of his hand. There was something wrong with the pen, as it seemed to have got thinner than he was used to, so he thrust it back in his pocket and strode into the dining hall. He was only startled out of his reverie when the whole hall erupted with laughter and he realised he was wearing someone else's clothes. Wang Xuan was the kind of person who got completely lost in his work that way. This kind of work really demanded proper nutrition but sometimes he was so wrapped up in his work, he didn't give it a thought, and often went hungry.

From the spring of 1959, in order to save time, Wang Xuan moved all his stuff into the laboratory; at night he slept on the desk, and in the morning he rolled up his bedding and continued with his plans and designs. With the day divided into three shifts, he worked from seven o'clock in the morning to eleven at night. He dedicated the hour between eleven and twelve to reading foreign-language resources and catching up with current trends in computing. Come summer that year, after displaying his fledgling talent through a year of intensive work, Wang Xuan succeeded in completing a logical design. Then, just as he was rejoicing at having made the first step in completing the Red Flag Computer, some unexpected news arrived: in the course of the Anti-Rightist Movement, Zhang Shilong and two other Peking University professors had been identified as "an opportunist rightist clique within the party's specialist professionals".

After Zhang Shilong had been 'criticised', he was sent down to labour in a farming village. Just before he left, he handed over the vital task of testing and debugging the Red Flag Computer to Wang Xuan. Two years before this there had been another piece of unfortunate news: back in Shanghai, his father had had the dunce's cap of 'rightist faction'[1] put on his head, and from then on Wang Xuan had become rather taciturn and withdrawn, even more so now, and he plunged with abnormal intensity into his work, with eyes only for the computer. Then, in 1960, he could swallow down three bowls of steaming hot congee in five minutes and even that, given the standard of table manners in the people around him, made him really quite refined.

To add insult to injury, in November that year, food coupons for more than 10 kilos of grain that Wang Xuan had managed to lay his hands on, were stolen, so after that, there wasn't even any congee to eat. Formerly taciturn and reserved, Wang Xuan began to find his voice. He borrowed some grain from the dining hall which he would pay for in instalments. Wang Xuan was 1.73m tall, which was reckoned to be short by Beijing standards, but he was young and vigorous, still only 22, and the rations he had were not enough, especially since now he had to make monthly payments on the borrowed grain. So, he had no choice but to drop his ration to 400g a day.

The combination of semi-starvation and hard work finally laid the robot-like Wang Xuan low with intestinal oedema.

The work which Professor Zhang had entrusted to him on debugging the Red Flag Computer came to a halt. With one 'computer' ruined, the other one might follow suit, or so it seemed. Following this, Wang Xuan made one of the most important decisions of his life: he switched his focus from hardware to software. But he didn't give up on hardware completely. That said, however, he did abandon it temporarily as his illness forced him to leave the computer. Dragging his feet, he made his way reluctantly over to the library where he borrowed the Soviet scientist Andrey Ershov's book *Programming Programme for the BESM Computer* and began to read it attentively as his stomach growled with hunger. In it, he read a detailed introduction to the SOAP assembly language, and several chapters on FORTRAN. He studied them word by word and sentence by sentence. His heart was tripping with excitement, and in those palpitations a new way of thinking naturally opened up to him: he finally felt that he was beginning to understand computers.

At the same time he also began to understand himself. Let us say that one day Wang Xuan would discover a laser typesetting system for Chinese characters, ending a printing tradition essentially unchanged for a thousand years; all history had to do was just wait a while, wait for Wang Xuan, hailed as the modern day Bi Sheng[2]. The very beginning of it all was this transformation that took place in the midst of hunger and starvation.

But less than a year later, that is in the summer of 1961, not only had the oedema not diminished, a sudden rush of indeterminate intestinal ailments also attacked Wang Xuan with much the same effect as a computer software crash. He suffered with a persistent low-grade fever, chest pains, chest tightness and breathing difficulties. When he was examined in hospital, they discovered a dense shadow on his lungs, but the doctors looked at each other in bafflement and none of them dared make a firm diagnosis as to what the nature of that shadow was. The only thing to do was to keep him under close observation. Under that observation, his condition worsened: his blood pressure shot up, there was blood in his urine and his white blood cell count dropped to below 3,000. The doctors wrote all manner of urgent prescriptions but none of the drugs had any effect on Wang Xuan.

Everyone was perplexed by the nature of Wang Xuan's illness and even after many days of observation the doctors were unable to make a diagnosis. Eventually, Peking University 3rd Hospital made a reluctant preliminary diagnosis: systemic *lupus erythmosus*. This is a kind of auto-immune disease which attacks the skin but can develop into its systemic form and attack the internal organs too. Just hearing the name of the disease was frightening enough but the doctors also came up with some extraordinary proscriptions such as forbidding Wang Xuan to go outside into the sunshine just as he pleased.

What does not having access to sunshine do to people?

They become no different from troglodytes.

"Can I go out if it's cloudy?" Wang Xuan asked hopefully.

"No," the doctors said. "Not unless you wear a hat, even when it is cloudy. And it has to be a wide-brimmed hat." Wang Xuan really craved sunlight at that time, and he thought to himself that he could always look out of the window; but his health had weakened to such an extent he couldn't even look at a single ray of sunshine through the window. He wondered what fate was trying to tell him.

Wang Xuan eventually got hold of a wide-brimmed hat, which made him look an even stranger invalid than he had before. He was only 24 but he felt like an old man. No, not even an old man; he was as thin as a lamp post. If he was a 'robot', then it was a thirsty, starving 'robot'. In 1961, he was lying in bed in his dorm room. It had become a question of whether he would live or die. It was a question of general metaphysics; it was a question of physical metaphysics; it was a Shakespearean question.

Sick leave! That was the answer. Wang Xuan decided to go back to Shanghai. A colleague carried him to the bus and then transferred him to the train. From Wang Xuan's mother's point of view, those few years were a succession of misfortunes: his father had spent his whole life scrupulously following the letter of the law, entirely innocent in his conduct. But then he had said a few things when he was freely airing his views and he had been labelled a 'rightist faction'. Having their youngest son teaching at Peking University was a joy and a comfort to the old lady. Could it really be Wang Xuan being carried home by a colleague? She found it hard to believe. What could have happened to him in just a few years? Of father and son, one had become a 'rightist faction', and the other was just skin and bone.

Father and son were not to be compared to one another, but they were reflections of each other.

Wang Xuan only received Rmb37 a month labour insurance allowance, which was not enough to cover medical investigations and drugs, so all he could do was make economies, do what he could and keep the lowest level of treatment going. For a 24-year-old to live off labour insurance allowance effectively reduced him to the level of a disabled person. With nothing else to do, Wang Xuan revived the love of Peking opera from his youth, so he sat listening to records and, by force of habit, researching Peking opera. Research was what he was used to and what he was good at, so he researched whatever he came in contact with. Even though it didn't show again in the many years that followed, he was actually something of an expert in the field, with a deep knowledge of the subject. But, of course, Peking opera was not the path Wang Xuan was going to take.

Just as happened in Beijing, the hospital in Shanghai was baffled by Wang Xuan's unusual illness. Most frustratingly, his medical notes were still in Beijing because he had forgotten to bring them with him. However, this was not a problem for Wang as he decided to write them out himself, and he produced a detailed account of every investigation as he remembered it. The end result was as detailed a medical history as an official hospital record that included his personal medical history, the fruits of several hospital diagnoses and even summaries of lab test results.

The doctors in Shanghai were astonished when they saw this document and asked whether Wang had ever worked in a hospital. He told them he was a computer specialist. At that time, very few people knew about computers, so the doctors were completely nonplussed. Taking in Wang's extraordinary loss of weight, they said: "It looks as though you must have received some kind of specialised training" which was them almost as good as saying that they thought Wang Xuan was actually a robot. There was nothing they could do for him, robot or not, and when Zhang Shilong went to Shanghai to visit him, he returned to Beijing and tearfully told Wang's colleagues at Peking University, "Just eating a meal exhausts Wang Xuan; he is extremely weak... by the look of it, there is not much hope."

His mother said, "Your illness is caused by exhaustion; if you look after yourself properly, you are sure to get better." Wang Xuan gave a wry laugh. His mother sought out a traditional Chinese doctor and took Wang Xuan to see him. The doctor prescribed a long-term course of treatment. Wang's mother personally collected all the ingredients, cooked them and turned them into all sorts of different dishes for Wang Xuan. Calling on a lifetime's experience she made every possible effort and, miraculously, Wang Xuan showed some improvement. At the very least, it was apparent that the shadow of death had been removed. "It seems I'm not going to die!" Wang Xuan said as he looked at himself in the mirror.

It was spring 1963. Spring is the season of birth for one thing, and for another, Wang Xuan was still a young man. He drew on his body's life force and the day came when he was able to sit up, get off his sickbed and walk a few slow steps, holding onto the bed for support. No matter how physically slow he was to get about during this time, his brain was always busy. Because he could now move about, he said goodbye to Peking opera and turned his mind back to computers. To tell the truth, subconsciously he had never left them, and all along he had been mulling over the architecture of computer systems, including high-level language processing systems. First came hardware systems and software. At the time, software wasn't a familiar term even in the West, and it was only in 1964 that it really made its appearance. What Wang Xuan was thinking about was a thoroughly researched high-level language processing system followed by a new architecture for computer systems. Or, to put it another way, he was thinking of researching hardware architecture by means of thorough research into software, so he could fully understand the effect software had on hardware.

People who work with computers all know that computer language is the language that computers at any given time can interpret and implement. It works through the combination of two input numbers, '1' and '0'. Back then, it was difficult to compile, difficult to record, difficult to read and difficult to alter. Symbol language, which came later, used symbols to replace the two input numbers, but it still had all the same shortcomings. High-level language is comparatively closer to human language and mathematical language; it is similar to computer language but more intuitive. It is also easier to write, easier to read and much more versatile. But computers cannot read high-level language directly, and it has to be converted into computer language by a high-level language translator first. The necessary translation programme is called a 'compiler'.

That same spring, Wang Xuan's counsellor Chen Kunqiu came back to Shanghai to see her family and visit Wang Xuan. Wang Xuan called Chen Kunqiu 'Little Teacher' and talked to her about software with which they were both familiar. In the summer, Wang Xuan wrote Chen a letter, once again discussing some mutually relevant data. Chen Kunqiu was working on computer programmes in the computing and mathematical teaching and research section, so she asked someone to send Wang some material on ALGOL 60 from America. Wang Xuan had an ulterior motive in writing to Chen, and when he saw her reply, and drew certain inferences from it, he wrote her another letter. It was a coded love letter, asking to 'maintain relations'. The first time Chen Kunqiu read it, she didn't understand, but the second time, she got it, and it was completely unexpected. She couldn't help smiling at someone apparently at death's door, who was still able to think of this.

ALGOL 60 was a comparatively complex high-level language for the time but, with astonishing perseverance and great endurance, Wang Xuan worked through every detail character by character and sentence by sentence. Because his health was still very depleted, he often had to stop and lie on his bed letting the Peking Opera flow through him. The opera stood in for Chen Kunqiu, like recharging a battery, and although Chen hadn't been pierced by Wang Xuan's Cupid's arrow, nor had she completely rejected it. It was as though it was in the incubation stage. It was pretty much while he was in bed that he resolved his understanding of the ALGOL high-level language system, and after that it was as if his health had been supercharged. He made a miraculous recovery; he was able to look after himself, even to the extent of going outside where he could enjoy the sunshine on the Bund. Leaning on a railing there, he thought of Beijing and now Bejing had something new for him: it had someone to 'maintain relations' with.

In 1964, supercharged by 'love', Wang Xuan began to push ahead with designing the ALGOL 60 compiler programme. Drafts piled up on his desk and when he had completed his proposal for the first stage, he wrote to Chen Kunqiu in Beijing again and consolidated it with the help of Chen, Xu Zhuoqun, Zhu Wansen and several other teachers. The following year, his health improved even further so he was able to travel and he began to nurture the hope of going back to school to return to research work. In the same year, the ALGOL 60 compiler system was officially included in the Peking University research programme. Chen Kunqiu wrote to Wang Xuan giving him the good news, and Wang said goodbye to his parents and returned to Beijing.

Chen Kunqiu: Let's get married

Because of the ALGOL 60 compiler system, Wang Xuan and Chen Kunqiu became what seemed like a match made in heaven, as though they were playing out a real-life computer game, while at the same time being part of the 'game', part of the system. They were ahead of their time in China at that time and were pretty much keeping step with the rest of the world. Wang Xuan excelled in choosing the direction of study and fixing the overall strategy while Chen Kunqiu's strength lay in designing all the software. Once Wang's initial plan was on the table, she swiftly and efficiently wrote the programmes, and formulated an excellent action plan for testing and debugging. The programmes she wrote were precise and reliable, and seldom developed any faults. Wang Xuan was not keen on any general-purpose hardware for implementing his high-level language plan, and intuitively began to hunt down the problems that were causing a bottleneck with the operation of the compiler and the target programme, such as how to handle subscripted variables and how to invoke subroutines. At stumbling block after stumbling block, Wang Xuan and Chen Kunqiu came up with a steady stream of innovative thinking and brand-new design.

Just as Wang Xuan's research was bearing fruit with a new high-level language compiler system, and just as he had fully recovered from the flare-up of that internal 'software system' (his mystery illness), the Cultural Revolution began and everything else stopped. Wang Xuan and all the other Peking University teaching staff were sent to the countryside for correction through hard labour. All the members of the department went too. Halfway there, Wang Xuan fell ill. The truth was he was still very weak, and his health wasn't up to strenuous exercise. When he was examined at the hospital, he had a low-grade fever and there was a shadow on his lungs, exactly as there had been in 1960. He was confined to bed.

The so-called 'great connection'[3] began, when every day saw more than 100,000 people arriving at Peking University and the corridors were full of Red Guards debating the 'revolution'. The shouting and raised voices went on night and day. It was hard for an ordinary person to endure, let alone an invalid. Much against his will, Wang Xuan had no choice but to move to the branch of the university way out in the suburbs near the Imperial Ming Tombs in Changping County where he lived on the fourth floor of a dormitory block. Although the surroundings of the branch school were a great improvement, Wang Xuan was so incapacitated by illness that he didn't even have the strength to go downstairs to buy food.

Chen Kunqiu was able to visit him every weekend, and these were the only days that made life a little better for him. Usually, Chen tidied up the room as soon as she arrived, washed a week's worth of dirty laundry and brought some food with her. All she could see in Wang Xuan's eyes was apathy; no other emotion broke through. Someone who is looking death in the face is unable to show emotion, let alone express any ideas. The seriousness of Wang's condition increased daily: his low-grade fever persisted and he had difficulty breathing, to the extent that he was often left gasping. His ability to look after himself declined in every respect, and it seemed he would never get out of his bed again. He felt that his end was near, and he wanted to go back to Shanghai, to go home as he did before, and never return to Beijing. But now it was different from four years before: the trains were all full of proselytising Red Guards and every carriage was like a pressure-cooker. How could he travel in those conditions and, in any case, who could possibly go with him? Besides, back home his father had been denounced and the house searched and stripped of suspect items. How could he expect his mother to cope with the return of a hopeless invalid too? All Wang Xuan could feel was numbness and apathy.

His mind had shut down and all that was needed now was for his body to go cold too.

One day, when Chen Kunqiu arrived at his side, she didn't tidy the room as usual nor do the laundry, but she just looked at Wang Xuan and said, quietly, "Let's get married and go back to the university."

Wang Xuan stared blankly at her for a long moment but then he felt the heat rising in him, burning through the icy cold.

"Really?" he asked.

"Really!"

It was like a computer language, a programming language.

The language had a peerless truth, but also a warmth beyond truth.

Wang Xuan sat up, like someone returning to life from death.

The tears flowed.

Chen Kunqiu was a year older than Wang Xuan. She was born in Shanghai in 1936. She graduated from the Peking University Department of Mathematics in 1957 and she joined the same department after graduation a year before Wang, which was why he called her 'Little Teacher. Even though they were only a year apart in age, their relationship was rather like that of an older sister to a younger brother, or a teacher to her student. Although the characters Yang Guo and Little Dragon Maiden from the pen of Mr Jin Yong[4] are literary creations, they are certainly not so far removed from fact. Even though *The Return of the Condor Heroes* had not been written back then, its essence already existed in the reality of Wang Xuan and Chen Kunqiu.

On 1 February 1967, Wang Xuan and Chen Kunqiu got married in a room of about 10sqm on the third floor of Peking University's No. 6 Big Red Building. It was a north-facing room, and you could see Weiming Lake from the window. No one could understand why Chen Kunqiu would marry a 'walking corpse' like Wang Xuan who, with his emaciated body, stertorous breathing and unsteady gait, looked as though the next puff of wind would carry him away. But even looking at it like that, there was a flavour of the romance of eternal love about it; it had the feel of the 'Once in a Thousand Years', with a mysterious spiritual link to Bi Sheng[5], a millennium before. A new Bi Sheng was to be found residing in these two people.

But we are getting ahead of ourselves.

1969 saw preparations for war[6], a dispersal and a movement order, so Chen Kunqiu was once again sent scurrying around to find somewhere to live.

In the end, she found a small courtyard opposite the Shaoyuan Guesthouse called the 'Tong Residence'. There were three one-storey buildings in the courtyard, and the new household moved in, with Chen Kunqiu leading Wang Xuan to Number 8B. It was an old-fashioned, old-style courtyard, and although it was old and in poor repair, it still had the feel of better days long ago about it and it perfectly suited Wang Xuan. In fact, he himself rather resembled that courtyard, especially when he stood out there in the sunshine.

Chen Kunqiu felt inexpressibly content; so content that tears came to her eyes.

At the end of 1969, Peking University provided support for the development of a one million instructions per second (1 MIPS) computer called Machine 150. Wang Xuan was too seriously ill to take part in the project. Chen Kunqiu was the software technician and also made the mainframe hardware; to join in the development, she brought back to the university the main work force which had been sent down to the countryside for hard labour. In light of this, Wang Xuan told her, "If one of the two of us is involved, that is enough." From then on, he collated all his own thinking on the subject and gave it to his wife for the project team.

Wang Xuan's colleague, Ma Bingkun had a good family background, and was born and raised in very fortunate circumstances. He joined the Machine 150 development team right at the start and often went to see Wang Xuan. He had no fear of being implicated as a child of one of the 'Black Five'[7] reactionary factions and paid no attention to any of the many different confidentiality measures and prohibitions placed on the development team. There was one occasion when he came to visit Ma Bingkun, however, with a frown on his face. There were problems with Machine 150: the quality of the domestically produced magnetic tape was not up to standard, nor was the quality of the tape drive, and the error correction code they were using at the time could only correct a single error in any given line of commands.

When Wang Xuan heard this, he had a burst of energy as if the main engine of his mind had suddenly restarted, and he decided on an experiment. Since he had no computer, he did the whole thing manually, filtering and proving several hundred different programme codes. He was still running the same low-grade fever, but there was nothing for it but to work day and night and not let it get the better of him. Although he was confined to bed at the limit of his strength, often like an empty battery, within half a month he had come up with a programme. It just required eight supplementary valid commands and it could correct double errors in 16 locations. He checked it time and again, and it proved reliable. Ma Bingkun had been waiting and waiting for the day when Wang Xuan gave him his programme; he handed it over to the team, but he didn't dare say it was Wang Xuan's work. If he did, it would be seen as part of "the new direction of the class struggle".

Wang Xuan's programme was quickly applied to Machine 150's magnetic tape with instant success, greatly increasing the reliability of the machine. It was an anonymous invention, but Chen Kunqiu couldn't help smiling to herself. Many years later, the secret was revealed, but not until the 1980s.

East, West

In 1975, the unforgiving march of time brought Wang Xuan to the age of 38; as he closed in on his 40th birthday, the years had left deeper scars on his face than on most people. His breathing difficulties too had marked his ribcage. Even though he was indeed 38, he seemed to be of indeterminate age, neither old nor young; his body might be weak, but there was still a gleam in his eyes which had never been extinguished since Chen Kunqiu came into his life. Sometimes that light in his eyes was especially bright, as if all his life force was concentrated there. This was particularly so when he was working and researching material. Of course, because his energy was concentrated there, sometimes the rest of him seemed very weak. Or, to put it another way, in order to concentrate his energy in this way, what he was doing was taking bricks from the east wall to shore up the west, but he was unable to find a balance between the two. Nevertheless, it was by making this kind of transfer of energies that he was sharp and quick enough to be sensitive to the most important aspects of that era, revolutionary aspects.

In 1971, Intel developed the world's first 4-bit CPU (central processing unit), the 4004; in 1974 they launched the 8080 which was 20 times quicker than the 4004; in the same year, the American company MITS used the 8080 as the basis for the world's first microcomputer, heralding the arrival of the revolutionary age of the micromachine. Computers were a Western invention and were based on the English alphabetic system. They were simply on another planet from where China found itself, so far out of reach. How could Chinese, which was still using the same pictographic script it had been using for thousands of years, possibly be input into these microcomputers? The impossibility seemed axiomatic. Most people thought Chinese characters were too primitive, left behind by the rest of humanity: in the age of the micromachine, this was the general opinion of a whole host of so-called wise men. But that was not how Wang Xuan saw it or, at least, he thought that view should be challenged. What could he do? It was to determine this, that his extraordinary but paradoxical body had pursued a kind of preordained celestial course that had given him possession of certain things which now seemed as though they had been readied by god for the tradition of Chinese characters.

As the spring flowers opened in 1974, Peking University had its own computer which needed to be put to use. This precious 'microbloom' could not always stay a bud about to flower, it had to produce something. It was decided it should be used to take over the university's administrative processes. So, one day, a large number of the university administration team made their way to the university print shop. The supplies department and the finance department conducted an inspection in which Chen Kunqiu participated. Several months before, at the beginning of the year, she had contracted Menière's disease which flared up from time to time, making her head spin, so she was unable to teach her classes. She wondered whether she might somehow have been affected by Wang Xuan's illness. The teaching department relieved her of her teaching duties and assigned her to a variety of low-grade jobs in charge of resources and arranging student activities. People were irresistibly reminded of Wang Xuan's situation, and some of them would joke: those two really are a match made in heaven - they look like each other and they get ill like each other. It was in these circumstances that Chen Kunqiu had joined the inspection of the print room in order to understand what needed to be done. Fortuitously, while she was in the print shop, she was surprised to learn that there was an important national scientific research project looking at the technology for Chinese-character data processing, known as 'Project 748'. She told Wang Xuan about it when she got home. Wang Xuan had a keen nose for such things, and the more ill he was, the more acute that sense became. His mind engaged like a computer receiving a command. He suddenly felt like a long-idle main processor springing to life, and he could almost hear the whirring. The truth was that he had been running his internal processor all along over those many years and now his eyes lit up, just as he saw his wife's do. From then on, there was something more in those glinting eyes, and although it was hard to say exactly what it was, a laser perhaps or something similar, it was something that appeared only when the two of them looked at each other.

In all, Project 748 encompassed research into an accurate Chinese-character phototypesetting system, a Chinese-character information retrieval system, a Chinese-character communications system and Chinese-character end devices. Wang Xuan believed that the specialised system for Chinese-character phototypesetting was the key element as this would do the work of compiling and typesetting all manner of publications. It had particular significance for the Chinese-character writing system that had already lasted for five thousand years; it was in line with world trends and could enable Chinese characters not to be left behind in the revolution. Chen Kunqiu knew that within Project 748 there were already five work units engaged with this system; these were the Shanghai Institute of Printing Technology, the China Printing Factory, the Beijing Xinhua News Agency Print Shop, the Tsinghua University Department of Computing and the Chinese Academy of Sciences Institute of Automation. These were five very powerful institutions and they all already had many collaborative partners.

This was a national project which had no room for individuals, especially invalids.

But Wang Xuan could immediately see the flaws and deficiencies in those five work units, and he prepared to go out on a limb.

His internal central processor whirring away, Wang Xuan entered into a whole new type of computer-like working. By his own efforts he ferreted out a great mass of information: the world's first manually operated phototypesetting machine was launched in America in 1946; the second generation was an optical-type; the third generation was a cathode-ray-type. The most recent development, the fourth generation, was the laser phototypesetter: the digitalised dot-matrix forms of the letters were stored on a computer, and when they were exported, they were scanned and ordered directly on to the photographic plate by laser guidance. In the West, the progress from first generation to fourth was a slow process, taking 30 years. Of course, the five work units and their associated experts knew all about this process. But Wang Xuan was challenging all five institutions to a duel; he was challenging the national project. He did not believe this kind of thing could be achieved through cooperation or collectively. This was something for an individual, or rather, for a genius. But to others, Wang Xuan's insistence on the individual was just an *Arabian Nights* fantasy or like Don Quixote tilting at windmills. And this Don Quixote wasn't just mad, he was ill as well.

As for the project to produce accurate Chinese-character phototypesetting, the above-mentioned five institutions had shortcomings in three aspects which were key to its success: creativity, intrinsic achievability, and the feasibility of project completion. Wang Xuan really wanted to tell them that, in the West, the third generation of phototypesetting machine was already in mass production, and that development of the fourth generation was being accelerated in the technologically advanced countries; and what they had chosen to concentrate on were the second and third generation machines, so no matter how much blood they sweated over them, what would they actually be worth? On top of this, he had thought of something even more important to say, and that was that the system they had chosen for Chinese-character form storage was completely analogue, not digital, and could an analogue system really solve the problems of storage and export? But would they really change anything if a year-long invalid told them all this? Far from changing anything, someone like him, who couldn't even talk without getting out of breath would make that crowd of 'experts' on those five work units look on him not as Don Quixote, but as nothing more than an out-and-out invalid.

But Wang Xuan was not Don Quixote, nor was he in any way an invalid; he was a genius.

He was the kind of man Mencius[8] talks about on whom heaven places a great responsibility... only more so.

Wang Xuan bypassed the first, second and third generations of phototypesetting machines and set his sights directly on the fourth generation of laser machines that foreign countries were developing. He knew (just as the five work units didn't know) that the English company Monotype, which was the first to start developing these machines, was already at the product trial stage, but not yet ready to start commercial production. Although Japan was concentrating on third-generation machines, it was not meeting with complete success and could only successfully handle a few Chinese/Japanese characters. This was the challenge, but it was also an opportunity. Following behind is often the way groups choose to work; it is a recognised way of doing things but it is a mediocre way of doing things too. This was the difference between Wang Xuan and the five institutions. We can see from this that creativity seldom comes from groups; quite the opposite, in fact, as groups very often stifle and waste the genius that is in their midst. Very often an individual values freedom, but if creativity and freedom are interrelated, why is creativity so seldom set free? They are a pair of heavenly twins. A thousand years ago in the Song Dynasty, Bi Sheng, who invented movable type printing, was an individualist, but no matter how you look at it, our own individualism was too lacking to build on his idea. So for the next thousand years there was no one qualified to take printing technology forward into the future.

Starting in the 1940s, old-fashioned printing techniques met modern machinery, electricity, optics and so on with advanced technological results which took phototypesetting into its fourth generation. This coming together of technology and computers to form a compiling and typesetting system replaced lead type (Bi Sheng's movable type), implemented automatic typesetting for books and newspapers, and enormously increased productivity. Nowadays, the prospects for direct-to-plate laser-typesetting machines are even more alluring: the laser beam strikes a light-sensitive plate and through dynamic processing can directly perform offset printing; the image-developing, fixing, plate-making and so on, a whole series of processes, can be done away with, resulting in higher labour efficiency and productivity. But in Bi Sheng's ancient homeland, they still relied on the German Gutenberg's method dating back to 1488: this involved smelting lead and casting lead characters, for lead typesetting and plate printing, all relics of Europe's 'fire and lead' era five hundred years before. Wang Xuan was a direct descendant of the Song Dynasty's spirit of creative individualism, stepping up to challenge the world. Although, to tell the truth, there was in fact no one for him to challenge; he was challenging himself.

Of course, no one is suggesting it was easy to take the ancient pictographic characters – three thousand in common use and seven thousand less common ones – and merge them with computers, thus spanning a gulf of a thousand years. Moreover, there were a huge number of fonts and font sizes, with each font requiring seven thousand characters as a bare minimum, and each one also having sixteen font sizes from very large to seven point. If you take the different fonts and the different font sizes together, the number of characters needed for Chinese character printing reaches in excess of a million. Because of this, the storage capacity necessary for the corresponding character dot matrices exceeds 20Gb (gigabytes). This is an astronomical number, more than enough to frighten people off, so it was hardly surprising that the assembled experts of the five work units joined forces to perform the task. If Bi Sheng were alive today, would he have been able to rise to the challenge?

Yes, he would, that was Wang Xuan's feeling. Paradoxes like this are not uncommon: ordinary people feeling that something is impossible, while a sick person feels the opposite. The crucial first step was to find a way of massively compressing Chinese-character data. Wang Xuan's only worry was his own health. His spirit was strong but his health was often inadequate, so was it going to prove robust enough to keep him going? Ever since he fixed his eyes on his target 'windmill', he had often gone night after night without sleep; when he found he couldn't work sitting down, he would lie on his bed and continue that way. Luckily, he had Chen Kunqiu, as the two of them were so alike, so she could be his missing half. Because love is a kind of chemical reaction and because it was the most positive energy of that period, the combined capabilities of those two invalids was beyond comparison with an ordinary person's. Chen Kunqiu had quickly become used to Wang Xuan's ways and the two of them were extraordinarily compatible; so much so that sometimes they seemed like a single person. Wang Xuan worked as though he was possessed, checking dictionaries, reading newspapers and periodicals as he tossed and turned on the bed toiling over his research into the vast ocean of Chinese characters: the characteristics of their forms, the rules governing them, rules for the exceptions to the rules and the logic behind the illogicalities. They couldn't be classified using Western logic: that would never be possible, as Chinese civilisation had its own particular logic.

It was not all as strange as it seemed, as it was a self-contained system. What was needed was to use the system itself to tease out something that conformed with its rules, something that conformed with Western methods and something that conformed with computerisation. If the truth be told, in the whole of China, it was only the miraculous team of Wang Xuan and Chen Kunqiu who could achieve this task. Why was this one opportunity in a thousand years? Why was it doubly so? This is why. Because China had to wait for the one chance in a thousand years to cross the threshold into computerisation. Wang Xuan and Chen Kunqiu did not pass their days as normal people did; all they did was work, and that meant their lives couldn't have been simpler. Slowly they rationalised the rules for the different strokes that make up Chinese characters, each of which has its predetermined course and curvature.

Lying on his bed one day, Wang Xuan said breathlessly to Chen Kunqiu, "Can you think of a way of entering these strokes into a computer to see whether it is possible to choose some of them and apply them across the whole set of characters? Then we can look into how to use even less data to describe them." Chen Kunqiu was very sensitive to the insight this gave into the logic of Chinese characters, into Chinese logic, and she also brought a woman's innate facility with spatial imagination. On that basis she thought that what Wang had said was feasible. She showed the same spatial awareness in other tasks she had to perform such as knitting a sweater or mending a cap. She brought draft versions of the character patterns from the print shop and used them to produce enlarged versions of each one, transferred them to graph paper, drawing out the dot matrices and their statistical stroke classification, so she ended up with something like a knitting pattern. She discovered that the basic parts of the different strokes were comparatively consistent and that the changes occurred at the top and tail. Additionally, the variations at the top and tail were not too numerous, so it was possible to choose a certain number of archetypes that could be used across all characters. It was only with the left-slanting downward stroke, the downward right concave stroke and the dot, strokes which fell outside the normal rules, that the variations were too numerous. For them, it was very difficult to find any forms that could be used as archetypes in the same way.

Wang Xuan took a copy of the template for the character 张 (*zhang*), looked at it from every possible angle, tossed and turned through the night thinking about it, then, at that point, ever so slowly, within the ancient logic of Chinese characters, that is to say Chinese logic, Wang Xuan's knowledge of Western logic, derived from higher mathematics, began to play its part: the two sides miraculously and seemingly impossibly joined up, fused, melded and interacted. The point of fusion came with the use of quasi-mathematical topology to describe the form of a Chinese character: this involved using a dotted-line outline to approximate the form of the character, then choosing appropriate points on the outline, and joining the dotted line into a solid line, but keeping the dotted line where it represented a curved line in the form of the character. As long as you chose the right points to start with, then you could guarantee the accuracy of any enlargement or reduction in size.

This, then, was Wang Xuan's realisation: that there is a link between mathematics and Chinese characters.

There is no doubt that ancient Chinese characters are obstinate and unyielding but, even so, they can be described mathematically.

However, when they experimented with enlarging the form of a character, its strokes appeared coarse and uneven, and this was particularly pronounced with strokes such as the horizontal, the vertical and breaking or corner strokes. This clearly adversely affected the overall quality of the character. In order to guarantee the proportions of the character, these strokes required particular control. Wang Xuan and Chen Kunqiu made a rough calculation: about half of all the strokes in Chinese characters fell into the category of regular strokes, so a set of seven or eight thousand dies would include several tens of thousands of horizontal strokes and the same number of vertical ones, and after this categorisation there might only be a dozen or so types that combined both the horizontal and the vertical. Wang Xuan's agile brain had got him this far when a supremely elegant new plan seemed to form almost of its own accord. Puffing and panting and gasping for breath, he broke it down several times and then explained what was going through his mind:

"We can describe the regular character strokes using the parametric method; that is to say, we take the length of a stroke, its width, its starting point, its finishing point, the shoulder where it turns a corner, its head and its tail, and also its starting position, and give them all parametric reference numbers. The remaining irregular strokes can be represented in outline. This way we can not only guarantee the balance of the different strokes when they are enlarged, and settle the problem of their proportions under the same circumstances, we are also taking a step towards even greater data compression..."

Wang Xuan took a great gulp of water, lay down in his bed, and continued:

"Another aspect is that, because we can now enlarge without losing accuracy, we don't have to compress the data for all the different font sizes to store in the computer; we can just choose one or two representative sizes to input, and then we can enlarge or reduce to any font size using them. This way, we can achieve an even higher degree of compression!"

Chen Kunqiu was not only helping with the calculations at home, she was also taking the compressed data and entering it into the departmental computer to test it under various simulated conditions. To her delight, she discovered that this 'outline plus parameter' method of representing compressed data, took them to the limits of data economy, and provided the simplest of solutions to the input of Chinese-character data into a computer.

Chen Kunqiu told the breathless Wang Xuan the news.

He almost choked with emotion. The light in their eyes was exactly the same: it was the light of a laser.

The two of them did not slacken their pace but planned the compact shape of the compressed data; Chen Kunqiu took 10 different font sizes of Hei, Song, Fang and Kai fonts, and included ChangSong BianSong, Chang-Hei, BianHei and others, and compared the full-form dot matrix size with the storage size after compression. She discovered that the overall compression factor was pushing 500 times or more. They had reached the most critical point, which was how to return the compressed data to the original character dot matrix format. Chen Kunqiu still had to teach her classes during the day, so Wang Xuan was left alone, sitting, reclining, pacing the room or tossing and turning on the bed. One day, when Chen came home, Wang Xuan shouted out, "I've come up with a way!" He had to wait for a while before he could speak again after the shout. "We can use derivations from mathematical formulae to get a recurrent formula for restoring the compressed data!"

They pressed ahead with double-checking Wang Xuan's suggestion and were delighted with the results. They tried a whole batch of characters and, whether enlarging or shrinking, they got exactly the same result: nothing missing and nothing altered. Numbers and characters, East and West, two different cultures, fused in scientific form inside Wang Xuan. Who could have imagined that this fusion would choose an invalid like Wang Xuan? And who could have imagined that heaven would send him a goddess to help him?

It really is just as Einstein said: "The Lord God is subtle…"

The Night Before

In May 1975, Wang Xuan wrote his manuscript proposal *A Complete Electronic Phototypesetting System* proposing the use of the technique of digital storage and high-power compression for the storage of Chinese characters with keypad input.

When the head of the mathematics department at Peking University, Mr Huang Luping, saw Wang's proposal, he was amazed. He thought it really was "a big deal" and called a one-off meeting to present the proposal. The meeting was attended by representatives of the Peking University Radio Department, the university library and the print shop. The proposal should have been presented by its author, Wang Xuan, but he was too weak; he was normally continuously out of breath and had difficulty talking, so there was no way he could do it. So, was Wang Xuan's toughness of character not still intact? It was, but if he were to present his proposal in such a weakened state, might it not cause the people who were attending to be suspicious of it? But Chen Kunqiu reckoned that this was a one-off chance for Wang Xuan to present himself, and it might never come again. The two of them talked it over and over, but in the end, Wang Xuan decided that he would not put in an appearance himself; the proposal would be presented by his other half, Chen Kunqiu. The key thing was not to jeopardise the proposal through suspicions caused by his own ill health, and Chen was totally capable of representing him. Everyone there knew what it was like for someone to live on labour insurance allowance for a long time, so it was fine for Wang Xuan not to go, and besides, it might add a layer of mystery, having an absentee invalid who had achieved something that healthy men couldn't. That certainly had an air of magic about it. If Wang Xuan went in person, that mystery would be destroyed. Wang and Chen carried out the final precise calculations, then Chen printed out the manuscript and handed it over to the university management.

The meeting went very much as expected; the proposal was outstanding and started off spirited discussion. In particular, however, the personnel from the print shop took the proposal back to show to their technicians, who objected to it strongly: "Hey! Have you heard? There's an invalid in the radio department who's come up with a master plan. It doesn't use an indexing system, it doesn't use lead type, it just prints straight from a keyboard!"

"Really? So, us printers are Taoist immortals now are we?"

"This invalid fellow is just some kind of dreamer, isn't he?"

"Not at all! They formally accepted it at that big meeting…"

News of the printers' opposition quickly reached Wang Xuan's ears. He was reclining on his bed, continuously wringing his hands in agitation, his emotions abnormally stirred up and both his cheeks flushed. Although the flushed cheeks were those of an invalid, they quite clearly indicated unprecedented anger. Well, not quite unprecedented, but the last time he had been that angry was in 1954 when he was 17 and packed his bags to go north, and then again once before 1959, but this was the first time since then.

Wang Xuan's proposal made its way through the levels of university management and *A Complete Electronic Phototypesetting System* was formally adopted as a project by the Peking University Science Institute.

The university decided to transfer personnel in from the radio department, the education department, the physics department, the Chinese department, the electronic instrument factory and the print shop, to form the research team. So an invalid and long-term recipient of labour insurance allowance had set up a formal project, brought in a whole community of workers and was now considered one of the marvels of Peking University: a far more extraordinary result than even Wang Xuan had anticipated.

Wang Xuan's proposal got passed on to the officer in charge of the Fourth Ministry of Mechanised Industry's 'Project 748', Guo Pingxin, who was a computing expert. He was already well aware of how big a problem the five work units had with analogue Chinese-character storage, and that digital storage was much more in keeping with modern trends. He was also keenly aware that the success of Wang Xuan's research was due to the core technology used for processing the Chinese-character data, and if this really was a major breakthrough, it was of enormous significance, with immeasurable potential for the future.

But this was 1975, the eve of the end of the Cultural Revolution. Peking University did not have an air of genuine academic research about it and there were quite a few people who didn't approve of this invalid recipient of labour insurance allowance. The mathematics department aside, the radio, physics and Chinese departments, on whom he had been pinning his hopes, mostly reacted with coldness or indifference. There were only the two teachers sent from the maths department: one of them was Chen Kunqiu, and the other was another youngster. From the summer of 1975 to the end of 1976, the rank and file of researchers were still completely unable to start reorganising themselves. In addition, the workforce that had been transferred in was not particularly familiar with computers and was having to start from scratch. The only two people there who properly understood computers were Wang Xuan and Chen Kunqiu.

Wang Xuan and Chen Kunqiu had long ago got used to the way each other worked and from time to time they would look at each other and smile, then continue working just as they did at home. The draft proposal that had been handed over last time was only a tentative plan, a rough draft, and if they wanted to see it carried out, first they had to reinforce it, just as they reinforced each other on a daily basis.

Every day, Wang Xuan would lean over the desk, wearing his spectacles and also using a magnifying glass to examine the regularity of the characters' structure. More often than not, he would be lying on his stomach on the bed, or lying on his side, occasionally moving only as much as his health allowed. For many years now this had all come easily to him and there was nowhere he couldn't work. So it was in this way that Wang Xuan precisely calculated the changes in curvature in the different strokes of Chinese characters, sorting and collating, and step by step increasing the degree of compression for character data. This kind of topographical work turned Wang Xuan into the complete Chinese-character expert, a different kind of expert from the ancients, and an epoch-making expert. In their 5,000-year history, there had been no one who had really researched them properly – who previously had seen that Chinese characters were a branch of science?

Since no one had considered them a science before, they had to be turned into one.

This was Wang Xuan's mission.

Indeed, the truth is that there is nothing which doesn't involve science, and science was an innate part of Wang Xuan, his means of survival and even his reason for living. The application of a scientific point of view to Chinese characters did not belong to Wang Xuan alone, there was also his extraordinary other half, the heaven-sent Chen Kunqiu, who most certainly had her share. Although Wang's health was not good, it did not get any worse, almost as if science was holding back any deterioration.

After several months of hard work using his startling intelligence and tenacious willpower, he finally succeeded in winkling out the secret of the structure of Chinese characters. The terrifying volume of data for characters was abruptly reduced by a factor of five hundred! But could this massively compressed data be accurately restored to the original form of the character? To address this, at the same time as Wang Xuan discovered how to compress the data, he also worked out an ingenious method of restoring it. On top of this, he also discovered a minimal-distortion method for enlarging and shrinking characters, allowing the all-character matrices to make '72 transformations' just like Sun Wukong, the Monkey King: fat could become skinny, tall could become short, and large could become small. Wang Xuan was like a magician, using the mysteries of mathematics as his wand, and after he had compressed the massive army of Chinese-character matrices five hundred times so they could freely and easily be input into a computer, with the sleight of hand of an illusionist, he answered the summons of his bosses and swept away the biggest barrier to the project to develop accurate phototypesetting for Chinese characters.

In September 1975, Wang Xuan's techniques for the major compression of Chinese-character format data and high-speed restoration took another step towards maturity. Chen Kunqiu took the programme set to the departmental laboratory for testing and, by running it through the software, produced the analogue of the first left downward slanting stroke, the *pie*, of the character 人 (*ren*, person).

Although this stroke looks very simple, so simple an infant can reproduce it, that is when it is done using a brush; for Wang Xuan and Chen Kunqiu to emulate it using computer software made it a truly earth-shattering first stroke! This first stroke of the character 人 has a symbolic significance, as it was appearing through the medium of science for the first time in the history of our civilisation, and Wang Xuan and Chen Kunqiu's construction of this character 人 through the courage of their own convictions carried a whole host of connotations.

Wang Xuan was the *pie* (丿), and Chen Kunqiu was the finishing right concave downward stroke, the *na*. Together they formed a complete person (人).

Moreover, it was a 人 writ large.

After this, the two of them went on to produce the complete characters 方 *fang* (square) and 义 *yi* (righteousness), which represented an astonishing success. The production of these two characters was like them giving birth to a son and a daughter, and it proclaimed to the world: "Against all expectations, this represents the fusion of science and Chinese characters! The fusion of Chinese civilisation with the modern world!"

It was seemingly Wang Xuan's and Chen Kunqiu's fate never to have real children of their own but Chinese characters became those children. They were extraordinary people and if they did not actually come from another planet, they were certainly born to a different destiny from ordinary humans. In 1975, most people didn't even know what computers were. Even if they did, they certainly didn't understand their significance for Chinese characters. But there were two invalids who, with miraculous prescience, were already working for the future of civilisation, and their significance was truly out of this world.

In October 1975, at the Beiwei Hotel in the Xuanwu District of Beijing, the curtain was raised on a meeting of unprecedented size held to present the phototypesetting system project. Project 748's 'Precision Chinese Character Phototypesetting System' project and the more than Rmb1 million research funding had already devolved to the Beijing Publishing Office and the Xinhua News Agency print factory, and it was these latter two institutions that were hosting the demonstration. It continued in the Beiwei Hotel for several days, first with an introductory report on the project and then with an analytical demonstration of the progress made so far.

In truth, the meeting was like a kind of grand tournament. Every work unit across the country that was working on precision phototypesetting systems for Chinese characters had congregated in Beijing, bringing their own projects and results for presentation on stage in a kind of battle of the project plans. As well as a general introduction to the Japanese phototypesetting system, the meeting also heard about the project plans of the five aforementioned research institutes.

Peking University sent Wang Xuan and Chen Kunqiu to attend the meeting. On this occasion, Wang Xuan had to attend and couldn't argue; the meeting was too important. Wang Xuan and Chen Kunqiu slaved away for many days until one was dizzy and the other gasping for breath. As they toiled away in that room in the Beiwei Hotel, it was almost as if a curious cooperative harmony developed between their two different conditions that made them indispensable to their work. With great determination, they produced their latest success: they used a wide-format line printer to print out the character 义 which had first undergone character matrix data compression and then been run through the restoration software programme.

The character was spread over two sheets of wide-format printer paper and was 50-60cm square when fully displayed. The reason they had chosen the character 义 was because its compressed data was very simple, but it included three different types of stroke: left downward slanting *pie*, right downward concave *na* and a dot, *dian*.

At the meeting, the Academy of Sciences Automation Institute presented their current plan for a third-generation flying-spot scanner, the Xinhua News Agency Print Factory presented the second-generation machine they were working on in collaboration with Tsinghua University and so on, until all five of the work units had finished their presentations. Then Wang Xuan and Chen Kunqiu took to the stage. Of the two of them, one was dizzy and the other panting for breath. Wang Xuan reckoned that being dizzy was not so serious, not as bad as being completely breathless, which meant that no one could hear what he was saying, so he let Chen Kunqiu lead the presentation. To Chen it felt as though she was in a world with no people, or somewhere up in the clouds, but the sound was unusually clear and distinct: it was a surreal sound, an angelic sound.

Compared to the other work units, Peking University's plan was innovative and unusual, and demonstrated exceptional skill and talent. Its high-level data compression technology and the character dot matrix restoration technology galvanised the meeting room. As the chairman of the meeting put it, "Peking University has captivated all the technologists here."

But you must bear in mind that that was a technologist speaking.

The people from the world of publishing, however, were rather baffled. What they had in their heads were the long-familiar plans for second-generation machines. When confronted with two "heavenly messengers" in the form of Wang Xuan, Chen Kunqiu and others, catching them unawares with these mathematical proposals, they expressed grave doubt that these plans could actually work. Although the technical staff from Peking University who had accompanied Wang and Chen used computers to demonstrate the results of their simulation experiments, the conservative-minded in the audience still reckoned that the Peking University plan was just some kind of weird fantasy.

The publishing faction had a lot of influence and, in spite of everything, Wang Xuan's proposal was eliminated from consideration.

This meant the research funding might also be lost.

They really needed that funding, as they had done all the work up to now without any, and one of them had only his labour insurance allowance to live off. In his hunt for resources, Wang Xuan dragged his ailing body onto the No. 302 bus and hustled between Peking University and the China Institute of Scientific and Technical Information in Hepingli. The bus ticket for the journey from Peking University cost 25 cents, but getting off one stop short saved five cents, so that is what Wang Xuan did each trip, walking the rest of the way to the institute. Even though he was still under 40 years old, almost every time he got on the bus someone offered him their seat, and if no one did, the conductor would shout out, "Will some revolutionary comrade please give this passenger a seat?" When someone did give up their seat, Wang Xuan could only thank them weakly, not out of lack of gratitude but out of lack of energy. When walking the extra stop, Wang Xuan had to stop and rest frequently, and if he needed a longer rest, he would lean against a telephone pole for a while.

No matter how weak he was, Wang Xuan never looked as if he was asking for pity. He didn't feel that he was old, nor indeed was he, as he stood, leaning against a tree, wearing his large, black-framed spectacles, and gazing straight ahead of him. Perhaps there should be a painting of him in that pose, leaning against a tree (a telephone pole is not pretty enough for a painting) looking towards the information institute, but I don't know which artist could properly capture that likeness.

It is a real shame we don't have such a painting.

The truth is, though, we don't have such an artist.

Wang Xuan's research was certainly not at an end; once he had discovered something, he was not going to let it rest. Scientific exploration does not just have a practical aspect, it has an idealistic one too. Indeed, it is the latter that better represents the nature of science and human nature itself. As soon as we are born we want to explore the world, to explore the unknown, because we hope to explore ourselves there and even to complete ourselves.

"Next time, you do the introduction!" Chen Kunqiu said.

"It's not a question of the introduction," Wang Xuan replied. "That's not where the problem lies."

The irony is that at the end of that year, everyone was required to participate in the counterattack against 'the trend for rehabilitating rightists'[9]. Even the smallest 'combat unit' had to join in the movement, so all work came to a halt anyway. Wang Xuan told Chen Kunqiu, "Even though I am officially attached to the radio department, I am on the sick-leave list as requiring total rest and receiving the labour insurance allowance. No one is going to take any notice of me, and even if they do, I'm not going to join in." Wang Xuan was resolute, and although it was hard to know where the strength for that resolve came from, he had a kind of fearlessness. In the past this had only manifested itself in his scientific explorations, but now it showed through in his spirit and demeanour. If the truth be told, in that period in 1975 and the beginning of 1976, quite a few people had this same kind of resolution. Wang Xuan was not alone, and this showed in the events that took place in Tiananmen Square[10].

Wang Xuan told Chen Kunqiu, "I am not going to take part in any government movements; there is no point. The best thing I can do is marshal my strength and complete our plan."

Wang Xuan's entry for 1976 in his work log reads: "The technologies for high-level Chinese-character data compression, for high-speed decompression and for precise character size transformation are all comparatively mature as we have made breakthroughs in methods for the treatment of character strokes, data compression, high-speed decompression and character enlargement." Going through repeated validations, with the cooperation of the Chinese department, Wang Xuan conducted a large number of experiments on characters using many different methods of testing in every technology and chose the optimal plan from the results.

As Wang Xuan was completing these amazing inventions, he also made another innovation with a multilevel memory scheduling algorithm. With this, Wang Xuan removed the principal stumbling block to developing the 'Precision Chinese Character Phototypesetting System' on the eve of the end of the Cultural Revolution.

After the meeting at the Beiwei Hotel, the Xinhua News Agency was the main client for second-generation machines, but after putting them through a test period, they discovered some major problems. Not only were they slow and inflexible, they also suffered a string of malfunctions and proved fundamentally unable to meet the needs of newspaper production printing. This was something that Wang Xuan had understood long ago and had, in fact, often pointed out. The director of the Fourth Ministry of Mechanised Industry's Project 748, Guo Pingxin, had never given up on Wang Xuan's proposal, and even after it had suffered all kinds of setbacks, and been subjected to all manner of investigations, he still had complete faith in it.

It is true of any kind of monolithic entity that, once the cracks begin to appear, it is easy to split apart.

On 11 June 1976, Director Guo Pingxin, Deputy Head of the National Publishing Office Zhang Shenliang, Mao Ying from the Project 748 office, Zhang Songzhi and a cadre from Xinhua News Agency came to the Beijing University Computer Centre to see Wang Xuan's and Chen Kunqiu's simulation tests. With his dual status as an official and a computer expert, Guo Pingxin looked in total silence at the characters being printed on the wide-format printer. He himself picked out 10 characters: 山、五、瓜、冰、边、效、凌、纵、缩、露, then added another: 湘. They were expertly chosen, ranging from the simple to the complex, and included all the important elements of composition and brush strokes. If they could print out these 11 characters, then they could print out any character, and there would be no problem making a report. Guo Pingxin's gaze was severe and discriminating, like the strictest of chief examiners, as he minutely inspected the characters one by one. Each character was spread across two sheets of wide-format printer paper, perfectly according to specification, every stroke sleek and even. Despite the degree of enlargement, he didn't seem to detect any lack of precision. More importantly still, Guo Pingxin required that any character had to be compressed to 1kb (kilobyte) or less than 120 bytes, for it to be acceptable. In fact, the compression was even greater, and the results much better than anticipated. Guo Pingxin smiled solemnly, that is to say, his severity still showed, but the smile was one of satisfaction. He shook hands, one by one, with the panting Wang Xuan, the dizzy Chen Kunqiu and all the other operatives, and told Wang Xuan to look after his health.

On 21 September 1976, on the eve of the fall of the Gang of Four, at Guo Pingxin's suggestion, Zhang Songzhi drafted a letter of notification formally handing over responsibility for the development of Project 748's Precision Chinese Character Phototypesetting System to Peking University.

With the approval of the deputy director of the Ministry of Industrial Electronics, Guo Pingxin signed and issued the letter. Then Guo personally stepped in to give Wang Xuan contacts to promote cooperation from the factory bosses to set up better conditions for official production later on.

This is how, in very difficult circumstances, the curtain was raised on the second revolution in Chinese printing technology.

Lofty Peaks

The high-level compression of Chinese characters was a lofty peak, and after Wang Xuan had successfully scaled it, the next one was high-precision output equipment. At that time, Wang Xuan had only one thing he could draw on for experience, and that was the third-generation cathode ray tube output machines which could scan a page of a newspaper onto a TV screen and then expose it onto a photographic plate. This method had the benefit of speed and the ability to produce both black-and-white pictures and photographs, but the technology for the production of the cathode ray tubes and the scanning circuits was very complex and the specifications for the sensitivity of the photographic plates were very high. Wang Xuan eventually rejected this method.

Wang Xuan and Chen Kunqiu continued their search. They learned that the Ministry of Posts and Telecommunications' communications equipment factory in Hangzhou was manufacturing a newsprint fax machine which was already in practical use. It meant that newspaper proofs could be sent via fax from Beijing to provincial cities to be turned into photographic plates.

This reproduction of photographic plates and printing newspaper provided Wang Xuan with a clue. But because the light source fax machines use is video light, the output quality was very limited or even useless. Scientific exploration is always like this: a succession of failures, a succession of theories disproved, continuously groping in the dark to progress. Wang Xuan discovered that the English company Monotype was in the process of developing a fourth-generation laser phototypesetting machine, but they hadn't yet mastered the technology and it was not yet ready for commercial production so they were at an impasse. Very soon, however, Wang Xuan and Chen Kunqiu were at an exhibition where they saw the Hangzhou Communications Equipment Factory's fax machine and they simultaneously felt the same surge of interest: this kind of newspaper fax machine used wide-format paper, had high resolution and excellent alignment. Wang Xuan immediately thought of the laser phototypesetting system, and an idea developed. He told Chen Kunqiu, "If we change the fax machine's video light source to a laser light source, won't that turn it into a laser phototypesetting machine?" But Wang Xuan was only a layman when it came to optics, so he needed to find an expert to consult. When he got back to the university, he immediately asked for guidance from Zhang Heyi, who was the optics specialist in the university's Department of Physics: "Is it possible to change the video light source in a fax machine into a laser light source? And can you increase the resolution from its original 20 lines per millimetre to 24 lines per millimetre? This would probably increase the output quality a step, so it not only meets newspaper publishing specifications but also those of book publishing. Do you think it is possible?" Zhang Heyi's reply that he was certain it was possible delighted Wang Xuan and his face once again flushed with pleasure.

The light in Wang Xuan's eyes inspired a similar reaction in Zhang Heyi. Chen Kunqiu noticed this, and the laser beam of delight from her own eyes intersected with the other two, to form the most extraordinary beam of light of that generation.

Wang Xuan immediately applied himself to researching a control mechanism for the laser output. It was not an easy task, but no difficulty was going to stop him. His health took a turn for the better and, although he was still just as breathless, his energy levels improved and he was now sitting up more than he was lying down, nor did he have to support himself with a wall when he was walking. Chen Kunqiu had also grown accustomed to her vertigo and it didn't hinder her in any way. Under her supervision, Wang Xuan developed the design for a "selective ribbon and drum reader and printer to increase the speed of the data restoration" and he also designed a method for "the selection and reading of indexed compressed character matrix data for input into magnetic core memory." But the biggest problem remained that the internal storage was not big enough for a page of newsprint. Wang Xuan studied the *Guangming Daily* all day long until one day his eyes lit up again as he came up with the masterstroke of "generating and buffering segmented character matrices".

But, as always happens, a new problem arose: in changing the Hangzhou Communications Equipment Factory's drum-style fax machine into a phototypesetter, the drum speed couldn't be too great, with the result that it could only output 15 characters per second. That was too slow! The speed became a crucial problem. How could it be increased? With a succession of problems also came a succession of inspirations, as they are two sides of the same coin, and at this point, Wang Xuan's life energy was at its peak: the rhythm of his laboured breathing was no longer an indication of illness, it was a kind of music, an inescapable accompaniment to his life.

The way he generated energy was not something to be found in ordinary mortals, it was a gift from heaven. Deep into autumn, in November 1976, when the fiery red persimmons were hanging on the branches, the sunlight that bathed Peking University seemed like light from the Song Dynasty, bright and clear, ancient and eternal. One day, following the course of that sunlight, another inspiration popped suddenly into Wang Xuan's head: if the one laser beam that swept the machine's drum became four beams, the output speed could be increased by a factor of three!

This was an ingenious idea, or rather an ingenious intention.

Of course, it was only an intention but are not intentions sometimes the mark of genius too?

Great music starts with an intention and so does great literature; this is true of so many great things. Even so, Wang Xuan was still faced with barrier after barrier to negotiate, and he now knew for sure that the problem was not with the laser generating mechanism but with the optics.

A few days later, Wang Xuan attended a big meeting denouncing the Gang of Four and he bumped into Zhang Heyi outside the office building where it was being held. That autumn, Zhang Heyi had joined the Project 748 strategic planning team with special responsibility for laser output, and he was fired with enthusiasm when he heard about Wang Xuan's inspiration. Zhang had a profound theoretical and fundamental knowledge and was an optics specialist with formidable practical abilities. After only a little thought, he confirmed the viability of using a four-beam sweep.

Once he got going, he produced a design in double-quick time. He used optical fibre coupling to ensure the accurate orientation of the beams. This design for the even sweep of the beams meant that, just as Wang Xuan had thought, the output speed increased threefold: it was immediately increased from 16 to 60 characters per second, completely meeting the standard for practical use.

Wang Xuan devoted his efforts to breaking through barrier after barrier with the hardware, and Chen Kunqiu was like a battlefield commander on the front line, racking her brains over the software, and rushing hither and thither in pursuit of solutions. This slightly built woman with her exceptional intellect must be regarded as Zhongguancun's – indeed China's – first generation of software expert as she took on the overall design of the large-scale software for the laser phototypesetting system. At that time, the majority of American and Japanese typesetting software could only output galley proofs and use those galleys to piece together a whole page; there were only a very few systems that could output a whole page, automatically format it and automatically add the page number. The software Chen Kunqiu designed was aimed at equalling the very latest foreign standards so it could not only output a whole page with automatic formatting and page-numbering, but also added online modification capability and a fluorescent screen to display the proofs after modification.

At the end of 1976, Wang Xuan finished writing *A Complete Precision Electronic Phototypesetting System* and *A Complete Electronic Chinese Character Typesetting System* and Chen Kunqiu had designed every aspect of their software, and the digital architecture for the hardware-software interface (the latter being very much a reflection of Wang and Chen themselves); she also completed the design for the batch file typesetting language for book publishing and broke down the typesetting programme for double scanning. With that, the planning programme for the Chinese character laser typesetting system was fundamentally complete. The two of them had relied on second and third-generation machines for the mechanics; when it came to the major stumbling blocks with optics and so on, they had gone where no one else would dare to tread, and chosen fourth-generation laser phototypesetting. In going from lead-font typesetting to laser phototypesetting, the West had passed through first-generation manual typesetting, second-generation optical machinery typesetting and third-generation cathode ray tube phototypesetting, but Wang Xuan and Chen Kunqiu had bridged the deep 40-year chasm between them and the West in a single stride.

Was that the work of an invalid? No! It was the work of two invalids!

Heaven had not favoured those five work units, nor the crowd of experts in them. Perhaps it was heaven that had led those experts off on divergent paths while leaving its chosen path to these two invalid lovers. So did their illnesses come from heaven? Not at all! But if one insists that illness is ordained by heaven, that insistence is surely a product of the hardships of the age. But who then would be inclined to take pity on the suffering of others? Of course, this is all part of the myth, and that kind of mythical thinking does not accord with science – it does not accord with the precision of the most detailed software or the utmost delicacy of the hardware. Even so, the reader should hold onto that mythical thought because there are some things which certainly can't be explained any other way.

The myth remains as to how Wang Xuan managed to work so much and so hard when he only had the labour insurance allowance to live off. At the time of the New Year, in January 1977, Wang Xuan unexpectedly received more than Rmb100 in back-dated pay. Everyone thought this was a highly unusual occurrence, but the fault didn't lie entirely with his work unit. Wang Xuan and Chen Kunqiu might have been completely focused and aware of the finest detail in their work with computers, but they had completely forgotten that Wang Xuan could have gone to the management to apply for a suspension of his labour assurance allowance, and converted it to a regular salary. In the end, it was his work unit that thought of this.

Wang Xuan stared blankly at the extra Rmb100 for a long time.

If the truth be told, he had got used to living off the labour insurance allowance and had accepted it as his lot.

Swan Song

Early in the morning of 27 July 1979, with the bright sunlight reflecting off the waves on the lake, the computer room of Peking University's Chinese character data processing research team was benefiting from the double rays of light refracting off the surface of the water; but at the same time it was pulsing with nervous energy and filled with an air of expectation. The workers in their white smocks were standing in total silence round the prototype, watching the miraculous machine with rapt attention. No one moved, no one spoke, and the only sound was the continuous clatter of nimble typing on the keyboard. In the blink of an eye, they saw the laser phototypesetting machine output the photographic plate for an octavo sheet of newsprint. Two youngsters couldn't resist crowding in closer. All they saw was a photo-plate cassette being taken over to the dark room, so they went over and waited excitedly by the dark room door as people kept calling out anxiously, "Is it all right?"

Finally, the dark room door opened, and everyone jostled for position trying to get a glimpse of the newly developed negative.

His face flushed red all over, Wang Xuan struggled to steady his heart and gasped for breath. Standing beside him, Chen Kunqiu was paying close attention both to the negative and to Wang Xuan though, at the same time she was having a temporary hallucination of seeing three different types of sunlight. The negative passed from one set of hands to another as cries of admiration and delight burst out around the room. At this moment, the galley proof of the newspaper was finally printed out. The six characters '汉字信息处理' (Chinese character data processing) miraculously filled the masthead of the newspaper. The horizontal and vertical paragraphs in something over 10-point font were artfully arranged to fit precisely within the page frame and borders so the whole page was stylish, dignified and pleasing to the eye. Everyone was cheering excitedly, celebrating this new birth, a thousand years on from the time of Bi Sheng.

On 11 August 1979, the *Guangming Daily* had a boxed front page story: *Research into Chinese Character Processing and a Great Breakthrough in its Practical Application*. The sub-heading read: *"Our Nation's Own Design of Computer, the Main Engineering Development of a Laser-Guided Compiling, Editing and Typesetting System, has been Successfully Completed"*

The front page also had articles by commentators and photographs from the tabloid newspapers.

Everyone now knew about Wang Xuan; he was an overnight sensation.

No one knew about Chen Kunqiu. No one knew about her achievements. Wang Xuan didn't know how famous he was, or how all the fame was concentrated on him. When that fame was at its height, a reporter came to visit him and, out of the blue, he mentioned his wife. His reputation was at its height at the time as he had just received the gold medal at the Geneva Exhibition of Inventors, a UNESCO award and China's highest award for scientific and technological progress; he had been made a 'three academy academic' by the Chinese Academy of Sciences, the Chinese Academy of Engineering and the World Academy of Sciences. He was also simultaneously vice-chairman of the Chinese People's Political Consultative Conference (CPPCC) and deputy central chairman of the Jiusan Society[11].

Wang Xuan suddenly said to the reporter, "While I was responsible for the system and the hardware back then, my wife Chen Kunqiu was responsible for designing all the software. She performed that task for more than 10 years and her contribution to the project was pretty much as important as mine; she was also the innovator responsible for laser typesetting. If she hadn't always been so modest and retiring, the person you should be focusing on is actually her!"

The reporter said that in general people were used to focusing on only one person. Wang Xuan replied, "That's not right, because that's not how things really are. On his journey to fetch scriptures from India, Tripitaka faced 9,981 difficulties. We were just the same on our journey. I have always felt that I have exploited her, and the honours due to two people are being heaped on my shoulders alone."

In the summer of 1980 the core part of Chen Kunqiu's software was fully tuned. The computerised Chinese character laser compiling, editing and phototypesetting system successfully produced a proof copy of the book *The Sword of Wuhao*. The whole book only had 26 pages, but the form of the characters was clear and elegant, and the cover was simple and refined; it was the very first book produced using the Chinese laser phototypesetting system. It was input from manuscript form, edited, compiled and typeset, and the whole process from proof reading and correcting to adding the page numbers and so on was done under automatic computer control. Not a single piece of lead font was used, nor was there any of the otherwise indispensable checking of rows of fonts, making up of plates, brush matrix moulding, lead casting and all the other time-consuming processes. Especially welcome by their absence were the poisonous substances such as molten lead and lead castings.

It was the first time in the history of Chinese printing that no lead products at all were used, and the first time that laser phototypesetting was used for a complete book. When Wang Xuan and Chen Kunqiu saw that elegantly tinted pale green proof copy, they once again heaved a deep sigh of relief, and a healthy smile of victory showed on their faces. When Vice-Premier Fang Yi was presented with a copy, he couldn't suppress his delight. He leafed through it in admiration and then took proof copies to the Politburo of the CPC Central Committee and gave them individually to every politburo committee member. These modest-looking pale green booklets were the bearers of the most important possible news to the highest leadership of the nation: Peking University has an unknown young teaching assistant who has triggered an epoch-making revolution in Chinese character printing in the capital!

Nor did this news escape the attention of Deng Xiaoping, who immediately appended the comment: "This merits support". In October 1980, Fang Yi took Deng Xiaoping's note to Peking University and expressed his wholehearted thanks to Wang Xuan and all the rest of the development team. Chen Kunqiu stood smiling in amongst the team; Wang Xuan began to speak to the vice-premier but then stopped and looked at her.

When they got home Chen Kunqiu said to Wang Xuan,

"Alright, let's settle this: from now on, don't mention me. It's just you."

"It's both of us!" Wang Xuan murmured.

"Two people makes it too complicated," Chen said. "Do you think we can be separated now?"

She was right. The two of them couldn't be differentiated since from the time they first got married, Chen Kunqiu had made herself disappear.

Wang Xuan had also disappeared as the two of them became one person.

Either one of them was actually both of them, even if outsiders didn't realise this.

In October 1980, the Hong Kong Electronic Computer Society and the International Chinese Electronic Computer Society hosted the 1980 International Electronic Computer Conference at the Excelsior Hotel in Hong Kong. More than a hundred scholars and experts from America, Canada, Japan, Korea, Germany, Denmark, Hong Kong, Taiwan and other countries and territories gathered in one hall to exchange experiences and scholarly materials concerning the electronic computer processing of Chinese characters. Wang Xuan was accompanying a delegation representing the Chinese electronics industry, led by Professor Qian Weichang.

Wang Xuan had never left the country before and he had learned all his English from the radio, so this was the first time he had ever used the language publicly and to address such a large group of people. He was particularly uncomfortable because he did not have Chen Kunqiu at his side. The result was that 15 minutes into his lecture, he rather breathlessly and very nervously said, "My English is really not vey good. Please forgive me. Thank you everyone."

In May 1985, more than a hundred famous experts from the worlds of Chinese computing, news and publishing attended a National Appraisal Meeting hosted by the State Economic Commission. These experts conducted a rigorous test and examination of the Huaguang Mk II, a Chinese character laser compiler, editing and typesetting system, after which they solemnly stated that, "In terms of our nation's successful development, Wang Xuan's Huaguang Mk II Chinese character laser compiler, editing and typesetting system is a highly significant project that advances our country to a new level on the international stage, and takes Chinese printing technology into a new era."

In April 1986, the Guanghua Mk II system was exhibited at the 14th Geneva International Exhibition of Inventions and brought back the gold medal for China. On 22 May 1987, the *Economics Daily* print factory's laser phototypesetting machines printed the first broadsheet Chinese newspaper; in amongst the glittering machines, people could no longer hear the monotonous clattering of the type-casting machines or the rattle of typewriters, nor was there any of the toxic fog from molten lead to be seen or even the black silhouettes of the type-setting frames. The former type-checking girls were now all wearing snow-white smocks in front of monitor screens dexterously pressing buttons to enter 130 to 150 characters of draft text per minute into the computer; then it was formatted by the format editors who instantaneously arranged it in into headlines and text, turning it into a perfect page layout. If they weren't satisfied with it, then they could add, delete and modify as they pleased via a keyboard, until they were. Then the final page layout was entered into the main machine of the laser phototypesetting system to produce an exact copy on a photographic film. Finally, the film was sent to the photographic plate room to be turned into a PS (pre-sensitised) plate or a photosensitive resin plate which could then be used to print out the full-size page. This was the whole typesetting and printing process simplified to such an extent that, in that day and age, if you hadn't seen it with your own eyes, you wouldn't have believed it.

At the end of 1988, after Peking University had made substantial improvements to their original laser phototypesetting system, they launched the new Mark IV system which was officially called the Peking University Founder Electronic Printing System. By 1993, total sales of the Founder System reached Rmb400 million and in 1995, the Founder Group's turnover had reached Rmb2.5 billion. At 6:30 in the evening of 6 November 1995, at its headquarters in Paris, UNESCO held a grand award ceremony at which the Deputy Director Adnan Badran awarded Wang Xuan a certificate, a medal and a prize purse (Wang Xuan felt the whole thing was illusory without Chen Kunqiu, and he didn't understand why she couldn't have been up there with him as well). In his speech before the actual award, Dr Badran praised Professor Wang Xuan for the research and development of the Chinese character computerised phototypesetting system which had brought about a technological revolution in the Chinese newspaper and publishing industry, and had made an outstanding contribution to scientific and technological development and application. Less than three months after Wang Xuan had returned from Paris to great acclaim, on 29 January 1996 he again represented the Peking University Founder Group in the Great Hall of the People to participate in the 1995 National Science and Technology Awards Ceremony, where the Peking University Founder Electronic publishing system received first prize. No one knew it, but all these prizes and honours were shared by another person.

Wang Xuan felt that he was exploiting his wife but Chen Kunqiu would have none of it.

After another bout of illness, Wang Xuan wrote on 6 October 2000: "We are all going to die. This time when I fell ill I exerted my utmost strength battling the illness in the same way I would grapple with a problem. I once said that in my life I faced 10 important choices, and of them, my most fortunate one was marrying Chen Kunqiu. Without her, there would be no laser phototypesetting. When the day comes that my illness can no longer be treated, I definitely want to undergo euthanasia. My wife, Chen Kunqiu also wants the same."

Wang Xuan had long ago understood the nature of life and death, and even in his improved circumstances he continued not to indulge himself: he was accustomed to thrift and frugality. In the 1990s he was a triple academic and chairman of the board of Founder Holdings Co Ltd, but he still lived in the 74sqm apartment allocated to him by Peking University; his most important piece of furniture was a bookcase and there was vinyl on the floor. He gave away most of his awards and prize money; items of low value in the form of pens and notebooks, more valuable items like watches and cameras, and sums running from several thousand Rmb to more than Rmb10,000 to SARS research and the Tsunami Disaster Relief Fund. In 2002, he used the prize money from the highest national award for science and technology and the university award, a total of Rmb9 million, to set up the Wang Xuan Science and Technology Innovation Fund to support continuous innovation by the younger generation and encourage them to scale the heights of science and technology. In 2005, Wang Xuan who had been plagued by illness throughout his life, found his condition worsening and the intense pain of his illness continued to gnaw away at him.

His legs swelled up enormously, so he had difficulty walking, making it very hard for him to attend to his official duties. But still he fought through the pain, using the last of his energy to write *A Few Thoughts on the Export of Automated Technology Products*, *A Discussion of the Factors Leading to Success in Scientific Research*, *The Need to Surpass Other Nations in Determination and Belief* and other essays of more than 20,000 characters, continuing his research just as before.

When he learned that the deputy director of the Ministry of Science and Technology wanted to investigate the Founder Group's 'Internet Publishing Project', Wang Xuan took some painkillers and dragged his illness-racked body over to the Founder Group. There he told the men from the ministry, "Innovative industries must have the ability to innovate independently, but the development of the science and technology industry cannot be separated from government support. Internet publishing represents the future direction of the printing industry, and I very much hope that it will receive the vigorous support of the Ministry of

Science and Technology so that this technology, just as happened with laser phototypesetting, will play a leading role in the new technological revolution."

This was the last time Wang Xuan went to the company offices, and the last time he was seen in public.

Wang Xuan said: "Starting when I was 55, I went suddenly from having only one academic's cap to being a triple academic and becoming a person of consequence. But I realised that people had got their tenses wrong: evidently, I was a man of the past, but had somehow become the present to them; they even thought that I was the future and could show where our future lay. When I was 38, our research into computerised phototypesetting was at the cutting edge inside China, and it could be said to be within the top 10% in the rest of the world. It represented the second lofty peak in my life, but at that time I was a nobody and my voice had no influence. At 58, there I was, a triple academic, but I was even further away from being at the cutting edge then, and I was relying on the name I had made for myself in the past. All my life I have remembered the words of one of the great physicists of the past, Baron Rayleigh, who was awarded the Nobel Prize in 1904. He said that after the age of 60, he would offer no opinion on any new thinking because he believed that after that age, our thinking loses its vigour and originality. There is one academic here who is approaching extreme old age but who, just a few years ago, gave his opinion in the newspapers that our country has no need of the information superhighway because China doesn't have that much information. This particular academic's own specialisation was a million miles away from information technology, in a completely different field. Academics should be very careful about pronouncing on areas outside their own field of expertise and should not just randomly express opinions."

Wang Xuan never said very much, and when he did speak he didn't waste any words.

Wang Xuan died on 13 February 2006.

On 9 March the same year, the Chinese printing industry held a solemn memorial meeting for this giant of the time who had taken China in one great bound from the age of 'fire and lead' to the age of 'lasers and electronics'. The meeting lasted four and a half hours, and 20 scholars from all different fields stepped forward to address it. The guest most eagerly awaited by all there was Academic Wang Xuan's wife, the Peking University professor and doctoral supervisor, Chen Kunqiu.

But Chen Kunqiu did not attend. Many there could not understand why this should be and guessed that something must have happened to her. In fact, if they had understood why Chen Kunqiu had married the already severely ill Wang Xuan in the first place, then they might well have guessed some of the reason.

Back in 1981, Chen Kunqiu herself had been severely ill and almost died. Wang Xuan, who had never worried about his own illness, became intensely worried for his wife. While Chen Kunqiu was being operated on, he sat on a bench outside the operating theatre, counting the minutes as they ticked by. All thoughts of laser typesetting were forgotten; all he wanted was his wife. This man who apparently had no private life and dedicated all his time to scientific research, had his eyes firmly fixed, unblinking, on the operating theatre doors, as if he hoped to see through them.

Chen Kunqiu's illness had rendered Wang Xuan unable to find himself, as if he had lost a precious crystal ball.

Wang Xuan seldom regretted past events, but at that time he was filled with regrets: why had he so neglected Chen Kunqiu's health all these years? Because he himself had been ill so long, he was used to not caring about himself, and he had become accustomed not to care about others. It was as if illness had become a matter of no importance, just part of everyday life. For a long time, he had forgotten how it was that Chen Kunqiu had married him, but now he remembered, and the tears came gushing out.

He could hear Chen Kunqiu saying to him, "Wang Xuan, let's get married!"

"What?"

"Get married!"

Wang Xuan's illness was not even the first thing he thought of.

"My father is a 'double gangster', a rightist and a counter-revolutionary; he has a plaque round his neck and is being publicly denounced right now. You could get dragged into it in the future."

"My father is wearing a dunce's cap with 'historical problem' written on it, too."

"My illness is already..."

"So the sooner we get married the better."

Chen Kunqiu was crazy about music when she was a student and in 1959 radio stations were always playing Beethoven's Ninth Symphony. Her family didn't own a radio set so she was always running over to other people's windows and standing there until the music finished. After Wang Xuan and Chen Kunqiu got married, they never listened to music together once. Chen really did change into a different person.

It was like the combination of software and hardware, but does the hardware ever properly respect the software?

Tears were flowing down Wang Xuan's cheeks. Finally the operating theatre doors opened and Wang Xuan, staring blankly as if into outer space, asked the doctor, "How is she, doctor?" Half-jokingly, the doctor rebuked Wang Xuan, "Your wife is too thin; even her cancer cells are too weak and undernourished to have the energy to spread."

Thank the stars! Wang Xuan came back down to earth.

Wang Xuan completely abandoned his 'hardware' ways, and put his heart and soul into looking after his 'software', Chen Kunqiu, shuttling between home and the hospital every day. He was shamed by the doctor's joke about the cancer cells being too weak, and he humbly asked other people for advice about cooking, treating it as seriously as if it was science. As quickly as he absorbed a scientific principle, he absorbed the art of cookery, and cycled over to the hospital twice a day with rice and other dishes, something different every time: turtle steamed in broth, sweet and sour carp, dry fried eel threads; there were fresh vegetables with every meal too. The hospital ward filled with delicious smells every time he entered, and the doctors all said to Chen Kunqiu, "You eat better than any of the other patients!" Chen Kunqiu's body was a tangle of IV infusions and catheters, so she couldn't manage things unassisted; Wang Xuan fed her at every meal, mouthful by mouthful. Sometimes she wept at every mouthful.

At night, Wang Xuan slept in his clothes in a reclining chair he had borrowed from a neighbour.

In the end, Chen Kunqiu did not attend Wang Xuan's memorial meeting, but she did send a short message:

"It was Wang Xuan's intention that he should slip away quietly. He didn't want any kind of ceremony or other activity which would waste other people's valuable time and energy. Now, with every corner of society marking his memory at the very highest level, I think that if he were to hear about it in his grave, he would surely feel ashamed." No one was surprised at Chen Kunqiu talking like this.

Because only Chen Kunqiu *could* talk like this.

She probably didn't want to mark Wang Xuan's memory with other people because Wang Xuan belonged to her alone.

But maybe this wasn't entirely true.

DIARY NOTE 8: THE THOUSAND-YEAR INSTALLATION

In some ways, there is an element of installation art about non-fiction writing, as they both use real life material. To put it another way, all their constituent parts are real and actual. Installation art is an art-form that has become fashionable over the last 20 to 30 years, so now when you visit any art exhibition, you can't avoid suddenly being confronted by a piece of installation art. It is a little like sculpture, but it certainly is not that, and still less is it like painting. First and foremost it is an object like a ring-pull can, an old bicycle, an old piece of machinery, an ashtray, a tube of toothpaste or a shipping container, always an object – any everyday object can be turned into installation art. Thus we can see that every component of it is real and actual, but if the components are real, the whole thing is strange and unfamiliar. The components are one kind of thing, and the whole installation is another kind of thing. For example, a ring-pull can is a very familiar object but the space it occupies is unfamiliar. The component and the whole are not the same; the whole embodies its components, but the meaning is another thing entirely, and that thing is the artist's subject.

Non-fiction writing obviously wants its component parts and its whole to be the same, but is there not something to be learned from comparing an author's 'completeness' to an installation? That is to say, is it possible for a writer to take a public figure (an 'object' everyone is familiar with) and use the same material to write about something very different? To write about unfamiliar feelings? Judging simply by the end product, the unfamiliar feelings come from the person/object, whereas in reality they undeniably come from the author. Wang Xuan was a public figure whose achievements were widely known, but what I have tried to portray is the Wang Xuan that I see in my mind's eye. That Wang Xuan on the one hand comes from Wang Xuan himself: Wang Xuan's illness and his success are inextricably linked in the 'return after a thousand years' from the time of Bi Sheng. Similarly, Chen Kunqiu's love was also a 'return after a thousand years', glorious and earth-shattering, what might be called the 'love classic'. What was the connection between these two 'thousand-year returns'? What meaning is there to be found compressed between them by intractable illness?

Wang Xuan is a very mysterious figure, but his past mystery alone is far from enough, and when I considered this mysteriousness, I felt obliged to write about it. My literary skill is not adequate to the task – but that is another matter. What I want to say is that I was obliged to think this way at the start, to recognise Wang Xuan in this way, to conjecture about him, to explore him, to make him into an 'installation'. I cannot claim to have described the complete 'real' Wang Xuan because the truth is, he had no boundaries, but I can guarantee that I have been able to offer up his true depth. Indeed, to a certain extent, truth is a construct which displays the underlying identity of the 'constructor'. A construct is not at all the same thing as a fabrication, and it has nothing to do with fabrication except in the way that fabrication and installation art are two different means to achieve the same end: truth does not only come from an 'object', it also comes from the recognition of the juxtaposition of truth and individuality.

In mourning Wang Xuan, it was perhaps easier to get close to the real man by using my writing as a form of installation art.

[PART 4]
Lenovo China (2)
联想中国(二)

The Chinese Character Processing Card

History sometimes has a way of looking after itself, and when a company is looking for a direction, that direction appears. For example, when Lenovo was looking for a core technology and something to give it a competitive edge, when it needed a cornerstone to build on like the Lenovo Chinese character processing card (汉卡 *hanka*): there was Ni Guangnan and there, in truth, was 'history'. Later on, when Ni Guangnan was talking to a reporter, he said that when he and Zhang Zuxiang started working together on Machine No. 119 in 1962 they immediately became comrades-in-arms with a shared purpose. In 1974-75, they were fellow 'students' at the May 7th Cadre School with Liu Chuanzhi and were then also in the same research group. Wang Shuhe originally worked in the institute's business office and was Ni Guangnan's boss, so there was complete confidence between them all.

At first, Liu Chuanzhi and Ni Guangnan didn't know each other at all well, but when they were both undergoing re-education through hard labour at the May 7th Cadre School they were in the same room and became friends that way. When they talked about things other than the hard labour, such as the reality of their situation and their lost lives, the two of them found that they had many views in common and even expressed them in the same way; their relationship away from the labour was also much closer than it had been at the institute in Beijing. Ni Guangnan's health wasn't very good, with intermittent fever and low energy, but even with a temperature of 39C, he still went to work on the threshing floor; he completely ignored the flies that buzzed around him as he ate and his stoicism made Liu Chuanzhi feel that he and Ni Guangnan were kindred spirits in that respect. Ni Guangnan, too, unashamedly showed his admiration for many aspects of Liu's character. He was, for example, very taken with Liu's story-telling ability. One evening, when the lights had gone out, and everybody was lying in bed, Liu Chuanzhi told them the story of the film *The Count of Monte Christo*. Ni Guangnan had read Dumas' book, so he already knew the plot and wasn't particularly interested in hearing the story of the film. But Liu Chuanzhi's narration was so vivid and colourful that Ni listened with rapt attention for almost two hours. His admiration for Liu's scholarship and dramatic abilities knew no bounds.

Liu Chuanzhi had heard that Ni Guangnan had an exceptional memory and could recite Maxwell's Equations by heart – these are a set of equations that state the fundamentals of electricity and electromagnetism; they are very long, long enough to put most people off. On one occasion, Liu and some others decided to test Ni Guangnan, so they feigned ignorance of the equations and diffidently but mischievously asked Ni if he could write them out. "What for?" Ni looked at Liu Chuanzhi suspiciously.

Suppressing a grin, Liu said, "Can you write them down? I can't remember them properly." Ni picked up a pen and began to write; he left out the constant terms at the beginning but wrote down the rest, correct to the last detail. Liu Chuanzhi was immediately convinced, thinking how formidable the man was. In Ni Guangnan, he could see what was missing in himself, quite apart from the fact he didn't have Ni's astonishing memory. A great memory is unquestionably a talent.

In fact, the Ni Guangnan of 1985 was just the same as the Liu Chuanzhi of 1984: inside there was a kind of frustration despite the undoubted talent, an immovable sense of oppression. As a researcher with a profound knowledge of the field of computing, Ni Guangnan had achieved many successes; when a research project was finished he was always delighted and he would write out a report. The report would be passed on to his superiors, and once they had read it, they would send it on to the top-level leadership whence it would be released to the nation. The nation would give Ni an award, but after that no one took the results and put them to practical use in manufacturing anything. In the end, all these results were just locked away in a safe, as if they had been put in prison. With his results in prison, he was just like a prisoner himself, and he had no idea anymore how long he had been there.

But if taking the plunge to escape meant selling electronic watches, riding flat-bed trikes and selling trifling consumer goods, Ni Guangnan decided that wasn't for him. That was where he was different. Liu Chuanzhi could do it. After being cheated over the colour televisions, there was nothing he wouldn't do as long as it was legal. That was the difference between Liu Chuanzhi and Ni Guangnan. But after the company made its first pot of gold, there was no need to sell watches anymore or tout for business selling small consumer goods; of course, there was still no avoiding the flat-bed trikes as pedal-powered trikes were the most important means of transportation for the scientists and technicians of Zhongguancun, pretty much like the peddlers of Tianqiao[1]. But there were places other people feared to tread where Ni Guangnan was willing to go, and it was a treasured ambition to bring Ni Guangnan into the company, as that was the best way of honouring him appropriately. Besides there was a significant technological content to the company's first business success;

computers were a big part of it and the time was right to bring Ni Guangnan into the fold along with the results of his latest research.

At that time, outside China, personal computers were already 10 years old and Bill Gates' statement that he was going to "put a computer on every office desk and in every household" had already been realised in America. Ed Roberts established the first 'nuts and bolts' computer company in the world, taking a microprocessor chip and a ramshackle bunch of components and putting them in a metal box. Consequently, the computer assembly industry had already started. There were 110,000 computers in China in 1984, almost all of them apparently made by IBM. Computers were becoming part of everyday life here, but the shame is that, from their beginnings up to the present day, China's personal computers (PCs) could only work in an English-language operating environment; indeed, in the whole of China there wasn't a single computer than could identify Chinese. Language had become a natural barrier, and allowing computers to 'identify Chinese characters' had become the tireless objective of all the country's scientists, including Ni Guangnan.

There is no doubt that Chinese characters or a Chinese character system formed a bridge without which ordinary Chinese people were unable to enter a different world and were excluded from it. Ni Guangnan's 'Chinese character system' is known as the 'Chinese character processing card' (or 'Chinese character card' for short), because it incorporates three printed circuit boards formed from a number of integrated circuit chipsets and a software system. The three circuit boards are connected by planar cables and all the standard-form Chinese characters are permanently held in their font library; so when you enter a Chinese character on your keyboard, the control system takes the character you want and converts it into a digital value that can be read by the computer. That digital value is then transmitted to the relevant section of the font library and read into the memory via the processing system. From there it is sent to the monitor or printer where it is turned into a dot matrix Chinese character. At that time there were already a dozen or so 'Chinese character systems', which all worked along the same general principles with only minor differences.

Ni Guangnan's 'Chinese character card' was just another of China's many 'Chinese character systems' at the time, but its distinctiveness lay in its word prediction and auto-complete functions. These functions reduced the duplication rate of two-character words and phrases by 50%, that of three-character words and phrases by 98%, and for words and phrases of four characters or more there was practically no duplication. This doubled the speed of input for Chinese characters and this 'associative connection[2]' system gave rise to an epoch-making change in 'Chinese character systems'. Liu Chuanzhi recognised this for the miracle it was and foresaw that it was an opportunity to change China itself.

Not everybody is able to glitter and flicker with light like a pearl but they can still be the thread that links the pearls together to make a spectacular necklace. This was Liu Chuanzhi's experience, and he knew where his value lay. In this respect, he says of himself, "I think I am that thread". And in his eyes the absolutely indispensable pearl was Ni Guangnan.

On the day we are talking about, Liu Chuanzhi, Wang Shuhe and Zhang Zuxiang arrived at Room 322 in the Computing Institute's main building. This was the office of the Chinese character system research team and Ni Guangnan was sitting at a desk by the window. Liu Chuanzhi and the others put on somewhat unnatural smiles: genuine but overenthusiastic, eagerly respectful, polite and faux-relaxed smiles that seemed to be born out of awkwardness. Of course, they couldn't cut straight to the chase so they chatted idly about other things, such as how the development of the LX80 Chinese character card was progressing, and only after they had spent an age singing its praises did they finally broach their real subject, which was asking Ni Guangnan to join their company and promising to devote all their energies to launching the LX80 onto the market. Liu Chuanzhi was good at spinning stories and also had a natural talent for persuasion. His physique, his open-heartedness and his logical mind all showed in his smile and in his eyes, making him a man it was impossible to refuse. But the real question was whether what he had to say would strike home; if it didn't, any personal charm would be useless. On the other hand, even if words are effective but personal charm is lacking, it is still often difficult to get what you want and you lose out on that score. But in Liu Chuanzhi, the two aspects were inseparable.

"It's not just your 'Chinese character card'," Liu Chuanzhi told Ni. "We guarantee we will take the results of all your research and turn them into marketable products as quickly as possible." Ni Guangnan had sweated blood over the development of a mainframe computer; he had done everything there was to do in terms of national-level achievements; he had won the Chinese Academy of Sciences Achievement award several times. But until now, all of this had only ever ended up on prize certificates and not a single thing had made it into commercial production. This was Ni Guangnan's greatest source of regret and it was also a source of regret for the whole nation. Ni Guangnan didn't say anything about all this at the time, but it was a regret that gnawed away at him.

In fact, Liu Chuanzhi didn't have to make 'three humble visits to the thatched cottage³', as Ni Guangnan didn't hesitate but immediately accepted the invitation. Of course, looking at the big picture, it was the right time. Whether at the national level, or at the individual level of Chen Chunxian, Wang Hongde and Liu Chuanzhi himself, it was always a matter of circumstances, and if it hadn't been for 'circumstances' Ni Guangnan might not even have had the feeling of being a neglected talent. But Liu Chuanzhi's outstanding quality was his meticulousness and rigour of thinking; he could always see three moves ahead, and he told Zhang Zuxiang, "The two of us still need to visit Ni Guangnan at home. I don't think there are too many problems with Ni himself, but his wife is the key. If his wife's work isn't going well, then Ni might not come and join us." This was the voice of experience from someone who understood life, someone who understood people. If a man understands life, then there is nothing he cannot understand. Don't think I am saying that scientists don't understand people; their understanding on that score is exceptional, but on another level, science is a scary thing. At that moment, Liu Chuanzhi embodied that 'scariness'. Indeed, when he and Zhang Zuxiang arrived at Ni Guangnan's apartment in Hepingli, they discovered that Ni's wife was indeed a problem. Ni and his wife were arguing over the matter, and the appearance of Liu and Zhang was very timely. Naturally, Liu Chuanzhi was able to answer all their questions and dispel all their doubts. He didn't just understand the way men thought, he understood women too and he was able to win Ni's wife round with his silver tongue.

Ni Guangnan's arrival meant the arrival of the 'Chinese character card' too. Lenovo had a direction.

Liu Chuanzhi had got the engineer he had set his heart on. It was especially cold that winter, with heavy snow, and in an office of only a dozen or so sqm, building on the foundation of the 'Chinese character card', a development of Ni Guangnan's improved version, the Lenovo Mk I 'Chinese character card', began. This was what the company had pinned all its hopes on, the kernel of its existence, and Liu Chuanzhi was very satisfied with everything going on in the office. He was very clear that the world of Chinese computers was facing three choices: one was to direct all research at computers in a Chinese-character environment, cutting themselves off from the mainstream of world computing; the second was to put Chinese-character technology into software, but they were in the computing Dark Ages of 16Mb hard discs and internal storage of a few dozen kb, so the processing speed was very slow and it was very fiddly to operate. It seemed the only way was to use a combination of software and hardware, but the Lenovo 'Chinese character card' was not only a Chinese-character input method, it was, in fact, also a whole software-hardware Chinese character system. In 1985, Ni Guangnan's development team launched the Lenovo Mk I Chinese character card for the first time and although, looking at it today, it was a little bloated and slow, at the time it was a breakthrough innovation leading to a new era. Its unwieldiness was because it had been rushed out. The market doesn't wait for anyone, so they had reduced the workload to a bare minimum.

The Mark I card was an ugly duckling but without it there would have been no Mk II, Mark III and so on. In October that year, the Lenovo Mk I card underwent inspection by the Chinese Academy of Sciences and in January the following year, in a face-off of Chinese-character systems held in Beijing, the Lenovo card won out and became instant hot news. To be on the safe side on the day, it was Ni Guangnan who operated the system. To guarantee the successful production of the card and successful sales, Liu Chuanzhi restructured the company, fundamentally changing it by forming a team of more than a hundred specialists focused on supporting the 'Chinese character card'. The team spirit was very strong, developing and marketing as if their lives depended on it until finally, in 1987, they achieved a decisive victory. That year, the Lenovo card sold 6,500 units supplying the National Sports Commission; the Ministry of Agriculture, Animal Husbandry and Fisheries; the National Bureau of Statistics and the Heilongjiang Municipal Bureau of Finance and Taxation with supplementary sales of a thousand foreign microprocessors. The company's financial reserves mounted rapidly. The Ministry of Industry and Finance's end of year audit showed that the company had a sales revenue of Rmb73.45 million; Rmb5.5 million in free cash flow; Rmb4 million in fixed assets and Rmb3.47 million in taxes paid to the government. Within three years of being put on the market, Lenovo's 'Chinese character card' achieved sales of 20,000 units, generating an output value of Rmb60 million. The Lenovo Mk I 'Chinese character card' took the top prize for national technological progress. On the back of its core product, the Lenovo Company had officially taken off.

Fined A Million

The 'Chinese character card' was hugely popular but was facing a totally unexpected fine, and a huge fine at that. In those days, if your product was failing or dying, no one bothered you, but as soon as your product really took off and was all the rage for a while, then you found yourself surrounded by important new 'friends'. All your audits, all your sponsorship from contacts, your advertisements… but who would have thought that the men from the Commodity Prices Bureau would come to your company and say that your prize product, the Lenovo 'Chinese character card' was overpriced, that it constituted profiteering behaviour and contravened national commodity prices policy; and then impose an on-the-spot fine of Rmb1 million?

"On what grounds?" Liu Chuanzhi asked furiously.

The company was in an uproar, and the staff said one after the other that they shouldn't pay, that they should protest, that they should call a news conference to let the media judge and get their version of things out there. As the staff got more and more agitated, Liu Chuanzhi began to calm down.

"What do you want to do?" Liu Chuanzhi asked, looking at his staff, then turned to the officers from the Commodity Prices Bureau with a smile and ushered them out of the door. In the interests of the company, Liu Chuanzhi suppressed his feelings of injustice. He knew that if they made a big fuss, even if eventually sense prevailed, it would still cause a heap of trouble.

But Rmb1 million really was excessive. Liu Chuanzhi searched everywhere for contacts that might help him and several times went in person to the office of the director of the Bureau of Commodity Prices. He never got to see him though; if he wasn't told the director was in a meeting, he was simply told he wasn't in. Finally, when he thought he had exhausted all his contacts, he found out where one of the department heads of the bureau lived. One evening he took a female colleague and cautiously knocked on the door. The official and his family were having dinner, so Liu and his colleague's timing was very poor. He hadn't thought they would be eating so late. Or maybe it was just a very long meal. Ah, of course, it was Sunday, and the department head liked a glass or two of wine. Still, there was nothing for it; he had to go in: Rmb1 million was all their net profit. Even on a turnover of several tens of millions, they didn't make very much profit. After they went in, it should have been Liu who spoke first, but not a word came out of his mouth and he just stood to one side, his arms hanging at his sides – although, of course, he was putting on a bit of an act. Liu Chuanzhi was very expansive by nature and was always ready for any difficulty; he could act very modern or very traditional as the occasion demanded. But this kind of situation demanded a woman's touch, and Liu's female colleague nodded to the official with a smile, then softly stated their case. They were in someone's home, after all, not in the office.

Liu was looking rather sheepish so, naturally, his colleague temporarily stepped into the breach. The whole thing was very relaxed and the department head said he would look into reducing the fine. Later on, Liu took his colleague back to the bureau director's office, and this time they were shown in. Making that home visit had made all the difference and, in the end, the Bureau of Commodity Prices reduced the fine by Rmb400,000 which took it down to Rmb600,000.

This was no small achievement, getting more than half a year's profits back.

Liu Chuanzhi has a famous saying, "You have to know who you are."

This may not be a very exciting sentiment, but it is very realistic. It is much in the same practical vein as "a good man knows when to give way" and it is not talking about any lofty moral stance. None the less, it is correct, especially if practicality is what is needed.

Running Around Like A Headless Chicken

So the technology had its direction but the necessary money still had to be earned otherwise how else could they support the development and promotion of that technology? As to whether it should be technology driving commerce or commerce driving technology, there was plenty of heated debate within Lenovo but the truth is, the company's development and expansion proved that Liu Chuanzhi's comprehensive strategy of 'commerce leading technology' was what was right for the time. In some ways, this was the same route as the policy during the Chinese Revolution of 'surrounding the cities with the countryside' or even 'attacking the cities to seize power' and Liu Chuanzhi's 'commerce leading technology' owed a deep debt to the essential strategy that combined Marxism with Chinese practicality.

But the business world is like a battlefield and although they had already experienced being cheated out of Rmb140,000, in 1987, Liu Chuanzhi and Li Qin were once again swindled in a huge Rmb3 million business deal. When Liu Chuanzhi talked about this experience many years later, it was clearly still fresh in his memory and he remembered the date very clearly, "It was 20 April 1987: our agent in Hong Kong had struck a deal with IBM; if we wired them US$1 million by the 20th, we could have got a 40% discount so, of course, I was very keen to get the money sent before then. Li Qin hurried over to the academy to borrow the money as a loan. After he had obtained the signatures of 18 directors, he got his hands on the Rmb3 million. For my part, I went looking for an import company in Shenzhen, and someone introduced me to a Cantonese businessman who said he was certain he could arrange the importation for us. Even though I had been cheated out of Rmb140,000 once before, I still hadn't learned my lesson, so I believed him. I was delighted by his assurances and, after Li Qin had wired me the Rmb3 million, I then wired it on to my Cantonese contact. He said he would certainly be able to send the money on to Hong Kong around 10 April, and everything was in place."

Liu Chuanzhi happily went back to Beijing, leaving a colleague in Shenzhen to wait for the confirmation letter. This colleague was one of the workforce and not a very sophisticated thinker. He decided he would wait until the Cantonese fellow had wired the money to Hong Kong before contacting Liu Chuanzhi. So he waited and waited without hearing anything, and by the time Liu Chuanzhi telephoned Shenzhen again, he had already completely lost contact with the Cantonese importer. When he heard this, Liu Chuanzhi's head swam and his eyes reddened. He took the first plane to Shenzhen. He found his colleague and they telephoned their contact's company. The company told them he wasn't there and hadn't come in to work for many days! Liu Chuanzhi began to get very agitated when he heard this and by one means or another found out where the man lived. That evening, Liu Chuanzhi and his colleague went over and kept watch over the man's front door, with Liu looking more like a bailiff than president of a major company. Indeed, the truth was Liu Chuanzhi would happily have taken a brick to the man's head if he had had to. He hadn't considered the possibility that the fellow wouldn't even go home, but that is just what happened. After squatting outside the man's home all night, Liu Chuanzhi went back to where he was staying in a cold sweat: if the worst happened and he had lost the Rmb3 million, how was he going to pay the company back? How was he going to pay the academy back? Fortunately, it turned out the Cantonese fellow's family had been in touch with him and he telephoned the next day.

A few days later Liu Chuanzhi caught up with the Cantonese guy. When the man saw his bloodshot eyes and his determined expression, he said with a laugh, "I just moved that three million around for a few days, that's all. You're not a state-owned company, are you, so what are you so worried about?" The truth is, though, that if Liu hadn't found the man's home, and hung around waiting for him like some kind of gangster, it was by no means certain he would ever have seen the money again. But the funds were returned, and after all the trials and tribulations, the computers made their way to Beijing where, because they had been bought so cheaply, they made a very tidy profit.

"But three months or so after I got back to Beijing," said Liu Chuanzhi, "I was at a celebration banquet with Li Qin. Everyone was enjoying themselves, talking away, when there was a sudden crash and Li Qin was stretched out on the floor. This was the first onset of heart disease as his heart went into atrial fibrillation because of stress brought on by that loan. Actually, the stress had made us all ill and it was my turn, after Li Qin's spell in hospital, until the crisis had passed. I really didn't feel very well. I had been terrified from the moment I first heard the three million had been wired then had disappeared. Sometimes the fear kept me awake until two in the morning, and even then my heart was thumping so much I couldn't sleep for the rest of the night. It went on like that right up until the matter was settled, but even after we got the money back, I was still having palpitations. Later on, I was admitted to the Navy Hospital and people said I looked like Yokomichi Keiji's character in *Manhunt* at the time, and I wasn't making much sense when I talked. I don't mind talking about it all now, even though it was very scary at the time. Still, I gained a lot of valuable experience from things like that."

What he said is quite true. Some people become legends because of just one extraordinary deed, and others because of repeated feats. It is like the difference between the magic of lakes and the magic of rivers: lakes are still and limpid but rivers flow and are constantly changing. Liu Chuanzhi was like a river. It is hard to imagine such an assertive and confident man as him breaking down in tears and suffering so deeply, but that is just what happened to him in his dealings with the Bank of China (Hong Kong).

Although an agreement about the split of profits had been agreed in Lenovo's collaboration with the Bank of China (Hong Kong), it was only a verbal agreement, and hadn't been formalised in black and white. The Bank of China (Hong Kong) is an SOE and when the name of the CEO on the letterhead changed, the new CEO didn't know anything about any agreements his predecessor had made. So when the business account was being settled, with a stroke of the pen, US$20,000 of Lenovo's rightful profits just disappeared. "This is obviously an error," Liu Chuanzhi said.

"There is no error," he was told. "You have had your proper share." US$20,000 is a heavy stroke of the pen for a newly established company. In such a company people are normally scrimping and saving just to get by and have to watch every penny, even to the extent of giving up smoking. Liu Chuanzhi was so angry he rushed to Hong Kong, but he couldn't get a connection and had to stop in Shenzhen. He didn't dare spend the money to stay in one of the big hotels and eventually, as he turned a corner on Hongling North Road, he found a small hotel for Rmb8 per night where he clambered up to the third floor and spent the night in a shared room with a number of strangers. That night, Liu Chuanzhi couldn't sleep as he thought of all the miserable things that can happen when you set up a business. With all these thoughts whirling around in his head, he got up and wrote a letter to his contact in the Bank of China (Hong Kong).

In the letter he related all the problems he had encountered in his dealings with Bank of China (Hong Kong), including how he, a middle-aged man in his 40s, had had to fawn on and flatter some stripling of a youth who was representing the bank, in a way that made him cringe to listen to himself; and how one of his female employees had knocked on the fellow's door with trembling hands so she could plead with him for the sake of the company. He also talked about how another man in his 40s had gone running around for a whole working day with a fever of 39C, just to get hold of an import permit; and how he had made two return trips to the other side of Beijing, and had run himself ragged going up and down stairs on rubbery legs between the fourth and fifth floors, until he got that permit; he went on to tell how the same man had braved the rain to go and meet his guest from the Bank of China (Hong Kong) at the airport, and how he had been running to the bus stop to save money on a taxi, and had slipped and fallen down a manhole where the water was so deep he almost drowned, and how everyone was scrimping and saving, and doing whatever it took, regardless of their dignity, just to make sure the company cleared a profit. Liu Chuanzhi wrote and wrote, his eyes filling with tears. He could just about hold them in when he wasn't writing, but once he picked up his pen he couldn't stop them; all the time he was aware this was a last-ditch battle: he couldn't make it to Hong Kong, but now he was in Shenzhen he couldn't let the trip be for nothing. Everything depended on this letter. Was he being overdramatic? Of course not; he had a genuine motive and there was a lot of pain and suffering underlying that motive, and it all came down to a stroke of the pen. Liu Chuanzhi was just about able to contain his pain but he couldn't help thinking of his wife, far away back in Beijing, who was suffering with hyperthyroidism and, at that moment, was being operated on at the Friendship Hospital, yet he couldn't go back to see her...

Liu Chuanzhi's letter did indeed do the trick. The Bank of China (Hong Kong)'s new CEO had never heard of anyone staking everything for their business like that, not baulking at anything. Astonishingly, he went back and checked the bank's internal records and, to his great surprise, he discovered that everything Liu Chuanzhi had said was true. With a sigh, he reimbursed Liu Chuanzhi the US$20,000.

To tell the truth, I'm rather afraid that if Liu Chuanzhi were to write a love letter it wouldn't be as emotional as the one he wrote to the bank; it was all true, and accurate and honest, but he is a man who knows how to use those things to his advantage. He believes that the heart is just another muscle; it is a kind of conviction, and without that conviction, a person certainly cannot turn suffering to their advantage but, rather, they just let it settle deep inside them.

Three-Stage Process

In 1987, despite almost being cheated out of Rmb3 million; despite having to write an urgent letter in Shenzhen to avoid losing US$20,000; despite narrowly escaping a Rmb1million fine from the Commodity Prices Bureau; despite suffering ill health, the symptoms of which included dizziness, weird dreams, and frequent urination that pretty much amounted to insomnia; also not being able to switch his brain off night or day, so there was no difference between having his eyes open or shut, or if he did manage to doze off, waking with a start after only a few moments; being full of fear and having a heart that pounded incessantly; all of which led to him be admitted to the Navy Hospital; and despite being definitely diagnosed in hospital with the nervous disorder, Menière's disease; despite all of this, he still considered that year to be one of record performance. When he first set up on his own three years before, he had boasted to Director Zhou Guangzhao that within three years his business would be making Rmb2 million. And now, three years later, it was making Rmb70 million, with a tax bill of Rmb3.47 million, fixed assets of Rmb4 million, and Rmb5.5 million of working capital. As he lay in his hospital bed with all these thoughts surging around in his head, all he really wanted to do was get some proper rest and not think about the company. But his brain just wouldn't stand still and, whether his eyes were open or shut, all he could see was the business. Liu Chuanzhi himself thought that there was something 'inhuman' about the way he was.

In 1987, Lenovo was facing innumerable choices which Liu Chuanzhi had no option but to think about even if it made his head spin and his eyes go blurry as he lay in his hospital bed. If he didn't think about them, who would? And in any case, what would be the use of someone else thinking about them? It was his lot to do the thinking. Each one of the choices facing him could have changed the history of Lenovo and each change in direction of its development would have had a different ending. Undoubtedly, computers or something to do with computers were the way ahead for the company, and to the 'inhuman' Liu Chuanzhi, there was one clear and obvious choice: stick with the 'Chinese character card'. But the market was limited; Chinese-character software was still developing, and it was only a matter of time before the 'Chinese character card' was made redundant. The next thing would be to develop their own brand of computer, but although there were clear advantages to this, they had neither the funds nor the manpower and, besides, for the time being there was no way they could get the necessary manufacturing permit from the Bureau of Electronic Industries. The third thing would be to act as agents for foreign computers, build up capital, establish an online business and get a proper grasp of all the latest technology, all in order to lay a solid foundation for establishing their own brand of computers.

Thoughts from a sick bed often have a particular clarity and a particularly lively imagination: a cool-headed openness that can't be achieved in an office environment. Illness doesn't necessarily cause confusion or despair, and there is a school of thought that says the hospital is a place of hope. If it isn't, then what are you doing there? Sometimes, there are really important strategic decisions that are improved by having been made in hospital. It is certainly the case that, in this instance, being in hospital increased Liu Chuanzhi's 'superhuman' qualities. It was almost entirely while he was in the Navy Hospital that he devised Lenovo's 'three-stage progress' strategy which was to prove so reliable in the future. This is often the case with people: the ideas that are born out of extreme circumstances, when the person may be at death's door themselves, are often imbued with a particular life-giving energy, and later prove to be particularly robust and to be the foundation for something even bigger than previously imagined.

On the one hand, Liu Chuanzhi was thinking about retrenchment, but on the other he was giving birth to something new. What might be seen as a paradox was actually two sides of the same coin. Liu Chuanzhi's thinking was this: stage one was to set up a trading company somewhere overseas, France perhaps. In this way they would be able to obtain agency credentials that they couldn't get in China. At that time there was an 'agency permit' system in place, and only a handful of the most powerful companies in China had the right to one. Most of the companies in Zhongguancun could only get merchandise through an agent abroad or by smuggling, which was how the original four big Zhongguancun companies managed. Jin Yanjing was actually sent to jail for this, which gave a real fright to all the other companies in Zhongguancun who relied on smuggling to make their money. In the past, if you agreed an agency deal with a foreign company, according to the rules, the middleman had to give a discount of at least 15%; but if you had your own company abroad you had the freedom to conduct business as you pleased and could forget the 15% rake-off.

The second stage of Liu Chuanzhi's strategy was to extend the company's sphere of activity from the purely commercial into production as well, by moving on a grand scale into integrated industry, and using this as a foundation for developing their own computer. The third stage was to get onto the Hong Kong stock exchange as a listed company. This was a very coherent blueprint, and it wasn't an easy thing to have such a blueprint in such a turbulent marketplace; when people talked about a man of 'great talent and bold vision', this at least was what was meant by 'bold vision'. Over 30 years, most of the original companies of Zhongguancun have disappeared, and how many have continued to go from strength to strength? How many have grown into worldwide companies like Lenovo?

It was the second stage of the 'three-stage progress' strategy that was the most pivotal and the most ingenious, illustrating Liu Chuanzhi's imagination, daring and insatiably ambitious attitude, like the snake that wanted to swallow an elephant. Many years later, Liu Chuanzhi's purchase of IBM's worldwide PC business was not the first time he had tried such a thing, and was just another example of the 'snake swallowing the elephant' that constituted the second stage of his long-term strategy.

The autumn of 1987 was a pleasant one – autumns always are, but this one seemed particularly so. It was not long after Liu Chuanzhi had been discharged from hospital that he went south again to Shenzhen where there was a knot of foreign computer companies. He took three different models of computer back to Beijing with him and handed them over to Ni Guangnan's research team to try out. The researchers all reckoned that a model called the AST had the best compatibility at a competitive price.

Liu Chuanzhi decided to abandon IBM and sign an agency agreement with AST. It wasn't that he didn't like IBM, he liked them a lot, but he didn't think he could swallow up IBM at that time, but he did think he could, AST. At the same time as he was cosying up to AST, he had a plan to take them over and replace them: a tactic he rather grandiosely called "advancing on the shoulders of giants".

Once Lenovo Hong Kong was registered, it was well placed to freely start acting as an agent for AST computers. At the time, there were only five or six American brands on the Chinese computer market, and when Ni Guangnan linked the Lenovo 'Chinese character card' to the AST computer it became very popular with Chinese buyers and often sold out. AST was originally only a small company in America, but Lenovo gave it the chance to take off, and it soon came to dominate the Chinese market. At the time, computers were eye-wateringly expensive and the profit margins very high. But this wasn't the most important thing; the most important thing was the significance that cooperation with AST had for Lenovo's development. As the sales agent for AST, Lenovo gained an understanding of the internal workings of the computer, microprocessors and all the different connections between the components. Lenovo grew its own engineering team so that, by the 1990s, it had made great strides towards establishing a solid base in the world of computers.

In 1989, in a cramped laboratory in Lenovo Hong Kong, chief engineer Ni Guangnan was engrossed in designing Lenovo's own Model 286. Working night and day with three assistants, he hoped to have a glorious follow-on success to the 'Chinese character card'. Ni Guangnan and his team knew the AST pretty well inside out by now and were preparing to try their hand on the market with their own Model 286. At the time, personal computers were advancing by leaps and bounds in America, Europe and Oceania, and even in the Far East in Japan, Korea, Taiwan and Hong Kong. Liu Chuanzhi and the others had to match that pace. Liu chose Hong Kong as his battleground and spent HK$1,000 (US$128) buying shares in a Hong Kong company. Using this as his manufacturing base, he began to design and produce the motherboard, since the keys to victory were the micro-motherboard and the overall assembly. The motherboard is the circuit board that contains all the integrated circuits and microchips for the microprocessor and its complexity lies in the fact that it contains almost all the important elements of the internal workings of a computer: the central processor, the digital memory, the video card and a set of buses and ports. Ni Guangnan was obsessed with hardware and designing boards was just what he liked doing.

The man in charge at Lenovo Hong Kong, Lü Tanping, and Ni Guangnan got along pretty well together. At first, Ni hadn't wanted to use components made in Korea and Taiwan, preferring American-made, but Lü patiently explained to him that conducting business and conducting research were not the same thing: if they didn't use Taiwanese components, how were they going to compete on price? On another occasion, Lü Tanping told Ni Guangnan that, in business, using the best components to make the best product did not constitute success; using the cheapest components to make the best product did. To be a businessman, Lü made it clear, you had to reduce costs to the absolute minimum because that was the way you could guarantee the biggest profits. It almost didn't matter what components you used in your research, as long as the core idea and theory were sound, that was enough to start production. As long as the quality was there and the consumer was satisfied, that constituted success. When Ni Guangnan was designing the motherboard, of course the problems came thick and fast, and as soon as one was solved, another one became apparent. Because they didn't have a systematic testing regime, this was quite normal, and it was the reason Lü and Ni drew up together the first Lenovo QDI (motherboard) testing criteria.

At the same time, AST were delighted to see that Lenovo had inserted the 'Chinese character card' into their computers, and thought Lenovo were the most reliable of partners. They told themselves how wise they had been to give Lenovo sole agency for the Chinese market; so much so that they had no qualms about sacrificing any other sales paths. As for the establishment of the north-south combination of Lenovo Beijing and Lenovo Hong Kong as the perfect pairing to monopolise supply, AST were aware of it and accepted it. They even thought it couldn't be bettered. As far as AST were concerned, as long as their microprocessors were selling that was OK. But what they didn't know was that on his hospital bed, their partner Liu Chuanzhi was already aggressively opening his yawning maw to vomit out all that 'good will': Liu was in the process of taking all the profits from the AST agency to make up the deficit on the development of his own motherboard, and had ploughed Rmb13.5 million into producing the 'Lenovo computer'.

Of course, even if AST had known what Lenovo was up to, they wouldn't have taken the Lenovo computer seriously. There was such a difference in scale of operation, they couldn't believe that a little snake like Lenovo could possibly swallow a huge elephant like themselves. The huge elephant had confidence in itself, and not without reason. What is the main difference between an elephant and a snake? The difference is that they are two different kinds of creature; the difference is that one doesn't think and the other does; moreover, the one that does is particularly daring in the way it thinks.

On 30 January 1989, the Lenovo Group held its opening ceremony in the recently completed Haidian movie theatre. During the ceremony, Liu Chuanzhi told his staff, "From 1984 to now, Lenovo's cumulative turnover has been in excess of Rmb100 million, our fixed assets have surpassed Rmb50 million; we have 360 staff, 16 different companies, two research centres, three production sites and 34 service outposts covering the whole country. But the most important thing is that we are already manufacturing our own brand computer, the Lenovo 286." The opening ceremony was really like a general making a vow to his troops, and after it the Model 286, which Ni Guangnan's research team had designed, was ready to exhibit at the Hanover International Fair in Germany.

In March 1990, the Lenovo 286 computer passed its inspections and received a permit for a production run of 5,000 units in the first year. Having already wrested control of AST's computer market, Liu Chuanzhi looked around and decided to swing into action. It was a beautiful day with the spring flowers opening, when Liu gathered his sales staff together and let the deputy managing director of the company, Li Qin, make the solemn announcement, "We have come to the decision that we are no longer going to push sales of the AST 286, but are going to launch our own product onto the market!"

It was like the raising of a rebel standard or a revolt, and just as all such rebellions have an element of secrecy, so did Liu Chuanzhi's and Li Qin's decision. Accustomed as they were to selling the AST computer, the sales staff didn't really know what was going on; some of them looked at each other, some just stared blankly, some of them didn't like the way things seemed to be going and the few of them who knew the secret, whispered to each other.

Li Qin continued, "We are just going to leave a few of you handling the AST stock, but all of the main body of the Lenovo team are going to switch to the production, procurement and sales of Lenovo computers. You don't need to worry, the capabilities of the Lenovo 286 can match and even surpass the AST microcomputer...." When Li Qin finished, all the previously doubtful sales staff voiced their approval. The truth was that Lenovo was riding on the coat tails of AST's success and was like a cicada that escapes leaving only an empty carapace behind. The meeting lasted four days. It was one of the few extended meetings in the history of Lenovo because they needed to unify a philosophy, unify a strategy and change the standard they fought under. The market was used to the old products, why should it accept a new one? Because its operating capabilities could match the AST 286, and its price was lower.

But does cheaper mean better? This is something that needs further discussion.

Liu Chuanzhi attended every day of the four-day meeting, listening earnestly to every opinion and voicing his own, accepting debate of them just like any others. It was the consensus of opinion that the only advantage the Chinese market had at the time was a price advantage, but that four-day meeting not only laid down the course to victory in that particular 'rebellion', it also laid down the course for Lenovo's future victorious campaigns. What came out of the meeting was that they should first have a transitional period and not just drop AST outright. The best-case scenario would be that they hedged their bets by keeping the AST cash cow whilst their own product was also successful; the middle option would be for them to have a successful product of their own, but lose AST; the worst-case scenario would be for their product to fail and for them to lose AST too. Dependability, meticulousness and daring had been characteristics of Liu Chuanzhi all along, and these qualities gradually transferred themselves first to the management team, and then to the company as a whole. If a whole company acts as one, then that company will succeed. When the Lenovo 286 reached the final debugging stage, the last lap, Ni Guangnan was practically foaming at the mouth with agitation as he rushed to the airport with the prototype machine. As soon as he got back to Beijing, on (Chinese) New Year's Day, he and a dozen or so colleagues were in the test laboratory at the crack of dawn, working away, regardless of the early hour. They knew that if they didn't make it to the Hanover International Fair in March, it would set them back at least six months.

The Hanover International Fair has the most demanding standards of any exhibition in the world of computers. In the 10 days it ran from 10 March, 3,300 teams from 40 countries exhibited the cream of office, news and communications technology. In terms of building a business, the Hanover fair was uniquely situated to be the gateway into the world market for new products and new systems. Lenovo brought the 286 computer to the trade show, along with a set of compatible software, a diagnostic disc, a test card, the XT microprocessor and the Lenovo FAX facsimile communications card. In the computer hall, the Lenovo computer matched current worldwide microcomputer standards with better functionality and a lower price than other comparable products from the Hong Kong and Taiwan market. When the final curtain came down on the exhibition after 10 days, after its first appearance on the international market, the Lenovo computer took orders from customers from more than 20 different countries in Europe and the Americas for a total of 2,073 complete computer suites and 2,483 individual computers.

In May 1990, the company sent two 200 Lenovo 286s to the National Exhibition with explosive effect. A week later, they advanced on the Beijing Computer Fair, where they took Rmb12,478,568 in orders making them the most successful of the 220 computer companies that took part in the fair. During this time Liu Chuanzhi welcomed to the company office a delegation from the American company DEC, led by its company chairman. His American guest clicked his tongue in envy at Liu Chuanzhi's achievements over the last six years. Liu didn't dare be too pleased with himself, but he did have a certain feeling of gratification that he found rather moving. He knew that his company had succeeded, had a direction and had its own brand product. But that was only the foundation, and if he wanted to build Lenovo's grand tower block there was still a long road ahead.

DIARY NOTE 9: ALL THE SHADOWS

> There is a lesson to be learned from the four volumes of *The Selected Works of Mao Zedong* and even more from Sunzi's *Art of War*. Liu Chuanzhi was talking in the office with panoramic views enjoyed by Lenovo in the Raytech Information Park. Regardless of the time and the place, I found these words rather startling as they had a timeless quality to them; at first, they also seemed a little vague, but then they sprang into focus. I had read Mao's *Selected Works* too; indeed, at that time, who wasn't familiar with the famous 'Four Volumes'. There is a section in them about the *Three Great Campaigns of the Chinese Civil War* that had fascinated me as a warlike youngster. The military thinking behind the Three Great Campaigns is well known around the world, and as he lay in his sick bed in the Navy Hospital dreaming up his 'three-stage progress' strategy, Liu Chuanzhi clearly drew heavily on the four volumes of *Selected Works*. Volume Five of the *Selected Works* is a later addition from after the fall of the Gang of Four, and the other four volumes pre-date it by a long time. So, although I was a little hazy about the history, I had no trouble following it, eyes wide with enthusiasm. Given the history they cover, there are always people who can draw inspiration from them. Certainly, you could see the shadow of everything Liu Chuanzhi had been through writ large on his body, but even from within those shadows you could see that he was in command of them all.
>
> The story of the founding of Lenovo is like many other stories in that it can be made to sound like crisis piled on crisis requiring the nine lives of a cat, and snatching victory from the jaws of defeat at every stage of its progress. The most perilous times for Lenovo, when it was teetering on the edge of ruin, were often the times of its most daring

actions. Difficulty and danger serve to stimulate the imagination and the power to dream; when Liu Chuanzhi was in his hospital bed, just when he was thinking of retreat, the idea for his 'three-stage progress' was born, and his dreams bore fruit and drove out the defeatism. Where else do the biggest dreams come from, if not out of the greatest challenges? Challenges are the incubators of dreams and if you have a host of challenges it means you have a host of dreams. The Chinese for Lenovo means 'mental association' and if you just change one character in the name, you get the word for 'dreams', and Liu Chuanzhi was surely the product of a series of dreams. At first, the 'three-stage progress' seemed like a daydream but looking back now it can be seen as a grand vision and the clearest of dreams. So much so that it is now one of the case histories amongst the several hundred that a Harvard MBA student studies on its two-year MBA course.

I also appreciate Ling Zhijun's assessment, "The reason Lenovo stands out from the crowd is because of the way it interacted with the establishment, and the perseverance, patience and skill with which it handled the associated corrupt practices, gradually breaking their shackles and moving towards a new world."

Wangma

王码

ONE DAY IN AUGUST 1962, a confused and disoriented Wang Yongmin was on a train bound for Beijing. This child of a farming village had passed the entrance examination for the mighty University of Science and Technology of China but, because there were no trains to Nanyang at the time, he had had to go by bus to Xuchang first. It was four in the afternoon when he reached Xuchang, but his train wasn't until seven in the morning the next day, so he had a wait of 15 hours. He had never been to Xuchang before, so he didn't dare go anywhere and just spread out some newspaper in the station as a sleeping mat and went to sleep. He had never even seen a train before then, or a city or multi-storey buildings, so he was both expectant and incredibly nervous about what lay ahead: he had no idea what Beijing would be like. Finally, his farmer's eyes wide-eyed and dazzled, Wang Yongmin arrived uncomprehendingly in the capital.

His accommodation was in Room 421 of the university's dormitory block 7 but he had great difficulty just finding the university, let alone finding his room, as they all looked the same. In a daze, he fished out his tea flask and went to the boiler room for hot water. When he got back to his room and sat down at his desk, he suddenly discovered that his luggage had disappeared and was nowhere to be seen. He went white with shock and felt as though he was in the middle of a nightmare. How could this be? It would never have happened back in his village, but in the big city…? He had no idea what to do next. He pinched himself to make sure he actually existed, but the room made him feel unsure of himself, as though he was lost in some fantasy. The room itself did nothing to confirm his existence because none of his things were there. His things were the proof of his existence, but the room was denying him that certainty. But he didn't dare move, fearing he wouldn't be able to find the room again if he left it. It was only when someone came along and told him that he was in room 8, not room 7, that he came back to his senses and realised he had gone into the wrong room.

The affair remained etched in Wang Yongmin's memory. The experience had nothing to do with his intelligence; he had all the innocent openness of a country boy, but perhaps that innocence had spilled over into a kind of excessive sensitivity. But sensitivity is the gateway to many things and, seen that way, his innocence might be considered a kind of gift from heaven. Of course, it can also be a gift that brings suffering, and some people never get past that stage.

Many years later, after experiencing the vicissitudes of life, Wang Yongmin returned to where it all began for him in Nanyang. He had been through the turmoil of the Cultural Revolution with nothing good to show for it and, as if by karma, was returning to his origins, returning to a state of innocence. Of course, it wasn't the same innocence as before, it was the innocence of 20 years' experience, an innocence with many scars and bruises, but which retained its simplicity.

Wang Yongmin's major that year at the University of Science and Technology was wireless laser technology, and the work he went on to do for many years in Sichuan had all been connected with science and technology in one way or another. Going back to his hometown of Nanyang afterwards felt to him as though he was bringing his whole life back with him. He went to work at the Regional Science and Technology Commission in Nanyang with responsibility for a few specific projects; he was just another ordinary civil servant and it seemed that he would spend the rest of his life like that. He was a different person from the innocent who had gone up to university. Sometimes he would recall his teachers from back then, people such as Hua Luogeng, Yan Jici, Qian Xuesen and Ma Dayou, but really they were just figures in a dream by then.

Moving on to 1978, the Japanese invention of the phototypesetting or photocomposition machine, also known as the 'character implanting machine', was all the rage, and Nanyang had imported one. But there were a lot of shortcomings with the machine: you couldn't proofread and correct the Chinese characters once they were entered, and if they came out wrong, you had to start the whole phototypesetting process over again, which was a real hassle. How could they be coming out wrong? But that's what happened, time and again, so the Sichuan Regional Optical Instrument Factory spent Rmb90,000 building a 'slideshow format' keyboard to solve the problem. Wang Yongmin, who was in charge of the project, felt that this 'slide format' keyboard was a bit of a joke, and he asked the chief engineer at the factory, "Who do you think can remember which 273 characters to put on each frame of 24 slides? Do you know which frame of those 24 slides you would find your surname on?" Although it was a straightforward question, it made the chief engineer feel as though he was being made a fool of. He got annoyed and put Wang Yongmin on the factory's prohibited visitors list and even had him officially expelled.

The keyboard was a straightforward issue, seemingly almost beneath the dignity of someone like Wang Yongmin with his background in studies at the University of Science and Technology. He didn't think it was any great problem. He did want to solve it, though, but it turned out that the problem wasn't with the keyboard but with first finding a decent input programme to make it work.

Wang Yongmin's idea got the support of the Science and Technology

Commission, but because it didn't seem to be a particularly big project, they only allocated him a budget of Rmb3,000. He scurried around the Science and Technology information offices in Shanghai, Suzhou and Hangzhou consulting all the resources, foreign and domestic, that he could find. The input methods available at the time were: Wang An's 99-key triangular encoding system, but the large-format keyboard was not particularly attractive; there was the large single-character keyboard, and the large-format primary-auxiliary-key keyboard with nine characters to each key which used nine auxiliary keys to choose the character. This latter was the most popular at the time, and it was the programme that the National Science and Technology information office used. Wang An's programme used *pinyin*, but *pinyin* is imprecise, and no use if you didn't know the relevant character.

As Wang Yongmin delved deeper into the matter, he discovered that this wasn't a minor problem at all. Broadly speaking, it involved a revolution in Chinese characters, but on the other hand he felt that this was something he himself could do something about, as if fate had decreed this to be his problem. He sought out Zheng Yili, the chief editor of the *New English-Chinese Dictionary* and explained his thinking to him. The two men got on very well, talking character deconstruction, encoding and input as if they were discussing the arcane mysteries of some kind of martial art. Wang Yongmin benefitted enormously from these conversations through which he was able to meld his scientific and technological background with the vast ocean of ancient knowledge about Chinese characters whilst maintaining his scientific outlook and rigour. It was indeed a rare opportunity. It was then that this talented alumnus of the University of Science and Technology began to feel that he was at the dawn of a new scientific breakthrough that was his and his alone. It wasn't something that anyone else could own or stumble across because, however you looked at it, it was unique to him.

He even invited Professor Zheng to Nanyang and arranged accommodation at the best hotel in town.

Professor Zheng Yili's Chinese character encoding was a 94-key system that used a radical[1] chart. Drawing on local resources, Wang Yongmin hired a dozen or so girls to transcribe all 11,000 characters in the *New English-Chinese Dictionary* onto cards and encode them according to radical. When he inspected the cards after the encoding, he found there were 800 duplicate codes and, moreover, the programming also needed upper and lower case, which necessitated the equivalent of 188 keys. It was another defeat and was fundamentally unusable. But it is often said that defeat is the mother of success, and this defeat did indeed have its uses. Wang Yongmin had a thorough understanding of Chinese characters and could see from this that he was headed in the right direction and that compressing the key mapping was the crucial element. Wang said goodbye to Professor Zheng, and set off on his own voyage of exploration.

He toiled away, day and night, following the path he had decided upon, gradually reducing the number of keys: 138, then 90, then 75, then 62... on 15 July 1980 Wang Yongmin had compressed the key mapping to 62 keys, with only 26 duplicate codes. At this point, he was very close to success. In 1980, there was a conference on Chinese character coding in Wuhan, Hubei, at which Wang unveiled his 62-key programme. It caused quite a sensation there and was hailed as one of the four best programmes in the country.

With the encoding done, Wang Yongmin turned his hand to the integrated circuit. Drawing circuit maps and designing circuit housings were his forte, but he hadn't tested himself on them for quite a few years. In 1981, not only was the design for his keyboard complete, but it had also been tested. But, as he was about to launch it for practical use, he discovered that the keyboard was missing its editing function key. Designing function keys was an entirely different proposition, and proved to be a real headache as, once it was designed, it still had to be matched up and joined onto the existing keyboard. As he was tearing his hair out over it, Wang Yongmin suddenly came to his senses: why did he have to make this function key himself? Wouldn't it be much better to use one of the existing function keys already on the keyboard? Previously he had been thinking about how to transfer the function keys from a standard keyboard onto the Chinese character keyboard, so why shouldn't he do the same in reverse with an existing function key from a Chinese character keyboard?

This was a very significant line of thought! And one that belonged absolutely to Wang Yongmin's new dawn. There are some dawns that you lose sight of after going only a little way down the road.

Wang Yongmin was standing on a horizon that the ancients had never reached, nor was there now anyone following on behind him. A standard keyboard has 48 functioning keys, and it is only a short step from 48 to 62, so Wang thought to himself: "If I can reduce 62 keys to 48, then I can use a standard keyboard and there would be no need to waste time and effort designing a new one." It was already crowded with other people on the keyboard design highway, but in pursuing it to its end, only Wang Yongmin had the inspiration to abandon the idea of designing a new one, and focusing all his attention on the standard keyboard.

One might ask, if he hadn't got down to 62 keys, but was still a longer way off, would Wang Yongmin still have thought the same?

To get a 62-key programme down to a 48-key programme, the first problem that had to be solved was the one of duplicate character codes. Wang Yongmin got hold of some No. 0 tracing paper and laid out 150 radicals in a horizontal row and 150 in a vertical column. He then filled in all the first-rank character codes on one sheet of paper, all the second-rank ones on a second sheet of paper and all the third-rank ones on a third sheet. Then, with the three sheets of tracing paper on top of one another, he put the pile onto a glass sheet which was lit from underneath by six fluorescent lamps. That way he could see, for all the GB (National Standard) characters, which ones were duplicated and which were not; which ones were compatible and which were not; which ones were related and which were not. It was all crystal clear. Before this, in order to revise one radical, you had to flip through more than a thousand character cards, but now you could see almost immediately which radicals could be grouped together on one key.

Having succeeded in reaching 48 keys, Wang Yongmin reduced the number further, to 40 keys.

Then, with a final great effort, he got the number down to 26.

On 28 August 1983, Wang Yongmin's '26-key *Wubi* (five-stroke) Chinese character model input method' was revealed as a marvel of Chinese character computer input technology. On 27 September, the *Guangming Daily* reported this great invention with a front-page headline.

Although the invention itself was a success, the popularisation of it had to start from nothing. As an inventor, this wasn't really Wang Yongmin's thing, but once again he set out to do it himself. That was the kind of man he was, never afraid to start from scratch and always with an open mind. In 1984, he took his PC up to Beijing and, with the help of Yan Yuanchao, the inventor of CCDOS (Chinese Character Disk Operation System) he installed Wang's five-stroke character model input method (hereafter referred to as 'five-stroke') on his machine. For the next two years, Wang Yongmin occupied basement room no. 7 of the United Front Work Department of the CPC at 135 Fuyou Street. He couldn't even afford the Rmb7 per day rent. But he popularised the five-stroke input method in Beijing, and the way he did it was by explaining it to one ministry or commission after another. But although many of these establishments installed the method on their computers, the majority of their staff needed training to use it. Wang Yongmin went everywhere explaining the method, free of charge; if someone asked, he went, not bothering whether he had time to eat or not. If it took three days to explain it fully, that was fine; if it took five days, that was fine too. Starting with his kernel of openness and optimism, he 'captured the whole empire'. In the two years that he occupied that basement room on Fuyou Street, he went to more than a hundred related ministries, commissions and universities promoting his five-stroke method. As he was living, poverty-stricken, in his basement, DEC (Dongfang Electric) paid US$200,000 for the licence to use the five-stroke method. On 6 March 1987, Wang Yongmin moved out of the Fuyou Street basement into the Yuanwanglou Hotel in Zhongguancun and established the Wangma Computer Company. In the same year the five-stroke method won the gold medal at the 1987 China Exhibition of Inventions. In 1992, the Wangma Computer Company's revenues reached Rmb10 million.

But Wang Yongmin's open and innocent ways didn't change; he still often took a taxi to work, and always maintained his simple, country character.

One day in April 1994, Wang Yongmin took a taxi to his company headquarters in an office block in the Experiment Zone of Zhongguancun. When the driver learned that he was going to the offices of the Wangma Company, he started chatting to Wang about it, "The Wangma Company is famous! It has a turnover of more than Rmb100 million and the boss rides around in a Cadillac!"

Wang Yongmin asked the driver, "Do you know him?"

"I don't know him," the driver replied, "but I've heard that he is an inventor from Henan. A really clever man."

Wang told him, "I am Wang Yongmin. I don't own a Cadillac; I've driven a Volkswagen Santana for the last six years, but it's in for major repairs so I usually take a taxi at the moment."

The driver didn't believe him. Wang Yongmin had been putting on a heavy Henan accent and the taxi driver, who was an old Beijing hand and had seen a thing or two, glanced at him and could see that he was pulling his leg. He didn't get annoyed or make much of it, but just said, "You're a real joker, aren't you! But the accent's pretty good." Wang Yongmin was in earnest though and handed the driver his business card.

Beijing folk are straightforward and forthright by nature, and the driver was no different. He wrenched the steering wheel over and stopped at the side of the road. He grasped Wang's hand in both of his and kept saying, emotionally, "I'm so honoured! I'm so honoured! I never dreamed I'd ever get to drive a big boss like you, a real big boss, a great inventor!"

The driver wasn't joking on this occasion either, although he was known as a bit of a wag. The next day, he brought his wife and child from their home in Shijingshan, to the west of the city, to the Wangma Company offices to deliver a letter. Inside it there was Rmb10. The driver had written, "Dear Professor Wang, you are a celebrity but you still take taxis. That's amazing! You have changed the way I think about people with real ability. I am returning the Rmb10 taxi fare. I will always remember you and try to be like you!"

Wang Yongmin's openness and innocence often got a reaction like this from ordinary people.

The more you move other people, the more you have belief in yourself.

DIARY NOTE 10: THE ESSENCE OF CHINESE CHARACTERS

The five-stroke character input method was undoubtedly a turning point for Zhongguancun. At that time, with the initial rise in computer use at the beginning of the 1990s, it is my impression that, without the five-stroke system, there would have been no computers, as the two things were inseparable and, effectively, developed in tandem. Yinghaiwei had just appeared, but there was no Sina, Sohu or NetEase and getting online wasn't what was important; it was managing Chinese characters that mattered. Even though it already felt very modern and magical, the first time I tapped out a character on a keyboard I felt as though I was crossing 5,000 years in a single stride, and I felt like a truly modern man. I don't believe I was the only person who felt like that; I think I was just one representative of countless others. Although there was *pinyin* entry at the time, there was nothing novel and fresh about it, and I felt that using pinyin and writing characters were two fundamentally different things. The principles behind the five-stroke system and principles behind the way we are taught to write characters as children are pretty much the same, they both work stroke by stroke, breaking the character down into the different radicals. There is something of the 'essence of the nation' or the 'national character' about this. This is where the magic lies: you can 'write' ancient Chinese characters on a computer. How magical is that!

Characters are Chinese people's only writing system and the symbol of Chinese civilisation. In our daily life, Chinese characters are ubiquitous and we see them everywhere all the time. You could say that where there are Chinese there will always be Chinese characters. The significance of Wang Yongmin's five-stroke Chinese character input method lies in the fact that, compared to other input methods, it better preserves the essence of Chinese characters and their original flavour (which are to be found in the brush strokes). Additionally, it broke through the contemporary thinking that was fettered to the idea that a speedy Chinese character input method necessarily involved an oversize keyboard. In using a 26-key standard-format keyboard for the first time, it put Chinese in line with Western keyboards. It is hard now to imagine the PCs we use today linked to a giant Chinese character keyboard, as Wang Yongmin's invention banished forever the deformity of Chinese PC keyboards.

Nowadays, lots of people use the five-stroke format as a matter of course, and all sorts of world-famous companies such as Microsoft, IBM, Hewlett-Packard, Casio and so on, have all bought licences from Wangma. The five-stroke format itself has also progressed with the advent of digitisation. What has most pleased people is that, in recent years, Wangma has made tremendous innovations such as the Wangma Key Touch which they invented and designed: it is a three-way combination of the digital Wangma system, an electronic dictionary and an optical mouse. It has a Wangma microchip and can switch between simplified and traditional characters as desired; it can voice two-way Chinese-English translation; it can process 27,533 simplified Chinese characters and conforms entirely with the strict criteria of GB (National Standard) 18030. Overall, it embodies the vitality of Chinese characters and reflects their true essence.

As soon as I started using the five-stroke system, it was clear to me that Y represented a dot, G represented a horizontal stroke, J represented a vertical stroke, and that W was a stand-alone 人。 From the abstract Latin alphabet letter to the concrete original brush stroke and on again to a complete ancient Chinese character, this integrated process employed the rationality of the Latin alphabet, whilst at the same time preserving the sensibility of the original. It was a recognition of the sometimes startling inclusivity of Chinese culture and its capacity for regeneration.

Feng Wukuai

冯五块

MANY YEARS LATER, it is the afternoon of 10 October 2000 – the precision of the internet age allows us to give the time precisely as 14:41:47. If Feng Jun had happened to be walking along Zhongguancun Avenue or driving, for that matter, and had stopped at a red light by the Zhongguancun Post Office at the mouth of Hailong Road, he probably would have been able to see the Yibin Building come crashing down with a great rumbling boom and seen a great cloud of grey dust surge up into the air; the Yibin Building, the first great symbol of Zhongguancun, took its leave in that instant.

If that really was how things were, what Feng Jun saw in that cloud of dust was the end of an era.

There were countless such demolitions in Zhongguancun, and all across China for that matter. With so many going on, there is no time to regret any particular one, before the next one is upon you. A few days before, it was the Four Seas Market that had gone to make way for the construction of the Fourth Ring Road, losing a big chunk of Zhongguancun. The market had stood right in the middle of what is now the ring road, and now it was the Yibin Building creating a similar dust cloud. The ramshackle and chaotic Four Seas Market was no great loss, but the Yibin Building was a symbolic building of the age, and not being able to see it (and it had been next to impossible to miss) was like not being able to see Zhongguancun itself.

When the Yibin Building was first built, Zhongguancun didn't have any buildings to be particularly proud of, just the Four Seas Market in the north. In the 1980s, the market existed in embryonic form, and in the mid to late 1990s, other than a few big shop fronts facing the street, it was mainly occupied by second-string brand names such as Hisense, BaYi Space, GuoHe Computers and so on, and as you went deeper into its narrow lanes it turned into a sprawl of booths selling pirate CDs and DVDs, and so on. There you could buy anything from radios and hi-fis to classical music CDs, and surplus stock tapes and cassettes, some of them the kind of chromium oxide and other metallic tapes that you couldn't get elsewhere. Back then, the Four Seas Market was a chaotic place, much like the 'urban villages'[1] that were to appear later. Someone died there, one day: the old night watchman at one of the computer company warehouses was killed and more than a hundred RAM units and several dozen hard discs were stolen. 'Five Yuan Feng' turned up on the scene. That was the nickname of the boss of the Four Seas Market and Yibin Building complex. Back then, despite headline-grabbing events like the death of the old night watchman and the market's rather forbidding reputation, the puny Feng Jun was always shuttling ceaselessly to and fro between his hundred or more customers in the Four Seas Market and the Yibin Building carrying keyboards and computer cases. He wasn't worried by the murder of an old man, but he was worried about his keyboards and computer cases, and the only reason he had stopped by was because his customers were all chattering away about the case, and he had no option but to try and make conversation about it while his customers in their little shop fronts or behind their stalls desultorily looked over his goods. If one of them told him his computer cases were no good, Feng Yu would straightaway drop his conversation about the murder case and move on to the next customer. The next day, he would go back with a different case and try again. There were lots of different brands of computer case, twenty or thirty of them, and he showed his customers a different one every day.

To start with, Feng Jun was always being shown the door as he moved from one customer to another, but he never felt bad about it, as he told himself that if they were showing him the door, they were doing the same to other hawkers (mainly handbag sellers) as well. But if, one day, one of them took him at his word about his wares and dealt with him exclusively, once he had his hands on a customer like that, he never let them go and did everything he could to look after them. This was the logic of how Feng Jun worked and that was in 1993.

"Just have a look, it's the latest model!" Feng Jun thrust the computer case in the shop owner's face, his own face wreathed in smiles. He had already tried this particular shop several times, and he was beginning to wear the boss down.

"This one's not too bad. If any of my customers want one, I'll give you a shout."

Feng Jun was all too familiar with the sub-text of Zhongguancun conversations, and he took no more notice than he did of any murder case. He just stood his ground. He knew that he would lose his chance if he left; besides, the shop owner had actually engaged him in conversation so it was clear he was in with a shout.

Feng Jun squinted at the man and said, "How's any customer going to know he wants it if he can't see it?" The shop owner laughed and agreed to take the case on commission.

Selling on commission means you leave the item behind and get your money when it sells; every stall holder was overstocked, and Feng Jun never saw any money. Besides, he paid cash when he bought his stock so why should he hand it over for someone else to stockpile? He needed cash in hand to keep turning over stock. So he stood his ground and said, "I'll only charge you five yuan (yuan is the same as Rmb). If you haven't sold it in a month, I guarantee I'll refund the money to you. I'll look back in every day so you know I haven't done a runner..."

Feng Jun's honesty and openness were very persuasive, but the main thing was that there weren't any fools in Zhongguancun, and Feng Jun's computer cases were a fraction under the market price. Almost all the shop owners and stall owners were hooked by his good-quality merchandise at competitive prices. What happened next was really only natural. When he left his stock, he left his contact details and he also got his hands on what he most wanted: ready cash. Although the sums were tiny in comparison with the group of independent computer-builders around at that time, having liquid funds was Feng Jun's life-blood, because every time he paid cash for his stock, he got it at an advantageous price.

"That's right, I'll only charge you five yuan, guaranteed refund or replacement if it doesn't sell."

He was as good as his word, because he was an honest and trustworthy man who didn't make up stories.

Sparing no effort and with unflagging patience, he went round all the stall holders telling them the same thing.

The nickname 'Five Yuan Feng' caught on and was soon heard everywhere.

This was a kind of conviction with Feng Jun, and people with convictions are not run-of-the-mill. Although to look at, there didn't seem any difference between Feng Jun and his competitors who were also selling the same kind of computer cases and keyboards, all smiling faces and fake humility, there was still something different about him. There was a look of tranquil tenacity in amongst the smiles that the others didn't have.

People with a modicum of experience and perception could see the word 'education' written on Feng Jun's honest and open features. It was the mark of the kind of man he was, and a mark that his competitors lacked. No matter how worldly wise they might be, and despite their sneaky undercutting of his prices, selling for four yuan or even three, they could never out-compete him or see him off. Other than his "only five yuan" motto, he always had suitable alternatives, offering a different model every day to the same shop owner. "Look, this is today's new model!" That was his other catchphrase.

Feng Jun was from Xi'an, and as he drifted around the lower levels of Beijing society, he seemed pretty much the same as the people selling knock-off tapes and DVDs. But, in fact, he was an alumnus of Tsinghua University: in 1987 he graduated top of the school from Xi'an Yucai Middle School and went up to the Department of Civil Engineering at Tsinghua

University. He was rather proud and arrogant, and didn't particularly like that department. As a freshman, he wanted to switch to the Department of Construction and do a joint degree with the Department of Fine Arts. Not being allowed to switch was a major blow to Feng Jun: he didn't want to be a civil engineer for the rest of his life; nor did he want his life to be laid out so clearly. In his sophomore year he took to going into the city to the notorious Silk Street to act as a translator for the foreign students who were doing business there, earning US$5 an hour. In his junior year, he studied international trade and finance in preparation for leaving the country. In his senior year, he passed the TOEFL Test with a 639, but he didn't go abroad because he couldn't raise the Rmb50,000 training fee. As you can see, Feng Jun spent his whole four years at university looking for ways to change his life and his future. In August 1992, he formally graduated from Tsinghua University and, although he himself felt full of frustrations and dashed hopes, as though he was constantly having the door slammed in his face, from other people's point of view, as a graduate from a prestigious university, he was a blessed son of heaven. He could be assigned to a top-notch work unit, bring home a good, steady income, not have to worry about food and clothes, and work as an engineer. The head office of the Beijing Construction Engineering Company was expecting him and, on top of that, once he reported there, he was going to be sent abroad, to Malaysia. It was an opportunity not afforded to many. But when Feng Jun heard about this, he didn't hesitate but stood straight up and walked out on it. It stirred up too many painful memories. His father had been working abroad on the foreign aid programme for the last eight years but in 1992, not long after he returned, he died. Feng Jun had thought about his father night and day while he was working abroad, feeling totally alone. When his father finally came home, he fell ill and never recovered. Feng Jun didn't have a moment's hesitation in walking out on the Beijing Construction Engineering Company.

When he walked out, he only had Rmb26 in his pocket. He made his way straight to Zhongguancun where he decided to be an independent entrepreneur and work his way up from the very bottom of the pile. Zhongguancun didn't have too good a reputation in 1992 and was a long way from being 'China's Silicon Valley'; 'Cheat Street' was the more familiar sobriquet. Rejecting a steady job in a state enterprise, Feng Jun hid himself in the completely opposite world of the chaos of 'Cheat Street'. His thinking was this: of all its uncommon and extraordinary characteristics, mankind has the ability to dream, otherwise life would be full of tedium and despair. If those at the bottom of the ladder did not have these courageous, daring and determined dreams, how could society have its mysterious driving force? Where would the next Feng Jun come from? That's right! Even when everything else is obscure, that mystery persists and what we can see through it are what we call hopes and dreams. Although there were a few companies in Zhongguancun at that time which had already made a name for themselves, like those four giants of the early days, and the more recent arrivals such as Lenovo, most of the shops on the street were peddling pirate DVDs and software and dealing in smuggled computer parts and other goods; it was like a giant bazaar. Many of the people who had chosen to work there had not done so to develop Zhongguancun's IT industry or to challenge their own ambitions, but because this apparently high-end industry offered many low-end opportunities to scrape a living.

Once you arrived in Zhongguancun, you had to find somewhere to set yourself up, but Feng Jun couldn't afford a shop or even a stall. He set himself up with a table in someone else's 6 sqm stall, and paid half of the rent although he was only occupying a third of the space. The man he was renting from was one of his classmates, and his attitude was that, half the rent or not, just letting Feng bring in a table was pretty good going, and not something he would ever get from a stranger. It wasn't easy to find any space to rent in the Four Seas Market or the Yibin Building, even if you had the money. Once he had got his spot, when Feng Jun began to select his merchandise and buy it in, he knew that he was never going to make any money sitting there and waiting for passing trade. Although it was his first venture into the marketplace, he was very ambitious, and he targeted the stalls and shop fronts as his clients. He wanted to supply them with goods and establish his own client base there. The vast majority of the shops and stalls were dealing in computer accessories. The profit on a standard keyboard or computer case was Rmb15-30, but because computer cases were heavy and cumbersome, a lot of the shops didn't want to handle them. This gave Feng Jun an opening. He knew that if he was to break into the market, it had to be with something the others didn't want to deal in, whereas he wasn't fussy.

He began to take goods round to his customers, perched on his bicycle, one hand clutching a computer case, the other grasping the handlebars. With keyboards strapped to the back of the bike, he would weave unsteadily between the pedestrians. If he accidentally ran into a car, as he fell off the bike, he would risk his life by using his own body to protect the computer case. If he happened to run into a pedestrian, he would apologise for all he was worth, and if the collision hadn't been too heavy, the other party, as often as not, would take in how heavily laden he was, curse him mildly, then let the matter drop and move on. Wind, rain, searing heat, freezing cold, ice or snow, nothing stopped Feng Jun shuttling to and fro between his clients in the Yibin Building and the Four Seas Market. He had bought his bike, every bit of which made a noise except the bell, from a migrant worker, and he knew as soon as he saw it that it was stolen. When his business had picked up and he didn't need to ride a bike anymore, he didn't sell it, but left it on the side of the road as a way of returning it to its rightful owner. Where other people worked to a profit margin of Rmb10-20 on each computer case or keyboard, Feng Jun took only Rmb5 and he always had the latest model so, slowly, the shopkeepers all began to give him their approval. Their cry of "Five Yuan Feng's here again" always sounded a little disparaging to begin with, but as more and more of them discovered that he was their most reliable supplier, they stopped looking down on him.

Feng Jun switched to using a flat-bed trike to shift his stock: not a new one, of course, a second-hand one. This time he didn't buy it off a migrant worker who wasn't its rightful owner, but from a proper second-hand dealer so he could use it with a clear conscience. Although he could carry more stuff on a trike, it was still a nuisance, as although he could take four cases and keyboards at a time into the electricals market and the Four Seas market, when he got to the Yibin Building, he had to park the trike on the ground floor and carry his stuff upstairs. He only had one pair of hands, so he could only carry two items at a time and had to leave the others on the trike. What was going to happen if he had no one to watch them? Opportunist thieves would have them away, wouldn't they! This caused Feng Jun a lot of worry, because he wasn't happy paying someone who just happened to be there to guard them. How would he know who to trust? Wouldn't they just run off with them? It was all very risky, and he reckoned it was going to cost him more money than he wanted to get someone he could trust. So he didn't hire anyone, and decided to play it by ear.

He unloaded his goods and locked up the trike. Then he took two boxes as far as he could whilst keeping in sight of the trike and went back for the other two. When he had them all together again, he repeated the process. In this rather primitive manner, he shifted everything from the ground floor to the first floor, from the first floor to the second floor and then took his keyboards and computer cases one by one round to his customers in their shops.

What did this method of doing things actually entail?

One man going to and fro, sweat pouring from his head so he was drenched with it from head to toe.

"Only humans can shift things like that…"

There, in the autumn of the year 2000, as Feng Jun stopped his car watching the Yibin Building collapse in a cloud of smoke and dust, he could see an image of himself back then. He didn't drive past, but turned a corner. Even round the corner his head was still filled with the sight of the dust cloud and in that dust cloud he could see himself climbing those stairs.

So heavily laden! And that was eight years ago! It had all gone so quickly!

Zhongguancun was moving so quickly: too quickly. And he was moving too quickly as well!

Should he stop? But that train of thought was abruptly ended and disappeared without trace in the course of some negotiations in the office building he was visiting. Even the Yibin Building was forgotten, just like that, and he was soon quite used to the sight of a Zhongguancun without it.

DIARY NOTE 11: THE SPIRIT OF THE LOWEST RUNG

Wang Hongde from the early period of the history of Zhongguancun, and Feng Jun from its middle period, both had a particular kind of energy: 'Five Ways Wang' and 'Five Yuan Feng' were equally significant. The two of them were from a different dimension and of a different mettle. People today find it hard to believe that during the planned economy age, everything was planned out for people; their talents were under the ownership and control of their work unit, and they had no autonomy of movement. If you wanted to change work unit, your original work unit had first to agree and then it was a matter for discussion between the two work units in what was called a 'negotiation of transfer'. Nowadays it is different, and the difference began with Wang Hongde: that is the significance of Wang Hongde and the four original Zhongguancun giants. Feng Jun was a beneficiary of this, totally free in his actions and his choices, a man swimming alone in the great ocean. Within his own existence, he created his own mantra for survival, "I'll only charge you five yuan". Don't underestimate those words; although, on the face of it, they are much simpler than the 'five ways of leaving', they are a holy scripture for business, and actually also embody the basic standards of humanity: if you take honesty and trust as your creed you have the fundamentals of an ethical existence. You have to make money in business, but I can assure you that, no matter how much you make, in the end, the line between buying and selling becomes blurred. In no time at all, you reach the mutual honouring of contractual obligations that is common to the fundamentals of both business and human existence. Of course, this was not something Feng Jun invented; traditional Chinese shoestring businesses have always been like this, taking honesty and trust as their creed, and carrying that into life in general. Feng Jun's creed was a continuation of that tradition, and in the end, it led him irresistibly to success. The corollary of this creed of honesty and trust is the need for endurance and spirit, and it inevitably gives birth to the kind of spirit that drives a man up and down staircases, lugging his wares step by step.

Feng Jun was a top graduate from Tsinghua University, but the majority of the people he was doing business with were peasant farmers from Anhui and Henan. The CPU businesses prevalent in Zhongguancun at that time were predominantly, at least 60%, locals from Fengjing township in Huoqiu County, Anhui. They all mucked in together and it was no easy task to gain their acceptance and approval but, university graduate through and through as he was, Feng Jun transformed himself into one of them. When he was breaking into the world of the Four Seas Market, he addressed them all respectfully as "grandfather", regardless of their age, ducked his head and bowed, smiled ingratiatingly and spoke respectfully. You can detect a hint of mockery in Feng Jun's nickname, 'Five Yuan Feng'. But never forget, he was a university graduate: he had entered the market at the lowest level, and that was his status; in fact, if anything, he was at a basement level, below the lowest level. The fact that he only brought his low-status clients the very top-quality goods was a mark of his wisdom, logic and general benevolence – benevolence being the highest form of intelligence.

All the keyboards and computer cases that Feng Jun was selling were *Little Sun* brand, and after two years of hard work, his honesty and his "only charge five yuan" mantra had won over a lot of people. The sales of *Little Sun* keyboards alone had hit 30,000 units a month, which constituted 70% of the market share in North China. After this, he became the first person to unify the brand names for colour display units, computer cases and keyboards, in this case under the name *Little*

Sun, which he later changed to *Aigo*. The name *Aigo* is now known all over the world. When the Chinese Shenzhou 7 spacecraft took off successfully, on 25 September 2008, in the cabin of the craft, the equipment that recorded and stored most of the data and communications was supplied by Feng Jun's flagship *Aigo* company. Feng Jun has not just spread the spirit of 'Five Yuan Feng' across the globe, he has sent it up into space too.

[PART 5]
Feng Kang's Plan (3)
冯康构图(三)

Feng Kang's Disciple, Ya-Xiang Yuan

"My name is Ya-xiang Yuan: the 'Ya' is because I'm the second oldest child and the 'xiang' because I come from Hunan. I am from a farming family, and in my heart I will always feel that I am a farmer. I went to school aged five, and when I was 11, I took a year out of school to look after our cattle. After I graduated from high school at 15, I went back to my village to farm. I really wanted to be a poet, but sadly I didn't have the gift. At 18, I went up to Xiangtan University, and four years later I was accepted as a graduate student at the Chinese Academy of Sciences' Computer Centre; in October 1982, I did my PhD in the Mathematics and Physics Department of Cambridge University, supervised by Professor M.J.D. Powell. In 1988, I came back to China to work in the Academy's Computer Centre. My field of research was non-linear optimisation, and it was hard work. I loved playing contract bridge, and I still play it occasionally now. I am not a good manager, and I didn't want to be one. But fate likes to play tricks, and I did end up running a research institute. Now I enjoy my freedom from official duties; I supervise students, think about mathematics, write articles and travel the world. What a pleasure it is..."

That is how Ya-xiang Yuan introduces himself. His entry on Baidu is much more solemn and formal: "Ya-xiang Yuan, research fellow of the Chinese Academy of Mathematics and Systems Research, vice president of the Academy, Fellow of the Chinese Academy of Sciences, Fellow of the World Academy of Sciences, Associate Fellow of the Brazilian Academy of Sciences, SIAM Fellow (American Society for Industrial and Applied Mathematics), AMS Fellow (American Mathematics Society). Currently director general of the Chinese Mathematics Society, vice chairman of the International Federation of Operational Research Societies and Chairman of the Association of Asia-Pacific Operational Research Societies. He has made outstanding contributions as a leader in the fields of non-linear optimisation calculation methods, the trust region methods, the conjugate gradient method and others; the results of his work in the field of non-linear programming have been internationally recognised as 'Yuan's Lemma'."

Ya-xiang Yuan's self-introduction is perhaps a little breezy and self-deprecating, and you need to know that he wrote it on the occasion of his being made a fellow of the Chinese Academy of Sciences. Some people compare him with Feng Kang, but in truth, that is like comparing Gu Long[1] to Jin Yong. Ya-xiang Yuan reminds people of Ximen Chuixue[2], but

1. FENG KANG'S PLAN (3)

Feng Kang is the great knight errant hero and a generational hero. Feng Kang was born for mathematics and from birth all he was concerned with were the mysteries of mathematics; Ya-xiang Yuan was both other-worldly yet at the same time remained within the world of ordinary mortals. On the face of it, this was the difference between them, but there were some similarities. Although the temperaments of master and disciple were far apart, you couldn't say one was out of sight of the other, and with both of them, their closest associates couldn't catch even a glimpse of their innermost thoughts. There was a big age difference between them, they were simply of two different generations, but those generations allowed the two of them to travel them together.

In the 1960s, when Ya-xiang Yuan was still a boy herding cattle, Feng Kang was already one of those mysterious back-room heroes working on the 'Two Bombs One Satellite' project who had, at the same time, created the finite element method and was one of the pre-eminent mathematicians in the world. Simultaneously, one was performing unrivalled feats of martial skill and the other was herding cattle but, distant as they were, the passage of time was bringing them closer together. It was time that was ordering events so that, when the young farmer went up to Xiangtan University at 18 and graduated at 21, there was Feng Kang standing close at hand to this elegant and handsome youth.

Ya-xiang Yuan had originally wanted to stay on at his university in a teaching post; this was something that, normally speaking, would have remained just a dream for a young cowherd from a farming village but, once having broken into the world of mathematics, Yuan's eyes were fixed on the stars and he was determined to broaden his horizons. He prepared to enter the exams for a place as a graduate research student. There were two schools of thought in the university about this young phenomenon. The administrative authorities had an exalted opinion of Xiangtan University and felt that letting Yuan stay on would be watering down its talent pool; the mathematics department, on the other hand, felt that they were lacking just such a talent as his. In the end, the two sides compromised: Ya-xiang Yuan would be allowed to enter himself for a place as a graduate research student, but only under China's most exacting supervisor, otherwise it would not be permitted. That supervisor was Feng Kang, at the Chinese Academy of Sciences.

The mathematics department's rather niggardly thinking was this: Feng Kang is the country's number-one mathematician, and the hardest of taskmasters as a supervisor. You, Ya-xiang Yuan, may be the best in Hunan, but how will you fare in comparison to the whole country? How can Xiangtan University compete with Peking and Tsinghua universities? In fact, you wouldn't even pass muster at Hunan University, let alone Peking or Tsinghua so, when you don't make the grade, you'll be bound to come back here, won't you? It came as a complete surprise to everyone when Ya-xiang Yuan came out top of the academy examination and came face to face with Feng Kang.

For Ya-xiang Yuan, arriving at the Chinese Academy of Sciences, the highest seat of scientific learning in the land, was like Xuanzang arriving at the Leiyin Temple[3]. When he met with Feng Kang, as master and disciple, it was the crossing point of two generations, the old and the young, with each appreciative of the other's talents. As far as Ya-xiang Yuan was concerned, Feng Kang had already taken his place in the heavens, but those heavens were not the ones he had anticipated: his master's heavens were even greater. Feng Kang told him, "You shouldn't be studying with me, Ya-xiang; you should leave the country and go and study at Cambridge!"

Ya-xiang Yuan was astonished. When he had filled in the application form for the research student examination, there had been a question that asked, "Do you want to study abroad?" He had answered in the negative.

"Why don't you want to go abroad?" Feng Kang asked.

"Do you think I should go?" asked Yuan. Stunned as he was, the question was quite clear.

"Of course you should!" Feng Kang replied. "Our country has been shut down for a long time; we need people to go abroad to learn and get used to their ways. But if you do go abroad, Ya-xiang, don't research the finite element method. If you want to do that, stay in China."

In 1982, to be speaking like that with such certainty was astounding and extraordinarily prescient about what was going on in the world. Feng Kang could see what China needed, but at the same time he did not make the mistake of underestimating it. What he was telling Ya-xiang Yuan was that if he wanted to study Feng's own line of research, then there was no point going abroad, as Feng himself was already the leading expert. How many other scientists in China at the time would have dared say the same thing? At the same time, what kind of ambition did this demonstrate? Releasing his graduate student and sending him abroad: who else but a great master would do that? Now, 30 years later, the memories still come flooding back, and Ya-xiang Yuan is still incredibly grateful to Feng Kang, deeply aware of what remarkable vision he showed.

The academy had a great deal of autonomy at that time. It had allocated itself the money in 1982 to select 30 graduate students and it was preparing to send them abroad to pursue a variety of research subjects. This group of 30 students formed a cohort called the 'Foreign Study Preparatory Cohort' and they had been making their preparations for almost 10 months. The most important of these preparations was foreign-language practice and Ya-xiang Yuan was top of the class at this.

Although he didn't follow his teacher in the study of the finite element method, Ya-xiang Yuan still considered that Feng Kang was his revered master. There was one occasion during his preparations when Professor M.J.D. Powell, a Cambridge University mathematics professor, came to China at the invitation of Hua Luogeng and Feng Kang. When Feng Kang went to visit him, he took Ya-xiang Yuan along to meet him, to lay the groundwork for when Yuan packed his books to go to study in Cambridge. In fact, 10 months later, Professor Powell became Ya-xiang Yuan's supervisor. Experts always find other experts and great masters always find other great masters: Feng Kang invited the greatest international expert and introduced him to his top student. How could such an exalted combination not produce great talent?

Feng Kang took his 'high-flying bird' view of the international scene in choosing Ya-xiang Yuan's direction of study. "Currently in China we are comparatively weak on problems concerned with the question of 'optimisation', but the field has great promise for the future; so that is the direction you are going to take." Looking back at it now, Feng Kang did most certainly have the strategic overview of a 'high-flying bird', and what he called 'optimisation' is now the core question that needs to be solved in the burning topic of today, 'big data'. He foresaw this 30 years ago. A country is fortunate indeed to have a man like that.

Big data is all about processing all the available data together and using "optimisation" to achieve the best result for humankind. Since the start of the 21st century, more particularly since the beginning of the year 2012, the term big data is one that has been cropping up with increasing frequency, and people use it to describe and define the huge volume of data generated by the information explosion of the current era. As people mine deeper and deeper, their excavational ability on every front highlights deficiencies and potentials that were not known about before. In industry, economics and other leading fields, strategic and policy decisions will increasingly be made on the basis of the analysis of big data. This will bring about a revolution and the mighty resource that is big data will begin the quantisation process in every field. It is beyond doubt that the worlds of academia, industry, politics, and all the others will begin to make this journey.

Ya-xiang Yuan says, "Optimisation is a branch of mathematics that must be utilised and the most important thing to research is the question of where to pre-set the restrictions under which (the quantities of) certain elements should be sought so that a given target (or targets) is/are met in an optimal manner." This way of establishing a starting position is also called 'mathematical programming', exemplified by linear programming. Many practical and theoretical problems can be addressed with this kind of general framework. In aircraft design, for example, the shape of the wing is a question of optimisation, with no need for head-scratching and wracking of brains. Why do today's aeroplanes all look the way they do? It is because the wings have been 'optimised' by scientists. Normally, when you drive along the road in a car, you feel the bumps and jolts, but when you are in a plane in the sky, you don't feel anything, almost as if you weren't moving. Why is this? It is because science is ceaselessly progressing constant optimisation. Along with the development of high-speed computers, the arrival of the age of big data and the methods of computational optimisation, the problems thrown up by the ever-increasing scale of optimisation have become even more important, and have also been the subject of the highest degree of scientific prescience.

There was an age difference of 40 years between Ya-xiang Yuan and Feng Gang. "It was rather like the age gap in a family between grandfather and grandson," Ya-xiang Yuan says, recalling how things were at the time. "Logically speaking, there should have been much more contact between the academicians Lin Qun and Zhong Ci with Master Feng Kang. But he was of a different generation, and I am afraid that traditionally in China, the grandson is in awe of his grandfather. Lin Qun and Zhong Ci were very much in awe of Feng Kang, but I was not. We bridged the generations and talked about everything with mutual care and respect. He didn't hold back over anything."

Certainly, this is a particularly Chinese set of circumstances, or rather, an aspect of Chinese culture that is particularly rich in human warmth. Human nature expresses itself differently in different people, and often it can be not particularly mutually accommodating. However, it is always mutually inclusive. This is what makes Chinese culture exceptional. (Of course, we have to recognise that sometimes human nature inhibits both itself and rationality, and sometimes it can change. One can never arrogantly take it for granted, but always critically re-examine and make accommodations to allow it to reach its greatest heights.)

When Ya-xiang Yuan arrived at Cambridge, he was supervised by Professor Powell, but he kept in close communication by letter with Feng

Kang, reporting on his own academic progress and on the directions of research at Cambridge University. He lived up to his master's expectations and received his PhD after three years; he continued to work at the university for a further three years. Whether to stay on and what to study when he did, were both decisions he discussed by letter with Feng Kang. Feng encouraged him to continue his work at Cambridge so that he could gain a deeper understanding of the mathematical research that was being carried out in England and bring the most cutting-edge methods back to China, whilst at the same time putting into practice what he himself had learned.

Feng Kang made a trip to England while Ya-xiang Yuan was still at Cambridge, and he took the opportunity to visit his disciple. Yuan took his master on a tour of Trinity College and St John's College. Cambridge itself is a small English town with a population of about 300,000, through which runs the River Cam. The scenery on the banks of the Cam is very fine, green and luxuriant, and the river is spanned by several elegantly designed and beautifully constructed bridges. The university doesn't have a campus as such, or any boundary walls. The great majority of its colleges, institutes, libraries and laboratories are situated in the town along the banks of the Cam. The aura of the history of human affairs blending harmoniously with nature was particularly striking and made both master and disciple sigh with delight and wonder. Feng Kang talked about learning English as a child; in 1938, the school library at Suzhou Middle School was bombed by the Japanese. The air was filled with flying books; some were burned and some ripped apart but among the ashes, he found a tattered copy of an English book called *Anthology of the World's Best Novellas*. In the midst of that scene of desolation, he began reading avidly...

As they were strolling around Cambridge, Feng Kang talked about the plans to build the State Key Laboratories and how he was making preparations for the task. The State Key Laboratories were a major component of the national movement for scientific and technological innovation; they represented the highest level of state organisation of fundamental and practical research, the assembly and nurturing of outstanding technological and scientific talent, and the highest level of academic exchange to constitute a major base for the deployment of advanced scientific resources. The most important task of the laboratories was to conduct innovative research focused on the front line of academic and scientific investigation, and on the national economy; and on the vital areas of the current state and future direction of social development and national security. They were to employ cutting-edge exploratory research to bring together systematically innovative results with international resonance; with regard to the major scientific and technological problems currently facing national and social development, they were to develop new approaches and methods, and demonstrate innovations in fundamental principles by making breakthroughs in crucial technologies or by consolidating existing ones. Through the collection of fundamental scientific data, they were to supply and support relevant areas of scientific research and, at a national level, they were to furnish an overarching strategy based on science. Laboratories and research establishments were to coordinate their efforts to form a comprehensive and coherent set of facilities using the most advanced apparatus and equipment under integrated management for efficient operation and mutual benefit.

Physics figured largely in the make-up of the State Key Laboratories, as did chemistry, but people did not believe mathematics needed 'laboratories', so it was omitted. This was short-sighted almost to the point of blindness. Feng Kang submitted an application to the government, and were it not for his strategic foresight and prestige, it is hard to imagine that a State Key Laboratory for mathematics and related subjects would ever have been established. Looked at this way, Feng Kang can be seen as the founder of what is now the internationally influential Key State Laboratory for Mathematics. In 1988, when Ya-xiang Yuan returned to China, he went to work on the preparations for the Key State Laboratory for Computing and Mathematics, and became one of Feng Kang's most important assistants working on constructing the laboratory; he was responsible for drafting many of the relevant documents. The bill of materials and equipment alone for the laboratory came to several million US dollars, which was an astronomical sum for the times.

In the late 1980s and 1990s, Feng Kang was in his 70s but still continuously at his studies in a constant search for knowledge and innovation. Ya-xiang Yuan was a frequent visitor. His most abiding image is of Feng Kang going to the library with his satchel slung over his shoulder. It was an old-style canvas satchel, not army issue, but the dark-blue kind that folk take to go vegetable shopping, just an ordinary canvas bag, in fact. Feng Kang was still unmarried in 1982 and lived alone, so the library was his most frequent destination. He would make his solitary way, satchel over his shoulder...

Feng Kang's Disciples: Yu Dehao

Yu Dehao was Feng Kang's first doctoral student. He went up to the Chinese University of Science and Technology in 1962, where he was taught by Guan Zhaozhi and Yan Jici. In 1978 he passed the examinations for the Chinese Academy of Sciences Computer Centre where he was supervised by Feng Kang, first for his master's degree and then for his doctorate.

From when he first got to know Feng Kang through his written teaching materials at the University of Science and Technology to when he decided to become his research student, almost 20 years passed as if in a flash for Yu Dehao, a period which encompassed the Cultural Revolution. All this time, Feng Kang remained a towering presence in his heart, tall and imposing as a mountain, but with an air of mystery. During that time, Feng Kang moved from the Academy's Computing Institute to be director of its Computer Centre. From the Mathematics Institute in the North Building, Yu Dehao made his way to the Computer Centre in the East Building of Zhongguancun to register his name. He was very unsure of himself, because Feng Kang was not like Guan Zhaozhi. Guan Zhaozhi had taught him in person, but Yu Dehao did not dare just go up and knock on Feng Kang's door. Still wondering what to do, he went back to the factory where he worked in Miyun and wrote Feng Kang a letter, introducing himself and his circumstances. He was surprised by the speed with which Feng Kang replied. He still remembers that it was a very small envelope, and an old one at that, that had been turned inside out to be re-used. He struggled to imagine a great professor of mathematics opening up an old envelope, gluing it back together, writing the address and the name on it and then sticking the envelope down. At the time, re-using envelopes like that was an everyday thing to do but somehow Yu Dehao had never thought of Feng Kang doing it. The letter itself was very short, too, no more than a memo on Computer Centre headed paper. In it, Feng Kang told Yu Dehao, "We only accept the top candidates from the examination; this cannot be changed."

The note conveyed two messages: one was that there was no point asking Guan Zhaozhi for help, and the other was that nobody and no circumstances could influence selection and you had to rely solely on your own ability. It was the best way and Yu Dehao was more than happy with it. In the first exam, and in the second stage, although he was keyed-up he also remained calm and everything went swimmingly. He didn't see Feng Kang at the first exam, but he did at the follow-up: he was sitting in the central position of the board of senior examiners, right in front of Yu Dehao. When the results of the second exam were finally posted, Yu Dehao had placed first. When he received the notification of acceptance, his heart lurched: after more than 10 years that had slipped away from him, he was about to succeed.

The most important thing when studying under Feng Kang was the seminar schedule. There was a seminar class every week and when Feng Kang gave lectures in other academic institutions, his students were allowed to attend. Additionally, he took his master's students and doctoral students to all the other meetings he attended, including ones out of Beijing in places such as Xiamen, Guilin and elsewhere, all over the country. He also often received fellow academics from overseas, either just on visits or on exchange programmes, and he always arranged for his students to meet his foreign guests. This was an excellent preparation for them for any future research trips, exchanges or study visits abroad they might make.

In 1978, at the start of the reform and opening up, there was a comparative dearth of internal study materials and of scientific exchanges with foreign countries. But because of his position and his international reputation, Feng Kang had rather more opportunities than most for making foreign contacts, and he often made trips abroad or welcomed visits from foreign guests, both of which aspects naturally fostered closer and closer links. In the same year, it was Feng Kang who welcomed delegations of mathematicians from both the US and France. He was able to talk directly to them and amazed his visitors with his ability to talk for more than five minutes simultaneously in three different languages. Although he was physically quite small, his charm and personality were enormous, so he always left a deep impression on his foreign colleagues, something which also stood his own students in good stead. Because Chinese mathematics at that time had great masters such as Hua Luogeng and Feng Kang, although the country was closed down for many years, foreign visitors all felt that China was still up with the best of them. For instance, when the American delegation returned to the US and made their report to their government, they started by saying that, despite the Cultural Revolution, Chinese mathematics had been able to maintain itself at a very acceptable level. Yu Dehao particularly remembers that the delegation mentioned the finite element method, saying that China had successfully completed its formulation despite being isolated from the rest of the world. One member of the French delegation, an academician and a mathematician of high standing, became friends with Feng Kang after meeting him. He rated the finite element method very highly and greatly admired it. Quite apart from Feng Kang's academic excellence, his language ability and communication skills also proved to be of vital importance.

When Yu Dehao took up his research studies, Feng Kang gave him a huge stack of foreign-language documents, enough for several dozen books, and reference books. Other than English, there was also material in German, French and so on. Yu Dehao had studied Russian before, but there was very little in Russian, the majority being in English, German, French and Italian. Much of this was material Feng Kang had brought back from his travels abroad. His linguistic ability was such that he could understand what the material was about just by leafing through it, but for his student, it was not that easy. Yu Dehao could get by with the English, but he needed constant reference to dictionaries to get through the French, German and Italian. During his time as a research student, he studied a year of English as a foreign language, plus a year of French and a year of German. He had no option, otherwise all those books would have been of no use to him. He benefitted greatly from all this and later on, when he had his own students, he prepared a lot of foreign-language material for them too, saying that if there were bits that they didn't understand, it wasn't important; they should just skip them and pull out what was useful. It was quite possible that what they didn't understand today, they would come to understand later, that what they couldn't see any use for today, would later prove useful, so at the very least they would know where to go looking. Being a research student is not like being an undergraduate, and there is no need to understand a book from cover to cover. Although this was advice Yu Dehao gave from his own experience, it all stemmed originally from Feng Kang.

Yu Dehao had studied applied mathematics at university, but he went on to study computational mathematics. Feng Kang told him he should straddle the two disciplines. If he were to drill down into them, he would find what are called the numerical solutions to differential equations. There are many different kinds of numerical solutions to differential equations. Feng Kang's special field was the finite element method, which he put in the same category as what was then called the boundary element method. Feng Kang combined the two to make the "finite element boundary element method" and this became Yu Dehao's principal direction of research. It was part mathematical theory and part computational. He could refer back to his applied mathematics for the theoretical element, but the computational element came from computational mathematics, and that was why Feng Kang told him to straddle both disciplines.

Yu Dehao knew that his master had done a lot of work on the finite element method, and as a student he could not hope to reach that level, so Feng Kang let him work with him on the boundary element aspect. When Yu Dehao started out, there was not a single academic paper on the boundary element method, until Feng Kang wrote the first one in 1986. It was a very short paper, but it provided the foundation for Yu Dehao to make the boundary element method the subject of his master's thesis. After the thesis was completed, it was delivered with Feng Kang's name also on it as a speech at the China-France Boundary Element Symposium. It was simultaneously published in the magazine *Computational Mathematics* which was an English-language periodical on the subject that Feng Kang had just set up.

At the China-France Boundary Element Symposium, Feng Kang was in the chair, but as a bilateral Sino-French event, it actually had two chairpersons. Feng Kang took Yu Dehao along to attend the first meeting of the symposium in Beijing. The chairman's address on that occasion was in fact Yu Dehao's thesis, carrying the names of both master and disciple. The outline was Feng Kang's work, but the main body of the actual calculations was Yu Dehao's with Feng Kang adding the finishing touches. Feng Kang's speech at the symposium, and the penultimate speech of the whole event, was the chairman's report, which lasted an hour. Since the paper carried both their names and it was Yu Dehao's master's thesis, Feng Kang's delivery of it was equivalent to his launching Yu Dehao onto the international stage, and the effect it had was enormous. Questions were invited after the paper had been delivered, and Feng Kang told Yu Dehao to answer several of them. As well as the various French professors who attended the symposium, there was also a professor from the US, and one each from Japan and Italy. An entry about the event was also included in the *Encyclopaedia of China*.

When Yu Dehao was studying for his doctorate in 1964, Feng Kang's direction of research turned to geometric algorithms for Hamiltonian systems, and all future work on the boundary element method was done by Yu Dehao. Once again, Feng Kang gave his student an excellent academic opportunity and space for his own research.

At the end of the 1970s and into the 1980s, Feng Kang's living accommodation was very small but later, as it got bigger, he was able to devote a room entirely to his books. Yu Dehao remembers that when Feng Kang was in his smaller place there were books scattered everywhere over the floor, and there were piles of them under his bed and beside his bed; even the bed itself was covered in books. He recalls that there was never anywhere to sit down and that he just had to stand up to talk to his master, or maybe they would shove aside some of the books and sit on the edge of the bed. It was as if the two of them were meeting in a library or, more accurately, deep in the bowels of a library's stacks. Feng Kang did not seem like a householder, more the manager of a library. Or perhaps you might even say that he himself was one of the books.

Feng Kang was very strict with his research students, and after Yu Dehao had finished as a student, there were old research personnel at the Computer Centre who greatly admired his guts and determination because, as the saying went, "It was very hard to graduate as one of Feng Kang's students". There was a mentally ill middle-aged man living in the communal dormitory in Zhongguancun's Building 87, who had failed to graduate as one of Feng Kang's students before the Cultural Revolution. This always caused Yu Dehao considerable unease, and he felt that his master had been particularly kind to him.

In 1985, when Yu Dehao obtained his doctoral degree, Feng Kang advised him to go abroad to broaden his international horizons. He personally typed out two letters on an English typewriter. One was to an American professor who was an internationally famous specialist in the boundary element method and who had attended the China-France Boundary Element Method Symposium. The other letter was to the German Humboldt Foundation, which is one of the world's most famous foundations that funds about 6,000 doctoral research places every year for students under 40 years of age and offers scholarships to foreign scientists with outstanding records to enable them to spend a significant length of time conducting scientific research in Germany. The selection committee is formed from a hundred famous German scientists from every discipline and, under the direction of the chairman of the German Research Federation, it is responsible for selecting the cream of the applicants without restrictions on nationality or field of study. At the beginning of the 1980s there were not many Chinese recipients, only a dozen or so every year from any discipline. At that time, state-sponsored scholars who were sent to Germany received a state allowance of 600 Deutschmarks per month. A few other German foundations offered 1,000 Deutschmarks, but the Humboldt Foundation offered 2,400. When Yu Dehao first went, it was still 2,400 but, not long after, it was increased to 2,700. All the other scholars in Germany, including overseas students, were very envious of the recipients of the Humboldt funding.

While Yu Dehao was working in Germany in 1987, Feng Kang arrived there on a visit at the invitation of the Humboldt Foundation to give six months of lectures. He had just got married that year, and he had originally wanted to bring his wife but, for some reason or other, she was unable to make the trip. The foundation had prepared an office for Feng Kang to allow him to pursue his specialist research. When Yu Dehao and his wife went to visit him, they invited him on a trip to Switzerland. The three of them went by boat, took hundreds of pictures, and visited Geneva, Lausanne and Berne. The most extraordinary thing was that, on a hillside in Berne, Feng Kang bumped into his older sister, Feng Hui, whom he had not seen for many years. When they were at the top and bottom of the hillside respectively, at a distance they couldn't see who the other was, but as they walked on, it was as though they were walking through time until they stopped close to each other, and there they were, younger brother and older sister! All manner of emotions welled up inside them: they were both old now and hadn't seen each other for many years and here they were, meeting by chance in a foreign country. It was like the conjunction of two planets.

Feng Kang had no idea his sister was in Europe, although she knew he was in Germany. She didn't know he was coming to Switzerland. Feng Hui was married to Ye Duzheng[4] who, that year, was president of the World Meteorological Association which was holding the World Meteorological Conference in Geneva. Feng Hui had gone to America to visit their son and was returning to China via Europe to meet up with her husband. She had originally gone to Geneva but, once in Switzerland, had decided to make the most of it and make a tour of some other cities. It was pure chance that brother and sister arrived in Berne at the same time, like a chance meeting arranged by fate, with the two of them coming from different directions and bumping into each other. They stayed together on the hillside for 20 minutes or so, then went their separate ways. Yu Dehao took their photograph for them. Afterwards, Feng Kang told everyone he met about this "statistically highly improbable event". He was thrilled by it and asked Yu Dehao not just for a print of the photograph, but for the negative too.

Feng Kang's Disciples: Tang Yifa

Among the disciples of Feng Kang, Tang Yifa is the least well known. Although he is a noted researcher, he is not an academician, nor has he ever been director or deputy director of any institution. His entry on Baidu is very simple, "He graduated from Fudan University in 1987. He was

1. FENG KANG'S PLAN (3)

supervised by the Academician Feng Kang, taking both a master's degree followed by a PhD. Area of research: geometric algorithms for mechanical systems. Major academic achievements: significant influence in the areas of 'Multi-step algorithm existence', 'The form and capabilities of symplectic algorithms and their uses' and 'Symplectic algorithms for non-linear Schrödinger equations and time-dependent Maxwell equations'." The sub-entries are minimal both in number and content, but academically-speaking of great importance.

Tang Yifa loved mathematics from when he was little, and by the time he was at middle school he was already determined to be a mathematician. He went up to university in the mathematics department of Fudan University. He met Feng Kang while he was still a student as, in the winter of 1985, Feng Kang came to Fudan to give a lecture on 'Geometric algorithms for Hamiltonian systems'. At the end of the lecture, two of the professors from Fudan, Jiang Erxiong and Bai Zhaojun, each asked questions. Both the questions and their answers were so erudite that most of the audience only half understood them. Professor Jiang summarised Feng Kang's lecture by saying that he felt it "came from a lofty viewpoint which gave everyone a completely new understanding". Tang Yifa noticed that while he was lecturing, Feng Kang was constantly feeling in his pocket. Bai Zhaojun asked him if he wanted a cigarette, and he replied that he did.

In 1987, Tang Yifa graduated from the mathematics department of Fudan University and decided to enter his name for the examinations for a graduate research place at the Chinese Academy of Sciences Computer Centre. Feng Kang had already retired from his leadership roles and was no longer director of the Computer Centre. In April 1987, he returned to Fudan University to give another lecture, at which time the list of successful graduate examinees had already been published. Tang Yifa learned that he had been accepted by the Computer Centre but had not yet been assigned a supervisor. His cohort leader encouraged him to go and see Feng Kang. Although Tang Yifa had come top of the examinations, he was still hesitant to do this. His cohort leader told him forcefully that he must go, "Even if he doesn't accept you, he might still choose a supervisor for you, and that would still be an excellent outcome."

The weather was unusually fine that afternoon and Tang Yifa was in the Fudan University guest house, plucking up the courage to go and see the great 67-year-old master mathematician. To his surprise, however, he found that his nervousness was completely unnecessary. Of all the research Feng Kang had conducted, Tang Yifa started off by asking about the finite element method. Feng Kang just laughed and said that although he had put the finite element method on his recruitment notice for research students, he had, in fact, already changed the direction of his research to symplectic geometric algorithms for Hamiltonian systems, and that this academic year, he might be on the lookout for a couple of master's students in that field. Tang Yifa said that he really wanted to study under Feng Kang and asked whether that would be possible. Feng Kang replied simply that it would and added, "You Fudan students are very strong in mathematics, particularly in computational mathematics. Your inner qualities are excellent too, so you are always very welcome as research students at the Computer Centre." He went on to ask, "Do you want to follow me in this new direction? What is your background knowledge of physics and mechanics like? Do you have a basic understanding of fluid mechanics and elasticity?"

Tang Yifa had only done basic physics in his first and second years at university, and had just finished a little theoretical mechanics, but Feng Kang didn't give up on him or lose interest. "There is a book I recommend to you. It is Arnold's *Mathematical Methods of Classical Mechanics*. Actually, it is part of our post-graduate teaching materials and is an excellent book. You should read it carefully." The whole meeting only took 20 minutes and, although Tang Yifa felt there was a lot that he had to learn and it wouldn't be easy, Feng Kang's inspirational words had given him a lot of encouragement. He also noticed, moreover, that at no stage of the conversation had Feng Kang mentioned where he had come in the examination. As for the great mathematician Arnold's book, with the current restrictions in place, he hadn't yet been able to get hold of it.

Several months later, Tang Yifa arrived in Beijing to officially begin his studies as Feng Kang's research student. Feng Kang gave him a copy of *Mathematical Methods of Classical Mechanics*, which he had signed on the fly leaf. Now, almost 30 years later, Tang Yifa's memory of this book is still very vivid. He also recalls how attentively he read the whole volume and completed almost all the exercises. The book has been handled so much it is a little tatty, especially the dust jacket, and there are lots of places where tears have been repaired with paper and gum.

Feng Kang particularly admired Arnold. Valdimir Arnold was recognised as one of the greatest mathematicians of the 20th century and had been vice-chairman of the International Mathematical Union. Throughout the 1960s, Arnold concentrated his research on Hamiltonian mechanical systems and was one of the authors of the KAM theorem. The KAM theorem gives deep insight into mechanical systems and is one of the most challenging of theorems. Its background lies in that most difficult of ancient problems, the stability of the solar system. During those same years, he also discovered a hugely important phenomenon, which is now known as 'Arnold diffusion'. Essentially, between stable islands and a constant torus there may exist a number of ghost-like trajectories that can drift very slowly in a quasi-random manner; however, the mechanism of Arnold diffusion still remains unclear. Arnold's work revolved around drawing up an archetype for complex systems. There will always be uncertainty in the intertwined coexistence of regular and irregular motion, regardless of magnitude or level, and the necessary information to master that uncertainty is hidden in deep and immeasurable darkness. It was also around the same period that Arnold produced a particularly elegant illustration of the equation of motion for the perfect incompressible fluid. He visualised this equation as a geodesic equation for the motion on a Lie group of volume-preserving diffeomorphisms, and clearly demonstrated the geometric origin of the internal instability of fluid motion. Arnold had a particularly interesting point of view which was that mathematics is a branch of physics, and that the essence of physics is geometry. His famous *Mathematical Methods of Classical Mechanics* uses the framework of geometry to give classical mechanics a whole new form. It is known as the 'sacred text of geometric mechanics'.

Throughout 1988, Feng Kang and Arnold met and exchanged ideas in both the Soviet Union and France. Tang Yifa still remembers Master Feng returning from Europe early in the summer of 1988 when he, Tang Yifa, had just finished his foundation studies in his first year at the Chinese Academy of Sciences graduate school and was returning to the institute. He met Feng Kang who had brought back the text of Arnold's lecture on 'Symplectic Geometry' (it was not a book, just a lecture script). Feng Kang immediately photocopied it and handed copies out to his students. Feng was 17 years older than Arnold but, although this was a significant age difference, the two men had quite a lot in common. Back in the 1950s, Feng Kang had spent two years studying at the Steklov Institute in Moscow (the equivalent of the Chinese Academy of Sciences Mathematics Institute), where his supervisor had been Lev Semyonovich Pontryagin, an amazing blind mathematician, who was also vice chairman of the International Mathematical Union. Later on, Vladimir Arnold also went to study at the Steklov Institute, where he was supervised by Andrey Kolmogorov. Kolmogorov was of a similar age to Pontryagin, and also met Arnold.

Tang Yifa was with Feng Kang for six years and a number of events have stayed vivid in his memory. Because he often helped with Feng Kang's mail and such like, he often encountered him at meal times. Feng lived very simply and the meal his housekeeper most often made for him was eggs and bok choy with a small bowl of rice, and that was all. Previously, he had had no real interest in money, but there was one occasion when he did ask, unexpectedly, "Have my wages been paid yet this month, Xiao Tang?" This was after he got married.

"When we were together," Tang Yifa said, "some very simple things made one aware of his profound principles of living. There was a Spanish professor called Vasquez from Madrid University who visited us, and Master Feng invited him to a meal at a little restaurant near the Beihai. As well as Master Feng and Professor Vasquez, there were also Qin Mengzhao, a teacher from our work group, and myself." At that time, Tang Yifa was a young student and it was the first time he had eaten with his master, and it was also the first time he had had a meal with a foreign guest. When the waiter at the restaurant asked him what he wanted, his mind went blank and he just said, "I'll have the same as he's having."

Feng Kang reproved him solemnly, "Ha! Order what you want, don't just follow someone else!" Given Professor Vasquez's presence, this was serious stuff, and Tang Yifa never forgot those words. Interestingly, Tang Yifa later made a reciprocal visit to Madrid University and worked with Professor Vasquez.

Tang Yifa spent the winter of 1988 studying in great detail Arnold's complete proof of the KAM theorem on the stability of integrable Hamiltonian systems and then, in his master's thesis, he applied Liouville's theorem on integrable Hamiltonian systems to the geodesic flow on the surface of a three-axis ellipsoid. In the numerical simulations he advanced for the circumstances of periodic flow, he discovered that the similarities were of second-order accuracy and did not correspond to the single-step midpoint format (Feng Kang discovered in 1984 that it was a symplectic format in relation to Hamiltonian systems) or the two-step leapfrog format. When he reported his findings to Feng Kang and Qin Mengzhao, they were both very surprised, but Feng Kang quickly accepted these results and even said in one of the weekly seminars, "It now appears that we (meaning himself and Ge Zhong) were wrong in our original interpretation of the leapfrog format as a symplectic format." In the same seminar, Tang Yifa asked, "In that case, Master Feng, how do you think we should define the symplectic nature of the leapfrog format and even the linear multi-step format?"

This was undoubtedly a challenge to the teacher, but great teachers have no place for yes-men.

Even at the dinner table, Feng Kang was pointing out to Tang Yifa that challenge is an integral part of science itself, and science is a kind of spirit; without challenge there can be no spirit. Feng Kang spent his whole life challenging things.

In the seminar, Feng Kang wrote Tang Yifa's definition on the blackboard. "Using the step operator for your definition, look at the multi-step method as if it was the same as a step-by-step operator, and decide whether the multi-step method is symplectic or not and then whether the operator is a symplectic exchange or not."

With Feng Kang's encouragement and with a great spurt of energy, through repeated experimentation, Tang Yifa produced his final proof of the numerical value simulation for progression under the conditions of cyclical motion. "Under Feng Kang's new definition, not only was the leapfrog format not a symplectic format, nor were any linear multi-step formats either." This was a series of very daring questions and proofs. Thirty years later, Tang Yifa remembers that he used the time from sometime after five in the afternoon, through dinner and right up to one in the morning back in his dormitory to thoroughly settle this problem. The next morning, he got ready to make his report to his supervisor and when he asked when he should deliver it, Feng Kang told him to come to address the seminar at his home that afternoon. When he was making his report, he saw his master industriously taking notes. It was the first time he had seen Feng Kang do this in all of the six years he had been attending the seminars as a research student. It was also the only time. Tang Yifa's address to the seminar was certainly impressive and constituted a breakthrough. Afterwards, under Feng Kang's instruction, he completed the first task of his research programme. His results began to reach a wider audience; he completed the first draft of his related thesis *The Symplectic Nature of the Multi-Step Method* at the start of 1991 and, at the beginning of 1993, it was formally published in the American international periodical *Computers and Mathematics with Applications*. It attracted widespread attention in America and Europe alike, and people in many different forums of academic discussion began to talk about 'Feng Kang's Definition' and 'Tang Yifa's Theorem'.

The Symplectic Nature of the Multi-Step Method was the catalyst for Tang Yifa being given the opportunity to go to America to work at the Los Alamos National Laboratory. In 1991, someone took the as yet unpublished first draft to the University of Geneva in Switzerland and gave it to the famous numerical analyst, Gerhard Wanner, for consideration. Wanner's student, Ernst Hairer, gave the subject a lot of time and energy right through until 2008 when the results of his investigations were widely disseminated in the *Journal of Computational Mathematics*. At the same time, Tang Yifa's work received ongoing refinement through Hairer and Wanner's own 'B-Series Theory'.

Tang Yifa's success with symplectic algorithms was achieved entirely with Feng Kang's instruction and encouragement. "Master Feng took the lead and showed us the way. Looking back at it now, it is still a wonderful journey." He also has great admiration for another aspect of Feng Kang, "It wasn't just mathematics; the other thing that constantly amazed me and which I could never hope to emulate, was Feng Kang's facility with languages. He had not only mastered six languages but, when he spoke them, he was also inspirational, charismatic and at home with contemporary vocabulary. You could say there was a boldness about him, a boldness that won you over completely and irresistibly. In the late 1980s and early 1990s, email was not yet in general use and I remember his great friend, Jacques-Louis Lions (who was both president of the International Mathematical Union and president of the French Academy of Sciences), sent him a fax in French. I saw him with my own eyes reply also in French. He once told me that when he was young and a student at the National Central University (now Nanjing University), his passion for mathematics was so great that he would pick up foreign-language mathematical texts that interested him in the library and not be able to put them down. Sometimes, he got so engrossed in the books that he forgot they were public property, and he would scribble notes and calculations on them. He didn't just read books on mathematics either, but also the original foreign-language texts of works by Tolstoy, Shakespeare and others. His self-motivation, boldness and linguistic ability, along with the large quantity of well-known foreign literature that he read, were not isolated phenomena: Soviet mathematicians had a tradition of reading aloud masterpieces of literature, and Feng Kang continued that tradition.

DIARY NOTE 12: A BRONZE STATUE FOREVER UPRIGHT

> In 1980, the Chinese Academy of Sciences augmented its academic committee members (later called academicians) and Feng Kang, Feng Duan and their older sister's husband, Ye Duzheng, were all simultaneously admitted, an event that fired the imagination of the whole scientific world. Feng Duan was a physicist and, like his brother, an alumnus of Suzhou Middle School who had also gone on to study at the National Central University. Ye Duzheng was an important pioneer of

1. FENG KANG'S PLAN (3)

contemporary Chinese meteorology and an innovator in Chinese atmospheric physics. When the three of them were simultaneously admitted to the academy in 1980, the acclaim of the scientific world conveyed its astonishment: for one household to provide three academicians made it truly one of the aristocratic families of the academy.

In 1993, at the age of 73, Feng Kang was still probing the depths of science in his own individual manner, tireless and diligent as ever, investigating the unification of the finite element method with symplectic algorithms. In 1998, the American mathematician Jerrold E Marsden and his team established the 'Theory of a Multi- Symplectic Algorithm for Hamilton's Partial Differentiation Equation', and this new algorithm precisely coincided with Feng Kang's thinking on the unification of the finite element method with symplectic algorithms. Feng Kang's thinking enlightened later generations and his bronze statue stands in the Institute of Mathematics outside the doors of the nationally important Computational Mathematics Laboratory which he founded.

Standing in front of his statue, you feel he is looking out expectantly on Zhongguancun.

Looking out expectantly on the East, on the world and on humanity.

[PART 6]
Lenovo China (3)
联想中国(三)

Price Wars

IN MID-AUTUMN 1995, when Compaq announced a price-cut of 13-25%, IBM responded decisively within two weeks by cutting the prices of their range by 20%. Hewlett-Packard (HP) were a little slower off the mark and announced a new worldwide price structure on 1 November. As competitors in the same marketplace, Lenovo Computers felt the chill wind of being played at their own game. When it entered the market as a newcomer, Lenovo had price as their trump card; they held their costs down and their prices low, keeping their heads and fighting hard all the way, they overcame all difficulties to battle their way ahead of Compaq, HP and IBM. But now these highly-experienced major players had shown their hand, and backed the young upstart Lenovo into a corner. But this wasn't the first time such a thing had happened to Lenovo Computers, and backs-to-the-wall was a position they were quite accustomed to. Compaq and IBM and the others were used to being undisputed kings of the computer world, but over the last few years they had suddenly found themselves matched against a young upstart which was proving to be full of youthful energy and extremely tenacious. They couldn't kill it off cleanly or grind it down. In fact, not only did they fail to kill it off, it very quickly recovered from their attack, took the initiative and threw down a challenge of its own.

Not long after Compaq and IBM slashed their prices, at the beginning of 1996, Liu Chuanzhi, backed into a corner as he was, responded with his own seemingly suicidal price cuts: he reduced the prices on the whole line of Pentium computers under the Lenovo name. In particular, he put the entry level '75MHz' at Rmb9,999. This was the first time a Pentium computer had been priced at less than Rmb10,000 anywhere on the world computer market. At the time, the media called 1996 the year of the bolt-from-the-blue from the Chinese computer market.

To call it a 'bolt-from-the-blue' was no exaggeration: when the new price appeared on the market, it caused extreme disquiet amongst the world's computer manufacturing companies. Where it was different from anything that had happened before was that, in the past, price wars had been fierce and waged by foreign companies. This time they were rather slow to respond as they hesitated, not knowing what to do. They were completely unprepared: what were the Chinese doing, risking their lives with rock bottom prices? Was that even proper business? Wasn't business about making money? How could they make money like that? It was the other Chinese manufacturers who responded first, like a swarm of angry hornets. On 10 April, TopTry Computers reduced the price of their Pentium 75MHz machines to Rmb9,700. On 12 April, Founder announced they were dropping the price of their Pentium 75MHz machines to Rmb10,000. On 15 April, Inspur cut the price of their Pentium range by 20%-30%.

Liu Chuanzhi's trusted lieutenant, Lenovo's sales manager Yang Yuanqing, read daily reports from their sales force across the country, hoping that the consumers would go with Lenovo and understandably nervous as he awaited news of victory or defeat. Moreover, at that time, Lenovo's warehouses still had a big stock of '486s' which had begun to sell at a loss. With Pentium machines all now at Rmb10,000 or less, what would they now be able to sell the '486' for? Yang Yuanqing's plan was to use the Pentium machines to cover the losses on the '486'. This was a very risky strategy and if it failed, Lenovo would have suffered catastrophic damage. The results exceeded all expectations, and orders for the under-Rmb10,000 Pentium machines swept into the office like a blizzard. In the first month of the reduced price, Lenovo Computers' daily production exceeded a thousand units and, even more astonishingly, even the '486' sold out completely. Not only was the shortfall made up, they even showed a Rmb5 million net profit. The whole company was jubilant. This fabulous outright victory was entered into the annals of Lenovo history.

By that summer, no matter whether it was from Compaq, IBM or HP, there was no significant response to the sudden counteroffensive started by Lenovo and taken up by the 'allied forces of the Chinese computer army'. Incomprehensibly, they held their fire and continued to sell '486' machines for Rmb15,000 and Pentium machines for upwards of Rmb20,000. Could it be they didn't know what was going on in the Chinese marketplace? Or was it possible that the foreign manufacturers were brewing up something even bigger? All the signs were that this was something quite abnormal. In fact, nothing at all came of it and Yang Yuanqing discovered for the first time that the foreign brands' strategic decision-making process was very cumbersome and inflexible, and comparatively slow, especially when facing guerrilla war and unorthodox tactics. "All warfare is based on deception": this dictum from Sunzi's *Art of War*, is something that China has much experience of, and it is written into Chinese people's DNA.

Yang Yuanqing had fully absorbed Liu Chuanzhi's principles: strike first and don't give your opponent a chance to get their breath back. In fact, Lenovo's decisive battle plan was to be in constant motion. With Liu

Chuanzhi in the command post "they waged 10 years of war and after 50 years knew the decrees of heaven". By this time, AST was no longer a consideration and Lenovo had clambered up on the giant's shoulders as the next generation of young hopefuls took control: Yang Yuanqing, Guo Wei, Sun Hongbin, each one of them brave and skilful warriors. Every generation's commander-in-chief must have his trusted generals, otherwise he would never become commander-in-chief. Liu Chuanzhi was extremely gratified that "the landscape ahead seemed to be expecting him[1]" and within 10 years Lenovo had already supplanted AST and was in a position to challenge the likes of Compaq, HP and IBM; and Yang Yuanqing and the others had even vowed to overtake those companies and become number one in China within three more years. These youngsters were even more pushy and ambitious than he was, and Liu Chuanzhi was very gratified by this. However skilled and valiant the troops and generals, they must always have another quality: unyielding obstinacy. These young generals were not like the old guard of Zhang Zuxiang, Li Qin and the others; sometimes even Liu Chuanzhi's extreme affection was not enough to hold on to someone, Sun Hongxi is an example, and he had no option but to wield the knife. But that is another story.

In October 1996, Yang Yuanqing launched the fourth price war, lowering the cutting-edge Pentium 133 machines below the Rmb10,000 threshold, bringing joy to retailers all across the country and creating the legend of Lenovo's 'four wars, four victories'. In that year, only the situation in the Guangdong market area controlled by Chen Shaopeng remained unclear for a while, but that was the leading edge of the computer market, and not so easy to seize control of. Later on, however, the new dawn arrived there too: Chen Shaopeng and the president of the Rightway Company, Cao Nengye, signed a distribution agreement, rather in the manner of a besieged city being forced to sign a peace treaty. Although Cao's was not a small-scale company in itself, its uniqueness lay in the fact that it was Compaq's market agent. Cao was very dissatisfied with Compaq's and other foreign manufacturers' slow and inflexible response to the rapidly evolving Chinese market, but had as thorough an understanding of Lenovo's 'four wars, four victories' as if it were the valuables in his family strongbox. He had complete confidence in Lenovo's microcomputers. After he and Chen Shaopeng signed their distribution agreement (which effectively meant Lenovo had gained a hugely important sales agent), the two men sat in a car heading out of Guangzhou and leading the advance on the Pearl River Delta. There was an atmosphere of triumph in the car. By the beginning of 1997 at the latest, everyone could see Lenovo's two great contributions: one was arresting the decline in the domestically produced computer market and turning defeat into victory. If it hadn't been for all Lenovo's efforts in 1994, 1995 and 1996, China's PC market might have been completely destroyed by foreign brands. The other was the bold and decisive reform of marketing in the microcomputer division that Yang Yuanqing had enacted. He had established a highly efficient distribution system, aimed directly at getting the products to household users. Lenovo Computers' microcomputer division's 'four wars, four victories' strategy increased Lenovo's sales volume by 101% with a market share in excess of 10%, making it number one in the Chinese market.

In May 1998, Lenovo's millionth computer rolled off the assembly line and the company held large-scale celebrations. You could describe that computer as the masterpiece of the Chinese IT industry. It certainly had extraordinary significance. Yang Yuanqing was not content with what he learned from HP and was continually coming up with new strategies. He planned a nationwide 'make new friends' exercise for Lenovo, inviting every hundred thousandth customer to a celebration. This was a large-scale affair at the New World Restaurant. Yang Yuanqing remembers the event on 6 June: when he finished his speech, and a government official had read out a congratulatory message, Yang announced that he was presenting a Tianqin 959 Model computer equipped with a Pentium II processor to the chairman of Intel, Mr Andy Grove. In his acceptance speech, Grove said that he was going to put the computer into Intel's museum. After the event, the company's top-level executives sat down for a meal with the employees. At the dinner table they talked about everything from the millionth computer to the challenges of 1994, about the turnaround in 1996 and the wonder-year of 1997. As they talked about the joys and sorrows of those years, not a few tears were shed. In September 1998, Lenovo and IBM signed a cooperation agreement covering the whole software field, established a strategic partnership with Yonyou, took out a contract with the world-famous market intelligence company ITC for market reports, bought a 30% share in Kingsoft and set up regional offices in east China, south China, the northeast and the southwest. In the same year, Liu Chuanzhi was named by *Time* magazine as one of the world's 25 most influential business leaders, ranked at number 14.

The Agency System

Even if the price-cutting war was the trump card, it didn't have the back-up of a well-developed organisational system, and just having a single trump card is not only inefficient, it can also prove fatal. The principle of 'distribution' which has already been mentioned several times was the back-up, as it allowed the trump card to prove its worth and succeed in every situation.

If you are going to talk about the secret of Lenovo's success, you have to talk about retail distribution. HP was undoubtedly the first foreign company to introduce the idea of retail distribution to the Chinese computer market, and when Lenovo became part of their global internet marketing, they saw that the idea could be applied to themselves. The young general Yang Yuanqing immediately grasped the whole concept of the 'agency system' and, by extension, that retail was the key to commercial success. It was 1992 by then, and Yang was no longer in the microcomputer division but had moved on to the CAD department. CAD stands for 'computer-aided design' and, in fact, Yang's main job was as marketing agent for HP's plotter. From their marketing he could see the potential of another sales pattern as well as individual units and bulk trade: agency and retail distribution. This sales pattern had its own specialised marketing channels and specific client base, and, with reliable agents and relatively solid marketing channels, it could become a powerful sales network. The most important thing was that a solid marketing system would grow exponentially but, if there was any weakness in the system it would become disorganised and uncoordinated, limiting any potential for growth. Yang Yuanqing understood that, at that time, the CAD department that he headed up was just a segment of HP's huge sales network but that if they used the agent/retail distribution pattern to form their own global sales network and used the smallest amount of manpower necessary to build the broadest possible market, they would reap the biggest possible profit. It was a moment of personal enlightenment for Yang Yuanqing and he began to think about making Lenovo the very heart of that sales network.

The first month that Yang Yuanqing took up the management of the CAD department, he signed a retail distribution agency agreement with a company in Zhongguancun. This company undertook responsibility for the retail distribution of the HP plotter and the Lenovo CAD department would take 3% of the turnover in return. This was the first agency agreement of this type in Zhongguancun and was undoubtedly of enormous significance to both Zhongguancun and to Lenovo because it marked the arrival of the genuine distributor in the Chinese IT industry. To begin with, people found the idea of 'agents' and 'retail distribution' very strange and unfamiliar, and they were sceptical of the many benefits it promised. But after the first company, another one followed and the new marketing philosophy quickly took off. It wasn't long before the Lenovo CAD department began to think about gathering all the agency companies together and they convened a small-scale agents' conference. Although the numbers taking part were small, this had great significance for Yang Yuanqing and Lenovo. It was from that conference that Yang formed his new theory of marketing and it was when this model was employed in Lenovo's computer sales, that Lenovo Computers' fortunes were radically changed. When Yang Yuanqing applied this retail distribution model to his CAD department, sales took off, doubling in 1992, and doubling again in 1993.

It was because of his glorious achievements in the two short years he was in charge of the CAD department between 1991 and 1993, that Yang Yuanqing attracted Liu Chuanzhi's attention. At Lenovo Computers' most critical juncture, Liu promoted Yang Yuanqing to CEO of the microcomputer division, placing the future of Lenovo Computers on the shoulders of this young general. In 1994, in his new position as CEO, Yang brought radical change to the division; his first action was to follow the 'HP model' and take the division from a direct marketing system to a wholly agency sales system.

The Road Not Yet Taken

Later, Yang Yuanqing often recalled the accidental but inevitable road he took. In 1988, he remembers himself writing his graduate thesis at the Chinese Academy of Sciences Institute of Automation and thinking about his future. He was only 24 at the time, and his firm intention was to go to the US to do a PhD in computing and then go on to work in the mighty Silicon Valley. He felt very envious of any of his contemporaries at university who were already settled in Silicon Valley, and he could hear them calling him. At the end of the 1980s, if a science and engineering graduate from one of the top universities chose to stay in China he would be looked on as some kind of freak, because the vast majority of such students opted to leave the country. At that time two-thirds of a group from one year at Shanghai's Jiaotong University went abroad, with far more in Silicon

Valley than in Beijing. Needless to say, this was even more the case with the Science and Technology University of China, where sometimes people had pretty much left before they were even out of the classroom. Although it is not a massive distance from the Institute of Automation to Silicon Valley, it is still a more than 10-hour flight, and before Yang Yuanqing could go there he had to find a job to earn some money: for one thing he had to raise the tuition fees, and for another he needed to pay for classes to bring his limited English up to the standard needed for his specialised subjects. He needed a springboard, and his first thought was Zhongguancun. In 1988, Lenovo publicly recruited 58 new employees out of 500 applicants, Yang Yuanqing being one of them. The Lenovo Company was famous as a high-tech company in China and was a good match for Yang's specialities but, when it was announced, he was not very happy with the post the company assigned him to. He had been given a job as a salesman in the marketing department, promoting other people's products. Although he had spent seven years studying computing as his specialist subject, his knowledge was not being put to much use. But Yang Yuanqing learned something new in the marketing department: he learned that efficiency is born out of the market, and the market is born out of service. Many years later, when Yang was a top-level executive in the Lenovo Group, one of the business philosophies he espoused was to make Lenovo 'Lenovo the service company'. In the end, he never went to Silicon Valley but stayed in Zhongguancun. It is hard to say whether this was by chance or necessity, and equally hard to imagine what would have happened if he had gone to America; as the American poet, Robert Frost wrote:

THE ROAD NOT TAKEN

Two roads diverged in a yellow wood,
And sorry I could not travel both
And be one traveller, long I stood
And looked down one as far as I could
To where it bent in the undergrowth;

Then took the other, as just as fair,
I shall be telling this with a sigh
Somewhere ages and ages hence:
Two roads diverged in a wood, and I—
I took the one less travelled

- ROBERT FROST

Internal Affairs

In 1996, just as Yang Yuanqing was waging his fourth 'price war' and even the Pentium 133 machines had been brought below the 'Rmb10,000 barrier', and as Lenovo Computers had overtaken both HP and IBM to occupy the top spot in the Chinese market, one evening Yang Yuanqing received an order from the company telling him to join a meeting in the group's Conference Room 505. Usually, it was Liu Chuanzhi who phoned Yang Yuanqing, but this time it was the president's office that called. The 'order' was very sudden and highly unusual: it requested Yang to bring all his top executives – his battle-hardened brave troops and intrepid generals – to attend together.

Conference Room 505 is the most important room in the company, and all the most important decisions were taken there. No one knew what was going on, and the atmosphere in the room was very tense. Only Yang Yuanqing had an inkling what was going on. He and his brave generals sat on one side of the long, green velvet-covered table and everyone else was chattering away and laughing – the victorious troops had reason to be happy - only Yang Yuanqing seemed to have something on his mind. Suddenly the doors opened, and Liu Chuanzhi, Li Qin and Zeng Maochao walked solemnly in. Their expressions were serious, and they looked neither to right nor left.

With Li Qin and Zeng Maochao on either side, Liu Chuanzhi sat at the head of the table. He didn't offer any greetings but unleashed a barrage of reprimands which left everyone except Yang Yuanqing dumbstruck. Liu Chuanzhi abandoned his former imperturbability and dignified and imposing manner; he seemed to be completely out of control. This had never happened before. He tongue-lashed the microcomputer department for their complacency in resting on their laurels, sparing none of the assembled company's feelings and, as he spoke, his gaze slowly fixed on Yang Yuanqing. Showing no quarter, he said, "You should have no reason to think any of this is undeserved or unexpected! This stage was erected for you under great pressure by the company leadership. Do you understand that? If you do, then no matter how great the conflicting circumstances, with everyone working for a common cause, you should be consolidating your position step by step, fighting for an even bigger stage, and even bigger territory. You cannot just rush headlong into things and you should let me, Liu Chuanzhi, say what is fair and what is not. If you won't compromise, what do you think I should do?" Liu Chuanzhi's icy gaze swept over the others, then came back to rest on Yang Yuanqing.

Yang Yuanqing's face was ashen. He didn't say a word but sat, head down and his palms sweating.

As Liu Chuanzhi finished speaking, he announced two decisions: first, that within a year, Yang Yuanqing must make several compromises; second, that Liu Xiaolin should take immediate charge of the Planning Department.

Yang Yuanqing could bear it no longer but he only managed to say, "We put in a lot of hard work and we never expected…" But he couldn't finish; his eyes reddened and the tears began to fall as he wept uncontrollably. The whole roomful of his subordinates looked on stupidly, on the one hand scared out of their wits and, on the other, feeling as aggrieved at the injustice to Yang Yuanqing as if it had been done to themselves. Liu Xiaolin hurried to declare his position: he would follow the leadership's orders and arrange to take over at the Planning Department. But then he went on to defend Yang Yuanqing saying that he, Yang, had done his utmost every day, and he persisted in the view that it had all been done in the company's best interests. Liu Chuanzhi ignored Liu Xiaolin's excuses and kept his gaze fixed on Yang Yuanqing, not relaxing its severity in the face of Yang's uncontrolled weeping, but because he was waiting for him to state his position too. Gasping for breath, Yang Yuanqing gradually began to calm down. He wiped away his tears and stated that he accepted the criticism.

The three elders stood up and left, leaving the crowd of youngsters behind them in the room.

After the meeting broke up, the youngsters didn't go home, but went out to try to lighten their mood. From Zhongguancun they went to Baishiqiao, then on to a nearby restaurant where they drank wine and talked. They were at the end of a year-long campaign during which they had taken cities and seized territory and were no longer co-workers but were more like brothers. They cried out at the injustice to Yang Yuanqing, and they cried out at the injustice to their department.

That night, Yang Yuanqing's emotions were still in turmoil and he couldn't sleep.

Liu Chuanzhi, too, had trouble sleeping.

When We Have Experienced Many Troubles[2]

In the spring of 1990, Liu Chuanzhi convened a management training class. Ostensibly it was to give everyone a chance to discuss the question, "Fundamentally, what kind of company does Lenovo want to be?". In reality, Liu Chuanzhi wanted to settle the problem of Sun Hongbin, the manager of the Corporate Development Department. In his introduction to the class, he talked about the *Lenovo Corporate Report* produced by the company's Corporate Planning Department itself, which had shaken the whole company, and which criticised the department's manager Sun Hongbin for his gravely self-centred attitude. He had also read in advance the proposal in the Corporate Report that all Corporate Planning Department managers should have the authority to hire and fire and make appointments in branch offices and so on. During the class, he said firmly that the Enterprise Department could not have its own set of rules but was subject to the management system approved by the chairman's office.

Sun Hongbin had no sense of impending danger, and even objected to the criticism. His achievements were outstanding, and the Corporate Planning Department was held in high esteem in the company, quite exceptional, in fact, so it has to be said that Sun had grounds for his arrogance. After the training session had finished, Liu Chuanzhi went to the Corporate Planning Department officially to further admonish Sun, but he wasn't there. Liu Chuanzhi was fully aware of Sun's achievements, but he was critical of the 'secret society' element of his management, and the fact that he lacked a 'big team' attitude and subconsciously favoured a 'small gang' approach. As a result of this, what alarmed Liu Chuanzhi was that when all this was raised in the class, there were some people who stood up and said, "Chuanzhi, we are not a secret society, but you say that is how we are organised. Can you be more specific? We are directly responsible to Sun Hongbin, and if he curses us out we listen, but what has it got to do with the chairman?" Liu Chuanzhi had not expected that.

When one man had finished talking, another one took up the complaint until it all descended into a free-for-all. There was no way the meeting could continue, so it ground to a halt. Liu Chuanzhi was astounded to discover that the nature of the problem was not at all as he had thought. He looked up to the heavens and sighed.

Why was he sighing? Was it because he had realised he wasn't as smart as he thought he was?

With things having progressed this far, it was no one else's problem but his own. Prompt action was needed, bold and ruthless action, or it would be very bad for the company. What was the explanation for the Corporate Planning Department being in open revolt like this? If he was too lenient, that could, contrary to expectation, actually end up being harmful to his employees. This was a serious lesson for him, and very timely.

Liu Chuanzhi sought out Sun Hongbin and tested the water by suggesting he cut himself off from the problem employees.

"I can't fire them," Sun Hongbin said.

So that's how it was. Liu Chuanzhi wasn't surprised, and asked Sun Hongbin softly, "Xiao Sun, do you want me, or do you want them?" He wasn't holding back but going right to the root of the matter. His tone was very cordial, as to an old comrade-in-arms but it was, in fact, an ultimatum.

Sun Hongbin replied, "I want them..."

After a moment, he went on to explain, "If I were to fire them, what would that do to my reputation in the department? I would lose my authority and wouldn't be able to do my job. But if there really was a problem with them, of course I would fire them."

He continued, "In my judgement, there is nothing wrong with them; you just don't understand them. All they did was give you their opinion, so how fair is it for them to be in fear of the sack? You should have another think about it."

Sun Hongbin had joined Lenovo before Yang Yuanqing, arriving in 1988. At that time, Liu Chuanzhi was busy with affairs in Hong Kong; before he put up HK$300,000 for a joint venture company, he specifically spoke to several management-level personnel, "From now on, Lenovo not only wants to recruit more young people, it also wants to be bold about promoting them. There is nothing wrong with getting the promotions wrong, but not promoting them and not nurturing them, that certainly would be wrong." He had his eye on Lenovo's future, so a large cohort of recent graduates and even some youngsters who had not yet graduated and were still studying, joined Lenovo and, following the company's rapid development programme, they too developed rapidly, so that between 1988 and 1990, a cohort of 'baby-face managers' appeared, the most consequential of them being Yang Yuanqing and Guo Wei. The third one was Sun Hongbin.

In 1990, in a breach of the normal rules, Sun Hongbin was appointed director of the Corporate Planning Department. His authority covered the 18 subsidiary companies he had opened all around the country. The old guard at Lenovo had had no part in that process, so the top men in all the subsidiary companies were essentially all Sun Hongbin's appointees. This meant that Sun had a lot of clout with those companies. But Lenovo's subsidiary companies, as well as being under Sun's direction, also had to maintain good relations with every department of the Lenovo Group, the latter circumstance being much more important than the former. However, the senior management at the group discovered that their authority over the subsidiary companies was gradually being eroded, and they began to keep Liu Chuanzhi informed about what was going on with Sun Hongbin. Eventually, they requested that Liu Chuanzhi return to Beijing from Hong Kong on the grounds that Sun Hongbin was becoming too influential, that a clique was forming, that cracks were forming in the company and Lenovo was being damaged. It was then that the 'training class' was convened. On his return, Liu immediately initiated an investigation and quickly discovered that the problem was far from imaginary: the staff at the subsidiary companies around the country owed their jobs to Sun Hongbin, their finances were not under the control of the group to the extent that some people wanted Sun to lead a breakaway from the group to set up an independent company. To begin with Liu Chuanzhi didn't take this too seriously, thinking that, although Sun was a little out of control, he was still a man of exceptional abilities and Liu believed that if he transferred him to where he himself could keep an eye on him, he would have ways of making him grow up and come to his senses. If he continued not to recognise when he was well off, it would still not be too late to deal with him. Sun Hongbin was a tough, tenacious street-fighter of a man and, although Liu Chuanzhi was well aware of this, he had a maxim that if he had to choose between a mediocre but generally good man, and a capable man with faults, he would always choose the latter. In fact, he would even go looking for such people. Liu considered it was a skill to be able to use dangerous men.

Sun Hongbin went further than Liu Chuanzhi expected, obliging him to re-examine his attitude of valuing talent over everything else.

Sun rejected Liu's overtures, and the next day his Corporate Planning Department held a meeting at Peking University's Shaoyuan Restaurant. News of the potential sackings had got around and the members of the department were all fired up and furious. Sun himself was in an excited state as he sat and drank his wine. Some people said they should just make off with the company's money, while others said they should immediately set up on their own and take the department's funds with them.

Whatever they said, the Corporate Planning Department was still part of Lenovo, not Sun Hongbin's personal fiefdom and someone reported the affair to the still somewhat undecided Liu Chuanzhi.

For the last time, Liu summoned Sun Hongbin to see him. Sun's Corporate Planning Department office was on Zhongguancun Avenue, in the same building as Stone. Previously, if there had been any issues, Liu Chuanzhi had gone to the department, but not this time. He ordered Sun Hongbin to go to the old Lenovo offices on Kexueyuan South Road. When Sun arrived, Liu Chuanzhi was unaware that a number of his subordinates had followed him to the headquarters building. Both sides had made their preparations, but neither side knew what the other had done. Liu Chuanzhi was alone in the chairman's office, not accompanied by any of the company's senior figures, so it was one-on-one, in a very tense and highly charged atmosphere.

It was reminiscent of a scene from *The Godfather*.

Modern materialistic China was all there, but what was missing was any form of culture or art.

Liu Chuanzhi didn't beat about the bush but told Sun Hongbin that he knew all about the meeting at the Shaoyuan Restaurant. Sun brazenly admitted it all.

"But that is not the way I see things," Sun Hongbin said.

"You are already beyond my leadership. You will have to go it alone!" Liu Chuanzhi replied.

Liu said Sun could choose any subsidiary company he liked to go off to.

"There's no need. I'm leaving," Sun replied.

The two of them had an equal sense of honour and were equally streetwise. There was a lot of subtext to what they both said, and neither believed things were as simple as they presented them. Neither agreement nor refusal was straightforward. But no matter what was said, Liu Chuanzhi was meticulous both in virtue and in sense of duty.

In the afternoon of 7 April, Liu Chuanzhi made his move. He gathered together all the personnel of the Corporate Planning Department and announced that he was dismissing the two most vehement members of the 'Shaoyuan Revolt' and he was freezing the accounts of all the subsidiary companies under the control of the Corporate Planning Department. He was asking officers from the Public Security Bureau to ensure the company's security. He himself was taking charge of the Corporate Planning Department and Sun Hongbin was to leave his current post to go to the Business Services Department.

This was equivalent to declaring a state of emergency. The mood in the room was very solemn, and the two men whose sacking had been announced joined the rest of the departmental staff in folding their arms in front of their chest as a gesture of protest at Liu Chuanzhi. Cigarette smoke coiled around the room as several people lit up. Sun Hongbin gave a loud shout, "Put your arms down!" Everyone unfolded their arms and dropped them to their sides. He gave another shout, "Put your cigarettes out!" Everyone extinguished their cigarettes. There was another shout, "Stand up!" Everyone stood up, like a phalanx of Spartan warriors.

The next day, Liu Chuanzhi received a secret warning that some people in the Corporate Planning Department were intending to make off with the company's money and telling him to be on his guard. Liu Chuanzhi knew that there were at least Rmb17 million in funds held by the subsidiary companies under Sun Hongbin's control. And if those people really did make off with them, it would put the company into both a financial and reputational crisis. He alerted the Chinese Academy of Sciences' security office. Obviously, this kind of situation did not just fall under the company's remit as it involved the breaking of criminal law, so Liu Chuanzhi also made a report to the Public Security Bureau and to the police. At the same time, he sent 20 people out on an urgent mission to sequester the funds of all the subsidiary companies. For the next few days, Lenovo assigned a powerfully-built young bodyguard to protect Liu Chuanzhi who was instructed not to leave his side at any time.

With all preparations made, the group went ahead with a meeting. Sun Hongbin still tried to defend himself, reluctant to admit any mistakes, but as soon as the final decision was announced that he was "suspended from duties to examine his conscience", he was escorted out of the company office. Initially, they took him to the Xiyuan Guesthouse under the supervision of at least two people. Sun Hongbin was at liberty to eat and sleep as he wished, and his guards said to him, not entirely joking, "What a character you are! You eat like a horse and sleep like a baby!"

Sun replied, "I'm tired. I'm so tired every day. I don't often get any time to myself."

A few days later, some of his men heard the news and they went over to where he was staying. The guards and the rescuers confronted each other with makeshift weapons in their hands, and it looked as though everything was about to kick off. Sun Hongbin stood in the doorway and berated his men in a stern voice, ordering them to leave at once.

On hearing this, the men immediately did what they were told. One of them still refused to accept what was happening and went back to the office. Although he was a southerner, he had the unruliness of a northerner. He started mouthing off any old how, and even threatened to "cut off the arms" of the traitors in the company. It wasn't Liu Chuanzhi's job personally to intervene with this crazy supporter of Sun Hongbin, but he had infuriated him. Liu was a man of diverse character, and was quite willing to use underhand tactics in a just cause. The next day Liu Chuanzhi seized the initiative, and stopped the man who had made the threats on Zhongguancun Avenue and, although he wasn't actually dressed in black, his sturdy build did give him something of the air of a gang boss. He said to the fellow, "You need to be clear about something: violence never outweighs what is right, and from today on, if anyone in the company starts something, I will hold you responsible." The man stiffened and shot Liu Chuanzhi a look. Liu Chuanzhi went on, "You can stop trying to play the tough guy with me. Who do you take me for? Let me ask you something. Suppose you are walking along the street and suddenly get knocked over by a bicycle. Do you think that's the kind of thing that might happen? After you've been knocked over, the two of you start a fight and both get taken to the local police station. The man who ran into you is quickly released, but you have to spend time in the cells. Do you think that is the kind of thing that might happen? If there are three men following you everywhere, night and day, would you be afraid?" The man's face went paler and paler as he listened, and he said on the spot that he wanted to leave Lenovo and wouldn't be involved in anything ever again.

Liu Chuanzhi immediately began to feel a little ashamed and wondered just what he thought he was doing.

But, at the same time, it felt good; it felt good because he had personally faced down violence.

It felt a little as though he was fighting for his life, but then that is what enterprise in business is all about, fighting for your life over everything.

Early one morning on 28 May 1990, Sun Hongbin was detained by the Haidian police. Ten days later he was formally arrested and charged with misappropriation of public funds. The Public Security investigation discovered that he had diverted Lenovo money into another company and the sums involved were far from negligible. Sun Hongbin defended himself, saying that he had had no intention of "using public money for personal gain"; it was just that the company's financial regulations were too inflexible and the procedures too complicated, and he simply wanted some liquid funds to "ease the way" for the company to do business. The investigation discovered no absolute proof that showed that Sun Hongbin had actually been corrupt in the use of this money but, even so, the movement of public money without the proper permission did constitute a legal problem. On 22 August 1992, after a long-drawn-out 27-month stay in the Haidian detention centre, Sun Hongbin received the court's final verdict:

he was sentenced to five years' imprisonment for misappropriation of Rmb130,000 of public funds.

The all-powerful Sun Hongbin became a convict, spending most of his time sharing a cell with more than 30 other people and introducing him to a whole different society. His life consisted of crossing off the days, one by one. Because he was a graduate of Tsinghua University – there weren't many graduates in prison in those days, let alone Tsinghua graduates – his fellow prisoners were amazed by his arrival and he received a fair degree of respect in the cell. He also learned quite a lot of underworld slang. After four years, on 27 March 1994, Sun Hongbin was released after serving his sentence and, as he walked out of the prison gates, he saw the sun again for the first time as a free man.

What did he get out of prison? Moderation, cool-headedness and the ability to consider problems like a philosopher. He didn't stay in Beijing long after he got out and he did not stop to drink and chat and talk about prison life with the folk who had been waiting expectantly to see him. He had said goodbye to the past and he went back to Tianjin that same day. Whilst in prison he had planned his future as a property developer. He experienced a lot of twists and turns in his quest for the appropriate licence but that did not pose any real problems for him. In the end, he decided on 'Shunchi' as his company name, 'SunCo' in English, which sounds as though it is short for 'Sun's Company'. Before Sun Hongbin was released, he met Liu Chuanzhi outside the prison on one occasion. One of the training officers in the prison sent him out to buy some computer software. He found someone who had links with Liu Chuanzhi and told them that he wanted to see him.

It had been four years, but Liu Chuanzhi hadn't forgotten Sun Hongbin. He met him in a Sichuan restaurant at the top of the New Century Hotel. He didn't bring any bodyguards or take any protective precautions. After four years, the two men looked at each other for a while; there was nothing of the chairman or the criminal in their gazes, just time and the man. Sun Hongbin told Liu Chuanzhi about his plans to become a property developer. Liu asked him coolly what he had going for him and Sun, equally coolly, explained his thinking. Wine broke through any awkwardness, and Sun went on to express his remorse. He clinked Liu Chuanzhi's glass, "I used to have the mistaken idea that if I hadn't done what I did, I wouldn't have been me." He took a mouthful of wine and looked at his former boss. "Later I thought about it again, and finally saw that wasn't the case. In fact, you don't need to change your essential character, you just need to analyse your circumstances so you see them a bit more clearly and understand them better, then you have a chance of not messing up." Liu Chuanzhi sighed softly and chinked Sun Hongbin's glass. Sun went on to say he had been thinking about these things every day for the three years and 10 months he was in prison, and now he had the chance to meet and talk them through.

It sounded like an apology and it sounded like someone speaking their true mind. It sounded like Lu Xun's poem, "When we have experienced many troubles, the relationship between us still exists."

It was an unimaginable scene, and unique in the lives of both Liu Chuanzhi and Sun Hongbin, one of them only just into his 30s and the other already past 50. Liu Chuanzhi commented regretfully to Sun Hongbin that it couldn't have been easy getting through his time in prison, "Remember these words, Hongbin, and repeat them to others whenever you like: Liu Chuanzhi is your friend. If you ever need any help, I myself, Chairman Li and Chairman Zhang, will all offer it. We would even buy shares if that…"

But Sun Hongbin tactfully declined Liu Chuanzhi's offer, as he did all offers of financial aid from his newly-returned friend. He wanted to start from scratch and, indeed, it was not many years before he had restored his own financial security as he prospered in the property development marketplace. Liu admired Sun Hongbin as he would admire a lofty mountain peak whilst still recognising its dangers.

Liu Chuanzhi understood quite well: he did not fear danger, but he did his best to avoid it. He could admire Mount Hua[3], and even go to visit it, but he preferred his own seat atop Mount Tai.

A Letter to Yang Yuanqing

With past events fresh in his memory after this stormy period, Liu Chuanzhi felt much more warmly towards the young people around him; Sun Hongbin's fault was his fault, and this wounded him deeply. He could never let such things happen again, especially as he was preparing to hand over the reins at Lenovo to Yang Yuanqing.

There were some things he had to tell Yang Yuanqing so, late at night with a robe draped around his shoulders, he picked up his pen:

YUANQING,

Even though work has been very arduous since my return from Hong Kong, I have still been worrying about your situation. After my investigations, I feel that I have not been in close enough touch with you over the last few years, and all that we have talked about has been specific problems that you needed resolved. Objectively speaking, it has been because we have both been so busy, but subjectively speaking, it is because we have not been paying specific attention to the importance of our relationship. I am using odds and ends of spare time to write you this letter in the hope that, by writing, I will be able to formulate things with a cooler head. But I don't want to be too formal and will write down what comes into my head. I would rather let my feelings flow spontaneously and not necessarily too logically. What lies behind what I have to say is very important, and if we don't get through it all the first time, we can pick it up again later. I like young people who have ability. The main reason the bosses of privately-owned companies like to have talented people around them is this: they make them money and that is all that matters. But for the bosses of state-owned enterprises (SOEs), that is not enough; they also want some kind of emotional bond. Nobody wants a successor who may be good at the job but is on bad terms with his predecessor. To put it more light-heartedly, if I am looking for a wife and find one who is only beautiful (equivalent to being 'good at the job') but doesn't love me, what use is that?

Lenovo is already a sizeable enterprise and, if we follow our fixed strategy, it will grow even bigger. If I don't, at this point, pay meticulous attention to nurturing the core leadership, then anything I say in the future will just be empty words. So, what kind of young core leadership am I envisaging? Most importantly it must have virtue or integrity. This encompasses several things: firstly, loyalty to Lenovo as a business, that is to say, the profit any individual makes should come only from the profits Lenovo makes as a whole. Publicly speaking, this is the most important thing. Privately speaking, it also means that they must whole-heartedly follow in the footsteps of the pioneers who preceded them – I believe this is one of the things that should be included in our understanding of integrity. In a purely commercial society, after the founders of a business have established their company, when they hand it on, they should be rewarded both materially and emotionally. But in our current society, the different mechanisms mean that this cannot be guaranteed. This encourages the older generation to cling onto power and delay things rather than hand them over.

My responsibility, therefore, is to quietly enable the old guard to hand over, whilst guaranteeing their benefits. On another front, I must build a solid backbone by comprehensive appraisal of the right people and from there, choose a core leadership that will stand up to any test. Additionally, falling somewhere in the compass between 'talent' and integrity', the new young leader must rely on his altruism, and the stringent requirements he places on himself, and even on his generosity and tolerance to his comrades; in short, on his own outstanding leadership abilities. He must be open-minded in recognising the strengths of others and constantly reflect on his own shortcomings. He must have a whole series of outstanding qualities that will make others follow him. You know my big-chicken little-chicken theory. Only when you are the size of an ostrich will the little chickens whole-heartedly accept you. Only when you have won such whole-hearted acceptance will you be in a position to meet the fundamental needs of your contemporaries. Of course, there are SOEs where the boss is chosen by the country's top brass and therefore not whole-heartedly trusted by the employees; that is why the management struggle to keep them solidly behind them. If I did not consider these things in advance, but just decided on the spot, as happens in those SOEs, if it didn't make life impossible, at the very least it could leave hidden dangers within the organisation just when Lenovo wants to forge ahead.

I hope that by proceeding down these lines I will be able to nurture and support you. When you moved from the CAD department to the microcomputer development division, and that department began to show real signs of improvement, not only was I delighted by the business success, I was even more delighted to see a real talent emerging and displaying its potential. Not long after you started work, a lot of intractable problems arose. I am firmly opposed to expecting perfection from people. If I had forced everybody else's experience on you, it would have made things very difficult for you. We strove together with a common purpose, as far as possible, to guarantee a favourable environment for the microcomputer development division. In fact, what we proved was your ambition and determination not to give up if, at first, you didn't reach your goal. With things at this stage, I should be giving you even more support in exploiting your advantages whilst, at the same time, pointing out to you your shortcomings, with the aim of advancing you to an even higher level. But what should be your priorities at this time? I think you should be taking stock of what are your true strengths and what are your weaknesses. When you get down to it, what support does the environment at Lenovo offer you (this should give you more cause to consider your own achievements)? What do you need particularly to be aware of as you move to a higher level? Once I have clearly decided on the necessary qualities needed for the people who will form the core leadership of the company, what I intend to do for you is:

1) Strengthen your overall understanding. For your part, you must take every opportunity to exchange all kinds of ideas with me. This applies not just to work, but to all aspects of your life. 2) Improve my communications with you, so you can better understand my own good points and faults, the flaws in my character and what is going on in the back of my mind. Only in this way can we develop genuine communication at an emotional level. 3) Mutual assistance, primarily for me to use the new methods you learn to remedy your shortcomings and progress towards pre-determined targets.

I wrote all the above in an hour on Saturday and an hour on Sunday. I have to go out soon, so I think I will stop this letter here. So, finally, this is what I want to hear from you: 1) Are you willing to endure the hardships and accept the grievances that are necessary to climb to a higher level? 2) Reflect on yourself and whether you have any failings that would affect your progression towards this aim. Once I have received your letter, I will write again. I have never spent this much time writing a letter to a young person before.

Very well, I will put my pen down now.

Best wishes
LIU CHUANZHI

After another sleepless night, restless with anxiety, Yang Yuanqing went to the office the next morning and was surprised to see a letter from Liu Chuanzhi. It only served to revive his anxiety. But this time it was different: it was an expression of something that had always been there, but unspoken: an expression of understanding and emotional support that would allow him to rebuild himself. Even now, many years later, Yang Yuanqing still carries this letter with him, and opens it to read again from time to time. After the Sun Hongbin affair, Liu Chuanzhi's life expanded to another level of consciousness, just as a martial artist achieves 'enlightenment' through practising austerity.

DIARY NOTE 13: MOUNT TAI

> In spanning the huge gap between seeing off Sun Hongbin and choosing Yang Yuanqing, Liu Chuanzhi's character and vision grew enormously, seemingly becoming almost all-encompassing. Because of this, the 'ruthlessness' of Liu Chuanzhi's training, its accuracy, the detail of its modelling, its rectitude, all combined to make him seem as awe-inspiring as Mount Tai. After he had seen off Mount Hua in the form of Sun Hongbin, the identification was even more profound, just as you only come to understand your true self through the way you handle other people. If it hadn't been for Sun's Mount Hua, he would never have found himself atop Mount Tai. From the 1980s up to today, there are very few companies that have constantly flourished without declining: white goods maker Haier, of course, is one, also Changhong, Vanke and New Oriental, but none of the second-generation leaders in them had the benefit that Yang Yuanqing had of the rational and structured guidance of such a well-known and successful entrepreneur as Liu Chuanzhi. The problems facing successors are not small and there is a kind of cultural element to the situation, as it embodies both an individual's personal development and their limitations. Some people are Mount Hua, some people are Mount Tai, and there are some who are both.
>
> It is interesting to note that China has an organisation of entrepreneurs called the 'Mount Tai Association'. It is a very independently-minded association of leading industrialists in the privately-owned science and technology sector made up of famous entrepreneurial CEOs and board members, including Lenovo's controlling shareholder Liu Chuanzhi, Stone Group's Duan Yongji, Alibaba's Ma Yun (Jack Ma),

Vantone Holdings' Feng Lun, China Oceanwide Group's Lu Zhiqiang, Broad Air Conditioning's Zhang Yue, Sinyuan's controlling shareholder Lin Rongqiang, Giant Group's Shi Yuzhu, Baidu's Li Yanhong and a dozen or so others. Liu Chuanzhi is the chairman of the association. It is an exceptionally low-profile group but with enormous influence. It admires the cultural tradition of Mount Tai, promotes a traditional cultural spirit, aspires to the lofty rectitude of Mount Tai, maintaining an aura of poise and refinement. Of their number, it is Liu Chuanzhi who has been the most effective.

KV3000

In 1996, Wang Jiangmin took a yellow minivan taxi to Zhongguancun to launch his offensive against computer viruses. At first sight, this offensive had nothing to do with his physical health and, in any case, was certainly ahead of its time. Computers were still a new phenomenon at the time, and computer viruses even more so, let alone an all-out attack on them.

Wang Jiangmin contracted poliomyelitis when he was three years old which deformed one of his legs.

"All I knew was that I couldn't go downstairs and once, when I tried, I tumbled all the way from the top to the bottom."

Because he was stuck upstairs, the young Wang Jiangmin used to sit by the window every day, looking out at the bustling crowds on the street below, looking out at the nearby free market, at the trams, the cars and the bicycles. Sometimes he would pick up a slip of paper, tear it in two, lean out of the window and, with a twirl, sent the paper fluttering down to the street below.

In his first year at primary school, his polio-withered leg was broken in an accident with a cyclist. Luckily it wasn't his good leg, or the consequences would have been much more serious. On another occasion, he was standing on a small bridge looking at the fish in the river and a passing pedestrian carelessly bumped into him and sent him tumbling head-first into the water. These incidents made Wang Jiangmin think he must be unusually light in weight and he thought of training in *qinggong*[1], but sadly he never followed through with the training and never again experienced that same feeling of weightlessness after bumping into someone. Later on, he went with his family to Yantai. He was fishing from a reef at the seaside there and, although he loved the sea, he had little experience of it and got cut off by the rising tide, unable to make it back to the shore. The sea quickly swept him under, and in that instant it felt as though the polio had disabled his whole being as well. He couldn't swim and, scared out of his wits, he struggled to make for the shore. He just managed to keep his head above water and, although he ingested a few mouthfuls of water, he finally made it back to dry land. When he looked at the ground, the setting sun and the clouds, he felt as though he had been reborn. The most extraordinary thing is that, although he had swallowed a lot of bitter sea water, the sea and his stomach seemed to have come to some kind of agreement because, awash as he was, he had learned to swim.

He felt that this new accomplishment was profoundly significant: it was as if there was now nothing he couldn't do.

He couldn't let the polio take over his mental attitude; he had to fight against it.

From then on, he began to set himself against himself: his leg was no good and he couldn't climb mountains, so he wanted to be a mountaineer; he couldn't learn to ride a bicycle, so he wanted to ride one. If there was anything he couldn't do, that is what he wanted to do. In some of these projects, he ended up being better than an ordinary person. He often ended up with a bloody nose and a swollen face, seeing stars, but his explosive energy and speed were quite astonishing.

Polio is caused by the poliomyelitis virus and manifests itself in muscle weakness and paralysis. It is asymmetric, and causes fading of the tendon reflexes and decline in muscle tone; the lower limbs and large muscles are more easily affected than the upper limbs and small muscles; or all four limbs may be equally paralysed. If the neck muscles, diaphragm and abdominal muscles are involved then combing one's hair and sitting up become difficult, breathing and movement are impeded, and paradoxical breathing and other conditions may result.

Wang Jiangmin fought against all this, apparently to great effect. Both the physical and mental struggles seemed to increase his fierce determination. When he was 11 years old and in the fourth year of primary school, without the help of his teachers, he put together a dual-waveband, eight-transistor radio, a transceiver and even a record player. In the early 1960s he was a little amateur radio ham.

But after he graduated from junior high school, no factories wanted to employ him. Even though he was willing to work for free with no wages, no one would take him on, because no one wanted a disabled person. They seemed to want to avoid him like the plague.

Back in those days, they didn't call disabled people 'disabled', they called them 'cripples', which was not at all polite or respectful. A lot of people were 'class enemies' intent on persecuting others. Whether they had committed an offence or not, 'cripples' were the detritus of society. Wang Jiangmin did not blame society nor did he feel that it was heartless. But heartlessness was the norm then. He did hate polio and the poliomyelitis virus, and he didn't understand how a disease like that could turn a perfectly ordinary person into something ugly and deformed.

Of course, nothing could hold Wang Jiangmin back. We won't talk about how oppressive things were, how severe the resistance, how often others pushed in front of him; we will only talk about the year 1989. Wang Jiangmin was working on developing industrial control software. Because the machinery which ran his software (which was entirely self-taught) often became infected with viruses, his customers thought that it must be the software that was no good. It was in that year that news reports first defined what a computer virus was, but before that, Wang Jiangmin had already discovered the 'Bouncing Ball' virus and the 'Stoned' virus, but no one had previously identified them as viruses. He had already marked them down as such, and he instinctively posed to himself the question: if my polio virus can't be cured, is the same true of a computer virus? Could it be that viruses were his generation's karma? Contrary to the way everybody else was thinking, Wang Jiangmin launched an all-out assault on computer viruses. He was energised in a way he had not been before he found out about them, and he felt this was what he was born to do.

Wang Jiangmin started by using Debug as a manual virus killer, but then wrote a programme to kill a specific virus. At the beginning of the 1990s, his first programme was designed to kill the '1741' virus. He wrote an article about it for a periodical, then released the programme. At that time the IT crowd were all energetic youngsters in their early 20s, English speaking, highly educated with high IQs: a generation pretty much custom-made by the internet, the so-called Generation X and very different from preceding generations. Wang Jiangmin was an exception, an outlier, and because of that, age and generation were meaningless to him: he acted entirely independently. Just as it is hard not to conclude that Steven Hawking is an exception, an outlier, to our generation, so Wang Jiangmin, regardless of age and appearance, was also just such an outlier.

But the status of outlier is not a chance matter, it is always connected with unusual suffering.

With great ease, Wang Jiangmin wrote a lot of programmes and killed a lot of viruses; to such an extent, in fact, that he began to feel much fresher and more relaxed in his own skin, and his body became like a constantly self-healing machine. After he had written a whole host of these programmes, he began to feel that the use of stand-alone virus-killers was very bothersome, so he took six of them and bundled them together, calling the new programme KV6. He went on to produce KV8, KV12, KV18 and KV20.

He started to participate in computer studies technical conferences, mostly in connection with computer viruses. At that time, the viruses that Chinese users encountered were all foreign produced but, as often as not, they were a kind of practical joke written by the programmers, not capable of doing serious harm to data. They were comparatively easy to deal with, and everything was fine once they had been dealt with. Later on, viruses written by Chinese appeared, and they were much more harmful, without any humorous element to them. They weren't just idle pranks, but cold-blooded and dispassionately evil creations. Most significantly, they could wipe out data. They threw the world into chaos, with evil begetting evil and competing to see who could be the worst. The first generation of virus creators was wiped out by these newcomers.

The second time Wang Jiangmin participated in a computer studies symposium, the problem of viruses was being talked about everywhere, and a number of experts' opinions combined into the statement: "Computer viruses are becoming more and more damaging, and research into them can no longer be done on an ad-hoc basis. But if it is being researched and sold commercially, it is hard to avoid the situation becoming a vicious circle of writing virus software then producing the anti-virus software to combat it. Can anyone deny this is how things stand?" In other words, it could be that the experts producing anti-virus software are the very ones creating the viruses in the first place. Wang Jiangmin started to be viewed with suspicion and to be viewed in a very different light.

Certainly, if you took that attitude, Wang Jiangmin did look even more like a virus engineer.

Or, more like a 'virus' himself.

This was a paradox that Wang Jiangmin had never even thought of.

No matter whether it was foreign or internal, Wang told the symposium, his face expressionless, it was impossible that people fighting viruses were the ones writing them; psychologically speaking it was impossible, and legally speaking, it was against the law. Moreover, he went on, just because someone knows how to kill off viruses doesn't necessarily mean they know how to create them. Writing a virus requires very careful study of lots of different factors, and it is much more complicated than writing an anti-virus programme. He even went as far as to believe that the virus creators were at a higher level than the anti-virus programmers, although ordinary people thought it must be the other way round.

"I am a polio victim, but do I have any control over the polio virus?" (Wang Jiangmin didn't actually say this. Saying it would have been very painful for him, but so was not saying it. In the end, however, he did not say it.)

Certainly, it is true that sufferers of this disease can also be carriers of the virus.

But Wang Jiangmin was not the kind of person who could do such a thing; his whole life, he never had been. He was not going to profit by being the creator of viruses for which he was selling the cure.

He was always fighting against things, even the form his body had taken.

One year, the Wuhan University Basketball Teaching and Research

Team sent Wang Jiangmin a sample of a metamorphic virus. It was a very unusual virus and it was the first time he had encountered it; it was also the first time a metamorphic virus had appeared in China. This wasn't something that could have been created by an anti-virus engineer; no, it just wasn't possible, even for someone as crazy as he was. Wang Jiangmin had heard about this kind of virus, but he had never actually seen one before.

He worked on it for a week, but he could not kill it. Standard anti-virus methods were simply not effective, and this fascinated him. In fact, to tell the truth, he didn't really expect that he would be able to find a way of killing it, and every route he took ended in defeat. Of course, at the same time, he spared no effort and his knowledge base expanded exponentially. He would conquer the virus in the same way he had conquered his own body and, in the end, he alighted upon the 'broad spectrum filter virus investigation method'. He gathered together several samples of the same type of virus and formed a theoretical summary of the characteristics of metamorphic viruses. The results were unambiguous, and he wrote a paper about them which received a national award for excellence.

Although Wang Jiangmin's KV series of anti-virus software was pretty ruthless it, like all the other software around, was still in the position of playing catch-up. Would it be possible to catch newly appeared viruses before they had spread and publish a weekly list of diagnostic codes in the newspapers so KV users could upgrade their programmes themselves? This would almost be equivalent to virus protection. Wang Jiangmin linked up, in free-form fashion, all his virus protection ideas, and sent them, together with the expandable KV100 software, to *Software News*. He even gave the package a name: 'Sucop' (short for Super Cop). *Software News* thought it was an excellent idea and, on 15 July 1994, published the first 'Anti-Virus Report'.

KV100 exploded onto the scene in *Software News* and in those days before internet and CD distribution, the 'Anti-Virus Report' was of enormous use. Many work unit directors ordered their computer department managers to cut out the weekly reports from the newspaper and upload the new anti-virus diagnostic codes. Wang Jiangmin became, to all intents and purposes, the lead scientist taking a stand for virus prevention; his reputation soared and people put their trust in him.

The first time Wang Jiangmin was introduced by friends to the Sinostar Company, the company was not particularly aware of the enormous value of KV100. But then, one day, the 20 or more computers at the Chinese subsidiary of a major foreign company were suddenly infected with a virus. The hard disc drives stopped as if they had cerebral palsy or a brainstorm, "their facial nerves were paralysed and they couldn't speak a word"; they were all as quiet as the grave. The company's staff were dumbstruck: several hundreds of millions worth of contracts couldn't be printed. In utter panic they searched high and low for someone who could save the situation and kill the virus. They even hunted down the most *avant-garde* foreign anti-virus software, but all to no avail. There was nothing for it but to call a meeting with all the local computer support companies and promise that in future they would buy all their hardware from whichever company could solve the current problem. The head of Sinostar, which was one of the hardware supply companies, put in a longdistance call to Wang Jiangmin in China and, at the same time, also contacted an American anti-virus expert, with an opening offer of US$20,000. When Wang arrived at the Beijing office of the big foreign company, he found the American expert already there investigating the virus.

Feeling like a spare part, Wang Jiangmin waited in the lobby for more than an hour. He went to the toilet several times because he was not feeling too well, and the receptionists wondered whether they should go to his aid. Of course, he refused any offers because he never wanted assistance from anyone. Even now, when things are very different, and Wang Jiangmin is well known everywhere, even though he is in a wheelchair, his manner is still extraordinarily forbearing. Back then Steven Hawking had already visited China, and people accepted and even admired his complex robotic presence. But with Wang Jiangmin, although his physical health was uncertain, he had a particular aura, both internal and external, an exceptional self-cultivated self-assurance. In fact, such people are the same the world over: their physical state marks them out but is also symbolic of their spiritual essence.

The poised and dashing American expert was rather less than poised and dashing at this moment, and inside the office he was shouting, "NO! NO! Format! Format!" Finally, he emerged, flustered and exasperated, presenting a total contrast to Wang Jiangmin. Wang encouraged confidence in others, as if they were reassured by the personal circumstances he himself had overcome. Of course, the atmosphere then was very tense, and everything he did was recorded by note-takers standing next to him.

Wang Jiangmin quickly determined that the virus that had infected all the machines was a Torch Virus, which only wipes out the hard disc partition table, but doesn't destroy data. In 10 minutes, Wang had coaxed all the affected machines back to life, and after 20 more minutes, he showed the staff of the company how to clean the virus off all 20 or so machines. Sinostar left the company 20 sets of KV100 and began to negotiate the rights transfer to market the product.

Previously, KV100 had been licensed to numerous companies, but to avoid such a confused market with KV200, Wang Jiangmin decided to include a standard laser anti-counterfeiting measure to standardise the market and standardise the price. This was a very clever move. Even so, he was quite clear that these measures wouldn't completely solve the counterfeiting problem so, to protect his own rights and interests, he came up with a system upgrade that would keep him one step ahead: as soon as the hard disc partition table restoration technology was perfected, he upgraded KV200 to KV300. Also, it was in the same year that the KV300 upgrade came out that Wang Jiangmin took that popular yellow Beijing minivan taxi to advance on Zhongguancun by taking Rmb500,000 in capital to register his own company: the Jiangmin Company.

Unlike many other people, Wang Jiangmin came prepared, and although the capital wasn't a huge sum, it was backed up by mature technology and was enough to start the venture. Of course, Wang also looked different from other people, but his maturity and reputation were enough to make people overlook that. The declaration of war against viruses was different from the one he made in Yantai. Beijing and Zhongguancun irradiated the whole country, they represented the whole country. He hadn't been in Zhongguancun long when he realised that the businessmen there liked to 'consolidate', that is to say a number of distributors would club together to increase their purchasing volumes in order to get a better wholesale price. Wang Jiangmin latched onto this and offered a very favourable wholesale price, so that if two big work units clubbed together, they could save a million Rmb. He couldn't have done this in Yantai, but Zhongguancun was so big that within a week of his arrival there he had chalked up his first victory.

His problem wasn't with sales, it was with the viruses. In themselves they might not have been problematic, but the challenges they presented by extension were. Wang Jiangmin was countering viruses, but the people in China who were creating the viruses and writing the programmes were constantly working on ways to circumvent him. The author of the famous 'Hefei 1' virus issued a direct challenge to Wang Jiangmin, not long after he arrived in Zhongguancun: he went as far as to decrypt KV300 and plant the Hefei 1 virus inside the programme, and then published the infected version of KV300 on internet bulletin boards. After the virus was activated on 1 January 1997, the author of Hefei 1 immediately spread the word far and wide on the internet that KV300 was infected with a virus. The battle between virus creator and virus defender was no longer going on backstage but was in the full glare of the footlights. This battle of the magicians drew a lot of attention from the industry, as a new 'Duel on Mount Hua[2]' manifested itself in the Badlands of the IT world. It was the Covenant of Mount Hua, and Wang Jiangmin, like Wu Qing (Heartless), the hero of *The Four Great Constables* from the pen of Wen Rui'an[3], as fast as lightning and with miraculous skill despite his handicap, overwhelmed Hefei 1 on the summit of IT's Mount Hua.

If these occasional challenges may be considered honourable affairs and quite proper, then what came next left Wang Jiangmin not knowing whether to laugh or cry. After Wang had seen off Hefei 1, its author went rogue, abandoning any pretence of being the noble outlaw. He said on the internet: "Why was it only Wang Jiangmin who could kill the virus, and not anyone else? Because it was Wang Jiangmin who created it! It should be called the KV300 Virus." With a twist of his tail, like a fiend in human form, he had turned the tables on Wang Jiangmin. At the same time as this devil incarnate was bellowing out his grievances, he was also launching the Hefei 2 virus. This was the fiendishly insoluble, incredibly destructive 'Joke' virus which had innumerable variations almost as though it was using every encryption technique in the encryption handbook. Wang Jiangmin's head ached for three days over it, but he found an encryption-breaking method of killing the virus.

The fiends behind the virus flew into a rage of humiliation (of course, there was more than one of them), and immediately successively produced the Shanghai 1, Shanghai 2 and Shanghai 3 viruses. With flying fingers and dancing feet, Wang Jiangmin followed the viruses everywhere, neutralising them wherever they appeared. The Shanghai Technology Centre quickly collected a sample of the virus affecting KV300, and Wang Jiangmin immediately killed it. The Shanghai 2 virus changed its display name to KV300C, but it was destroyed by Wang Jiangmin before it even got out of Shanghai. The Shanghai 3 virus quite simply changed its display name to the romanised *pinyin* form of Wang's name, calling itself 'wangjiangmin'. Wang analysed all three Shanghai viruses and produced a set of anti-Shanghai virus broad-spectrum codes. After that, there was no Shanghai 4 virus, because whatever alterations the creators made, however they revamped their technique, they couldn't get past Wang's 'Sunflower Manual'[4] of a broad-spectrum virus detector code. Wang Jiangmin completely destroyed the lair of the Shanghai virus, though, needless to say, there was an element of killing the goose that lays the golden eggs about it.

Wang Jiangmin was ruthless and made no attempt to hide it.

It was fortunate that Wang Jiangmin possessed this kind of ruthless determination.

At around 10 o'clock in the morning of 4 April 2010, Wang Jiangmin died suddenly, at the age of 59. Some people said God's computer must have been infected with a virus and he took Wang Jiangmin to fix it. You might just as well say that God wanted to learn the 'Moonwalk', so he took Michael Jackson to teach him or he wanted to read *I and the Temple of Earth* so he took Shi Tiesheng.

DIARY NOTE 14: ILLNESS AND CREATIVITY

The earliest anti-virus software came on 3.5-inch floppy discs when computers still had disc drives. They don't any more. I remember there was a lot of such software around at the time: Rising, KV300, Jinshan, Kaspersky, 360; and computer housekeeping was a thing of the future. I used a lot of them, but mostly Rising. There was one day, however, which I remember very clearly, when a colleague gave me a floppy disc which he said was a fearsome anti-virus programme called KV300. I thought the name was great, and indeed it was great when I used it. After that I always remembered KV300.

Anti-virus software was a key element in the rise of Zhongguancun, and people have all sorts of memories of computer viruses. You could say that computers were not around for very long before computer viruses arrived on the scene, and that the two naturally go together. But right at the beginning, from what I have heard, viruses were really not understood: after all, how could a computer have a virus?

At the time, I didn't know that this lethal virus-killer software, KV300, was the brainchild of an invalid, or that he had been fighting his own physical virus all his life. Of course, there is no evidence to show that the poliomyelitis virus and computer viruses have any connection. But it is not irrelevant here to suggest that illness clearly has a complex psychological relationship with human creativity. On a stage like Zhongguancun, how could there not be such a relationship? It is evident in Wang Xuan, in Feng Kang and in Wang Jiangmin.

However, I am not, of course, going to delve any further into this question. I will leave that to you, my readers.

Internet

In May or June 1995, a billboard was erected at the mouth of Baishiqiao Road in the Haidian District of Beijing: How far are the Chinese people from the information superhighway? 1500 metres to the north. Baishiqiao Road leads to Zhongguancun and the Yiheyuan (New Summer Palace). People in Zhongguancun call it Baiyi Road, and the intersection where the billboard stood was the starting point of Baiyi Road; it was also the starting point of the concept of Zhongguancun.

This was China's first open-air internet advertisement; 1,500 metres north of the spot was China's first internet company founded by the *avant-garde* pioneer of the Chinese internet, Zhang Shuxin: Beijing InfoHighway. In that year, there were 40,000 Chinese going online via InfoHighway, and actually connecting and communicating with the world. The concept of the 'Information Superhighway' was very new back then, and very much in vogue, opening, as it did, a window on the rapid progress taking place in the world. The name came from Alvin Toffler's book, *The Third Wave*, which was very popular in China in the 1980s. It talked about the society of the future being an information society. That information society emerged in embryonic form with InfoHighway.

Wang Zhidong was online that year too, but in America, not via Info-Highway. In California's already famous Silicon Valley, he immersed himself for three whole days in the internet, and was fascinated by the world he found there. On the internet, the speed of the world was so fast, the world was flat, and all time was synchronic so that it almost lost its significance. The third wave, the new tide were there in front of his eyes and he stood in amongst them

Wang Zhidong was at a crossroads: before he went to America, there were two things that had rather excited him: one was meeting Feng Bo, the assistant to an American investment banker called Robertson, and the other was meeting Microsoft's Tang Jun. One thing Feng Bo said then really opened up Wang Zhidong's imagination. He said that Stone Rich Sight was not really a Chinese software company; it was an international company with its headquarters in China. Other people were probably baffled by this observation, but it was a wake-up call to Wang Zhidong: he was going to run his company following the model of Silicon Valley.

At that time, Tang Jun, who was to become chairman of Microsoft China, was upper management in the new Windows NT department at Microsoft headquarters, and when he met Wang Zhidong, he said, "At the moment, we are building an engine, and when that engine is finished, your 'Chinese Star' will be redundant. By that time, Microsoft Windows

Chinese edition and English edition will be released simultaneously. Previously there was a time-lag but in future there won't be."

Wang Zhidong had made 'Chinese Star' a household name, and it was a business at its peak. He was the most influential and trendy of the 'Zhongguancun Second Generation'. Tang Jun's words made Wang, who was at the zenith of his success, suddenly see the final sunset of judgment day when he would undoubtedly suffer the supreme penalty. It seemed a cruel fate. But Tang Jun was absolutely right, and was being quite open and honest. He was also secure in occupying the strategic high ground, and sure of his backing. Wang Zhidong understood that Tang Jun was not speaking as an individual but representing the Microsoft Corporation. In the past, Wang had stuck close to Microsoft, and rapidly become famous on the back of it, but now Microsoft was about to shake him off its coat-tails.

Wang Zhidong was born in a water town in the south of China, and at the age of 17 went to study radio-engineering at Peking University. In his third year, he began to build computers and write software off-campus, earning more than his professors did. His story begins with him writing software. The campus at that time was famous for its poets, who were part of the 'Misty Poetry Movement'; these included Hai Zi, Xi Chuan, Ge Mai and others. Wang Zhidong was stirring up the same kind of waves as these poets, but in a different field: the software he wrote was making a name for him on campus as someone way ahead of his time. Other than poetry, software was the other thing at the cutting edge of society. One day, a stranger came looking for Wang Zhidong, bringing a Peking University electronic typesetting system and a computer he had just bought. He told Wang that the two things were not compatible but the software engineering teachers, Wang's own teachers amongst them, at the university couldn't do anything about it. In a matter of moments and without breaking sweat, Wang Zhidong cracked the software code, modified it and solved the compatibility problem. Wang Xuan, the inventor of electronic typesetting, got to hear about this and was both amazed and outraged that his coding had been broken; he sent someone to investigate. When he learned that the person who had performed this feat was a student, he found himself rather pleasantly surprised.

In the 1980s, the top priority for China's computer technologists was to build a mature Chinese operating environment. A string of innovations made by the first generation of master software engineers in this field quickly turned Zhongguancun into one of the standard bearers of the age.

But, by the beginning of the 1990s, the fundamental technology in China was still reliant on the 'sinification' of foreign software programmes, just as if an English language book was being translated into Chinese. But, because the software itself was advancing at such incomparable speed, developing a Chinese operating environment was a real headache. The few programmers working on the 'sinification' process were most afraid of the sudden emergence of new capabilities in the English-language operating systems. Because of that, a lot of the time they had originally devoted to adapting the older versions of software was wasted effort.

Wang Zhidong joined Wang Xuan's main team, where Wang Xuan gave him exceptional freedom: he didn't have to come into the office, but could work from home, and however important the task, he was to follow his own instincts in developing it. Wang Xuan was someone who valued talent above all else, especially unusual talent, because that was what he himself had. He knew the problems brought about by being different, and he thought Wang Zhidong was just like he had been in his youth. He had had a very torrid time of it when he was young, and he didn't want Wang Zhidong to have to endure the same bitter struggles and lack of freedom. He wanted the young man to be free to be himself.

When Microsoft's 'Windows 95' came out in the 1990s, it ruled the roost at Microsoft. Wang Zhidong paid very close attention to this new phenomenon as it was the only one among all the countless pieces of software that he had worked on, that genuinely stunned him. One day, Wang Xuan said to him, "I know you have got the ability to alter my stuff, but do you dare alter Microsoft's?"

There was really no need for him to ask. Wang Zhidong was already giving that matter his close attention.

Already thoroughly immersed in the world of electronics, after Wang Xuan got under his skin, Wang Zhidong became even more solidly ensconced at home, barely even going out of the door. The rattle of the printer could be heard at all hours of the day and night, and his all-out dedication was very like Wang Xuan at the same age, except that Wang Xuan had been even more extreme and had starved himself to the point of dropsy and had become seriously ill. Wang Zhidong had no trouble looking after himself properly, eating plenty and keeping his strength up. It was the times that were different. The pages of programming spewed out by the printer piled up on the floor and the room slowly became a world of printer paper, a world of white, a world of ink and, even more, a world of numbers. Wang Zhidong kept his head buried in his studies and spent all day every day in that little world. Like someone shut up in a world of the future of his own making (who is to say whether it was a little corner of heaven for him or a prison cell?), Wang Zhidong was just like that as he battled against the mighty Microsoft, the giant Microsoft. Much as you might say he was owned by Wang Xuan, he was just as much owned by Bill Gates. Of course, first and foremost he owed a debt of gratitude to Wang Xuan as it was Wang Xuan who had given him sovereignty over this kingdom of solitude. But it was Bill Gates who had given him a target, an elevated and difficult target. Zhongguancun had a spirit of individuality, of single combat, of a duel to the death, a battle with history. It was this kind of challenge that created the legend of Zhongguancun. In fact, China hides much great individual strength and all it requires is the right conditions - indeed, even if the conditions aren't fully met, it can still be unleashed.

Almost 70 days later, ghostly white himself, Wang Zhidong emerged from his white world, still leaving a chaos of white behind him. Like a performance artist in white, Wang Zhidong held in his hand the Chinese version of Windows 1.0, '视窗1.0' (Shichuang 1.0).

He had succeeded in the challenge and rewritten Microsoft. This was what Zhongguancun was all about; this was what Wang Zhidong was all about. Even so, there was no way it could be released onto the market, as it was simply turning English Windows into Chinese, like a book being translated, and there was no creativity or innovation involved . Even so, this success was revolutionary: it was matching Microsoft step for step, or rather it had caught up with Microsoft and caught up with the world. The problem was that before the shock of Wang Zhidong's 'Shichuang 1.0' had died down, Microsoft's Windows 2.0 appeared in Zhongguancun; and before Wang Zhidong could produce a Chinese version of that, Microsoft's Windows 3.0 was on the streets. Was he always going to be just imitating Microsoft? The market has no time to lock the stable door after the horse has bolted.

This problem had to be resolved; he had to be right up there with Windows, progressing at the same rate. Wang Zhidong was very happy working independently, and decided to set up his own centre, like those talented folks in Silicon Valley. But times had changed, and individual heroes were no longer what were required. Wang Xuan understood this and, like the lofty 'high-flying bird' that he was, he released Wang Zhidong. Wang Zhidong set up Stone Rich Sight to settle once and for all the problem of 'locking the stable door…' He went back into his closed white kingdom to continue what other people thought of as his 'performance art'. He locked himself away for several months, racking his brains. But this time he was unproductive and could not see his way through the problem; for a time he was close to despair. But there is always a glimmer of light in the darkness which can resolve a struggle like Wang Zhidong's. One night, a lightning streak of light flashed across Wang's dreams, and he woke up with a start. He sat bolt upright, looking deep into the vaulted dome of his imagination, "Aha! Yes! That's how it is!"

He jumped out of bed, switched on his computer and rattled out a short programme. His thinking was now that he should no longer be trying to mess around with Windows' internal programming, but he should hang his own Chinese platform on its external interface – it was like a martial arts manoeuvre you find in in *wuxia* novels called 'the scorpion climbs backwards up the city walls'. He called his new programme 'the trapdoor technique'. This was his 'core thinking' and it showed great originality. Simply put, he was cutting an opening into the Windows programming through which he could rapidly insert his information data, then extract it; but, because he had set up his Chinese platform in advance, he could scoop out armfuls of the data, turn it into Chinese, then return it to its original location and let it run according to the original programming.

This was an imaginary world, a world which even the poets of the time had trouble envisaging. Very few Chinese were capable of entering it. It was like a palace and when Wang Zhidong went in there, he became king[1] of his own palace. His contemporary at university, the poet Hai Zi, once conjured up the idea of 'being king of oneself' but ended up entering the kingdom of darkness when he killed himself on the railway tracks at Shanhaiguan. But, like a character from science fiction, Wang Zhidong built his own palace inside the very core of the Windows software and became the one and only king there. But the little programme for that 'trapdoor', or maybe we should call it a 'hook', was no more than 60 lines of code, so it was a very small palace. Small as it was, though, it burrowed deep into the internal workings of Microsoft, very much in line with the computer world's dictum: simplest is best. That night, Wang Zhidong succeeded completely in securing it on Windows 3.0.

He was well aware this was a pioneering achievement, an enormous achievement and he was elated by it. As the sky in the east began to lighten, he couldn't go back to sleep, he had no desire to sleep; he seemed to be ascending into the heavens with the sun and he said to himself, "No one else has ever done this before anywhere else in the world, only me!"

There Is Only One King

The next day, he put the programme on all the other versions and was successful in every case; so successful, in fact, that the results were compatible with every kind of monitor and printer, which was actually beyond his expectations. From Wang Zhidong's beginnings, this Chinese computer platform became a stand-alone programme known as a 'plug-in programme'. From then on, Wang Zhidong and all other software engineers no longer had to slog away modifying other people's programmes step by step. Wang Zhidong gave his discovery a name that was neither really Chinese nor foreign, calling it 'BDWin', which was short for 'Beijing University[2] Windows'.

This was an individual's challenge to Microsoft.

There was no other individual like him in the world.

Wang Zhidong's plug-in programme 'Chinese Star' spread rapidly across the internal market as soon as it was launched, speeding up China's computer use and promoting enormous gains in social and economic efficiency. It was reported that, in one month, 'Chinese Star' made a net profit of Rmb900,000. It was also said that its appearance, out of the blue, gave Bill Gates an enormous shock and he loudly lamented the fact that China had produced this marvel. Microsoft's senior management commented that at least 'Chinese Star' had brought Microsoft's products onto the Chinese market five years ahead of their schedule. Although its selling price was Rmb680, it worked so well with Windows 3.0 that no one considered it expensive.

Microsoft tolerated Wang Zhidong for three years until 1995 when, pleasantly surprised by the speed and strength of their entry into the Chinese market, they decided to release the English and Chinese versions of Windows simultaneously. Tang Jun had warned Wang Zhidong this would happen and the announcement had many obvious implications.

Wang Zhidong understood.

He also understood that his career as a programmer was over and there was no need for him to play Don Quixote with Microsoft any longer. He needed to broaden his horizons.

This was one part of those obvious implications.

Wang Zhidong went to America. He remembered Feng Bo telling him that Stone Rich Sight was not a Chinese software company, but an international software company with a Chinese headquarters. He wanted to follow the road begun by Silicon Valley; he wanted to seek out venture capital. At that time, Zhongguancun knew nothing about venture capital, and although Wang Zhidong knew a little bit about it, his knowledge was very superficial.

There was investment activity in Zhongguancun at the time, but it wasn't called 'venture capital', nor was there the concept of 'angel investment'. But, in fact, Wang Zhidong and the first generation of Chinese programmers did receive this kind of investment when Stone's chief engineer, Yan Yuanchao, launched Stone Rich Sight. As key players behind the scenes built the bridges, Wang Zhidong went to see Stone's chairman Duan Yongji and, using both his skills and his legendary reputation, he managed to persuade Duan to come up with HK$5 million of 'angel investment' for his own future software company, later to become Stone Rich Sight. Without investing a cent himself, Wang Zhidong held 20% of the shares in the new company. Duan Yongji also agreed to Wang's three extra conditions: the new company would be autonomous in controlling its personnel and Stone would not import a single member of its staff; it would only make software; and the employees would be given stock options.

Because he had not been able to find a candidate for the post of CEO, after two months, and with the support of Yan Yuanchao as instigator of the project, Wang Zhidong took up the post himself. In its initial set-up, the company rented a small building from Wanquan Primary School in the southern part of Zhongguancun and, because the location was so remote, Wang Zhidong had no option but to put up signboards at every intersection in the vicinity. The company's main project was to use Chinese Star as the central core for developing the Chinese language software platform Richwin, the first version of which was launched on 20 March 1994; but only a year later there was an even louder fanfare for the onslaught on the Chinese market of Microsoft Windows Chinese edition.

This fanfare for Windows was, in fact, just as much a death knell for Richwin.

The world has always had holy places, such as Jersualem and Mecca.

If the modern world has a holy place, then it is Silicon Valley, at least according to Wang Zhidong

The first time Wang Zhidong set off for Silicon Valley, he got lost and had to phone a friend to ask for directions, saying he was on Number One Street. The friend was baffled as he didn't know of any street by that name in the area. Getting impatient, Wang Zhidong said down the receiver, enunciating as clearly as he could, "One Way! The signpost says One

Way!". It was also at this time that Wang Zhidong went on the internet properly for the first time when he saw a website address in a magazine he had bought in passing at the airport. When he got to his hotel, using a dial-up connection, he easily upgraded to the local operating system and even succeeded in downloading the latest data from the factory website.

Nowadays, online upgrades are nothing out of the ordinary, but back then, Wang Zhidong caught the scent of something new: as the engineers of Silicon Valley were singing the praises of the internet, what Wang smelled was the scent of the future. From 1995 to 1997, when he found his first tranche of venture capital, he visited Silicon Valley three times, and repeated study brought understanding. He discovered that the vast majority of foreign venture capitalists had no understanding of China, let alone of the Chinese IT industry.

Over the next two years, Wang Zhidong spent a lot of time and energy trying to talk round the venture capitalists, explaining to them about China, Chinese culture, Chinese economics and Chinese government. At the same time, he also turned back to China to persuade internal investors by introducing them to the concept of venture capital. He also talked to company staff trying to make them understand how important the introduction of venture capital was to the development of the company, how vital it was. In the course of those two years he pretty much became an expert in the theory of venture capital and in the problems facing China. He was also learning for himself how to communicate with foreigners, learning about what Silicon Valley was really all about, and the rules of the Western capital marketplace.

In the course of this journey, Wang Zhidong's thinking became more and more mature. He decided to straddle time and space, and to straddle cultures by establishing a common internet platform for Chinese people all around the globe. The impact of this action exceeded all expectations. Economic connections between Taiwan and the mainland at the time were not very close. In terms of online business, Taiwan was a major exporter and streets ahead of the mainland, so the sudden appearance from a mainland company of the biggest internet site that linked Chinese communities across the world, was an almost unimaginable event.

To facilitate the setting up of this website, Stone Rich Sight bought an American company. At the time, the company had a lot of Chinese with a Taiwan background and through them they established the fastest-growing Taiwanese customer-based website anywhere. However, negotiations with venture capital businesses were proving very tricky, as the investment companies refused to accept Wang Zhidong's valuation of

Stone Rich Sight at US$15 million. But just as an exhausted Wang was giving up hope, the investment companies caught wind of something, and suddenly agreed to his proposals. It was a dramatic moment when the marketplace and capital woke up to what was going on

It does have to be said that the huge Chinese market was the last to take it up.

In October 1997, the Walden Investment Company, RSC Capital and the Ivanhoe International Group raised a total of US$6.5 million in venture capital for Stone Rich Sight. After this round of financing, the Walden Group became the majority shareholder and Wang Zhidong's holding was reduced to 13%. The Walden Group's investment interest was in the Chinese-language internet and, under the requirements of their investment, by 1997, Stone Rich Sight changed fundamentally into an internet company. Moreover, the one thing the investors could not tolerate was Stone Rich Sight's comparatively primitive management organisation. Before this, Stone Rich Sight had already been criticised in the news media as being a 'family company': Wang Zhidong himself was the CEO and his wife, Liu Bing, was in charge of company finances. Under pressure from the investors during the financing negotiations, Wang Zhidong decided to hand over financial control.

On 1 January 1997, an American called Mark was engaged as Stone Rich Sight's financial director and became the first American to enter Zhongguancun. His introduction caused a sensation in the Chinese business world. Later on, also at the instigation of the investors, Wang Zhidong established three deputy general managers in his 30-something-strong company, in charge of technology, marketing and administration respectively, distributing the authority formerly held by the CEO alone.

Stone Rich Sight was taking big steps towards becoming an internet company, and by this time SRSnet, under the supervision of Wang Yan, who had studied abroad in France, had already been in operation for a year. After SRSnet carried the 1998 FIFA World Cup, its reputation took off and it gradually became Stone Rich Sight's most important division. On 26 September 1998, at Beijing's Crowne Plaza Hotel, Wang Zhidong met the then CEO of the Chinese-language internet site Huayuan, Jiang Fengnian (Daniel Fongnian Chiang). The formation of Sina was a direct result of this meeting. In the course of it, Jiang Fengnian and Wang Zhidong got on as though they had always known each other, and when Jiang discovered that Stone Rich Sight also owned the incredibly popular SRSnet, he immediately suggested a merger. Wang Zhidong doubled the previous year's

US$15 million valuation of Stone Rich Sight to US$30 million, and Jiang Fengnian still accepted this astronomical figure.

After nine days of negotiation, on 27 October, the two sides reached an agreement and the sale of Huayuan to Stone Rich Sight was settled with one share in Huayuan pitched at 0.38 of one share in Stone Rich Sight. In the new company formed by the merger, Jiang Fengnian became simultaneously chairman of the board and CEO, while Wang Zhidong was director-general. After the agreement was signed, Jiang asked Wang, "What are we going to call the new internet site?" At the time, his planners had already taken Huayuan's English name, 'SINA' and changed it to '*Sainuowang*' (赛诺王. an auspicious name with a meaning something like 'king of competitive promise') and were even on the point of printing branded stationery and merchandise. Wang Zhidong didn't agree to this on the spot, and the next day, after a sleepless night, he told Jiang Fengnian that the new name would be, '*Xinlang*' (新浪 New Wave), which in English became Sina Corp.

Because Sina Corp had offices in America, Hong Kong, Taipei, Beijing, Shanghai, Guangzhou and many other locations, Wang Zhidong split his time so that each month he spent one week in Silicon Valley, one week in Hong Kong, one week in Beijing and the remaining days of the month he would share between Taipei, Shanghai, Guangzhou, New York and Los Angeles. As a result, he became a 'frequent flyer' roaming the skies around the world. It was just as Feng Bo had said, it wasn't a Chinese company, it was an international software company headquartered in China.

It had been a dream and now it was a reality. What kind of a dream was it for this talented programmer to turn into the founder of the famous Sina Corp? It was a dream in which Zhongguancun stopped being just Zhongguancun.

Zhongguancun was now the world as well.

DIARY NOTE 15: SHADES OF YESTERYEAR

> Although Windows 95, Chinese Star and Sina Corp are just memories now, they are also still present, as if they have the power to transcend time. And there is one man who connects all three, a miraculous presence within the miraculous. In Wang Zhidong's case it is not an exaggeration to say that the trend of events brought forth the hero. When Windows was launched, China was faced with the problem of how to

'sinify' it. Cometh the hour, cometh the man; and behold - Wang Zhidong appeared - creating the legend of his 70 days locked away breaking into Windows. In those 70 days, his world turned white and there stood Wang Zhidong on a floor covered in sheets of white paper; there he emerged clutching a Chinese version of Windows 1.0, a Wang Zhidong whose own body almost seemed to have turned white. His appearance made people think of Ximen Chuixue[3]. Like a Ximen Chuixue of the IT world he challenged Microsoft, and succeeded. The old tales of dragons may not be true, but we still have proud and valiant real-life heroes.

It was just such an expert who, out of the blue, created Sina Corp which, after the collapse of Yinghaiwei[4], allowed the Chinese internet to rise again like a phoenix from the ashes, to stride out and even be floated on the American stock market. But China's IT folk had better remember Yinghaiwei: it was first in the field but toppled to the ground before the sun even rose. Indeed, I believe there are quite a few writers who, like me, started publishing our works on the internet right at the beginning on Yinghaiwei. I can still see myself signing up with Yinghaiwei at the intersection with Baishiqiao Road, handing over the sign-up fee, providing my home landline number, buying a modem, and seeing my whole world change once I got home. It was 1995, and I remember it very clearly: how I dialled the number and heard the swift rhythm of the connecting tone given off by the connection icon on the Windows 95 interface display. I went into Yinghaiwei's 'Coffee Shop' chatroom and joined in the forum's countless discussion topics, amongst which, to my surprise, there was one called 'Online Literature'. That must have been the first appearance of 'Online Literature' on the Chinese mainland, and where I first uploaded and posted some of my written work. A year later, Yinghaiwei made an 'Online Literature' CD called *The Remains of the Day* which included some of my uploaded work. I still have a copy of that very first 'Online Literature' CD produced in China, and I have also kept a lot of the content from that early chatroom. Back then, my internet handle was '*kefesi*'. After Yinghaiwei stopped operating, in 1998 I continued to use '*kefesi*' for my Sina Corp email, and it is still in use today.

My memories of the internet are so many, but they are as ephemeral as smoke too. I clearly remember 13 September 2000, when my full-length novel *City of Masks* was uploaded onto Sina Corp after it had been turned down by traditional literary magazines. It was in serial form to begin with, and in one month it received half a million hits.

That was an astronomical figure for the time; it was later accepted by the well-known literary magazine *Contemporary*, and was even named overall champion in *Contemporary's* second Literary Rally Competition. The following year it also received the Lao She Award for a full-length novel. In me, traditional literature and internet literature join up like the confluence of two rivers. A man can't dive into the same river twice, but at that time I felt I was diving into two rivers simultaneously.

The serialisation of *City of Masks* finished after three months at 15:26 on 15 December 2000, and I appended to it an article entitled *Deserted by Tradition I Found a Friend in Sina*:

...almost as though I had had a premonition, over the next few days publishers came to my door, hoping to publish *City of Masks*. It wasn't just one publishing house; I was spoiled for choice. The respected author of *Red Poppies: A Novel of Tibet* once approached 13 publishers over four years, until his book was chosen at random, and proved to be a masterpiece. But how many such works remain buried? How many different people in 13 houses read *Red Poppies*? The same number who decided the fate of a potential masterpiece. But those days are gone now. Of course, there are some writers and authors who persist with the old ways, abiding by them with dedication and a feeling of loneliness, wading through the sediment of time, clutching a masterpiece in their hands and disdaining the public arena.

Let everyone do it their own way!

People ask me if I got paid or not? I tell them I didn't. But what I did receive was more valuable than any remuneration. I'm not going on about being paid now, as that goes without saying, what I am saying is that what I got from the days when my novel was being serialised in the public arena was the readers' emotions, their equality and participation, their criticism and penetrating insights which all made me experience a kind of equality and freedom, and an interactive modern day interpersonal relationship. Hermit-like scholars are full of bitterness in their solitude, and once they take up any kind of post, they put on airs, seek respect and expect rewards; that is the inevitable psychology, the psychology of bureaucracy, even. The truth is, we all retain a servant mentality in our repressed and lonely selves.

The public arena – the internet - is educating us; changing us.

When surfing the net, there is equality of opportunity: no complaints, no redress, freedom of communication, a normal balance of gain and loss. Reason comes not only from knowledge, education and book-learning, it also comes from heredity, habit and ordinariness. The

3. INTERNET

deep significance of this kind of change comes not, I believe, from enlightenment and the 1980s. The nature of the deepest change is to be found in what is happening day to day.

But that's enough theorising, let us return to my written oeuvre. Another aspect of my understanding comes from writing itself. When I read my works online, I critique myself from the readers' point of view. I feel deeply uneasy. I can see my mistakes: many places where I am harsh, implausible, unreasonable and imprecise. Sometimes I even stop making later corrections but go back and fill in gaps in what had come before, as though I am trying to hide my shame. A full-length novel is an adventure, brimming with misconceptions, forks in the road, well-worn clichés, old habits and unfamiliar worlds; sometimes I may even find myself out of my depth.

Other than all that, it is regrettable that I may discover that my original ending is not at all what is required and I have to rewrite it; this always causes me a degree of alarm. I may not have thought out the new ending even as the serialisation closes in on it. I may not be able to see where Ma Ge is going, so I can't arrange a proper ending for him: this is just like the uncertainty of my own future. I may consider having him killed or him committing suicide, but no matter how carefully I plot it, it just feels like a murder or an assassination. So what can I do? He's only 27! And I haven't even begun to think about the secondary characters. Fortunately, this is the public arena, and people see not only the end result but also the creative process and are active participants in what comes next. I think that is what modern writing is all about.

In the same way, I may tell the publisher, the work isn't finished yet and I'm not even sure when it will be.

I may think I have already said all the important things I have to say but, even so, there still has to be an ending, even if it is only a kind of stop-gap ending. It's still not easy, though. I am very grateful to my online friends for the encouragement they give me, and for their criticisms and opinions. I hope that I will continue to receive them, and through a process of ongoing refinement, arrive at an acceptable ending. I must redouble my efforts so that we can come together and upload a take-away-ready amended version onto Sina.

I am particularly grateful to my online friends teeming 先生 , 阿lulu_500 先生, 黑雪 01, 玄武岩 , wengjw123, iceburg15, wuhoya, 泡泡茶 , forrmb, zicq, 麦齐尔, sflii, waiiya and the others. Your indefatigable attention undoubtedly constitutes an inseparable element of this book.

I also particularly want to thank Sina for providing the arena.

Seventeen years later, my books are still on the internet, and I am still very grateful to Sina.

I am particularly grateful to Wang Zhidong and his legendary story.

I also want to thank Yinghaiwei and its emergence on BaiYi Road, 22 years ago. Indeed, Zhongguancun and I share an ineffable karma. I am part of Zhongguancun, or rather, we all are.

[PART 7]
Lenovo China (4)
联想中国(四)

Accumulation

ALTHOUGH IN 2004, Lenovo was famous throughout the PC world, its purchase of IBM's world PC business caused a lot of the Western news media to look askance at it: on the one hand they thought Lenovo was biting off more than it could chew, and on the other they thought it was buying a pig in a poke. Some of them asked, "Why has Lenovo chosen to buy IBM which is an American business with a brand that is operating at a loss? Some reports even asked caustically, "Can a frog become a prince just by putting on a prince's cast-off clothes?"

The chief analyst of an American IT consultancy company, Robert Enderle, even observed, gloatingly that, "This deal is like a Christmas present to HP and Dell; I have never seen two companies so happy. IBM is a very distinctive company in the US and its internal culture is extremely problematic. When HP merged with Compaq, they transferred a team of more than a thousand to work on the integration process, but Lenovo doesn't appear to be planning anything on that kind of scale..."

Michael Dell, chairman of the rival company that bears his name, said bluntly, "This is a loss-making acquisition. Dell has never had the slightest interest in IBM's PC division... I cannot see how Lenovo's purchase of it is any different from any of the loss-making acquisitions that have preceded it."

In truth, when people in China got to hear the news, there was also a lot of scepticism. Although Lenovo already had a substantial reputation in the country, when all was said and done, how could it really compare with a global giant like IBM, and how could it possibly swallow IBM's worldwide PC business? What if it couldn't? Some people even reckoned this was fake news.

At that time, Chinese were used to foreign companies and foreign investment coming into the country, and used to boast that however many Fortune 500 companies established a presence in China, that just meant there were that many joint-venture businesses. So what was Lenovo doing turning things upside down like this? Not long after, Liu Chuanzhi was giving a lecture as part of the MBA course at Peking University and when he started talking about the IBM purchase, there was a sceptical noise from the audience as no one believed it was going to prove a success. Actually, there were three people who did, two of whom were on Lenovo scholarships. Even when CCTV interviewed Liu Chuanzhi on the evening after the deal went through, the interviewer, Shen Bing, asked what he would do if the purchase went wrong. Liu Chuanzhi was very put out by this. At that time there were all kinds of quite reasonable ideas that people just weren't used to yet.

It was said at the time that it was Liu Chuanzhi's second-in-command, Yang Yuanqing, who had first brought up the idea of buying IBM's worldwide PC business, and that Liu himself was astonished, and couldn't get his head around it. Yang Yuanqing was CEO of Lenovo at the time, and Liu Chuanzhi was chairman of the board so not involved in the day-to-day running of the business. However, an earth-shattering deal like this needed Liu's seal of approval, and he thought it needed due consideration before he could come to a decision. Yang Yuanqing sought out McKinsey and Goldman Sachs to make a preliminary analysis, and they both gave the thumbs-up. But Liu Chuanzhi was still uneasy, and even at this stage, how to take the first step still needed careful consideration. It was not an ordinary kind of step, it was an historic step. It is often the case when history is being made that most people are completely unaware of it, and only a very few people who have studied the route carefully are ready to match their wits with history.

Liu Chuanzhi called a board meeting during which he and Yang Yuanqing kept a neutral stance, and all the board members vetoed the scheme. They were not without reason in doing so. The main points were:

1) After Lenovo bought the IBM brand, wouldn't foreigners not be aware and still think it was IBM?

2) In buying IBM, Lenovo wasn't buying factories as they didn't have any; they were buying sales teams and research teams; people, in fact. At the time, IBM had 400,000 employees worldwide, 200 of whom alone were lawyers. If we Chinese buy up the PC business and the staff all leave and don't stay on, what are we going to do?

3) After the sale goes through, Chinese will take up the executive posts and if the foreigners in the Chinese market pick a fight and fight dirty, are they going to take any notice of Chinese executives? These were the biggest objections.

Yang Yuanqing was greatly taken aback by the veto and very angry. He asked Liu Chuanzhi how Lenovo was going to grow if they didn't seize this opportunity. How was it going to go international? If it didn't go international how could it keep up with its competitors? These points were equally valid.

Yang Yuanqing was so persistent because he knew that the board members who were top brass at the Academy of Sciences and those who were representatives of the workforce put most store by Liu Chuanzhi's opinion. In the end, Liu Chuanzhi gave his final verdict: there was temporary uncertainty over whether to make the purchase or not, but it was permitted to consult with McKinsey and Goldman Sachs as to the next level, and to pay their several million US dollars' worth of consultancy fees. This was a crucial decision, and it demonstrated one aspect of Liu Chuanzhi's character: it took account of everyone's uncertainty and sowed the seeds for what was to come next.

After a feasibility study of the considerable cost involved, the first two objections raised by the board were resolved as they were not considered to be major problems. The third objection concerned whether, in five years' time, a Chinese would actually be able to run the company. It wasn't a problem for Yang Yuanqing to be chairman of the board, but the powers of a chairman of the board are not as great as those of a CEO. It is normal in China for the chairman of the board to be seen as the secretary to a municipal committee where the CEO is the mayor, and in practice, it is the CEO who holds the reins within the administrative apparatus. But, in allowing Yang Yuanqing to be chairman of the board while inviting a foreigner to take up the post of CEO, the main fear was that a foreigner would not have enough experience to rein in Yang Yuanqing. For example, supposing this deal didn't go very well in the first two years, the foreigner didn't listen to advice and the company's performance was down, come what may, it would be the CEO who was fired. The way Liu Chuanzhi saw it, however, was that making a foreigner CEO would give Yang Yuanqing a chance to see clearly how a CEO operated and for Yang, taking a step back would be an advantage, a chance to consolidate power, and run the office from the back seat, as Liu Chuanzhi himself did.

IBM's owners wanted to leave their original CEO in place and take over as CEO of Lenovo after the merger. This was one of IBM's conditions at the time, but after Liu Chuanzhi looked into it, he discovered that the man in question was not particularly competent and had limited knowledge of China. He wanted to get rid of him and chose someone else from IBM's senior management. It would still be an American, so there was no fundamental change to things but, to his surprise, IBM's chief negotiator flew into a rage and objected strenuously. Liu Chuanzhi made a speakerphone call with IBM's Greater China general manager, Zhou Weikun, there to interpret while at the same time having an open line to his own chief negotiator in America, so it was effectively a teleconference. It took a long time. The American was very serious about the question of changing personnel, and very angry. He made it quite clear to Liu Chuanzhi that if he wasn't willing to accept the current CEO, there was nothing more to talk about. When Zhou Weikun translated this, he left out a lot of the bad language. After a while, Liu Chuanzhi understood what was going on: there was a lot of important office politics in IBM over this deal, and the CEO was being used as a pawn in making this particular exchange. Liu Chuanzhi persisted in asking for a change, and after several phone calls, IBM's negotiator instructed Zhou Weikun to say this, "If you do this now, after six months I don't care what arrangements you make." Liu Chuanzhi understood and agreed. This is often the way things go in negotiations of this kind, particularly with Americans. After six months the CEO was, indeed, swapped out, without any repercussions.

Gil Amelio

The second CEO was invited in from Dell and was a senior vice-president of the company called Gil Amelio. He was Jewish and a very able man. It has to be said that it is very challenging for a Chinese company with a US$3 billion turnover to buy a US$10 billion American company, and such a deal presents considerable administrative difficulties. But Amelio was a tough character and a forceful businessman. He was also an archetypal professional administrator who had been in his post for five years and if he had taken his business acumen to the next level, he would have been America's top CEO. But as the company's profits grew year on year, and the company share price was taken as the most important measure of his ability, that was where he concentrated his energies. But after several years of this, a huge change swept through the computer industry as the volume of PC sales overtook the sales of institutional machines; the principal product in IBM's acquisition by Lenovo, was the ThinkPad, which was a high-end machine targeted at institutional use. If they didn't develop products aimed at the ordinary consumer, they wouldn't be able to compete with Hewlett-Packard and Dell, so that was an absolute necessity. But that required investment, and the necessary investment for the IT systems alone for a consumer-level computer, let alone anything else, would be US$700 million over three years. Where was that going to come from? From reducing internal profit margins, of course. For example, if the profit was originally US$500 million and the annual costs were US$250 million, the profit had to be reduced by that amount. Moreover, if the company profits were affected like this, that would also have an effect on the share price. As a professional company director, Amelio naturally had no wish to see a decrease in profits built into the business.

Amelio decided not to do it this way, and although the current chairman of the board, Yang Yuanqing strenuously objected, Amelio ignored him. So the paradoxical situation between them played out with Yang Yuanqing in the right and Amelio equally correct from a professional manager's point of view. There was nothing for it but for Yang Yuanqing to suggest a compromise to the board: he would look after the consumer-targeted PCs and let the CEO get on with the company's original business. There were two Americans at the board meeting, and although their shareholdings were comparatively small, they carried considerable clout. Amelio went to see his American boss and explained the situation. His boss felt that Yang Yuanqing was just a troublemaker: how could the chairman of the board personally do that kind of business? He determined to take Amelio's side in the affair. Although Liu Chuanzhi felt that Yang Yuanqing was in the right, this kind of confrontational, tit-for-tat, all-or-nothing way of doing things, simply wasn't his style. Liu advised Yang not to be so hasty but to keep calm and wait for his chance. In the meeting, Liu hadn't let his support for Yang Yuanqing show, because if he had, given the weight his opinion carried, the meeting could have become a stand-off, polarised between the Americans and the Chinese. If the stand-off was exacerbated and became more pronounced, there was no knowing what exactly would come of it, but it would be irreparable.

As Liu Chuanzhi hadn't given away his position, Amelio began pushing things and, whether deliberately or not, he made some of the key Chinese personnel feel that maybe their positions weren't secure; but Yang Yuanqing couldn't very well intervene. In Liu Chuanzhi's mind, two of Lenovo's senior executives, Liu Jun and Chen Shaopeng, had the potential to be groomed into all-round excellence, but when Amelio reported on their work to the committee, he ranked them outside the top 16 executives. This saddened Liu Chuanzhi greatly, but he put up with it because he couldn't make a fuss at that point. He knew that if he did, there would then be no going back. Additionally, because of the culture clash and the friction it generated, a number of other Chinese personnel, particularly those with a high opinion of themselves, suffered major setbacks and quite a few of them even left the company.

As Liu Chuanzhi watched what was going on, his hand often twitched to draw his sword, but he had to be sure of his strike, and that kind of certainty didn't present itself. So he stayed his hand. That was Liu Chuanzhi all over. He was able to contain himself, to the extent that sometimes he even felt he was being callous. So that is how things stood until, as 2008 approached, the financial crisis struck and the company fell into loss. But the crisis was also an opportunity, and Liu Chuanzhi made his move by swapping out the CEO. He sought out the two American board members, one of whom was one of the founders of TPG (Texas Pacific Group, one of the top 10 American VC (venture capital) investment companies) and also a founding partner. He raised Yang Yuanqing's plan to ease out Amelio with them, but they didn't feel that Yang had the authority to do this. However, Liu Chuanzhi stood firm this time, and the discussions between the two sides went on non-stop for a week.

The Americans were also obstinate until Liu Chuanzhi revealed his bottom line which was that he would take the matter to the company's shareholders' AGM. The Americans got the message, as shares were king in China, and if it got to that stage it would be bad for everyone concerned. In the end, the Americans came up with a way of resolving the matter: if Liu Chuanzhi would become chairman of the board, then they would agree to Yuan Yangqing as CEO.

Liu Chuanzhi had stopped being chairman of the board at Lenovo back in 2004 and handed the reins to Yang Yuanqing while keeping a controlling share in the company. He really didn't want the chairmanship as he was more than busy enough as majority shareholder, with a thousand things to occupy him, but he agreed, nonetheless. Next he had to talk to Amelio, and everyone thought there was going to be an almighty row because the American had a tough, crabby personality and was given to shouting; they also knew that Liu Chuanzhi was a force to be reckoned with, and if anything went against him his anger was an irresistible force. There would be no ambiguity about his response. It came as a complete surprise to everyone when the two men emerged smiling and shaking hands after less than an hour's conversation. Amelio was resigning and would not be taking up the chairmanship of the board.

Four Slides

Having seen off Amelio, Yang Yuanqing took up the post as CEO and Liu Chuanzhi became chairman of the board. With things settled in this way, Liu Chuanzhi had set up a genuinely east-west cooperative organisation in this now multinational company. He let Yang Yuanqing arrange things the way he wanted them, taking out a certain amount of the profit to invest in R&D and breaking new ground in consumer-targeted PCs. Once again, Yang was not only taking on the role of professional manager, he was also the company leader in planning future strategy. Lenovo's progress towards a fully international status was already very well advanced with 70% of its turnover coming from overseas. It had a presence in 160 countries and overseas territories, and in none of those countries and territories had Chinese staff been put in; they were all run by local teams. In 2009 CCTV interviewed Liu Chuanzhi, saying that Lenovo was on the edge of a precipice. Liu replied that Lenovo was his life and he was duty-bound not to turn back. When he came back out of retirement, he latched on to culture, he latched on to the fusion of contemporary Chinese and Western culture, he latched on to building a value system and he latched onto building an ideology. The latter was very important. Working in accordance with a company ideology was very effective both in China and abroad, and Liu Chuanzhi had great faith in it.

Lenovo had annual company loyalty meetings, and Liu Chuanzhi and Yang Yuanqing went to Europe to attend the one being held there. It was held in France and was attended by all staff at manager level and above, more than 200 people in total. Things were different that year because both the chairman of the board and the CEO were Chinese, and that had quite a profound effect. Lenovo rules said that anyone who arrived late had to stand to attention, but this custom couldn't be used with foreigners. When Liu and Yang arrived at the meeting, the audience was sparse and widely spaced. With the financial crisis at its height and the company in significant loss, the sight of two Chinese caused a certain unspoken atmosphere. This wasn't an internal discussion, it was an inspection. Liu Chuanzhi understood what was going on: forget about the standing to attention, what could he talk about? Would these people listen to him? With Lenovo's deficit the size it was and the future opaque, the junior staff were probably looking for a way out. What was more, he was the Chinese chairman of the board and what else was he going to do but preach at them, Chinese-style. He could hear all these thoughts in their whisperings and read them in the expressions on their faces. Liu Chuanzhi looked around him for a moment then, without a word, he put four slides up on the big screen, and began to talk through them, one by one. When he had finished, you could hear a pin drop in the room.

The first slide Liu Chuanzhi talked about showed the sheep and pig farm Lenovo ran back in 1988. At that time, commodity prices in China went through the roof and Lenovo was afraid its staff wouldn't have any meat to eat, so they ran a company sheep and pig farm. There was a man from Shandong called Ma Jingang working at the Computing Institute, and the company gave him Rmb100,000 to go and run the farm in his home province. At an appointed time, the beasts were brought to Beijing and distributed amongst the employees. The second slide showed the smiling faces of some old employees from the 1980s and 1990s on a tour of Europe. These retired staff all had stock options and generous company pensions, and were very content with life. The third slide showed Lenovo's 72 household tenants drawn from new employees: the new graduates who came to Lenovo straight from university in the 1990s and had nowhere to live. The old employees of the Computing Institute had a quota of housing and could join the waiting list according to length of service, but the new employees were not included in this. So Lenovo came to an agreement with the Bank of China for a down payment and mortgage scheme with the loans guaranteed by Lenovo. This allowed 72 new employees to have somewhere to live. The fourth slide showed the young employees' development platform at Lenovo.

When Liu Chuanzhi finished talking, and closed the meeting, no one said a word.

With these four slides, Liu Chuanzhi was illustrating Lenovo's 'people first' business culture. The stories all happened in China, but they were saying, "If you work hard, these things could all happen to you, too!"

Liu Chuanzhi attended the same meeting the following year and things were completely different. The host of the event was a shaven-headed young guy and when Liu arrived, the seats in the hall were all taken already by a densely packed, neatly turned-out crowd of employees. The shaven-headed fellow said to the newly arrived chairman of the board, "Chairman Liu, this time it wasn't you waiting for us, but us waiting for you. We were all here on time and a lot of us even got here early." When he had finished, the whole hall burst into loud applause.

Liu's face was wreathed in smiles.

After Liu Chuanzhi had been out of retirement for only two quarters, Lenovo's results were significantly improved and by the year end, they had turned around completely. Not only this, but staff salaries had also been increased. In the past, Amelio's prime concern had been with his own salary review, but with Liu Chuanzhi's return, particularly after the change in the company's fortunes, the profits were being distributed, like pepper in a bowl of noodles, and every employee could get a pay rise. In other words, Liu Chuanzhi had done exactly as he had said he would in every respect. With a combination of strength and charm, he had won over the newly internationalised Lenovo, and he had won over all the overseas teams.

Yang Yuanqing's style was completely different, and he was very forceful when Amelio was CEO. He wanted to start an enterprise in Brazil, and the question was whether to buy an existing company or set up one himself. He gave his own opinion and then let 40 or more deputy chairmen give their views in a worldwide conference call. The majority of them, scattered around the world, had no real idea of the circumstances involved and most of them said yes. Afterwards, Amelio took the matter to the full board meeting, saying that they hoped to spend such and such an amount of money buying such and such a company. With this kind of affair, Liu Chuanzhi understood what was going on and, of course, he overruled Amelio.

When Yang Yuanqing took over as CEO, Liu Chuanzhi helped him re-establish the leadership team, which was very much a Chinese way of doing things, the old Lenovo way of doing things. There were nine people in the team: four Chinese, four foreigners and Yang Yuanqing himself, all of them in senior posts. The team would meet in different places for three days every month; it could be in Moscow, or Paris, or New Delhi, or Sydney or Johannesburg, always in one of the world's principal marketplaces. For one day they would probe the market, and then hold a meeting over the next two days to explore each other's views and discuss the direction of development for the company, with each member having their own area of expertise. Lenovo had done this within China in the past, uniting everyone and pooling knowledge, and this was the traditional Chinese way of doing things. In Yang Yuanqing's new leadership team, everyone took about six months to get to know each other, so they were all very clear about each other's individual specialities, what views they felt free to express, and where exactly each person's responsibilities lay. It was completely different from the way the previous CEO had operated. With the whole, huge company acting as one, results improved dramatically, even turning around the losses, and Lenovo's growth path far exceeded that of comparable companies. Up till that point, only selling one line of computers, Lenovo had an annual turnover of US$48 billion but the internal Chinese market was approaching saturation and growing very slowly; increased turnover was all coming from abroad.

Before the purchase of IBM's global PC business, although Lenovo was the biggest computer manufacturer on the Chinese market, it didn't have any unique core competitive strength; it couldn't compete in control of production costs with Dell, which started out as a direct marketing company; and in technological innovation, it was a long way behind the ostentatiously unconventional competitor, Apple. By integrating the resources of the old-school company IBM, Lenovo was able, at a stroke, to accelerate its globalisation process and, after 10 years of scraping by, it

1. LENOVO CHINA (4)

became number one in the global computer industry and was listed in the Global Fortune 500. Additionally, and perhaps more importantly, the success of Lenovo's purchase of IBM's PC business was not just a corporate success, it was a success for the company's corporate culture, for its corporate thinking and for its corporate value system. China not only became part of the rest of the world, it also brought with it, as its contribution, its unique cultural experience.

DIARY NOTE 16: 'POTENTIAL'

In Liu Chuanzhi's office, with its panoramic views, there was a small bronze *zun* (ritual wine vessel) called 'Potential'. It was in the form of a bronze ox, delicate and refined, and it stood in the window with the whole panoramic view as its backlighting. The normal representation of a bull is head down and charging, representing the pioneering spirit, but 'Potential's' posture is one that is very rarely seen: it is looking back, not forwards, curved back on itself like a tautly drawn bow. It seemed to be a reflection of Liu Chuanzhi, of his unique creativity, the like of which I had never seen before. A retrospective ox and a charging ox are two completely different things, philosophically speaking: the former has enormous potential energy, pent up and not yet released, totally alert. You could say it represents the most profound aspect of Chinese culture.

Liu Chuanzhi's reading, which started with the four volumes of *The Selected Works of Mao Zedong* (the making of history) but broadened greatly over time and many unassuming but profound aspects of his world view, experience and literary influences were discernible in him. The first time I interviewed him, as a novelist, I respectfully presented him with a copy of my recent book *Three Trios*, but I had no definite hope that he would read it. Of course, I would not have been surprised if he did, and I thought there was a real possibility that he might. The next time I interviewed him, a week later, I had forgotten about the book and when I entered the blue-coloured Raycom Infotech office block, feeling very bookish and arty, I had dismissed all thoughts of it. As it turned out, Liu Chuanzhi had read my book. The receptionist took me to Liu's office, which was empty, so I had a moment or two to wait. As I waited, the receptionist told me that not only had Liu Chuanzhi read the novel, he had actually recommended it to others. Liu came in through a side door, smiling broadly (it seemed that he had heard us talking about the book, and his expression was completely different from his seriousness in our first interview). He came over to me and said that he had already finished my novel, and the first thing he wanted to do was talk about it, as he had a few questions he wanted to ask for my guidance on. His choice of the phrase "ask for my guidance" really intrigued me and I thought there was something rather wonderful about it.

What really astonished me was that they were some really very specialist points that he was "asking for guidance" on. *Three Trios* is almost 400,000 characters long, and even an expert reader might consider it an *avant-garde* novel with an innovative format. It has three interwoven storylines forming a three-dimensional space, so you could call it a three-dimensional novel and that is bound to be a challenge to the average reader. The central theme of the novel is not clear-cut, and although the characterisations are distinct, the thought processes are complicated, and nothing is conventionally black or white. There were some online readers who said they didn't understand it. What Liu Chuanzhi was asking for guidance on was his idea that the novel not only had 'three trios' but also a solo; didn't I think that after the three storylines were disentangled, the resulting single line of a trigram (from *The Book of Changes*) could be considered a solo? Without waiting for me to reply he went on, "Your novel should be called *Four Quartets*." I told him I couldn't use that title because we already had TS Eliot's *Four Quartets*. He also went on to talk about his understanding of the main protagonist of the novel, Du Yuanfang (an SOE entrepreneur), praising me for not over-simplifying Du's character (or his criminal enterprise). He even went as far as to compare his own capabilities with Du Yuanfang's, saying, without any false modesty, that he had all of Du's abilities. He said this very solemnly, in the manner of one man of talent appreciating another. He also talked about the language used in the novel, saying that he couldn't read a badly written novel, and use of language was the first thing he looked at. We talked about my book for a good half hour before starting the interview. This made the interview very relaxed, as if we had already known each other for many years. After the interview was over, the relaxed mood continued as we went to a dining room on the 18th floor with another panoramic view, where Liu Chuanzhi said that since I had written about wine, he would like me to have a little drink with him while we continued to talk about the novel. I should perhaps express my profound thanks to that novel and to books in general, as I had never expected a businessman like Liu

Chuanzhi to be such an avid reader, such a book lover and so affected by literature.

"It is easy for heroic figures to straddle the world!" I'm not sure what made me think of that saying. Sometimes, I will be walking along and the thought will suddenly strike me that it is hard to imagine a man like Liu Chuanzhi reading *avant-garde* novels. But how many other unimaginable things does Zhongguancun hold? If Zhongguancun is China in microcosm, the changes over 30 years are certainly unimaginable; and if Lenovo is Zhongguancun in microcosm, the way it has become the whole world over 30 years is equally so. And within all that, how many unimaginable details are there? Looked at like that I, as a novelist, am still left outside the door.

And how many other doors are there waiting to be opened?

Fingerprints of all Creation

万 物 的 指 纹

Light Years

THE SPANISH PHILOSOPHER, Jose Ortega y Gasset says in his book *Man and Crisis*, "If you tell me what interests you, I can tell who you are. Whatever you fix your gaze on, that's what you are." That is a rather exaggerated statement but, like many exaggerations, there is some leeway within it. Suppose you have fixed your gaze on something, it could be that that is what also fills your heart, perhaps with even more certainty. When Bao Jie enters a room or, if you are watching a video, when he mounts the stage, you immediately notice something different from normal about his eyes. If you don't understand him, this difference may not seem that special, but if you do understand him, then you understand Ortega y Gasset's dictum. His eyes are very black and he sometimes squints a little, as though he were short-sighted which, in fact, he is not. If you understand what he is saying you may well feel there is something of black technology about him

I will talk more about black technology in a little while. First I will tell you about Bao Jie. Of course, his eyes are not now as they were when he was born in 1983, but his gaze seems as long as a light year. In one video, he says, "On 10 May 2011, the Armenian astronomer Grigor Gurzadyan discovered that a star called HD82943 had swallowed its planets in a process comparable to the Sun swallowing the Earth. This star's volume is pretty much the same as the Sun's, and the planets it swallowed were about twice the size of Jupiter. Star HD82943 is 78 light years away from Earth.

When he is talking, you seem to be able to see the limitlessness of the heavens in his eyes, and if they are not narrowed in his habitual squint, then you can feel the infinity of space. But with one narrowing of his eyes, a light year seems to pass, and you are brought back to the present. In fact, however, light years are not the subject of Bao Jie's research; he studies quantum dots, things that are 100,000th the width of a human hair. The infinitely distant and the infinitely small have a kind of correlation, so Bao Jie says. It is through the infinitely small spectrum of quantum dots, that man can see a star swallowing its own planets 78 light years away. Someone who is always looking through the infinitely small spectrum of quantum dots, looking at things that are 100,000th the width of a human hair, cannot help but squint occasionally, and that squint is like a fluctuation of a light year.

Black Technology

Bao Jie is from Taiyuan in Shanxi Province and is an archetypal nerd. After middle school he took part, every year, in the National Chemistry Competition, winning medals and finishing in the top rank. He was recommended to study chemistry at Tsinghua University, but Tsinghua insisted on him taking the *Gaokao*. When they saw the evidence of his overall ability, it was clear that Bao Jie, who had done absolutely no revision for the exam, had more than enough marks to spare to satisfy them. Examinations and competitions only served to increase Bao Jie's enthusiasm and reinforce his feeling of superiority; he thought this was the kind of elation a giant must feel. After studying for four years at Tsinghua, without giving it any real thought, Bao Jie went abroad to Brown University in the US to study for a doctorate. After his Masters, he took the four-year Ph.D. course (the academic research model was the same as a standard Ph.D. in its knowledge category theory, and its content and extent were at roughly the same knowledge level; you undertook independent research and had to make a contribution to academic circles within your chosen field). When he had finished, he took up a post-doctoral post at MIT (the Massachusetts Institute of Technology). His doctoral field of research was femtosecond lasers (a femtosecond is 1×10^{-16} s) and he was observing and recording the molecular vibrations within laser bursts of only a few femtoseconds duration. In his post-doctoral research at MIT, Bao Jie began to study quantum dots, a kind of nanometric matter that had suddenly emerged at the cutting edge of this kind of research. A femtosecond is 1×10^{-16} s, a nanometre is 1×10^{-19} m; one is a measure of time and the other a measure of length and they are, of necessity, connected in the field of infinite divisibility; but to what extent, remained the question. That is to say, the concentration time of quantum dots and the duality of matter are the two properties that form the quantum spectrum.

In 2014, the 31-year-old Bao Jie returned to Tsinghua University as a Ph.D. adviser, bringing the research work he had been doing in America with him. In 2016, his name went on Zhongguancun's Black Technologies List. Black Technology has something in common with Japanese anime and manga: they are all new terms from the internet and all represent things far beyond the current state of science and technology, and human knowledge, and technologies or equipment that on the face of it violate natural law: things like Gundam GN Seed, Nether Energy and Twilight. Latterly Black Technology has been used to describe new wearable products and new technologies, innovations, software-hardware combinations and so on, that have evolved even further from the recent technological explosion, including upgrades and improvements made to existing technologies and the user experiences of the above-mentioned equipment. It is beyond normal imagination but currently under research and due to materialise within our lifetimes. Currently on the list of Black Technologies are flying cars, express delivery robots, augmented reality, smart helmets, the Martin jetpack and all those kinds of impossible things. They all come under the umbrella term 'Black Technology'. The best known of the masters of Black Technology was the scientist who had just taken over as head of engineering at Google, Ray Kurzweil. This man held 19 doctorates, took 150 vitamin supplements every day as well as having monthly doses of all kinds of vitamins via intravenous injection, took nutritional supplements, including co-enzyme Q10, phosphatidylcholine, glutathione and other such substances. He was expecting massive advances in life-extending technologies to make it possible to live forever. His complexion already had a metallic texture to it. He predicted that within 15 years, computers would overtake humankind and surpass it in intelligence - the Singularity. Black Technology has absolutely no connection with mundane things like black foods, black coal pits[1] and *Thick Black Theory*[2]; rather it is an illustration of the clear weather that comes after a storm.

Quantum Dots

In June 2016, an article was uploaded onto the internet entitled *Quantum Dots - the Black Technology of Zhongguancun: the Young Tyro of Nanometrics*. It talked about how Bao Jie had completed the project on the quantum particle spectrum that he had brought back to China from MIT, and was preparing ways of exploiting it commercially. Because of this, Bao Jie was not only Tsinghua University's youngest Ph.D adviser and professor, he was also the founder and chairman of the board of QDChip. It is significant that article was not couched in exaggerated terms; in fact, it even suggested that it could have been written for primary school students: with a swipe of your cell phone, you can tell whether your glass of milk has gone off; or what today's PM2.5 air pollution index is. This is all possible, but today that possibility is becoming a reality. It was Tsinghua University's QDChip team that realised these possibilities, with Bao Jie as its founder and Ph.D adviser, leading the team in its use of new forms of nanometric material and techniques to create 'quantum dot spectrum cameras' the size of a cell phone camera that could be mounted in cell phones. These allow ordinary people to analyse, differentiate and evaluate objects of all kinds whenever and wherever they like. In fact, this kind of Black Technology had first been reported on the year before when, on 13 July 2015, CCTV News carried a special item on Bao Jie's success. Although the TV report and the internet article appeared at different times, the content was identical.

So what are the implications of this nanometre technology in the everyday use of cell phone cameras? Well, Black Technology has a lot to do with it: the implication is that the world will become more 'genuine', as fakery will have nowhere to hide. It is best to get straight to the point and talk about the real and the fake: in our daily lives, when we are buying things in the supermarket or the free market, the most frequent questions we ask ourselves stem from our suspicions over whether something is genuine or fake. Can we believe in it? Is there a problem with it? Is it as genuine as it purports to be? Is it too good to be true? Has it been genetically modified? Is that green colour real? There are too many uncertainties, too many instant decisions required; sometimes we are angry with the commercial sector, sometimes with the regulatory authorities and we can't help feeling that we are living in degenerate times. To be realistic about it, we cannot rely solely on the regulatory authorities, but we are even less willing to admit that it might be the rent-seeking behaviour of the authorities that might be creating loopholes. But what if everyone becomes an inspector? Supposing everyone is able 'to analyse, differentiate and evaluate objects of all kinds whenever and wherever they like'? Is that possible? Bao Jie suggests it is.

Just with a photograph on your cell phone, you will know if that mineral water is genuine; whether that rice has been bleached; whether that oil has been illegally recycled; whether those eggs really are free-range; whether those tomatoes have been artificially ripened; is this safe to eat or not? Can I give this milk powder to my children, or has it been contaminated with melamine? With one photograph you will know if that furniture has been made out of recycled wood or not. Is that household paint environmentally friendly? Does that new-build house have a permitted amount of formaldehyde and does it contain any radioactive material? For the world of collectables, this technology liberates everybody: you don't have to worry about drilling into something to test it. If you buy something fake or that is a reproduction, you don't have to go on some specialist antiques TV show; you don't have to go searching for an expert; all those TV pundits (and there are doubts about how genuine they are too) will leave our screens. You will become your own most authoritative expert: an expert in Yuan dynasty *qinghua* porcelain; an expert in Xuande period kilns; an expert in ancient bronze vessels; an expert in Wu Daozi's paintings; an expert in Zhang Xu's calligraphy or Huai Su's; an expert in Ni Zan's paintings and Zhu Da's. You will be able to tell if something really is Hetian jade or Zi'er jade; whether it really is amber or agarwood or turquoise. You will even be able to challenge China Guardian or Sotheby's over whether the items they have in their auctions are genuine or not. Everybody will be able to become an environmental protection agent who can tell with one photo on their cell phone how polluted the river water is; where the pollution comes from; whether the water in a swimming pool or a hotel is chlorinated or not. You will be able to carry out your own health check-ups and health monitoring: determine what your blood-glucose levels are; what your blood pressure is; what your intestinal health is like and whether there are any abnormal changes; what level of helicobacter pylori you have...

So many things, so many things! So many that do you even begin to doubt whether Bao Jie himself is genuine or not?

That is a reasonable question, because it does all sound almost too good to be true; if it does actually come true, then all well and good but the question is, do we want it too much? The truth is, the question of authenticity is not just one for the marketplace, it is also an ethical question, and a question of society's cultural journey. If everyone can tell what is fake, and that becomes the norm, our whole psychological condition will improve. It is not without precedent for deep-seated problems of social ethics to be resolved by science and technology; throughout the 1970s and 1980s, even into the 1990s, short weight and short measure were perennial and ineradicable problems, which were totally resistant to an ethical solution. The accuracy of a steelyard and the secrets of its workings, the secrets of its weights and its zero-point indicator, all the things that make it better to be the vendor than the purchaser, all embody the time-honoured mystery of the measure. Come the end of the 1990s, however, and the advent of the electronic scale (before then people did have little hand-held electric scales) the problems of short weight and short measure were solved at a stroke. No one worries about them in the marketplace anymore. Is there any anxiety about them left? Not even in the slightest. The purchaser is no longer worried, and the vendor no longer pays the matter any attention.

1/100,000th of the Width of a Human Hair

Alright then, let us investigate the feasibility of Bao Jie's universally wonderful news.

"With one photograph on your cell phone, you can tell whether a glass of milk has turned or not. What is today's PM2.5 air pollution figure? How is your health? All these questions certainly far exceed the standard remit of a photograph, but this idea is certain to become a reality. And its realisation is inextricably bound up with what is called quantum dot nanometric material. Quantum dots are formed from a limited number of atoms, and are spherical or near spherical in form, with a diameter of 2-20 nanometres. They are a nanometric material that has become increasingly hot property over recent years; they are miniscule in size and usually appear in solution. Essentially speaking, they are a form of photosensitive semiconductor crystal that can carry out controls from within the tiniest space.

"The uniqueness of quantum dot nano-materials, their most amazing quality is that they can change their own colour according to the diametric size of a crystal grain; within a space of several nanometres to 10 or so nanometres, they can take on a different appearance. Whatever substance you want them to resemble, we break them in half, and they change their appearance; break them in half again, and they change again. Another special property is that they have excellent solubility: because of the miniscule size of quantum dots, with a thickness of 1/100,000th of a human hair, they can be turned into solution form so you can see even more clearly how they change according to size and manifestly take on a different appearance."

Bao Jie goes on to say, "First the quantum dot solution undergoes a specific process; the miniscule size means that it is used rather like printer ink and is printed onto a microchip as an array film which takes on the quantum dot component form. Then we take the quantum dot component and align it with the detector in the cell phone camera. By getting them to echo each other, we form a very simple spectroscope."

"The wonderful thing about the spectroscope is that it is inseparable from the specific medium of light waves. The light waves are formed by the movement of electrons within an atom, and because of this, the light waves emitted by different materials are themselves different. This is like having an innate identity card and is the simplest and most accurate way of differentiating materials. Even a non-specialist eye can see how the range of differentiated light waves is transformed into light on the optical scale. Materials are constantly emitting light waves, the majority of which can't be differentiated by humans (a scroll painting, a porcelain vase, a grain of rice all emit light, everything does, and that light mirrors the object's innate character). A spectroscope, like our five sensory organs, can help us perceive the world; it is the eye that helps us differentiate all the different light waves. People have fingerprints and objects have fingerprints too. An object's fingerprint is its light waves. The way our two physical eyes see an object is completely different from the way the same object is seen through a spectroscope. It is this special capability that means a spectroscope can read an object's fingerprint."

"One apple gets bruised and then left for a while, and another is completely unblemished: what do they look like under a spectroscope? When the machine is turned on the unblemished apple, the data from the light waves is passed through your cell phone, it undergoes wave form and wave trough comparison which can tell you that the apple is ripe and ready to be eaten," Bao Jie says. "But when you take a photograph of the other, bruised apple, the light wave comparison will tell you that it is no good and you should discard it in favour of a sound one. Do you want to know how sweet an apple is? Whether it was grown with pesticides? Where it was grown? What the soil composition was like? With this process, you can find out all those things."

"Take skin cancer for example: one in five people will get skin cancer in their lifetime. Americans, in particular, are very fond of sunbathing, and get their deep tans through a form of skin cancer; but this type of skin cancer can cover their bodies in dark freckles and moles, and these moles can become malignant. There are different colours of ultra-violet rays: some are more violet, and some are more red. The more violet ones can harm the human body, but the redder ones are many times worse and the same amount of exposure to them of the skin can cause incalculably more harm. So you need to know how these capabilities are distributed in any given place. The quantum dot spectroscope can use simulation to tell you the short wavelength make-up of the ultra-violet light at a given time; if the reading is very high, then you should not go out sunbathing. Another aspect is detection: your body is covered in several hundred stripes and moles, but how do you know which are malignant? This is actually something that is very hard to detect. The most accurate method is to take a small sample of flesh from the freckle or mole – a very small one, of course – and look at it under a microscope. This can be a very lengthy process as a person can have so many freckles, it is next to impossible to inspect them all. But now," says Bao Jie with a wink, "you take a picture with your cell phone, scan it, and you know immediately."

Bao Jie's eyes are like a spectroscope; how many light years are held within them? What degree of divisibility? Their gaze seems so ancient for such young eyes, more ancient than the Earth. Bao Jie is not just Chinese, he is a citizen of the world, of the cosmos. His journey started as a youth when he took part in the Mathematical Olympiad, in the National Chemistry Competition; he began with a small high-tech research group and moved on to lasers, femtoseconds and quantum dots, then soared on over to cell phones. In the future, the results of his research will be on everyone's body and will change the reality of the world. What kind of a man is that?

Bao Jie says that we can get information from data, and we can turn that information into knowledge; that knowledge can help mankind to attain wisdom. Faced with such vast quantities of diverse data, a large number of sensors can help us capture the information; in the near future, quantum dot spectrum sensors will become the solid foundation of a pyramid of wisdom.

In 2015, Bao Jie's technological achievements were on display in America's most influential magazine *Nature*, and in the same year he was named as one of China's annual greatest cutting-edge scientists, and his achievements as being amongst the year's 10 most cutting-edge achievements. The nomination read: "He introduced to the world a new form of spectroscopic miniaturisation - quantum dot spectroscopy. He simultaneously reduced the size and production costs by a factor of two to three times whilst maintaining a high level of performance; by introducing spectroscopes into cell phones, he opened up a new path for portable equipment and intelligent sensors. This must rank as one of the most revolutionary of technologies. His success will have an enormous influence on the research industry, medical treatments, national defence, daily necessities and many other fields."

These external honours mean nothing to Bao Jie.

Because his gaze does not rest on the same things as ordinary people; his gaze rests on the phenomenon of a star, 78 light years away, swallowing its own planets and on things 1/100,000th the width of a human hair.

Currently, Apple, Samsung and LG are all in discussions with Bao Jie, but there is no way of knowing yet where and how the prize will land.

2. FINGERPRINTS OF ALL CREATION

DIARY NOTE 17: NEW GENERATION MAN

Bao Jie was already seated in the coffee shop of the Four Seas Building in Zhongguancun 10 minutes before I arrived. We hadn't met before, nor had we agreed anything definite. Rather, if I happened to be in the area, I would give him a call and that would be fine. It was the afternoon, and there were only three people in the coffee shop. Two of them were sitting together and talking, so the other figure had to be Bao Jie.

Bao Jie was young; he looked as though he was born in the 1980s, but at the same time he seemed very 'old' because of his eyes.

His eyes had a slight squint, but he isn't short-sighted. As I have said, it had to do with light years. Just how old were those eyes behind their frequent squint? How many light years had he travelled to get to the coffee shop?

Even now, I still persist in seeing Dr Bao Jie as living in two different times: one is natural time, and the other is eternal time. Most often they take it in turns: the time of the present and the time of light years away. Bao Jie, like Wu Gansha and Zhao Yong, and also people I am going to talk about later such as Cheng Wei and Liu Qing, are god-like humans of the new Zhongguancun. They are not like Chen Chunxian or even Liu Chuanzhi. They seem to make Liu Chuanzhi's generation into the gods of the Cold War era. It is not a question of one person surpassing another, it is one generation surpassing another. Even though they are all essentially rather out of the ordinary, Bao Jie is even further removed from the norm in the fields of technology and Black Technology. In the same way, they are different from that outstanding mathematician Feng Kang, nor are they like Feng Kang's young disciples. And in Bao Jie you can discern impossible things, unimaginable things, things outside of time. They are like aliens visiting earth, or earthlings crossing infinite space. They are not part of the world of the Five Elements, they have surpassed that, and represent the most distant space created by the new Zhongguancun.

The possible beyond the possible.

Garage Café

车库咖啡

A Guest Stranger

IN 2011, Zhongguancun after rain was part cloudy, part clear and a double rainbow reflected off the walls of glass in its estern quarter. Zaizher IM's CEO, Xiong Shangwen, brought Vivek Wadhwa, a reporter for the *Washington Post*, to the Garage Café on a small street near Haidian's Book City. They were unusual customers, as they were neither entrepreneurs nor investors. Of course, the clientele wasn't limited to those two categories, and there were all sorts there; an open-door welcome is a Beijing tradition and Su Lan's bright and welcoming temperament ensured it was continued at the Garage Café. The place had only been open less than six months, but the place was always packed, and every visitor was warmly greeted by a smiling Su Lan. The most he had welcomed in one day was close to 30 different groups. To date, seven or eight thousand business cards had been exchanged, and he had chatted with more than a thousand business teams. As he did customarily, Su Lan treated Xiong Shangwen and Vivek Wadhwa as just another work group and told them the story of the Garage Café almost without drawing breath.

'Start-up cafés' began in America, and they are often referred to as 'garage cafés'. The beginnings of many of the outstanding companies in America's Silicon Valley are intimately connected with garages, amongst them, HP, Apple, Dell, Google and YouTube. In Silicon Valley 'garage' almost became a synonym for low-cost high-tech start-ups. As a reporter, the special columnist Vivek Wadhwa was naturally very familiar with this phenomenon, but not with the arrival of garage culture in China. More specifically, he wasn't prepared for the huge scale on which it manifested itself at young Su Lan's place in Beijing: computers everywhere the eye could see in 800 sqm of workspace, almost half a football field, with entrepreneurs and investors thinking up ways of working together, cell phones pressed to ears. Every day was a trade fair of dreams. Wadhwa didn't even write anything down or record anything as he normally would, he just listened, looking around him from time to time. It made Su Lan wonder whether he was just making a tour of China and thought he had found something fresh and new here; or perhaps he thought there wasn't anything to know about start-up investment in China yet. That was all Su Lan could think, at the time. Getting very excited, he asked the American whether they had this kind of thing in the US. "No," Wadhwa said, shrugging his shoulders. "But what you are doing here is very American in style." What he said was very true, even though, at the same time, he gave nothing away about his status as a famous American columnist.

The American left, and the Germans arrived: three of them in this case, also unexpected. They stood in the doorway looking around for a while, then sat down at a table near the door and ordered two cups of coffee. As he would with any other customers, Su Lan went over to greet them (in English). Two of the Germans who were chatting to each other in German, told Su Lan in English that they were reporters from the German weekly news magazine *Der Spiegel*. Su Lan did not know what a famous news organ *Der Spiegel* was, indeed he didn't even know that it existed. An entrepreneur sitting nearby told him that it was one of the biggest names in news media in Europe, and very influential around the world. The Germans were very serious folk and had come well prepared, armed with cameras and with their electronic notepads already switched on. They were a different proposition from the American. Su Lan was more conscientious this time, with none of the bluster that is part of the Beijinger's character, and answered all the Germans' questions seriously, weighing his words. Not long afterwards, *Der Spiegel* carried a seven-page report on the Garage Café, in the course of which it was mentioned that Su Lan had himself asked the reporters a question, "As German journalists, why is it you have come to China, to Zhongguancun, in fact? To report on the Garage Café?"

The Germans replied, "The one place that has the potential to eclipse Silicon Valley may well be in China, in Beijing, here in Zhongguancun…"

A Space of Dreams

From the outside, the Garage Café is very low-profile; it is on the second floor of a small hotel tucked away on Book City pedestrian street and there is no obvious signage to show that this is not a lovers' trysting place, but a 'place of work'. You go through the lobby of the very basic little hotel, up a flight of 20 granite steps, through a creaky folding wooden door and there, totally devoid of any metallic garage-like qualities, is the Garage Café. Its walls are covered in grey wallpaper, a dozen or so hanging lamps are suspended from the black-coloured ceiling, the tables and chairs give off a smell of timber, the fabric-covered sofas are soft and comfortable, the lighting is gentle and unobtrusive. It is a peaceful and comfortable open-plan environment, with black-painted exposed pipework across the ceiling and plain red tiles on the floor. The babble from the wireless speakers mingles with the rich smell of coffee and with the dreams of young entrepreneurs and their thirst for success. There is a glass-partitioned library, paid for by donations from successful internet entrepreneurs, where anyone can leaf through the books and periodicals, looking for inspiration. There are four separate meeting rooms, all decorated with rather arty starscape wall paintings representing the clientele's dreams.

The job opportunity wall next to the bar counter is the most popular spot, where several dozen hand-written or printed recruitment notices are pinned up in rows. Internet agriculture, internet medicine, internet social networking... it is an 'internet +' field of creativity where entrepreneurship, success and dreams all mingle together; it is a veritable feast of neologisms. There are notifications from as far afield as Shanghai, Guangdong and Shenzhen – recruiters come to Beijing to sit and keep an eye on the Garage Café. Some of them come once a week until they find someone who clicks. To the right of the main door is the bulletin board where there are photographs of Su Lan with big noises in the investment world and high-up government officials making a formidable background, but there are also announcements from 'garage groups' about weekend activities and outings.

On the 18th floor of an office block a few doors down from the Garage Café is Sinovation Ventures; half a stop to the south is Microsoft; turn right and there is Tencent; one intersection up to the north are Sina and Aigo. Situated where it is, the Garage Café is undoubtedly right in the sweet spot for the world of Chinese e-commerce.

If you spent Rmb20 on an Americano or a cup of green tea, you can work here all day and, most importantly, you can hook up with even more entrepreneurs and meet angel investors. Creating this kind of low-cost platform for conversations between entrepreneurs and investors was exactly what the Garage Café's owner was aiming for. The place provides printers, photocopiers, scanners and a business card service. For Rmb5 an hour, you get the latest beta-test cell phone, a projector and a desktop touch screen; there are even massage chairs to help people relax. From Monday to Friday, 13.30 to 14.00 is entrepreneurs' half hour which is a specific time set aside for start-ups to establish contacts, find source materials and make friends. Those people who delight in searching out promising new projects and creative teams in order to offer them financial backing, often have a very enjoyable time here; and there are often also people who are really keen to share with you their creativity, their plans and their dreams. From time to time in this 'garage', you can see small groups of total strangers sitting together in happy conversation; or it may even be a group of people crowding round a table, deep in discussion of some technical problem or market trend, or exchanging ideas on how to get in touch with investors, or talking about examples of successful entrepreneurial teams.

If you come out of the A exit from Metro Line 4's Zhongguancun station onto Zhongguancun Avenue, 20 minutes' walk takes you along four main streets. In the course of the walk, you can see all of Zhongguancun's changing history. It is a trip through the decline of the traditional electronics industry and the innovative changes of internet commerce. You can see the difference in the now somewhat dated-looking landmark buildings of the former wealth-creating factories of China's electronics industry, like the now totally deserted Hailong Building and the eWorld Fortune Centre which were Zhongguancun's first showcase buildings. The new generation's landmark building is Ideal Plaza which brings together Sina, Youku Tudou, iQIYI and others, representing China's internet commerce brands. From e-World to e-Generation, this route is still giving birth to new landmarks, and the main players are, perhaps, the youngsters on Entrepreneurship Street.

On any afternoon on the short, quiet length of Entrepreneurship Street, you can see small groups of young men and women with backpacks on their backs, walking along and chatting; the street signs advertise establishments in the four-storey buildings on either side of the road: the Dark Horse Club, Venture Capital, 3W Café… it is easy to enumerate the shared characteristics of these cafés: they are all simple, *avant-garde*, unruly and very enticing. The little street is very quiet and peaceful, like a picture postcard, but the same is not true inside the coffee shops; no matter how big or small they are, they are always bursting at the seams. Some people are staring at the diagrams on their notepads; some are sitting talking in twos and threes; some are talking animatedly down their phones in small-scale conferences, brimming equally with creative enthusiasm whether they are sitting listening or animatedly asking questions. It is like this every day. No matter what they are doing, everyone has three things in common: they are young, highly educated and full of energy. A year ago, this 200m-long pedestrian street was still called Haidian Book City. But recently, all the hurtling carts piled high with books have disappeared, and the several dozen book stores have been replaced by an apparently equal number of coffee shops. The smell of coffee has replaced the smell of books and the sales counters have become counters of dreams.

The trend-setting Garage Café is still very low-key, easygoing and welcoming to all comers. Su Lan himself seems always to be equally cordial as he spends every day there in the café which has now been open for four years, chatting with every young entrepreneur who comes here. Then, according to what he makes of their character and potential, he introduces them to investors whilst, at the same time, recommending their particular skills to other groups and teams already in the café. When it is really busy, he finds himself talking for up to 10 hours, late into the evening, so everyone in the café ends up knowing everything about everyone else.

A Beijing Lad

Su Lan was born in the western district of Beijing in 1979 and grew up in an intellectual family. He was not, however, a very hard-working student, but was given to all kinds of whims and fancies, and was easily distracted, attracted by every next new thing that came along. As a result, he ended up at a very average university in Beijing. Although he joined the lively electronics department for his studies, he still did not apply himself to his studies and remained headstrong and independent, just doing whatever he wanted to do. During his first year at university, there were two of his classmates from high school who had failed to get into university themselves and were selling computers in Xidan's BuyNow computer store. Su Lan was enchanted by the store, and he went door-to-door round the shops asking if anyone would give him a job moonlighting as a computer salesman. He thought moonlighting was a fun thing to do, and very edgy. In the end, one of Lenovo's reps in Beijing came across him and told him to come along for a trial. Su Lan accepted the offer, with no base salary, but a Rmb100 commission for each computer he sold. On his first day moonlighting, his gift of the gab helped him sell his first unit and he was delighted. He discovered that he had a real talent for sales. The concept of 'sales' was one being latched onto by a lot of young Chinese at that time. It was actually a kind of academic subject, and the inspiration, later on, for many industries and commercial concerns. Lenovo's success and rapid rise to dominance relied to a great extent on its sales philosophy, along with the strategies and competitiveness of its sales teams who had a profound understanding of consumer mentality. It really was a battlefield and if you won over a customer you had a feeling of self-worth, a kind of revelation, and that kind of satisfaction had a sense of immediacy and excitement. This was not something that could be learnt in school or university. Whether Su Lan actually saw it as warfare or not, the process certainly made him recognise his own value within it. Considerations of self-worth aside, his sales results just kept on improving: the most he sold in one day was 15 units, earning him Rmb1,500 in commission. In 1988, this was no small sum. Even today, how many people can earn Rmb1,500 a day? That makes a monthly salary of Rmb50,000 and an annual income of Rmb500,000.

For people of a certain temperament, or those with unusual talents, certainly it is not necessary to follow the norm by going to university, or to stay there if you do. Although Su Lan didn't actually withdraw from university, he might as well have done, as he spent most of his time immersed in the world of computers and selling them seemed to satisfy a need in him and make him feel comfortable in himself. Meeting with daily success, his sales patter became more polished, and he learned to be more sophisticated in his dealings with people. Overall, his understanding of the mentality of his customers became increasingly acute. As he saw it, every customer was a mirror image of himself and he could discern any differences in the minutest detail. He set up his first business before he had even graduated from university. In the course of his moonlighting career, he got to know several other people who were doing pretty well in the same line of business, all university students too, all about the same age and all with the same self-belief. They decided to set up shop together. Four of them rented a 16 sqm shop space in Xidan and opened their company. The rent was Rmb6,759 per month, which was a lot in those days. They were located on the top floor of a five-storey mall in Xidan, and the four of them pooled their resources totalling between Rmb30,000 to Rmb40,000.

Where do you ever find a first attempt at setting up a business that prospers? There are all kinds of unexpected circumstances that can nip a young enterprise in the bud, and it doesn't take too many setbacks to permanently stunt any growth. That is just the way of things. Before they had even been going five months, although their own business wasn't going badly at all, the field as a whole went bust because of the crisis in the property market. Their own company didn't collapse and was still earning money but, as the saying goes, how can any eggs remain unbroken when the nest is overturned? They went the same way as everyone else. It is interesting to note that, when Su Lan wrote his CV after graduating, his work experience referred to his own company, as it did in the CVs of all four of them. They all wrote their own recommendations saying that "this employee showed exceptional qualities during the period he worked for this company". That closed the chapter on them running their own business, but fortunately they were still in time to give recommendations from the company to others of their classmates who also asked them for their CVs.

In fact, they had no need of all that because, although they had provided their own references, everything they said was quite true. Now tempered by experience, Su Lan had no doubt about his abilities as a salesman, and what made him really happy was that, fundamentally speaking, although his first business venture had been short, it had been profitable. He knew that even a profitable business can be shut down by external circumstances or by some unforeseen internal event.

In 2001, Foxconn launched the FuBen motherboard onto the market, and Su Lan joined the sales team as sales channel manager for the north China region with a base salary of Rmb2,000 a month. Su Lan does not hold back about this experience, "In truth, a sales channel manager is really just a salesman; it is a very lowly position," he says, rather mockingly. A lot of successful people have a similar experience, starting at the very bottom of the ladder, and perhaps this is proof that the most basic work provides the firmest foundation for life. Su Lan went on to change jobs several times after this until, riding the wave of China's rapidly developing internet, he joined what was then the little-known website 8848. It was his first job with an online company. As he moved from being an ordinary sales channel manager to starting up the Nanjing branch from scratch, 8848 was the starting point for Su Lan's deep understanding of the internet. By chance, the point in time when he joined 8848 witnessed the first time the internet followed the trajectory from flaming glory to burst bubble. In the end, 8848 too went bust and closed down. The commercial experience he gained from this episode was undoubtedly profound. Even today when talking about the past, Su Lan is most appreciative of all about his time at 8848. Lü Chenwei, the then CEO of 8848, now CEO of Roxbeam Media Network Corporation, is the name he mentions most often in private conversation. Lü put a lot of trust in him and gave him a lot of support and those two things are probably the most valuable encouragement anyone can give a young man as he sets out on his career.

In 2006, Su Lan joined ChinaCache in Beijing. ChinaCache's main business was providing smart CDNs (Content Delivery Networks) and speeding up CDNs and internet sites. Its main competitors were internet companies such as Sina, Sohu, Youku and others, and it was in the middle of a recruiting drive, which was how Su Lan became one of its earliest team members. This was his last job before he set up the Garage Café and it was also his most important one from a networking point of view. Initially he worked in sales, and in his third month there, he signed up a big account with Roxbeam Media Network Corp, so once again it was Lü Chenwei who gave him this kind of trust and support. In one month, Su Lan signed contracts worth several million Rmb and, with such a promising start, he began to make quite an impression at ChinaCache. At the same time as he was enjoying the feeling of success, he was also very conscious that the contacts he was accumulating in the internet business were of enormous use in what he was doing. His wide circle of friends and his expansive aura of good karma over many years began to bring him their rewards and he soon became sales manager at ChinaCache.

Su Lan worked for ChinaCache for five years, a period which coincided with the internet's second great growth spurt. Because of the nature of his work, his main contacts were all with CTOs and CEOs of the various companies, many of which were start-ups, and as he watched the course of their development and maturity, he witnessed amongst them the life and death of companies and their rise and fall. The well-known companies 6.cn and Kaixinwang were both his clients in their early days when they only had a few employees, and both are now substantial businesses. Indeed, Su Lan's sales success at ChinaCache had a lot to do with the rapid growth of many of his clients. Before he left the company, he was already head of sales and had personally achieved an annual sales total of more than Rmb40 million, with the three people in his team adding another Rmb70 million. The total was equivalent to a quarter of the entire company's annual turnover.

Su Lan was very astute in his judgment of his clients. When 58 Tongcheng was still very small-scale and when Kaixinwang was just starting up, Su Lan accurately foresaw their very successful development. By 2010, sales successes were no longer enough to satisfy Su Lan's sense of achievement and he raised the idea of ChinaCache drawing up an investment strategy. The company was very supportive and created an investment strategy department. The department consisted solely of Su Lan. Every day, just as he had done with sales clients, he went to see teams in the early stages of starting up businesses, and in the process, just as he had found out with sales, he realised that Beijing was simply too big and the businesses too widely scattered. He was only able to make a handful of visits a day as he simply didn't have the time for any more. This prompted him to come up with an idea that was later to profoundly influence not just Zhongguancun but also the whole world: shouldn't Beijing have a place where all these entrepreneurs could get together? If there was such a place, it was bound to improve efficiency enormously. Silicon Valley didn't have such a meeting place, but that was no reason why Beijing shouldn't.

Su Lan was very excited by this idea: if a person has the energy, there is always something that he alone can achieve. What is yours? These things that are unique to you, are what make you who you are. In searching for your way forward, if you follow your instincts, with all the twists and turns that entails, there is always something individual and unique waiting for you. But if you spend your life just following the herd, then that is what you remain; part of the herd. In September 2010, Su Lan went to see his first-ever client at ChinaCache, Lin Xianzhen. Lin was the founder of SP Times Lele Interactive, and also one of the original investors in 58 Tongcheng, and Su Lan told him all about his instinctive idea for creating a meeting place for entrepreneurs. Lin approved of the idea and decided to give Su Lan his support. This support was crucial because Lin Xianchen himself was an investor. Su Lan went on to visit Lianzhong's founder, Bao Yueqiao, who had already been an angel investor for quite a few years by then. He too thought the idea would work, and the three of them began gradually to hammer out the details of the idea.

He had no sooner had the idea than he moved into action. Although he was still working for ChinaCache, his imagination had taken flight, and it was almost as if his legs had grown wheels. Su Lan beat the streets of Zhongguancun's western district, visiting every business. The reason he chose the western district was because it was there the cream of Chinese technological talent was gathered. Wowsai's Zhao Jingwen, Weibo's Hu Zhensheng and Special Price Hotel Tonight's Deng Tianzhuo were some of the important friends he met on his travels who made lots of suggestions about the location and format his enterprise should take.

The location he ended up choosing was the Co-Working Office Café, and this was not entirely influenced by the entrepreneurial stories of Silicon Valley. The main thing, in fact, was that the innumerable young teams Su Lan had made contact with were all to be found in UBC Coffee or Starbucks, and since coffee was a kind of 'high-tech' trend, would it not be possible to use the concept behind UBC and Starbucks to provide a workspace even better suited to the needs of these entrepreneurs, and better equipped with the kind of facilities they needed? Couldn't they furnish those entrepreneurs with the biggest possible meeting place? Looked at this way, for one thing the Co-Working Office Café didn't necessarily have to be right on the street front, nor did it necessarily have to have all the usual commercial coffee shop trappings. Rents on the street front were too expensive for that to be considered a necessity in any case; for another thing, related to the first, as the floor space had to be ample, at least 500 sqm or more, the rent could be kept down if they stayed off the street front.

Su Lan fixed on the street in Haidian known as Book City. With the rise in electronic books, Book City was no longer the place it had been and was a very desolate spot. He spotted the second floor of a bleak-looking hotel on the street. Opposite it was a stationery store, to the east was the Haiwanju Zhajiang Noodle Restaurant and to the west was a clothes shop. Because the street was so quiet and the space was on the second floor, the rent for the 800 sqm space was very cheap indeed at only Rmb2 per sqm per month. This was cheaper than anywhere else in the whole of the western sector of Zhongguancun. Even so, when Su Lan learned about the history of the place, he couldn't help feeling a little nervous. Every other business that had set up there had failed. The last one had been a club which ended up owing Rmb8,000 for electricity after it had only been open three or four months, and subsequently shut down. The business before that had been owned by a Korean who opened an internet bar. It had just taken off when SARS came along, and the Korean made himself scarce. Su Lan had his doubts, but one of his friends who claimed to be a *fengshui* master said to him that although the *fengshui* of the place was only so-so, he, Su Lan, could make it work and keep on top of the *fengshui*. The so-called *fengshui* expert was actually more of a psychologist and there is nothing wrong with the power of positive suggestion.

Everything was all set and all that was needed was the lease. At the end of December 2010, as soon as Su Lan and the hotel signed the contract, the refurbishment was done in record time; but by the time it was finished, he still hadn't settled on a name for the place. It was at this time that he made a trip to America. In the course of more than a month's travels in the US, he spent about half of the time shuttling along the 20-30km narrow strip between Palo Alto and San Jose in California. The famous Silicon Valley was the Holy Land in the heart of everyone in the internet business, and Su Lan was no different. As he sped along the freeway, with lush greenery flashing past on either side, he seemed almost to be able to smell the ubiquitous scent of freedom swept in by the pioneering spirit. Of course, he had to make a pilgrimage to the famous 'Garage' at 367 Addison Avenue in Palo Alto. This is the place where the two founders of HP first struggled to establish themselves 60 years before, and everything in the place is just as it was back then. The sombre-coloured old-fashioned furniture has a patina like you see on oil paintings. Su Lan felt that the place had the energy of the spiritual core of the business. As he walked slowly round the place, his brain played out the scene of his own constant travels around China setting up businesses, and in amongst the changing of trains and planes he saw pair after pair of eyes burning with the fervent desire for success, and youngster after youngster desperate to prove themselves.

After he got back to China, Su Lan officially registered his company. It was to be called 'Entrepreneur Street Coffee Co Ltd' but that proved not to be possible. One day, at his wits' end, when he was looking at Weibo, he saw a post about the rise of famous companies that started out in garages in Silicon Valley. He was irresistibly reminded of his own travels in America, and inspiration struck: what could be better and more natural than to call the company 'Garage Café'? The name was very American, but at the same time it was very Chinese, very Beijing and very Zhongguancun. This is how the world works: lives are inextricably interwoven and the whole world is interdependent, but dreams grow great in isolation and taking pride in one's own abilities is a generational way of thinking. Even as the world opens up, other people remain an integral part. Behind this tale of coffee shops are several grand and important themes concerning modern China's economic society's place in the world: technological innovation, economic transformation and international competition. Also involved, of course, are capital markets, capital investment, venture capital and angel investors. Without the backing of a strong capital market, there would be nothing to even talk about.

The large-scale but everyday platform that the Garage Café built didn't exist abroad; it was as though the Chinese were particularly adept at embracing a marketplace way of thinking, except that the trade was in ideas not in commodities. It was a great marketplace of dreams, concrete and abstract at the same time, invisible and intangible, yet alive with the flying sparks of ideas. It was one great dream that accommodated countless smaller dreams as the night sky accommodates the stars.

Any new development or advance is misunderstood and considered strange to begin with simply because it is different from what went before. With 800 sqm of business space, and a hundred or so seats, to begin with, the place looked empty and cold. Su Lan was like the conductor of a dance band except there was no band. Or rather, there was only the orchestra of ideas.

These are the fears and uncertainties that confront all dreamers and innovators.

Mo Xiaoyi

There must always be a warm-up act. When Su Lan was making his investment, he was in contact with two different groups he knew were looking for office space. He told them that his place was empty, it was pretty much as good as any office and he could set up the seating however they wanted; they should come on over. At least that would inject a bit of life into the 800 sqm space. One of the groups consisted of four people and the other of two; additionally, as the place was being refurbished, a number of other people turned up, rather like homeless people looking for somewhere to stay. Every day, Su Lan found himself staring hopelessly at people, unable to help them, and a month passed in a daze. Su Lan began to doubt himself, wondering whether he had set off on a journey he couldn't finish. But deep in his heart he believed that if he nurtured the parasol tree[1] properly, the phoenix was sure to roost in it.

Su Lan researched material on the internet, looking to see if such places existed abroad, and studied everything he could find to see if there were any problems with his 'parasol tree'. In the end, he realised he wasn't going to find another tree like it anywhere, or anything resembling it, so he gave up on those studies. At the same time, he still went onto his Weibo account everyday spreading the word and posting loads of stuff. Then, one day, someone finally appeared at the front door of the building. They made their way along the gloomy ground floor corridor, up the stairs to the second floor and there, suddenly, was their face peering round the half-opened door. Su Lan was as excited as if he had just seen a clear spring in a desert landscape.

As an opening promotion for the first couple of weeks, lemonade was being offered free of charge, and the 'homeless people' had been drinking it for 15 days straight. Chief amongst them was Mo Xiaoyi. Finally, on the 16th day, Su Lan had to ask, "Why do you lot never order anything?" Mo Xiaoyi replied that his team's capital was too small to hire an office, and they only had enough for the four of them to last out at the Garage Café for three months. In order to economise, they had rented a bungalow outside the Fifth Ring Road, which only cost around Rmb200 a month. But to get to the café, they had to take two buses and the Metro, a journey that took up the best part of two hours. If they didn't manage to attract any investment within three months, the team would probably have to break up.

Mo Xiaoyi was 23, from Hangzhou, and had only arrived in Beijing that spring. The poplar trees were flowering and the willows were fluttering with catkins. This wasn't the Beijing he had imagined: it was too big, the air was too dry and the weather was fluctuating between warm and cold. This kind of Beijing really didn't suit a southerner. But all these negative aspects were counterbalanced by one important thing: Beijing was the ideal place for a mobile internet business.

In 2010, there was a new surge of start-ups and most people consider that the spearhead of the movement was the mobile internet. There is pretty convincing proof of this in Kai-Fu Lee's involvement in the setting up in Zhongguancun of the mobile internet start-up project incubator company, Innovation Works. Mo Xiaoyi and all the other similar undergraduates, graduates and recent graduates assembled under the banner of the mobile internet, and set off along the path of their dreams. The majority of them had technology backgrounds and were concentrating on software development which opened up all kinds of possible uses in the mobile internet industry value chain.

Mo Xiaoyi was just one among many. He had been in Beijing for almost a year and, like most male engineering students, was almost too honest for his own good, or at least that is how it seemed. He was shy and spoke very softly and slowly. When he was working, he would stay huddled at his desk all day, and when he had some time off, he liked to play online games with his colleagues – though, of course, he only had one day off a week. He spent six months trying to find people he could form a start-up with, and in the end set up his first four-person team. Before the Spring Festival in 2011, Mo Xiaoyi resigned from his job and by March, he and his team were itching to move into the as-yet-unfinished Garage Café. They had heard how good the service for start-ups was going to be there and were desperate for it to open. In the first 15 days after it did, Mo Xiaoyi and the rest of his team hadn't spent a single cent. But what they had done is made hay with all manner of office equipment including iPhones, Android phones, beta versions of tablets, projectors and desktop touchscreen computers.

It was 15 April and Mo Xiaoyi was sitting at his particular seat, massaging his temples as he worked. To his surprise, the normally taciturn Su Lan beckoned to him as he came out of the meeting room. Mo looked blankly at him for a moment, until it dawned on him that Su Lan wanted to introduce him to an investor; not just any old investor, either, but a really big name, famous in investment circles: Lin Xinhe. Mo stammered out that he could only spare five minutes because another investor had arrived. This other man was Cai Wensheng, known as 'the king of domain-name investors'. The two men knew each other well, and they cut short

Mo's halting speech. This brief interlude dismayed Mo Xiaoyi, and he returned to his seat in considerable embarrassment, feeling that he had really messed up this first opportunity to gain some investment in the team's project. That evening he posted on Weibo, "Feeling rather unsettled as I've done something I shouldn't have and my insides are all knotted up with regret." The next morning, on his long commute into the Garage Café, he was still mulling over what had happened the day before when he got a phone call from Su Lan.

The second meeting with Lin Xinhe was completely unexpected, and this time it took place in the café's partitioned-off reading area. "What do you want to do? How much money do you need? What share can I have in the project?" These were the only three questions Lin asked Mo Xiaoyi. Mo didn't even have a PowerPoint presentation with him at the time, because he didn't think the opportunity would arise again to see the investor. But he did his very best to explain the project and introduce the team. Mo's team had chosen the internet-oriented name 'Onion' for themselves and, two months later, Lin Xinhe spent Rmb2 million to buy Onion's newly launched software.

After the news began to spread in internet circles that Lin Xinhe, previously the COO of Sina, now the founder of 58 Tongcheng, had invested in Mo Xiaoyi's team, the flow of customers into the Garage Café turned into a veritable flood. The café became *the* meeting place for start-ups looking for investors and investors looking for viable projects, and this was exactly where Su Lan had been directing his energies. He had prepared himself to run at a loss for two years, and was amazed when, after only six months, he was already pretty much breaking even. Although he wasn't going to make any money on people buying one cup of coffee a day, it didn't matter, as coffee sales were propped up by peripheral materials such as Garage Café t-shirts, cups and posters which could bring in several tens of thousands of Rmb a month. But this wasn't what was important to Su Lan; what mattered to him was the creation of an atmosphere of mutual support and an environment tailored to the needs of young start-up teams.

Utopia

In the course of his dealings with start-ups, Su Lan gained a clear impression of the importance these innovators placed on finding kindred spirits and cooperative partners, so every month he promoted a 'talent event' to help all the little project teams to recruit new talent. On top of this, he also often held 'salon' meetings and lectures in the café themed around entrepreneurship or investment, including investigations into new technology and discussions of legal practicalities. Also, from Monday to Friday, the hour between 1300 and 1400 was dedicated to the 'showcase' which gave start-up teams a chance to introduce their projects to the clientele and invite comments from well-known investors in the industry and from other participants.

Su Lan gradually increased the Garage Café's range of services to over 300, and set up joint-service agreements with more than 30 major companies. The café was officially recognised by the Zhongguancun management committee as a 'model innovation incubator'. The committee also joined the ranks of those offering services to the start-ups at the Garage Café by opening a fast-track company registration service. On two days every month, start-ups could submit applications at the café which would then help them with company registration thereby avoiding an otherwise tedious and time-consuming process. Su Lan also reached an agreement with Microsoft for every start-up team based at the Garage Café to receive three sets of beta-test results every year; there was also free Alibaba Cloud cloud storage and broadband, a complete free Android testing service, and a China Mobile App prototype cloud-testing platform, all of which served to optimise the office environment at the Garage Café.

Even more significantly, after a period of discussion, the Garage Café and the Agricultural Bank of China combined to promote the bank's 'Helping you grow: the customer always comes first' campaign, which opened an early fast-track service for low-capital companies offering reciprocally favourable terms for a comprehensive banking service, including bank settlement accounts, electronic banking, financial advice services, and so on. This was an innovation in banking terms which meant that, for an annual fee of only Rmb1,200, start-up companies could save between several thousand to several tens of thousands of Rmb. All this was of immediate practical assistance to the young entrepreneurs.

Some people say that Su Lan wasn't actually a venture capitalist but a rare kind of idealist, a visitor from outer space. A friend who knows him well says, "Su Lan wanted to turn the Garage Café into a kind of Utopia, an asylum for ideas." He had friends who helped balance the café's books so that a three-person team could spend Rmb1,000 per month on their daily coffee consumption whereas rent alone in a shared work-space in Zhongguancun would have been at least Rmb4,000. In the café, printing cost 20 cents per sheet and hire of the meeting room was Rmb10 per hour, essentially a loss leader, and the speed of the free wi-fi was astonishing, so start-up costs for the patrons were kept to an absolute minimum. So, from the point of view of entrepreneurs starting with nothing, and with no experience, it was hard to imagine anywhere more like heaven, anywhere more ideal, anywhere more utopian than the Garage Café.

Entrepreneurs

In 2011, after completing her high school education in London and graduating from university, An Qi, a girl of the 1980s generation, decided to set up a business in Beijing. Entrepreneurs all have a dream that their product will change the world and influence everybody's lives. At the same time, An Qi wanted to produce a mobile app to do with fine dining. But after several months and after having spent several tens of thousands of Rmb she came to realise that entrepreneurship has nothing to do with dreams and that, in addition to the apps pre-installed on cell phones, everything was essentially the product of major companies, mostly monopolised by Weibo and WeChat. The possibility of a small team coming up with an app that would be found on the opening screen of a user's cell phone was negligible.

Having come to that realisation, An Qi felt very disillusioned after sinking so much money into her project without any prospect of success. She felt it was partly down to lack of capital, but more importantly due to lack of experience. In trying to produce something with no knowledge of app-building herself, the programmer she had found turned out not to be very reliable. She had also borrowed the money from her mother who was, effectively, her angel investor. Nevertheless, she did not abandon her plans, as she remembered the story of the famous California Gold Rush: had not thousands of people gone off prospecting for gold? Very few of them actually struck lucky, but the people selling them food and water made a lot of money out of them.

An Qi decided to change her product plan. At the beginning of her project, she spent a lot of time in the Garage Café where she discovered a lot of teams working on the same product idea as she had had, and after quite a while, she realised that many of their products actually had no proper design or, at least, only sketchy design. If a product design is inadequate, the user experience is compromised but, at that time, there were no graphic design aids like the future User Experience Design and VI Design, which incorporated user experience.

The way she saw it, the Garage Café was a kind of high-speed hub for entrepreneurial communication, with all kinds of investors and start-ups all under one roof. On Tuesdays and Sundays there were special events for presentations from investors, and people such as Cai Wensheng and Kai-Fu Lee participated. The evening events were particularly enriching, like the IT 'chats' which were attended by well-known investment institutions in the field which sent their associates to talk about their investment plans and preferences, and about company strategy. They were followed by promotional talks by five start-up teams who introduced themselves and their product so that interested investors could go and talk to them directly. An Qi had majored in Fine Art and excelled in visual design, so she decided to form a company based on internet design software.

Interestingly, An Qi had got to know another of the young entrepreneurs who frequented the Garage Café and who sought out her team to design his product. The end result was that, when the job was done and dusted, he spirited her away and the two of them became lovers. This was the talk of the Garage Café, and even now is a topic of conversation amongst the clientele. Entrepreneurship is a hard road, and An Qi was delighted to have her new boyfriend as a travelling companion and mutual support on her second attempt. She often tells her friends that in the field of entrepreneurship, if you try and understand everything, you probably won't succeed. If you stop to think about it, you will see that you really can't examine the costs and risks too closely. The risks are so great that no one with any intelligence would even start out on the road. So, why are there people who do? Because, in their bones, they are not the kind of people who want to know today how much money they are going to make tomorrow; that is the kind of life 'other people' live. They work when they have to and stop work when they have to, and go off travelling when they have the free time. Entrepreneurship is a way of life; she needed that way of life and it was what defined her. Without it, she wouldn't have known who she was.

Entrepreneurs may come in all shapes and sizes, but the Garage Café itself is still a coffee shop, albeit an entrepreneurs' coffee shop, and it retains the character of a coffee shop: it is very sensitive about this. Here you will find idealists, speculators, anarchists, activists, entrepreneurs, occasional poets, reporters and rebellious programmers – though, of course, such subversive programmers are mostly lone wolves. As well as 3D printers and Bitcoins (cryptocurrencies), you will also find O2O (online to office), VR (virtual reality) and all sorts of other innovative industries that had their start here, playing out the new fantasy sagas of contemporary times. The future star of the Bitcoin world, Er Bao[2], the man who would eclipse the World Economic Forum (WEF) at Davos, was originally a beef seller in Pingyao in Shanxi, a young lord of the 1980s generation in that ancient city. When he left Pingyao, he stepped out of the past and into the newly internationalised Beijing, following his dream. Inevitably, his feet took him to the Garage Café. He had heard about the place on the internet back in Pingyao, and heard that it was the relay station of dreams. Dreamers are people who are never content with their lot; innately they are wanderers, displaced refugees, all looking for a relay station, a place to meet up; Su Lan's Garage Café is that place. Er Bao came to the café to find out how to sell his beef on Taobao. He came with his wife, who was already expecting their third baby. They drove a stretch limo with a minibar in the back, and in the front. It was seven metres long and, if it had been a Cadillac, it would have cost Rmb3-4 million. In fact, it was manufactured by the Great Wall company, and cost Rmb300,000. Only one batch had been manufactured, and they were converted from a people-carrier. Foreign visitors didn't know about the Great Wall brand and were very impressed.

Er Bao gave the Garage Café a case of his beef, which everyone ate as much of as they liked. They all said it was delicious, but what is there bad to say about free food? Er Bao was delighted. He always spoke in heavily accented Shanxi dialect, and he probed Su Lan over whether he thought people would eat the stuff if he stewed up his beef in the morning and took it to the food court for lunchtime. Regardless of how business was going, Er Bao's wife was captivated by the Garage Café. She had no interest in beef and ran an internet programme called 'Chat with Yangyang'. Her name was Jin Yangyang, and despite being pregnant with their third child, was much more modern and fashionable than her husband. The programme was on a new-wave (Weibo) microblog account, and every day she brought a small microphone or her cell phone to interview the people in the Garage Café who were mining Bitcoin, asking them what the current situation with Bitcoin was, and what they thought about it. She interviewed one person in depth every day, and as her popularity grew, she gradually became a person of consequence in the Bitcoin world. There were a lot of people messing around with Bitcoin in the café at the time, and the most famous of them was Li Xiaolai, the biggest propagandist for Bitcoin in the country at the time, and the biggest holder of the cryptocurrency. He spent six months at the Garage Café and was the biggest living legend in the place. Many people were influenced by him and followed him in all sorts of directions. Er Bao's wife was one of them.

Er Bao came to his wife's aid when she gave birth to their third child, making sure he was there for all the interviews so gradually everyone came to recognise him too. Er Bao thought it all looked rather good fun, much better than selling beef, and once he got involved, he became even more active than his wife. With nothing else to do, he drove the bar-equipped stretch limo, complete with banner advertisement, all over the country – he called it the Nationwide Bitcoin Tour – visiting Bitcoin enthusiasts everywhere. Little by little, he set up Bitcoin media and Bitcoin mines, and became the biggest investor in Bitcoin mining in the world. His own Bitcoin mining operation used up a large amount of the country's electrical energy, he was a major shareholder in a comprehensive Bitcoin advice website and he was considered a really big noise in that world. His trip to take part in the debate at the WEF in Davos is even more interesting as he was responding to an invitation from the chairman of the WEF to discuss cryptocurrencies. All the assembled guests were impeccably attired in Western-style suits and leather shoes, and there was Er Bao in a padded waistcoat, sweatpants and slippers, stepping up, clutching a brown paper package, and speaking with great assurance. He had his photograph taken with the chairman of the WEF dressed the same way, looking, to Su Lan's eyes, like a Shanxi tough guy. When Su Lan saw the photograph Er Bao brought back with him, she almost said, "I hope you didn't tell them you were from the Garage Café!" In fact, Er Bao had mentioned the café and also that you could use Bitcoin there, even just to buy a cup of coffee. So, as it turned out, Su Lan really wasn't too unhappy at all.

Mengde was originally just a village schoolteacher, not very highly educated but with an agile mind and very persistent. He had speculated in the second-hand mechanical digger market in Anhui, and made a bit of money. With that money, he went south to Shenzhen to sell knock-off cell phones – it was 2010 and this was very common back then. No one knew how quickly things were going to change, though, and in 2011 Xiaomi burst onto the scene and knock-off cell phones disappeared almost overnight. This had a huge effect on Mengde who lost all his profits almost at a stroke and went bust. But in the course of his dealings with knock-off phones he did discover what an excellent thing the mobile internet was. He sold the car and the house he had bought with his previous earnings. He got Rmb50,000 for the car which had originally cost him Rmb200,000 and took the money with him to Beijing where, once he made his way to the Garage Café, he never left.

When Mengde talked to Su Lan about projects and approaches, it made Su Lan uneasy.

For one thing, Mengde did not have a technical background, and for another, he had no notion of product design. He recognised this, and he began to teach himself about the production process. He didn't have anyone to teach him but did it on his own. A month later, he produced the blueprint for his product prototype. What he came up with was an Android smart phone. That is, he wanted to put an Android operating system into a standard phone to help businesses process the data and statistics they entered. There was nothing wrong with the idea, but Su Lan felt it wasn't the best time to bring something like that onto the marketplace. Nevertheless, Mengde, having gone ahead with producing his self-taught design blueprint, using the appropriate software, cobbled together his prototype model. He had taught himself well, and it looked surprisingly good. Su Lan was quite impressed by this but, even so, Mengde still made him uneasy.

Mengde worked long hours every day and once, when Su Lan asked him where he lived, he gave him quite a start by saying that he lived in the main lounge of the local bath house. The original hotel where Mengde had stayed, next to the Garage Café, had closed down two months before, and he had moved to another place further away. "Since your ancestral home is no more," Su Lan said jokingly to him, "why don't you rent a place? Isn't the bath house a bit noisy? I'm sure you could find people to share with." Mengde replied that it was very cost-effective living in the bath house: the entry ticket was only Rmb60 a day and, with the top-level membership card, he got a 50% discount which brought it down to Rmb30; he could wash and bathe there, sleep there, and have a late-night buffet and breakfast in the morning. If he made the most of the breakfast, he didn't have to eat for the rest of the day and could fill up with the late-night buffet. "But isn't the air in the lounge all humid and steamy? And when you're trying to sleep, what about the people next to you grinding their teeth and talking in their sleep? What about them thrashing about and belching and farting? How can you stand it?" Su Lan asked. He could stand it quite well, it seemed.

"I'm saving money!" replied Mengde. "I can stand anything if it's saving me money." Su Lan was very impressed by this. He found Mengde a job as a sales rep for a company owned by one of his friends. The job came with a monthly salary of Rmb5,000. In the course of his first month's work, Mengde invited Su Lan for a foot massage. As soon as they walked through the door of the bath house, Mengde was greeted by a row of attendants, asking how he was. Because he had been living there all that time, they all knew him very well, and every morning as he left, they would call out, "Take it easy Boss Shen!" And when he came back at night, they would greet him with, "Welcome back, Boss Shen!" Mengde was not the least embarrassed at being called 'Boss' and accepted the title happily. His real surname was indeed 'Shen' and it was Su Lan's little joke to give him the nickname Mengde, like Cao Cao[3].

Mengde worked away at the job for two months, earning a bit of money, but all the time he was thinking about his own stuff and his heart wasn't really in being a sales rep. He would do a few hours and then go back to the bath house or the Garage Café and get on with his project.

After he had been hanging around the Garage Café for a year and living in the bath house for the same period, there was an odd smell about him that was difficult to pin down. It wasn't the smell of the bath house, but it was a bit dank and musty. He wasn't aware of it himself. After he left the café, the smell tended to linger on there. People rather cherished it because it was an inspirational kind of smell and they all shared the same kind of perseverance. It was a kind of underlying smell, a tenacious smell. Mengde left for Guangzhou without telling anyone or saying goodbye. Being an entrepreneur is a way of life in which success is by no means a certainty, and failure is very common, in as many as eight out of ten cases, in fact. Really intelligent people shouldn't be entrepreneurs because all they see are the dangers, the unknowns and the uncertainties; they only like to travel tried and trusted routes and they don't like to make mistakes. Taking risks and not taking risks are two very different things, in the same way that going to war and not going to war are very different; really intelligent people don't rely on innate talent, but only work from practical experience. So Mengde's departure was quite normal, but what was surprising was the sudden text he sent Su Lan when he was in Guangzhou on business a year later, telling him that he had just received a Letter of Intent from an investor. As they exchanged messages on WeChat, Mengde said he had gone back to the thing he was best at: second-hand mechanical diggers. Moreover, the agency behind the investment approved of this direction for his business, and that agency was a nationally famous early-phase investment fund. The manager of the fund had previously worked for Mitsubishi in their heavy industry section, so he had a very good knowledge of mechanical diggers. Mengde said it was different this time because he was selling the machines on the internet, and there were already 20 or 30 people working with him.

He had gone back to his old line of work but, because he had had his entrepreneurial baptism at the Garage Café, it was no longer quite the same old line of work.

Before the café had even been in operation for a full year, off the top of his head, Su Lan could tell the stories of more than a hundred entrepreneurs.

There was the 31-year-old Tan Sizhe, nicknamed the Daoist Priest, who had come up to Beijing from a remote country village in Hunan. He had realised that the local farmers didn't have credit cards so they couldn't take advantage of Taobao. He decided to set up an e-shopping tool that was even simpler to use than Taobao so there would be an easy route to market for the farmers and their produce. The Daoist Priest said, "If you are looking for a zero-cost start-up, then the Garage Café is a good starting point." Beneath his heavy beard and eyebrows, his voice was curiously soft and unassuming.

After the Garage Café had been open for 15 days, 'The Gangster' Liu Huanqing became a regular there. He was making 'pocket museums' and virtual reality shops using gaming technology to give 360-degree 3D images of artworks on your cell phone. He said there were a million hidden treasures in the Forbidden City, only a few thousand of which were ever put out on display; 99% of them are locked away in private rooms, but with his system it becomes easy to view them.

Twenty-five-year old Lian Zhilin was a man of few words, and his usual spot in the Garage Café was a seat by the window. He wore a crumpled jacket the colour of the loess of the Yellow River and his dirty hair formed something rather like a cap on top of his head. The screen of his computer displayed the women's social networking platform that his team was developing.

He was from Henan and had gone to Shanghai after graduating from university to work as a programmer. After two years, his salary had gone up from Rmb8,000 a month to Rmb15,000, which wasn't a fortune, but was still pretty good. However, one thought kept nagging away at him, and the monotony of office life was not enough to suppress his entrepreneurial instincts. He resigned from his job and came up on his own to Beijing and the Garage Café, where he ploughed Rmb100,000 or so into a start-up. He felt very lonely sometimes as his life consisted solely of programming, his product and trying to raise money. He had no social life and no girlfriend.

Zhang Dalin was 24 and had a mania for all things Apple: Apple notebooks, iPads and iPhones. His family had been in business for three generations and was pretty well off. Three generations were looking to him to carry on the family tradition but after he graduated and was starting up in business, he found he really did not fancy getting involved in the family business. He believed that traditional handicrafts were on the wane and that the business was not suitable for growth and was unsustainable. He needed a business of his own. He had majored in computing at university and was very talented musically. He could play a dozen different instruments and wanted to develop some software to let every music lover live in their own musical world. It normally would take at least three years to learn to compose music but Zhang Dalin's software would teach you to compose and record in three minutes, and then upload the finished product onto an internet channel so everyone could listen to it. This was his dream.

During this time, the fame of the Garage Café spread like wildfire across all forms of the media: science and technology blogs, local media, national media, even foreign media, The *Washington Post*, Germany's weekly news magazine *Der Spiegel*... on 27 May 2012, the Garage Café was the lead item on CCTV's 'News Hook-Up' and that was the first time it had featured start-up services: the segment lasted six minutes, and the opening shot was of the café.

What Are the Americans Afraid Of?

Bill Gates once wrote in his diary, "Life is a conflagration. What the individual can and must do is try his hardest to rescue things from that fire." Undoubtedly, entrepreneurs all have the fire of their dreams burning inside them, and no matter whether in Silicon Valley in America or Zhongguancun in Beijing, there are always youngsters, unhappy with the status quo, building dream after dream and wonder after wonder. In both America and China, the world of 30 years ago was different beyond all recognition and back then no one could have dreamed that China would become the second biggest economy in the world, so closely connected to and so much on a par with the rest of the world, both economically and culturally. In March 2013, the economist Bin Qi gave a lecture at the Guanghua School of Management, Peking University, entitled: *The Next 10 Years – China's Economic Transformation and Breakthrough*. He mentioned the Garage Café three times, saying that there weren't any coffee shops like it in America and that in Silicon Valley venture capitalists and entrepreneurs met singly in lots of different places; the Chinese were very clever to come up with the 'mass blind date'. Bin Qi also mentioned that a reporter from the *Washington Post* had visited the Garage Café and written an article headlined: *What Americans Should Fear About the Chinese*.

The article was published in the *Washington Post* of 27 September 2011, more than a month after the reporter's conversation with Su Lan, and it was accompanied by a photograph showing a Chinese in Tiananmen Square, wearing a Peking opera mask and hiding behind a Chinese national flag. Bin Qi commented, "The allusion of the headline and the photograph is that China, which has already become the number two economic power in the world, is still booming and roaring ahead, and American society is worried and wants to know what is driving the Chinese economy. What secret weapon does it have?"

The overall gist of the article was that American policymakers were spooked by the enormous increase in the number of Chinese scientific papers and patent applications. The writer believed that those policymakers were right to be worried but were worried about the wrong thing. Americans do not need to be worried about Chinese patents, academic papers and its GDP; what they do need to worry about is that when young Chinese graduate from the country's top universities, they are leaving the college gates straight into the commercial world as innovators, and they have already become or are about to become entrepreneurs. The Chinese have already discovered America's secret. What is that secret? It is the bringing together of technology and capital. That is the secret that has allowed America's high-tech industry to stand alone in the world for the past 20 or 30 years.

This situation had first developed some time before, in the time of Chen Chunxian, in fact.

It was a month later that Su Lan discovered he had been in the American press, when a friend living abroad telephoned him to say that the Garage Café's fame had spread to the US. Su Lan was quite flustered, and spent a long time trying and failing to remember what he had said to that American. He was much clearer about what he had said to the German reporter. He learned that he had been in the American papers for a second time a year or more later at the time of Bin Qi's lecture. Someone reported to him what was said, and this time he remembered the day and the circumstances when IM's CEO Xiong Shangwen had brought Vivek Wadhwa to the Garage Café.

DIARY NOTE 18: ZHONGGUANCUN, BEIJING

Su Lan had a shaved head and wore a monk's gown and cloth shoes; he didn't even have to open his mouth for one to know he was a dyed-in-the-wool Beijinger and this made me look on him, as a genuine native, with a familiar affection. He made me remember my own

3. GARAGE CAFÉ

youth and reminded me of many of the neighbours on my street. In truth, however, he is very different from the Beijingers of my youth; he has a kind of concentrated essence of modernity in his old-Beijing style, a prescience; but at the same time, you could equally say that he has a concentrated essence of old Beijing in his modernity and prescience. It is only in Zhongguancun that you could find such an extraordinary composite; a kind of hybrid not to be seen anywhere else.

In the 1970s I lived through the Cultural Revolution, a time of total government control with the streets resounding with revolutionary slogans; there wasn't very much old Beijing atmosphere at all. It was all in complete contrast to Su Lan's current 'old Beijing', freed from the Cultural Revolution, and his modernity and prescience were something that I have never had. He is a Zhongguancun Beijinger, and I have to recognise that difference between us. He reminds me of Shopkeeper Wang in the film *The Teahouse*[4], just as the Garage Café itself reminds me of the establishment in the film, although these were really just vague impressions, and they are really not the same things at all. There may perhaps be some similarities, but the most fundamental difference is that Shopkeeper Wang had a kind of humility, sorrow even, that is completely absent in Su Lan. In contrast, he has a real sense of spirit and drive. But what still irresistibly reminds me of Shopkeeper Wang is the air of tragedy with which that character is played, an impression of being superfluous, that is redolent of old Beijing in every gesture and every move. No matter whether he's discussing black technology, series-A funding rounds, Bill Gates or mobile apps, it is the warmth with which Su Lan greets his customers, his expression, his tone of voice and his manner, all so practiced and instinctive, that irresistibly reminds me of Shopkeeper Wang. Although Wang never welcomed any foreigners into his teahouse, if he had done, I am quite sure he would have been just like Su Lan, always with the depth and mellowness of something long-steeped in rich wine.

Of course, when all is said and done, these are different times and the air of longstanding depression is much reduced in Su Lan, or rather it would be more accurate to say it is gone completely and he is very bright and open. He is the kind of young man Beijingers look on with approval, and without youngsters like him, Zhongguancun would be missing some of its Beijing atmosphere, its local feeling and it might also be lacking some of its harmoniousness. The harmony of Zhongguancun and old Beijing, their complexity, are things that other places don't have. The Garage Café itself embodies the tolerance of old Beijing and it allows people from all over the world to become Beijingers themselves.

Yes, that's it: the Garage Café is not just about high-tech, venture capital, finance and all those Zhongguancun kind of things, it is also the gathering place of dreams. Clearly on show here in a utopian ambience are idealists, speculators and all other kinds and colours of people. There are university students, returnees from abroad, beef salesmen, village teachers, artists, second-hand mechanical digger salesmen, major players, venture capitalists, reporters, foreigners. Beijing has its internationalism and globalism; indeed these are its specialities, and anything that represents Beijing must have them. But the Garage Café is not just a symbol of Beijing, it is also a symbol of the whole of modern China.

—————— **Sharing or Enjoying Together** ——————

分 享 或 共 享

The Chinese Academy of Governance

ON 26 MAY 2016, the 33-year-old Cheng Wei, who was born in 1983, delivered a lecture at the Chinese Academy of Governance entitled, *Sharing Economic Development in China*. His audience consisted of more than 400 government officials, all older than him, and some of whom were even his direct superiors. According to published data and information, 33-year-old Cheng Wei was only the second internet entrepreneur after Alibaba's founder, Ma Yun, to mount the podium in the great hall of the Academy of Governance. Just the day before, on 25 May, he had returned from a big data summit meeting in Guiyang and before that, he had been in Davos. He was the founder of DiDi Chuxing and, right at the start, both the youth of DiDi and indeed the youth of Cheng Wei himself, became the focus of intense debate among the officials in the audience; but for the people who came in after his talk had begun, his age quickly became irrelevant. What he had to say made it evident that a new age was being born in the person of this young man: the age of the mobile internet economy.

Four years previously, Cheng Wei was still an advertising man in an office building in the Central Business District but recently, particularly after the purchase of Uber, DiDi's valuation exceeded US$35 billion, a sum seldom seen in the internet world, and rare even in the 'real' world. This had nothing to do with physical age, which was a traditional and outmoded concept in Cheng Wei's eyes.

"China is quite possibly the leading nation in the worldwide sharing economy," Cheng Wei said with quiet assurance. "We were not leaders in the industrial age, but we can have confidence that China in the age of the sharing economy may well overtake both Europe and America. If we take DiDi as an example. In America Uber did not succeed in changing Americans' travelling habits and they still prefer to drive themselves; cars are cheap in America and so is gas, so the cost of a self-driven trip averages out at US$7. The basic cost of labour over there is high, so chauffeurs/drivers are expensive, making the average cost of a taxi ride three times that of self-drive at US$21 per trip. So people with less money drive themselves and rich people just employ a single driver, and don't bother with hiring taxis or getting other people to drive them. After Uber appeared on the scene in America, the average cost of a trip went down from US$21 to US$14, but it was still more expensive than self-drive because Uber drivers represented a high labour cost. The mobile travel service industry developed in North America two years before China, and it has already been going for six years. Even taken together, Uber and Lyft only service 2 million customers a day in the whole of North America, so how is it that after only four years in China, the industry has gone straight to more than 13 million customers per day and continues to grow at an even greater rate than America?"

Cheng Wei talked about the international competition China faces, and how foreign industry sees Chinese industry as a target for its expansion into new territory. When Uber arrived on our doorstep from America as a competitor, they came to DiDi's offices and arrogantly stated that DiDi only had two possible routes: one would be to accept a 40% investment from Uber, and the other would be to be swallowed up. Uber had already conquered America and Europe, and had an estimated value of US$50 billion; they arrived in China with several billion US dollars in hand and their gaze fixed covetously on the Chinese market. Two years before, Cheng Wei said, no matter that DiDi and Kuaidi were independent guerrilla outfits, Uber viewed them as one rag-tag army, and if they didn't accept Uber's offer, then Uber would just plough their several billion dollars into the Chinese market and throw their competitors into complete turmoil. If they still refused to be integrated into Uber, they would be destroyed. Cheng Wei could see quite clearly that this wasn't a negotiation. He told Uber that when the 'Great Powers' first came to China in 1840, they adopted the same course of action, threatening to annex Hong Kong, liberate Canton (Guangzhou) and fight their way all the way to the Forbidden City. He said that the Chinese internet was not the internet of 20 years ago, and he drew Uber a diagram, talking as he drew, "You were established three years before us and now you are worth US$50 billion. We came along a few years later than you, but I believe ours is the same as the story of Taobao and Amazon."

Uber's challenge was very serious, and not only did they burn through US$400 million in China in the second quarter of 2015, Uber's CEO came in person to oversee the campaign and stayed for more than 70 days. Cheng Wei prepared to meet the challenge, and this 30-something young man was like a high-ranking general poring over the map of a military campaign, carefully studying the fundamental differences between the Chinese and American businesses, working out the basis for defeating the enemy on his home ground. He was even seeking viable strategies for victory in future worldwide competition. He realised that American business's method of attack was pretty much the same as the one the American military used. When they were not fighting on home ground, they had to spread across the whole globe and for that they relied on air power. In the same way, to begin with, Uber fought a capitalist war, a public opinion war, a marketing war: this was the equivalent of their air power, as their actual strength on the ground was not great. Because they were fighting away from home, their ground forces were effectively all marines, reliant on air support and the fighting ability of isolated military units. The military analogy is very accurate.

So, where to come to battle? Cheng Wei consulted three businessmen from the previous generation. First, he asked the experienced strategist, Liu Chuanzhi: in Cheng Wei's eyes, Liu had always fought the most elegant campaigns. Liu told him that he should exploit his native advantage of superiority in guerrilla warfare and keep inconveniencing the enemy. Cheng Wei also went to ask Tencent's chairman, Pony Ma, who said he should square up to the enemy and annihilate them. Finally, he went to consult Alibaba's Ma Yun, who told him all imperialists are paper tigers, and if you keep obstructing them for two years, they will begin to cause themselves problems. With each of the three giving different advice, which one was it to be? A straightforward head-on Player Killing? Or guerrilla warfare? Or just let the enemy get on with it? In the end, Cheng Wei felt that these were different times and called for different methods.

So, this was the man invited to address the Chinese Academy of Governance, despite his youth.

No one questioned his youth, rather they were deeply moved by it.

Starting Out From A Place of Pain

In 2012, Cheng Wei booked a restaurant in Beijing's Wangfujing District to have dinner with some relatives from Jiangxi. They had landed at the airport at 5 o'clock and were waiting for a taxi, so Cheng Wei settled on 7 o'clock for the food to be served and went ahead and ordered far too much. In the end, his relatives called at 8 o'clock asking if he could go out and pick them up from the airport. Cheng Wei didn't know whether to laugh or cry; it would take him at least an hour to get to the airport, but his relatives had said there wasn't a taxi to be had anywhere. He was working for Alibaba at the time, dividing his time between Hangzhou and Beijing, and he had often missed a flight because he couldn't find a taxi. He had developed something of a neurosis about hailing taxis, so he quite understood his relatives' situation, but there was nothing to be done about it at the time. He urged his relatives to settle for taking the airport bus, but they were so confused by the airport that they couldn't find where to catch it;

all they could do was walk around the airport, phone in hand, looking for a signboard. On another occasion, in Hangzhou, Cheng Wei was going to a meeting only five or six kilometres away. It was raining and he walked all the way, trying to flag down a taxi. He arrived at the meeting looking like a drowned rat, but at least it took place.

Cheng Wei was born in Hekou township in Jiangxi's Qianshan County. His father was a civil servant and his mother a maths teacher. He was a very good student and went up to Qianshan Number One Middle School. He took the *Gaokao* in 2001 and his excellent results admitted him to the Beijing University of Chemical Technology. He graduated in 2005 and went straight off to work for Alibaba's subsidiary B2B Marketplace. Just like other university graduates, Cheng Wei started at the bottom, working in sales. He rose through the ranks over three or four years to become an area manager and was the youngest person in the company to hold that post in that year. In 2011, he was promoted to deputy general manager of the Alipay B2C division, with responsibility for the Alipay product and merchant interface. After this change in direction, Cheng Wei began to turn his attention away from the sales teams onto product management, and with the internet horizon ever widening, within a year he had rapidly developed a collaborative company working interchangeably across three sites with a workforce that increased from several dozen to more than a thousand. The mobile internet was growing like wildfire, and although outsiders may not have understood it, Cheng Wei knew exactly what was going on.

2012 was the first year of the development of the mobile internet; it was the year that smart phones like Apple's and Samsung's grew less and less expensive and began to be seen everywhere, when previously, Nokia products had ruled the roost. Smart phones meant that all you needed was a handset and you could connect to the internet; you could find out exactly where you were at any given time; and you didn't need to be in a room with a computer to get online. It was made possible by hardware developments and the ubiquity of 4G internet, and it made possible new and innovative formats. Observing all this, if it wasn't the time for Cheng Wei to start his own business now, he didn't know when would be! On this fast-moving new platform of the mobile internet, everyone was rushing to get online, and if he didn't make his move, he would regret it. A whole generation of people at the cutting edge of the internet felt the same, including Wu Gansha at Intel Labs China. This was a shared phenomenon which illustrated the hyper-reality of the relationship between the age and the individual.

Nine months before he resigned as deputy general manager of Alibaba's Alipay division, Cheng Wei had thought up six different projects but not gone through with any of them. Forming a start-up is an act of impulse, but that can't be all; in the end it is also shaped by the individual's own business acumen. Impulse is a kind of hope and business acumen is the control imposed on that hope; the two things work together in opposition, and intuition plays a vital role. Intuition is the product of accumulation and maturation, often superseding hope and reason in its return to the original. Cheng Wei's focus returned from the outside world to himself, to his innermost feelings: what was the most painful thing that had happened to him? What was the lowest point of his existence? He thought of food, of clothing and of accommodation, but none of these had ever been a headache for him. Whenever he was out and about, every time he was left standing in the biting wind, every time he missed a flight, these were his most painful times and that pain became his starting point.

Taxi-Hire Software

On 6 June 2012, the day after he quit his job, Cheng Wei set up the Beijing Xiaojie Science and Technology Company to provide software used for hiring taxicabs called 'DiDi Dache'. He invested Rmb100,000, and his colleague at Alipay now turned angel investor, Wang Gang, put up Rmb700,000, and with that, the company was launched. Although pain was their starting point, there was no problem with the basis of their venture, but the reason the place of pain was painful was precisely because it was a difficulty: a difficulty not just for Cheng Wei, but for society as a whole. People had been cursing the taxi industry for a long time, but no one had ever done anything to change that. Why not? Cheng Wei consulted all his friends over what they thought about creating taxi-hire software, and they almost all reacted as though he were delirious. Even those who encouraged him couldn't agree on what kind of software he should make. Everybody felt that China had never had a proper taxi system: you call for a cab which may or may not come; when the driver sees there is only one of you wanting to go to the airport, he may take on another fare; while the taxi is on its way to you, you may see another empty cab and take that one instead of waiting for the original one. Often, drivers didn't have smart phones; indeed at the time, only 10% of them could fish an iPhone or a Samsung Galaxy out of their pocket, and most of them were still using Nokias. Nothing that wasn't a smart phone could be loaded with software. Moreover, at the time, there was no online payment and people were most emphatically not used to the idea of paying the taxi fare when you made the hire. Although you could make card payments, that was certainly not the norm, and drivers were used to taking cash and would refuse this kind of internet payment. Then, of course, there was the political risk, the possibility of contravening government policy.

"Every day I asked myself if this thing was actually possible. I weighed it up, over and over again, asking myself, but I had started and there was no turning back. Even so I constantly doubted myself, always trying to refine my plans," Cheng Wei says. "At the Guiyang summit meeting, at Davos, at the Chinese Academy of Governance… how could one not have doubts facing such difficult situations? But I also knew that entrepreneurs are not thinkers or strategists, they are adventurers and very few of them have thought things through completely when they start out; if they had they wouldn't be doing it. But the things that you say should be thought through are all things that are subject to change and so are unpredictable. Besides, change is what entrepreneurs are seeking. If the market isn't ready yet you can't do it, is how people who think things through see it, but it is precisely in those conditions that entrepreneurs succeed. With smart phones commonplace, and both end users, drivers and customers properly educated, the market would be ready but it would be too late for you to launch taxi-hire software."

Don't think so much, just start from the fact that it is do-able; you are going against the current, so first produce the software. That is what is do-able, so get on and do it, and don't worry about anything else. Painful decisions have to be taken, that is quite right and the right direction to travel, so just do it and let the journey end how it will. This is how it has always been for entrepreneurs, and this generation of them are certainly no less impetuous than any other.

Cheng Wei had two possible courses of action, either to assemble his own team to produce the software, or to outsource it. Setting up your own R&D team was the traditional way for old-school entrepreneurs, but Cheng Wei decided to outsource and find a technology partner. This is the way of the internet entrepreneur. He met with quite a few potential outsourcers, one of which was the producer of what they called E Drive software. If they had made that, they must be alright, so Cheng Wei went to talk to them. They quoted three different prices: Rmb100,000, Rmb80,000 and Rmb60,000. Cheng Wei thought about it, and chose Rmb80,000. At that time, he did not know about the technical divisions of iOS, Android, frontend and backend. When the product appeared two months later, it was next to useless as it only had a 50% connection success rate. That is to say, for every two calls from customers, only one would connect at the driver's end. But Cheng Wei was in a hurry to get the app online, so he just had to make the best of it. At the time, there were 189 taxi companies in Beijing and DiDi's target was to break through the 1,000-driver barrier for the installation of the software. In the end, after 40 days, not a single taxi company had signed up. Every morning, the off-line co-workers set out full of hope, but every evening they returned downhearted. Every day, they were asked the same question, "Do you have a red-letterhead document from the Traffic Committee?" This was the first requirement when it came to assessing political risk.

No one can afford to mess around with political risk. In China, this is just the way things are, but Cheng Wei decided to test the water. He was a young man, and it is in actions like this that a young man's hopes lie; they are also sometimes where the progress of the age lie. He couldn't do anything in Beijing, as policy was too strict, so he decided to switch cities and try somewhere else. He felt that Shenzhen was a more open city than Beijing but, in the end, he hit the same problem. Just when he thought he had reached the point where further effort was hopeless, heaven opened a new window for him. On the 49th day, one of their peripatetic real-time agents phoned Cheng Wei to tell him that he had found a taxi company that was willing to work with them. It was a small firm in Changping with only 70 cabs, called Yinshang Taxis. The owner didn't really understand what DiDi was offering, but had had a merry time out drinking with DiDi's rep, and had agreed while flushed with wine.

This was a glimmer of light. With one company signed up, when they went out pushing for more business, they could say, "Look, Yinshang Taxis are already working with us, and if you don't do the same, you are going to lose out to other companies and before you know it, your own drivers will have gone off to work for them too." Used like this, that glimmer of hope could be a guiding light. In the course of the next week, the rep's colleagues signed up another four companies. As taxi firms slowly began to join them, the next thing to do was to organise training for the drivers. Cheng Wei undertook this in person. He told them that he himself had started out with Alibaba, which was a big-name company that everyone was familiar with. Lots of the drivers had bought things on Taobao and some of their family members had opened online shops on the site. He went on to say that, although he was an outsider to the taxi business, he had been working with the internet for a long time and had seen many different businesses improve their efficiency that way and increase their profits. DiDi's software could improve efficiency in hiring cabs and so help the drivers earn more money. Cheng Wei thought he was being very open and up-front, but the drivers in the audience just sat there, smoking cigarettes and chatting to each other, and not listening at all. They found meetings really boring and irritating as all they did was waste time during which they could be earning money. They had been cheated out of money by all the oil and petrol companies and thought that DiDi was just a new scam to do the same.

At that time, only 20 out of every 100 taxi drivers in Beijing had a smart phone and, as a rule, on any given day DiDi could only equip seven or eight. Then, one day, one of the reps equipped 12 drivers, and he phoned in delighted, saying that he had made a major breakthrough. It was indeed a breakthrough of a kind, but really it was a dispiriting one since the original plan was that they would have signed up 1,000 drivers in the first two months. If they could only get 12 a day, how long was it going to be before the company took off? But they couldn't waste any more time; they had to get on with it, put on a bold face and settle for the connections they could make. They still had to go before the Traffic Committee; they couldn't not go and, no matter whether they were successful or not, there was work to be done. Even if they only gained a basic understanding of what they were trying to do, that would be enough. Cheng Wei went in person to make the presentation to the Traffic Committee. Because it was something completely new, the members of the committee were full of curiosity, and stared attentively as though waiting for some kind of message from an extra-terrestrial. Cheng Wei made two attempts, each of 30 seconds, but neither connected. How amazing, how persuasive it would have been if they had, but as it was, Cheng Wei felt like a fraud, and just wished the ground would open up and swallow him. Fortunately, the members of the Traffic Committee were good sorts; they fetched a cloth for Cheng Wei to wipe away the sweat on his forehead and told him not to get agitated and to have a drink of water. If he hadn't been an ex-employee of Alibaba and a senior manager, he might well just have been thrown out completely at this point. He went back to give a second demonstration, and this time he took two cell phones with him: whichever one connected would be the one he used.

Outsourcing technology is not a very reliable way of doing things. You have to find technical partners, but if there aren't any to be found in the mobile internet industry, what do you do? Cheng Wei went to every possible length. First, he sought out a colleague from his Alipay days and got him to make up a list of all the technical people Cheng Wei might know who were working in Beijing. Then he went and talked to each of them in turn, but none of them wanted to leave to join him. Then he thought of an older cousin who had opened an internet bar back in his hometown and was a computer studies graduate. He asked him if any of his old classmates were working in Beijing and might want to become his technical partner. But none did. Then, one day, Cheng Wei heard some news about Sogou and Tencent, and thought to himself that if those big companies were going through changes, then there were bound to be some of their technical staff on the look-out for new jobs. He immediately did the rounds of Baidu and Tencent, asking people out for meals and for coffee, but all to no avail. There was no one who wanted to join him. He happened to be part of a WeChat group, one of whose members called himself a head-hunter. He asked Cheng Wei what kind of person he was looking for, but after he had told him, he heard no more from him. "When you have reached your wits' end, heaven may open a window for you!" These are words you will often hear Cheng Wei say. A month later, out of the blue, the head-hunter telephoned him to say he had found someone. He made immediate arrangements for Cheng Wei to meet this person, who turned out to be DiDi's current CTO, Zhang Bo. Sometimes people are brought together by fate, and as soon as Cheng Wei clapped eyes on Zhang Bo, he knew he was the man he was after. It was the same with Zhang Bo, who immediately recognised their shared talent. Cheng Wei was delighted after his talk with Zhang Bo, delighted beyond measure, and as soon as he was out of the door, he telephoned his angel investor, Wang Gang, telling him Zhang Bo was a gift from the gods. The fact that the Rmb800,000 seed money was almost exhausted, and the Series A funding was not yet in place, didn't affect Cheng Wei's delight in the slightest.

Even so, after his meeting with Zhang Bo, Cheng Wei did ask Wang Gang for an injection of funds. Both Cheng Wei and Zhang Bo were, in reality, inexperienced in the world of venture capital, but DiDi gave another presentation using their equipment with its unreliable internet connection, seeking US$5 million of funding. They tried everywhere among the mainstream venture capitalists, 20 or more different companies, but not one of them was willing to invest. In truth one couldn't really blame them given the discrepancy between what the company was worth and the amount it was seeking.

With no orders on their books and no one calling their cabs, despite Zhang Bo's superb technical knowhow, there was no denying this was a serious problem; not the most serious problem, because all their problems were equally serious and interconnected. But as a young man still, Cheng

Wei ploughed on regardless, like a new-born calf that hasn't learned to fear the tiger, like a cat risking all its nine lives, and kept searching for a way up like a man climbing a cliff face. Then, one day, a taxi driver came to the DiDi offices from quite some distance away to square up to Cheng Wei, waving his cell phone at him and calling him a fraud. He said he had used up more than a dozen megabytes of data without getting a single order. If getting no orders still used up data like that, the cab-hire software might as well not be there and was as useless as some crazy person's dream. In fact, many of the drivers saved data by not even opening up the software and one day, when he was checking it, Cheng Wei discovered that there were only 16 drivers online and only 16 lights lit on their map of Beijing.

If there were no orders coming in, they had to find people to go out and hire the cabs before even those little beacons of hope were extinguished. They needed to encourage them, give them some impetus. He had almost used up the last of the company's nine lives and it needed an intravenous drip. Recruiting people to hire cabs was something that had never been done before and Cheng Wei was forced into it as a last resort. The first person he interviewed asked what the job was, and he told him it was hiring taxis, and he would give him Rmb400 a day to hang around the Third Ring Road, hiring cabs. The man stared at him wide-eyed, struggling both to understand and believe that the work just involved spending money. It was certainly a novelty. He wasn't to go too far, Cheng Wei told the applicant, because his capital was limited and they needed to be economical. Cheng Wei said he reckoned this must be the easiest way in the world of making a living, and the man agreed. But a few days later, the taxi hirer was not a happy man. He told Cheng Wei, "You have no idea what a miserable job this is. I worked out my route when I left home in the morning and took a taxi to Sanyuanqiao. I intended to hire another taxi there to go somewhere else, but the first cab didn't drive off. It stayed where it was, waiting for another fare, and there I was, stuck at Sanyuanqiao. I couldn't flag down another cab in case the first driver saw me and took me for some kind of plant or stooge. Do you think it's nice being taken for a stooge? It's not an easy thing!"

"If you really don't want to do it," Cheng Wei replied, "you can hand out fliers instead. I'll come too." And that is what he did. He went to the World Trade Centre and started handing out leaflets, helping people to download the software on the spot, and hire a DiDi taxi. It wasn't long before he got a phone call from the other man, who had gone to do the same thing at Beijing West Station. He was standing under an overhead walkway and had only just taken out his bundle of fliers when he was arrested and was now down at the local police station being held for being a protester. Cheng Wei was very alarmed by this turn of events, and once again asked himself whether he was attempting the impossible.

In the midst of these difficulties, competitors began to appear, and stronger competitors at that. This was both a good and a bad thing. At least it meant that Cheng Wei was pointed in the right direction, that people had seen the future and were getting together to change the present. The first competitor was YoYo, which was a private car hire company. It had obtained US$3.5 million in Series A funding from Sequioa Capital and ZhenFund, so with US$3.5 million and Rmb800,000, its capitalisation was a hundred times bigger than DiDi. It spent Rmb300,000 on television advertising to introduce its own taxi-hire software, which DiDi simply couldn't compete with. Cheng Wei was at his wits' end, when one of his logistics people said they could see a way through. Cheng Wei was keen to listen: at the beginning of his start-up, someone saying they had a way of doing something was music to his ears. All the fashion shopping channels at the time ended their broadcasts with the same line: Phone xxxx now! The idea the logistics staffer had was that they should follow YoYo's advertisements with a short one of their own simply saying: "Now phone xxxx and download the software immediately." After all, the taxi drivers weren't going to be able to tell whether it was YoYo's number or DiDi's. The results exceeded their expectations, particularly when YoYo called a public meeting and no one attended. They phoned up loads of taxi drivers who told them: "We've already downloaded the software. Didn't you say all we had to do was phone xxxx?"

Of course this wasn't strictly honest, but given the difficult spot he was in, Cheng Wei didn't really care too much.

When Yoyo leased a stand at the airport, Cheng Wei was too short of money to follow suit, and all he could afford was a stand at the train station manned by uniformed staff who helped taxi drivers install the software. But still, most drivers didn't really understand smartphones and what they could do, so the staff asked them one by one if their phone was a Nokia (Nokias are feature phones, sometimes called dumbphones). If it wasn't, they took the driver aside and installed the software for them. Then they gave them a brochure to take away and read, to learn how to use it. This time they paid attention to every little detail. For instance, if they were stationed beside the toilets, they had to be careful about whether they handed out the brochures before the drivers went into the toilet or when they came out. If they did the former, then the brochure was nowhere to be seen when the driver emerged.

This was a tricky business to manage, and it had to be handled like this:

"Excuse me, is that a smartphone?"

"What's a smartphone?"

"Oh, I'm sorry; please excuse me."

or

"Yes, it is."

"Excellent. Let me give you this to read. It is guaranteed to make you money."

Unicorn

One afternoon in the summer of 2012, three young female office workers were walking past Beijing World Centre Tower 3 office block. They were what Cheng Wei had meant when he talked about "heaven opening a window". One of them told the other two, "I'm using software on my phone to hire cabs now. It's really convenient. You should try it." At the same time, an unremarkable middle-aged man brushed past the girls. The girl who was talking is almost certainly unaware even now that her words, which were carried along in the breeze, prompted a decision to make a venture into the internet investment field. The man's name was Zhu Xiaohu, and he had just had a meeting with Cheng Wei. A few days before, he had exchanged a few words with Cheng Wei on Sina Weibo, and the two had subsequently met. Zhu Xiaohu had taken a DiDi taxi to DiDi's offices some distance away, but Cheng Wei was very busy and, after a hurried greeting, had left him waiting for half an hour. Zhu said he wanted to invest but Cheng Wei didn't seem at all excited at the prospect, even when he said he had US$2 million to put in. This was because Cheng Wei didn't believe him or doubted his seriousness. Another thing that made him suspicious was that Zhu Xiaohu didn't haggle over the price at all, but just agreed to what Cheng Wei proposed. Perhaps he was a Shanxi mine owner? He looked like one but didn't sound like one. They had talked for no more than half an hour, and after Zhu Xiaohu left, Cheng Wei had basically decided he was a fraud. A week later, his finance department told Cheng Wei that US$2 million had been deposited in their account. Cheng Wei was so stupefied he almost passed out, but at the same time he could see a window opening in the heavens, and standing in the window was the unremarkable, plain-speaking figure of Zhu Xiaohu. And all the time, his colleagues were still desperately handing out fliers at the train station.

• • •

Cheng Wei almost burst into tears at the thought that heaven had come to his aid.

US$2 million! He had run into so many brick walls he had given up hope, so this really was manna from heaven.

Cheng Wei leapt back to his feet like a boxer who had been knocked down.

This Zhu Xiaohu who took just 'half an hour to decide on an investment' nonetheless described himself as a 'rational' investor. On the Jinshajiang official website he is described thus: "This man's main direction of investment is the internet, wifi and new media. Zhu Xiaohu was once part of a software sales team which he chose to leave seven years after start-up when the company had a sales team of over a thousand. He then joined Jinshajiang Venture Capital. Zhu Xiaohu has invested in many well-known cases: in the field of e-commerce he invested in online fashion boutique Moonbasa (Dream Bazaar) and global online shopping site 'LightInTheBox'; in the field of news media he invested in classified advertising site Baixing.com and in group buying he invested in Lashouwang."

He didn't go out and about much, and from when he started out in 2008 up to now, there have been less than a dozen online media reports about him. He is very low profile, verging on secretive. He seemed to have been secretly stalking trends on Sina, hunting a unicorn. He had been lurking on DiDi's microblog, paying close attention to this new company, watching how it fought its corner. He was clear in his mind that over the past 15 years in the world of Chinese internet start-ups, there had been a lull at three-year intervals. It was in one of those lulls at this time: China's venture capitalists were starting a new round aimed at the new field of O2O and beginning to loose off their rounds. O2O or Online-to-Offline/Offline-to-Online simply put is opening access between online and offline material, taking online data and channelling it into offline spending thus giving offline merchants the opportunity to link up with the mobile internet. Like a hunter secretly stalking his prey, Zhu Xiaohu had set his sights on the unicorn that was DiDi.

Things work in mysterious ways: just when you are in the greatest difficulty and think you can no longer support yourself, someone fixes their attention on you. In the internet age, people playing these kinds of computer game, or perhaps we should say shouldering some of the burden in this way, are even more now the creators of legends. 'Unicorn' is a term used in the investment industry, more particularly the venture capital industry (clearly influenced by computer gaming), to indicate those few start-up companies whose valuation exceeds US$1 billion. That is not to say that particular company will earn a billion dollars in a year, indeed it could well be running at a loss and on the verge of collapse. Being on the verge of collapse doesn't mean the direction it is going in is wrong or its technology doesn't work; it is just a question of investment, and venture capitalists don't see that as a problem. In fact, it is their leverage.

Zhu Xiaohu knew that the American ride-hailing software company Uber received angel investment funding in 2010, and took another tranche of US$64 million the following year. He saw an opportunity in the field of ride-hailing, and even before Cheng Wei came along, he had already taken a look at all the companies in the field and, in his opinion, Yongche had the private hire market sewn up. As for Kuaidi, his judgment was that the project 'had no CEO'. It was not until he saw media reports on DiDi and then sought out Cheng Wei on Weibo and lurked on the site there, that he finally arranged to meet Cheng Wei. It only took a brief meeting for him to decide that this was the 'unicorn' he was looking for and that Cheng Wei's vision, courage, insight and brains exceeded what he had expected. Zhu Xiaohu kept all this to himself and was as sparing with his words as if they were gold. All he did was ask a few questions, ascertain Cheng Wei's own thinking, and then stump up the money.

Zhu Xiaohu's way of pulling the trigger on the deal was so terse and succinct, it gave the whole business a dreamlike quality.

Zhu Xiaohu says, "I had had my eye on the travel sector for a long time. Back in 2010, we were very enthusiastic about local travel. We were paying close attention from the time Yongche received its first tranche of investment, and then we wanted to put money into its Series-A funding, even signing the investment agreement. But we pulled out after the due diligence. One reason was that smartphone usage among the drivers was very low. Yongche wanted to grow their driver community by giving them all phones, but that would have pushed the costs very high without a big enough increase in efficiency. Another even more crucial point that worried us was that we felt that the ride-hailing software really wasn't quite there yet so, in the end, we didn't make the investment. After that, we also made contact with the YoYo team. By that time, they already had quite a few customers in Beijing, but we went on to discover that the team was too weak and their approach to the internet was all wrong. Even from a distance, they didn't look like a good prospect. At the same time in Hangzhou, Chen Weixing (Kuaidi Dache's original CEO) was incubating the project which was to become Kuaidi Dache."

"In November 2012, DiDi came to my attention. I chatted with Cheng Wei on Weibo, and after meeting him for half an hour, I knew that he and his team were very clear in their thinking over what should and shouldn't be done. The general tone of the team, including their previous business development and on-the-ground marketing experience was very appropriate to the undertaking, so I decided after half an hour's chat that we were in complete accord with Cheng Wei's way of thinking. I later discovered that he had seen at least 20 other venture capitalists before he met me, but none of them had invested. He thought I was some kind of fraud because I decided to invest in him after only half an hour's talk. After I had been to see him, I was making my way back to the World Trade Centre when I passed three office girls, one of whom was telling her colleagues very enthusiastically how she had used DiDi to hire her taxi the night before. This convinced me that the software was a high-frequency on-demand app with a high level of viral spread, and we would be fools not to invest."

One evening, a few days before Zhu Xiaohu deposited US$2 million into DiDi's account, Cheng Wei spent the night sitting on the sofa in his office. He lay there, eyes closed, half-awake half-asleep, with all kinds of questions piling in, thick and fast, and flashing onto the black screen of his closed eyelids. It felt as though his brain was eating popping candy. Head bowed, he massaged his temples and when he looked up, he discovered a heavily-bearded young man had appeared in front of him, looking like something from the realm of augmented reality. Cheng Wei pulled over a chair and sat down on it. He glanced at the watch with the Apple logo on his left wrist. Reflected in the watch glass, the heavily bearded young man asked:

"Come on, there isn't much time. If you've got any problems, spit them out!"

Cheng Wei was momentarily taken aback, but then recollected himself, and continued as if there was no question of any of this being imaginary.

"We can't go on. The investors don't like the look of our set-up and we only have enough cash left for another week. Soon we won't be able to pay any wages, so is there any point in me carrying on?"

The heavily-bearded young man said, "It won't be too long before people are queuing up to thrust money at you."

"I have stood in a lot of queues begging for money."

"What you must do is fight your hardest to be number one in the market."

Cheng Wei gave a bitter laugh, "Oh yes? And then what? I got all excited about the idea of getting everyone to use their cell phones to hire cabs and that's what I set out to do. In the first month, not a single taxi company came in with me. I'm afraid it's just not possible to get the taxi driver community to accept this."

"That's not such a big problem. In the future, smart phones are going to get much cheaper, and if the drivers know that having one is going to make them money, they won't hesitate. It only takes one of them to start making money, and the rest will all join in. Then, the more drivers there are, the greater the success rate will be for the customers hiring cabs and it's all down to the internet. That is the crux of what you are trying to do."

"The trouble is, the way things are going, we'll go under before we are halfway there. It is too big an undertaking." Cheng Wei was rather discouraged; the other him in the reflection was just too young.

"Other people have the same destination in mind as you," the bearded young man said mysteriously. "That's all I have to say; the rest you will have to learn by experience."

"All right then. But you know that the taxi industry is very much its own world, and a lot of the normal market rules don't apply. I'm afraid we won't even get past the government barriers."

The young man in the reflection replied, "Sometimes the government can change according to the market, and respect the rules of the marketplace. Trust me, you can work together on future developments."

"The reason I first thought of taxi hire was because I wanted to make the process easier. Looking at it now, that's only going to happen if all the taxi drivers in the country download the software. Basically, setting out on a start up, you want things to be on as large a scale as possible, but I'm not sure if the taxi hire business can be big enough."

"Taxi hire is just the start, the real journey is to the whole huge transport market. Essentially, getting a person or a load of goods from one place to another is a problem that computers are ideally suited to solving. Within 10 years, world transport and communications are going to see an enormous change, and you have a chance to ride that wave. Just get on and do it."

"So my last question is, is everything you have just said, true?"

"What do you think?"

The room fell silent again, with only the low hum of the computer fan. Cheng Wei stared blankly round him for a moment, then drifted off to sleep.

The Snows of 2012

The next stroke of luck was the great snows of 2012.

At the Chinese Academy of Governance, Cheng Wei said, "Before I started my venture, I went to Badachu[1] with one of my co-founders. I am certainly not a superstitious person and I haven't even been back to give thanks. I just felt that if you really go all-out for something, it might bring good luck. And it worked. I've always had high-up people on my side who have joined in and helped us."

"There have also been many chance events, like the great snows of 2012 in Beijing."

In a city already as beset with traffic jams as Beijing, the combination of snow and wind left countless people craning their necks for a taxi, but there was not a single empty cab to be seen. Calamity often marks a change for the better, and this was the case with DiDi. On 3 November, the first day of the snows, they reached a thousand hires in one day for the first time and, looking on the app and on the map at the office, there were lights twinkling like stars everywhere. Cheng Wei and his staff were thrilled. They were all young, with an average age of 24, and they cheered excitedly: they were the representatives of young China. The unexpected news that you could hire a taxi in the snow, and without any extra charges, was gleefully posted on the Weibo blogs of innumerable office workers, and the name DiDi Dache was everywhere on the site. DiDi was suddenly all the rage. Weibo was the expressway of the mobile internet (soon, WeChat would be even quicker, with complete synchronicity of connection) and in some ways, it could also be seen as the development superhighway. Additionally, the snows of 2012 were particularly heavy, falling continuously for several days, almost as if they were a gift from heaven, as if there was someone even higher up than Zhu Xiaohu watching over DiDi, watching over the city and watching over the common people.

"When this is over, we must go and thank the gods at the Temple of Heaven!" Cheng Wei jokingly told his staff.

DiDi's numbers kept climbing as more and more people started using the software, as one became ten, ten became a hundred and so on, presenting the company with a most delightful prospect as they moved into the New Year. DiDi's story was like a fairy tale, and people love a good fairy tale. Of course, their competitor YoYo benefitted equally from the snowy winter. YoYo had got its product on the market ahead of DiDi and its financing had gone more smoothly; moreover, its early targets were the same as DiDi's and they got even more drivers to install their own software by promoting their product at the stations, the airport and all the other places taxi drivers congregate. Other than Terminal 3 at Capital Airport, DiDi also had spots at all the important places, but YoYo had signed an agreement with a third-party service company giving them control of the Terminal 3 building.

The Terminal 3 building was exceptional because its daily consumption of taxis exceeded 20,000, pretty much equivalent to all the other main taxi sites combined. It was a vital location, and not having a presence there was a real sore point with Cheng Wei, a hurdle he had to get over, an unnamed hill he had to climb. If he couldn't occupy that commanding height, there was no way he could gain the initiative in the battle and claim victory. After Cheng Wei had wracked his brains over this, he thought he might as well go and seek a similar agreement to YoYo's with the service company. The main thing he was worried about was that there were a lot of uncertainties about such an agreement. As it turned out, later on, the airport authorities received a complaint, and permission for YoYo's promotional stand was rescinded. As YoYo went frantically searching for another place to access the taxis, DiDi had a hard time hanging onto their own venues. As the data showed them gradually overtaking YoYo, they took the opportunity to launch a counterattack by starting their Series-B funding round.

This time, DiDi received lots of advances from venture capitalists, Tencent among them. Because DiDi didn't want to rely on handing over a majority shareholding for its B-Series funding, to start with they weren't going to take Tencent's money. But, just like Zhu Xiaohu, Tencent had accurately spotted the 29-year-old 'unicorn' Cheng Wei. With the powerful mediation of Tencent's vice-chairman, the members of the board of the Tencent Industry Win-Win Fund and the CEO Peng Zhijian, Cheng Wei and Wang Gang had a face-to-face meeting with Ma Huateng (Pony Ma). Before they went in, Cheng Wei and Wang Gang came to a solid mutual understanding that they would not give Tencent the opportunity to be the lead investor. In the meeting, Cheng Wei gave an analysis of all possible developments in the transport and travel field and of DiDi's opinion of Tencent's valuation. He also raised the question of control of the company, hoping that by pushing back against Tencent in this way, he would make Ma Huateng recognise the difficulties and back off. Just like Zhu Xiaohu, Ma expansively agreed to essentially all of Cheng Wei's stipulations, including not interfering with the company's development and not trying to gain control. The only thing he pushed back on was wanting a larger shareholding. After several discussions with Tencent negotiators, Cheng Wei gained the impression that Tencent were honest, straightforward and had friendly intentions, which was no easy thing for them to have achieved. He also learned from friends at Alibaba that Tencent too were keen to clear the way for the deal. Moreover, he could see quite clearly that, with one of his powerful competitors, KuaiDi, already accepting investment from Alibaba, if he didn't take Tencent's money now, and they got impatient, they might turn and take their money to YoYo, which would leave DiDi in the doldrums. On top of all this, DiDi 's strength lay with the internet, and if they lost the use of WeChat, the acme of online access, they would lose their most important tactical advantage. They also needed a powerful partner to confront the uncertainties of public policy and, in order to survive, the most important thing was not to let themselves be trampled underfoot.

Cheng Wei and Wang Gang continued their final discussions in a bath house (not the one in Changping), and as they came out and walked through the quiet nighttime streets, they came to their final decision: they would go with Tencent. Wang Gang favoured using them for follow-up investment and Cheng Wei preferred the idea of up-front investment. In the end, it was Wang Gang who compromised. It was a beautiful night, and it was on that beautiful night as they emerged from the bath house that they decided DiDi's formidable future success.

Burning Cash

In April 2013, DiDi DaChe received Tencent's Series-B funding.

At the beginning of 2014, after they gained access to WeChat Pay, the company was like a tiger that had grown wings. Cheng Wei saw this as an opportunity for a sales promotion such as offering both drivers and passengers a subsidy. Cheng Wei asked Tencent for a budget of several million Rmb, and Tencent told him that wasn't enough. The result was that they gave him not several million Rmb but several tens of millions, which was really pretty cool. Tencent's financial perspective gave Cheng Wei enormous support, and they became more and more generous. This promotional subsidy increased DiDi's business volume dramatically, and after just one round of it, their takings exceeded Rmb100 million.

The dramatic rise in DiDi's fortunes put a lot of pressure on its competitors. The day before Cheng Wei stopped the promotion, KuaiDi and Alipay put themselves on a war footing and also began to offer a subsidy to both drivers and passengers. Because DiDi's subsidy had come to an end, the situation quickly reversed and DiDi's numbers began to fall rapidly. Their opponents' timing was very precise, a counterattack just at the moment of the enemy's retreat.

Cheng Wei called a board meeting and announced gravely, "In two weeks, KuaiDi's figures may well overtake our own." This alarmed the board members and investors considerably. "We have an important choice to make: do we immediately follow up with another subsidy?" This was not a decision Cheng Wei could take by himself; it required a board meeting. All the investors' instinctive response was that they didn't want to just burn more cash, as no one wants to see money they have put into a venture go up in smoke. Cheng Wei told them that he had just come up with a 'red envelope product' which was more sophisticated but also more expensive. He explained his thinking, which was that they would introduce this new style 'red envelope' subsidy in a month's time. Both Wang Gang and Zhu Xiaohu stated their opinion that, although it was their own company that had started this subsidy war, now they had to counterattack immediately and, if they waited a month, their market share could easily drop to 7:3 in the opposition's favour, ceding the initiative and, quite possibly, driving DiDi out of the market altogether.

The committee members made their own deductions: when we issue the new subsidy, if KuaiDi don't respond within a week, but wait a month, DiDi's market share could be 7:3 or even 8:2. If this is what happens, the internet effect could come into play: if the customers feel that no drivers reply when they call, and the drivers feel that there are no customers using the platform, then the result may well be that the strong will grow stronger and the weak, weaker. In these circumstances, even if the opposition spend 10 times as much as us, they are by no means certain to catch up with us and the result will be that they find it very difficult to get further financing and go out of business. Or the same thing could happen to us.

Everyone came to an agreement very quickly that they certainly wanted to bring Tencent in on the subsidy. Tencent had picked up the whole tab for the previous promotion, but the agreement was that Tencent and DiDi should go 50/50 on this new one. Ma Huateng gave his verdict straightforwardly: "As to whether you start after a month or next week, the CEO should decide."

When Cheng Wei instituted a Rmb10 subsidy, Lü Chuanwei went to Rmb11; when Cheng Wei matched the Rmb11, Lü Chuanwei went to Rmb12. The battle raged up in the heavens and down on earth, until the sky clouded over and the earth went dark; but for passengers and drivers alike, they found themselves bathed in sunshine affording a magnificent vista. When the subsidy rose to Rmb12, Ma Huateng (the Grandmaster of

Heaven) drew on his many years' gaming experience and came up with another idea: offering random subsidies between Rmb10 and Rmb20 so the opposition couldn't just keep matching them. Cheng Wei immediately adopted the same plan. Ma Yun (the Primeval Lord of Heaven) had his response, and so it went on with the price war continuing to rage back and forth. By April, taxis had practically become free of charge, and the competition had to come to a halt, but if one side wouldn't stop, nor would the other, and the whole process became like a prison. Cheng Wei and Kuai-Di's Lü Chuanwei were watching each other closely but, as neither one would stop, the battle became faster and more furious. There was, however, a channel of communication between the two great deities and there was no personal animosity between them. While the battle raged wildly beneath them, all was peaceful with the two of them up above.

Cheng Wei was the first to drop the subsidy a little, and Lü Chuanwei immediately followed suit. Then they did the same in reverse, and in this manner, the subsidy got lower and lower until, on 17 May 2014, both sides simultaneously dropped their subsidies completely. It was this truce that laid the foundation for the merger that lay ahead.

Although there was no winner in this great war, nor was there a loser. It was, however, the first great shock to the system for the whole transport industry, and the decisive factor in the changes the taxi business would undergo in the future. With people getting used to hiring cabs on the internet, the traditional taxi industry, in a single stride, became an online industry, and in terms of personal transport, it leapt from the back of the queue straight to the front. It is not too much to say that this was a change that turned everything on its head. The traditional taxi industry with all its corrupt practices, so obvious to everyone and so long denounced, was beyond reform, but with the leverage of the mobile internet and one small piece of software, a tiny thing to achieve so much, the industry was deconstructed and reborn. Tempered by the experience of this battle, Cheng Wei's maturity as a businessman suddenly blossomed, not only exciting his several venture capitalists, but also mobilising the enthusiasm of his board members, who were more than satisfied. Cheng Wei quite naturally progressed to being the youngest pin-up boy of the internet generation. There was no one younger in the prevailing circumstances, and it was those circumstances that created the representative of the age. And with the heroes of the age being so young, it is not surprising that sometimes they resembled characters from computer games.

Cheng Wei said at the Chinese Academy of Governance, "The mobile internet turned cell phones into Rmb1,000 instruments and Rmb100 instruments, and lots of people who are not part of the internet crowd, blue-collar workers like taxi drivers, can now get online; 3G is so stable now, and so cheap, that the gates have been flung wide open. Lots of people are talking about the subsidy war, and the way I see it is that Web 1.0 was part of the free economy, and TaoBao and 360 used free access to undermine the paid sector. It is the same thing today, except that the competition has been even more extensive, and free access is redundant. Now 2.0 is the age of the subsidy: the threshold for customer acquisition is even lower and the education of customers is even quicker, so that within the last two years the whole industry has undergone a very rapid process of development, competition and cooperation.

She Knows How To Get People Going

"I get very excited when I think of Liu Qing (Jean Liu). She is undoubtedly a talented individual and knows how to get people going." After the great war between Cheng Wei, another 'visitor from heaven' appeared in the form of Liu Qing. I am not saying she had some kind of halo or heavenly radiance, but she certainly dazzled Cheng Wei. "I almost don't dare look at her," he sighed to Wang Gang. Excited as he was by Liu Qing, he still rejected her. This was Liu Qing: she came from a distinguished family, the daughter of Liu Chuanzhi, chair of the board and CEO of Goldman Sachs Asia with an annual salary of US$4 million.

When she was at high school, Liu Qing was influenced by Bill Gates's book *The Road Ahead*, published in 1996 and, following her dreams, she went up to Peking University's Department of Computing. After graduating, it was pretty much inevitable that she should go on to Harvard, continuing her studies in the same field. In 2001, two years' experience at Goldman Sachs Hong Kong steered her interest towards the investment banking industry and away from her dream of becoming a legendary computer programmer. In 2002, just as the 'internet+' bubble burst, Goldman Sachs reduced its annual intake of new applicants from 30 to just six, for which there was bitter competition amongst the graduates of the top universities. After going through 18 rounds of interviews, and after actually having to sing *My Heart Will Go On* at the top of her voice in the final round, Liu Qing joined Goldman Sachs Asia as the lowest level of analyst. She excelled at the work and she recognises that her experience at Goldman Sachs Asia was a journey in which she reinvented herself. Twelve years later, she became the youngest chair of the board and CEO in the company's 100-year history, at the very top of the financial industry pyramid.

One evening in June 2014, Cheng Wei and Liu Qing were having a meal together in a small restaurant in Beijing's Digital Valley district. Liu Qing brought up the subject of Goldman Sachs investing in DiDi, and although Cheng Wei was rather in awe of her, he turned her down. This was the third time they had met, and the third time he had refused. Liu Qing put on a show of petulance, "Are you refusing our investment because you want to make me work for you? Alright then! I'll put up my own money and that'll mean I am working for you!"

Of course, it was said petulantly and in jest, but it was all the prettier for that.

After the battle he had been through, although Cheng Wei was still young and comparatively inexperienced at the age of 33, there was nothing he was afraid of.

His steeliness made a deep impression on Liu Qing.

Before she decided to invest in DiDi, Liu Qing made sure she thoroughly understood the company. To begin with, she hoped to act as matchmaker to bring Cheng Wei and Lü Chuanwei together. She had close relationships with both Tencent and Alibaba, and if she could succeed in getting them all together, she could represent Goldman Sachs in making an investment at a good price and for an advantageous shareholding. Early on, several months previously at the end of 2013, Liu Qing had already brought DiDi and KuaiDi together for discussions once. Those discussions had been held at Hangzhou airport but nothing resulted from them. The two companies were at daggers drawn at that time, fighting each other aggressively in the marketplace, and were completely unable to come to any agreement over the proportion of equity shares and so on. So the proposed merger went nowhere, much to Liu Qing's disappointment. She was well-disposed to both parties, or rather, she was well-disposed to the online ride-hailing business. There being no way of realising her dream, she was ready to throw her hat in with Cheng Wei alone, but met with no success there either.

This was quite unexpected, and a great loss of face.

Cheng Wei knew quite well that Liu Qing's petulant words were just for show. When he told the board meeting his thinking about poaching Liu Qing, Wang Gang and Zhu Xiaohu had difficulty trusting him. They both thought of him as an ambitious CEO whose aspirations knew no limits, and they supported his search for a hot-stuff partner, but poaching Liu Qing went far beyond anything they had considered.

After the board meeting had considered everything, Cheng Wei launched his offensive. He telephoned Liu Qing. He told her that they had held their board meeting, and that he had taken to heart what she had said. Liu Qing was astonished to hear this and was caught completely off guard. It was as though her opponent had suddenly turned round and recanted. Cheng Wei agreed to meet Liu Qing. When Cheng Wei was the one being persuaded, he didn't dare look Liu Qing in the eye, but now he was doing the persuading, he calmly looked straight at her.

Their discussions went on continuously for a whole week.

"It's like they've fallen head over heels in love, spending 16 hours a day together!" Wang Gang said.

Liu Qing later told a reporter from *Forbes* magazine, "Joining DiDi was like finding my calling, as I saw the chance to be right at the heart of a fundamental change in the travel industry. Also, having the chance to grow up and mature with a group of young people who had change in their very DNA was a treasure absolutely to be cherished."

This was telling it as it really was. Before Liu Qing made her final decision to join DiDi, she went on a trip with Cheng Wei and his team. When the two of them had been in discussions for a week without her making a decision, Cheng Wei said to Liu Qing:

"Let's go to Lhasa together."

It was an excellent idea and, no sooner said than done, the plane tickets were booked.

There were seven young senior executives, mostly in their early 20s, plus Liu Qing, who first flew to Xining then immediately hired two cars and headed up onto the Qinghai Plateau, planning to drive to Lhasa in three days. None of them, including Cheng Wei, had ever been there before or even knew where it was, but it was a compelling destination, the difficulties of reaching which, they were only vaguely aware of. It was an archetype of internet thinking, of young people's thinking and of e-travel thinking.

On the first day, they reached Qinghai Lake. The original plan was to spend the night there, but darkness hadn't yet fallen so they continued on their way. But it was raining and they were on mountain roads, so it was with considerable difficulty that they reached a village which had a small hotel called the Black Horse River Hotel. They went in but were frightened straight back out again: the place was full of dogs. They resumed their journey, travelling a total of 1,700km that day and ending up, with considerable effort, at another small hotel up on the plateau. The two drivers were running fevers and one of them told Cheng Wei and Liu Qing, "I've been in trouble almost from the start, and I've driven the whole way leaning into the steering wheel just to stay in control."

In that isolated Tibetan-style hotel, the eight of them used up Rmb3,000 worth of oxygen. The next day, they reached the foothills of the Himalayas. Ahead of them lay the holy city of Lhasa, and all eight of them burst into tears. There was nothing more to be said: the trip was the essence of entrepreneurship. Cheng Wei told Liu Qing, "I handed our fate over to the drivers. I had faith in them."

In Lhasa, Liu Qing sent Cheng Wei a text, "I've decided. I'm on board."

Sad to be leaving Goldman Sachs, up on the high plateau, Liu Qing wept. She wrote each of her team members a long letter marking her final farewell to her 12-year career at the company.

The five top investment banks in the world are J P Morgan Chase, Goldman Sachs, Citibank, Bank of America Merrill Lynch and Morgan Stanley. Liu Qing was at the very top level of international investment bankers, walking up amongst the clouds; DiDi was a grassroots start-up company dealing with the harsh realities of life for taxi drivers and their passengers, and its future was full of uncertainty. Everyone was baffled by her departure from Goldman Sachs. It wasn't uncommon for people to leave investment banks for start-up ventures, but what made Liu Qing different was the loftiness of her position, and the huge drop in salary she was taking.

Liu Qing herself described her decision as "starting again from scratch".

There was the same steeliness in Liu Qing as was evident in Cheng Wei; it was just that the steeliness had been cushioned by 12 years up in the clouds, but how else would you describe the determination of someone who would abandon a salary of US$4 million a year to join a start-up company? Steeliness is the only word! Cheng Wei told Liu Qing, "I'll give you half DiDi's income. How's that?"

This was steeliness talking to steeliness.

Stephen Zhu was a colleague of Liu Qing's at Goldman Sachs for four years and went on to join her at DiDi as director of strategic planning. Stephen describes Liu Qing as a flag-carrier for Goldman Sachs' business culture, wanting to take everything to the peak of achievement, an extremist in business, very demanding of herself, always going the distance and never beaten. This was why Liu Qing was not worried about leaving but was worried about whether she would be able to fit in with a grassroots team. Stephen noticed that for six months after Liu Qing left the staff of Goldman Sachs, there was neither sight nor sound of her, almost as if she had disappeared completely, as she struggled to adapt herself to DiDi's free-wheeling style. She eliminated all trace of the elitist arrogance of the investment banker in favour of the timidity of the grassroots company. When she resigned, she moved voluntarily from the first-class cabin to economy, from staying at luxurious Four Seasons hotels to Hanting chain hotels and even made sure to stow away her luxury-brand handbags.

Even though she had graduated from Peking University and Harvard, and was born into the computer industry and had once dreamed of being a programmer, Liu Qing was far from being a typical science and technology clone. Her innate fear of failure made her drive herself to extremes from the start. She would stay awake all night, going over WeChat messages and emails, striving to meet everyone's demands, seeking validation from every quarter. In amongst all this, there were, in fact, several things that weren't necessarily of prime importance to the company and which she didn't necessarily have to work herself half to death over. She seemed to be always on the go, keeping busy for the sake of being busy. Cheng Wei gave her lots of psychological comfort and advice, advising her every morning to rank the three most important tasks to be done, suppress the urge to try to do everything and try to find some kind of emotional rhythm to her work.

Gradually, Liu Qing reached the point where she was enjoying herself and slowly she began to feel as though she was properly running the company. She couldn't avoid making comparisons with her previous life: being an investment banker was like being a member of a tribe of nomadic hunters: a few people on horseback could go out on campaign, finish one project then go off in search of another. Running a company was like running a farm, where you have to take care of everyone and everything regardless of size and importance; only if you work hard at the ploughing and weeding can you reap the harvest. "This total change in role was something that happened by a process of percolation. I had no doubt this was the team I wanted to work with, and it was amongst them that I would realise even more of my true worth." With her exceptional intelligence, and given proper direction, Liu Qing made many observations here and there, which she could then pass on to Cheng Wei.

There was no one better suited to being DiDi's second-in-command, and in December 2012, using her own resources and contacts, Liu Qing brought in all the investment funds with an interest in the industry and within three weeks had settled US$700 million of investment. This was one of the biggest tranches of investment in the history of the mobile internet in China.

After this tranche was completed, not to be outdone, KuaiDi also raised a comparable sum. Finances settled, the question for the two companies was whether to continue their trial of strength or whether to shake hands and come to terms so they could face up to their other competitors. With Liu Qing now amongst them, communications between the two of them began to be much more honest and cordial. In the course of this journey, Liu Qing became the key player. Because she was equally close to Ma Yun, Ma Huateng and Liu Chiping, and was in a situation of mutual trust with the team at KuaiDi, the biggest problem of commencing merger negotiations in this affair - Liu Qing's pre-eminent position led the media to call it the 'St Valentine's Day Plan' - was coordinating all the strategic shareholders within a settled framework. But she was entirely successful in her role as mediator. The merger proceeded smoothly and, at the signing ceremony at the start of the new year, Cheng Wei wrote a commemorative couplet that read, "Fighting shakes the heavens and rattles the earth; unity spreads loving affection throughout."

Cheng Wei announced, "We have completed the most successful merger the internet has ever seen, because never before in the history of the internet have two companies that fought so bitterly come to such an accord." In only two or three months after the merger, KuaiDi and DiDi swiftly achieved the disposition of their combined forces, unifying the entire team so smoothly that not a single management-level employee resigned. The frantic level of work brought its rewards and by February 2015 DiDi's valuation had reached at least US$10 billion, and its customer base passed the 160 million mark. Six months after joining, Liu Qing had advanced from COO to president of the company. In the public letter announcing this promotion, Cheng Wei said, "In the six months since Liu Qing joined DiDi, she has helped the company complete a US$700 million tranche of investment, the biggest ever for a non-listed company. She has also led the private hire team, the PR team and the government relations team in a hard-fought and bloody campaign, and carved a blood-soaked path away from the battlefield."

After Liu Qing's arrival, the company began to put out feelers in the private vehicle hire sector. This new 'product' changed direction from taxi-hire software to the purchase of car-hire companies and commercial vehicle leasing, so that private vehicle owners could effectively become 'chauffeurs', thereby circumventing the regulations that applied to the traditional taxi industry. In six months, DiDi acquired 400,000 private car-hire drivers as customers. Taxi drivers were realistic and always paid their dues, but private car-hire drivers were not. The car-hire industry felt that their rights were being infringed and one after the other, local governments began to investigate and prosecute private-hire drivers. In May 2015, private-hire drivers and taxi drivers confronted each other in the street, and the Ministry of Public Security set up a special operation to investigate the increasingly serious situation with private-hire cars.

Professor Zhou Qiren of the Peking University China Centre for Economic Research commented on the phenomenon saying, "Watching DiDi is like watching Xiaogang Village back then." In 1978, 18 farmers in Xiaogang Village, Anhui took an enormous risk by putting their chops to a land contract that opened the prologue to China's reform and opening up. Thirty-seven years later, here was DiDi, this start-up mobile internet company, becoming a major impetus for China's reform to enter the deepwater zone.

Just like the "person who was unwilling to be the sacrificial victim of the revolution" who her father, Liu Chuanzhi, once talked about, Liu Qing didn't like suddenly being cast as "the revolutionary". And also like her father, she was wise enough to understand that in an environment where old and new systems intertwined, DiDi had to be innovative but could not withstand all the powerful influences out there. Her many years of experience in the investment business had taught her to bring an impartial, coolheaded and meticulous approach to bear on any problem. In her communications with the government, Liu Qing emphasised the benefits DiDi could bring them in its role as a technology company. She always told the local authorities; "As we progress DiDi's exponential growth, we are going to gather big data on lots of cities, which will mean we can work with the government to plan a whole big city's traffic system."

A Shared Dream: A One-Stop-Shop Travel Platform

Talking about private hire, Cheng Wei told the Chinese Academy for Governance, "On the day DiDi and KuaiDi merged, we discovered that the taxi-driver community had changed from being the least internet-savvy[2] group imaginable into the most internet-savvy of all, more than capable in the use of online devices. The earliest taxi-hire software solved the problem of the informatisation of the taxi industry, and the subsequent arrival of private hire and express hire had the effect of boosting its marketisation. So, what were the biggest problems of the insufficient marketisation of the taxi industry? Firstly, the prices did not reflect supply and demand; secondly, the service delivered did not determine the drivers' income. It is not the drivers' fault that the overall taxi service is inadequate. The drivers who provide a good service are not in a position to have a greater income than those who provide a poor one. Conversely, the crooked and dishonest drivers who take roundabout routes can earn much more. This discrepancy in income and incentive to dishonesty are the sign of a failing industry. Good drivers can't be rewarded, and bad drivers can't be punished, so their service just continues to deteriorate. By promoting private-hire and express-hire services, we hope we can enable good and honest drivers to earn more money."

"We haven't needed to employ lots of overseers to manage them," Cheng Wei continued. "We determine a driver's income according to the assessment of individual passengers so if you, as a driver, receive a critical assessment, just as if what you are selling on TaoBao is adversely commented on, that criticism may well adversely affect your future income and bookings. If you receive serious complaints, you can be removed from the platform. If you are commended for your service and are a really conscientious driver you will get priority for bookings. This system encourages good drivers. If there is heavy demand and not enough cars, we up the prices, which is a way of selecting the most urgent customers, whilst at the same time encouraging more drivers to start taking fares. Take where I used to live in Shangdi: a few years ago, it wasn't a particularly flourishing area, and it wasn't easy to find a taxi but slowly, after a few internet companies sprang up there, there were more people hailing cabs so gradually the number of orders in the area increased considerably. What is more, because of the relative scarcity, the fares could be increased so that, by nine or ten o'clock, when lots of people were calling cabs after work, prices were at their highest, and more and more drivers were encouraged into the area. It is a self-regulating system based on supply and demand."

The 33-year-old Cheng Wei went on to say, "If there were only professional drivers, no matter how they were regulated, you would still never be able to get a taxi at peak periods, and this was what concerned me. This went on until I happened to be visiting Professor Zhou Qiren at Peking University and asked him how we could ensure that customers could get a cab during peak periods. He said it was an archetypal question of economics known as 'tidal demand economics'. There is a similar problem with increased travel demand around the 'Golden Weeks' of Chinese New Year and the National Day holiday. Just like the tides, passenger demand comes in waves, and bottlenecks occur at peak periods. Just think about it, everyone: all those hotels that have been built in Sanya (Hainan) to accommodate visitors during the National Day and New Year holidays – if they are full during those Golden Weeks, but are largely empty during the flatter periods, that is very uneconomic because they can't just provide service for those two weeks out of every year."

"The railways are another case in point," Cheng Wei continued. "If there are enough tickets for everyone to be able to buy them easily during the New Year period, how can the railway system cope during the slack periods? They are bound to incur huge financial losses. So how can we resolve these economic problems from an economist's point of view? Professor Zhou told me that the only resolution lay in the 'sharing economy'. How does this work then in the case of hotels? If hotels are built according to the demands of the off-season, they would guarantee a 70% occupancy rate during those periods. They would put their prices up in high season, and at the same time use the large number of neighbouring family guesthouses to supplement their accommodation. These householders normally have other businesses and professions, but during the Golden Weeks, they can put any empty rooms or houses to use, and then go back to their normal work when the peak season is over. This is a way of integrating the whole of society's unused natural resources to meet the seasonal rise and fall of demand in the marketplace. This is the 'tide' that DiDi too is concerned with.

"So we can't make do with just professional taxi drivers; at peak times, passenger demand is five times that in the quieter periods. At peak times, everyone is out and about and at quiet times they are all at work or at home. If there were enough cabs at peak times so everyone can get one, then in the quiet times the professional drivers would have nothing to do, couldn't earn money and couldn't even make a bare living. So we have begun to recruit large numbers of moonlighting drivers, so that they now account for 80% of DiDi's private-hire and express-hire cars. We also have a car-sharing or car-pooling service with 7 million registered vehicles across China. If you are driving by yourself on the way to work, or if you have an empty seat or seats, we can help you find people going the same way as you to ride with you. This is just like the Sanya family guesthouses: at periods of peak demand, the natural resources of amateur hoteliers and amateur white-collar drivers can be put to use so that people can carpool and enjoy their travels smoothly. After DiDi and KuaiDi merged in 2015, we began to promote our private hire, express hire and car-sharing services. DiDi's dream is to make travelling a wonderful experience and to set up China's biggest one-stop-shop travel platform that uses the internet to bring together all modes of transport, unify scheduling and encourage sharing. We can move all the demands of travel onto the internet, move all supplies and suppliers onto the internet, and match up and schedule everything through a cloud-based big data travel engine. This will increase the efficiency of the travel marketplace and improve the overall experience for every city resident and driver. Just as with air travel today, where however many passengers want to fly, and however many planes there are on however many flight routes, everything is precisely scheduled, so overall efficiency is maximised."

On 29 January 2015, based on the outstanding innovation and transformation he had brought about, Cheng Wei was named 'Most Influential Person in the New Economy of China 2014' by *China News Weekly*. The award nomination said of Cheng Wei, "He is a subversive who, relying solely on a tiny cell phone screen, has pried apart the crusted layers of decades-old interest patterns. He is a force for good who has used a client terminal to elevate the zeal of the provider and the comfort of the consumer. He is an outstanding talent who has changed the habits of the internet user and zeroed in on the pain of the urban office worker trying to hail a taxi. He is a vivid example of how technology can change lives, informing the paths of countless entrepreneurs and innovators, and with his finger forever on the pulse of the consumer."

At a press conference on 22 May 2015, acting as DiDi's representative, Liu Qing, wearing a white gown, unveiled the next three years' 'tidal strategy': just as you can't build more hotels just for the Golden Weeks, it is not practical to put more taxis on the street just for the sake of the peak times. Therefore, DiDi hopes that the strength of professional drivers can meet 80% of the demand during off-peak hours, and when peak demand comes, we can use private hire to augment that strength to meet the temporary needs of the customers. From this foundation, DiDi will take a step closer to sorting out the tangled threads of the travel industry. We will introduce an evaluation system for the taxi industry to provide passengers with an even better service; in the field of private hire, to satisfy the rather greater and more personalised demands of the passenger, we will introduce the value-added service known as ACE (Absolute Comfort Experience).

Liu Qing announced, "Starting from 25 May 2015, KuaiDi will introduce a subsidy of Rmb1 billion to promote a weekly 'Free Taxi Ride for Everyone' campaign in 12 cities across the country, in order to meet the offensive launched by Uber. Our car-pooling service has already recruited more than 600,000 drivers, encouraging customers to share their travel. We have established a 'substitute driver' section with the aim of becoming the biggest substitute-driver service platform in China". Liu Qing went on to say that Cheng Wei had a dream for the whole DiDi group: in the course of the 'netification' of the whole transport world, which includes bringing together online public transport, taxis and all directly connected travel and transport fields, to establish the world's biggest one-stop-shop travel platform.

This indeed is Cheng Wei's dream, and Liu Qing's too. One could call these two the mobile internet industry's perfect couple, who both admire and complement one another. As someone who, from the very beginning, has held onto his shareholding in the company, Wang Gang says, "Cheng Wei and Liu Qing are both exceptionally intelligent, upright and courageous. Cheng Wei comes from humble origins and has risen step by step from the lowest level as a salesperson, and his ability to penetrate the front line at the sharpest point of the marketplace is what is missing in Liu Qing. Liu Qing was born into a famous family and her aura of power and influence, her international vision and her vast array of contacts with which to summon the wind and call down the rain are what Cheng Wei lacks. This is why their coming together brought about an immediate 'chemical reaction' and supplementary effect.

"Cheng Wei is an extraordinarily far-sighted, ambitious, courageous man who wants to invest in his dream. His feet are firmly planted on the ground but his aims are lofty, and he moved me deeply back when we met," Liu Qing told reporters straightforwardly. "Everything that has come afterwards has only served to confirm my first impression. We are the best of friends because we appreciate each other's talents. In this age of the young entrepreneur, Cheng Wei is the best of the best in terms of his character, his heart, his vision and every other aspect."

Cheng Wei had only one short sentence to say in reply to this: "She is perfection in every way."

Clearly, she no longer needed to "know how to get people going"!

War With Uber

Going back to not long after Cheng Wei's unexpected rejection of Liu Qing in June 2014, one afternoon in July, Uber's founder and CEO, Travis Kalanick, arrived on the scene. He came uninvited, demanding either DiDi accept a 40% investment or Uber would mount a large-scale China offensive. Kalanick has a buccaneering style and has been described by the American media as "an armed robber and a gangster", and particularly when he is preparing for battle, his face has the appearance of a clenched fist. Uber, which was founded in 2010, was also the very image of a new technology internet 'conquistador', and within four years had vanquished not only America but Europe as well. It had launched services in more than 340 cities in 60 countries and territories, and was not only valued at US$50 billion, but also had cash holdings of US$1 billion. The story of Uber's beginnings is like a fairy tale: one snowy windswept night, Travis Kalanick and his friend Garrett Camp were waiting for a taxi on a Paris street. Because their wait had been unsuccessful, they vowed at that time to produce some revolutionary essential software that would solve this problem. It would be very simple: you could call a cab with the press of a button. Two years later, Cheng Wei was just the same as he stood in the rain. Perhaps because of the similarity, Cheng Wei opened the door to see Kalanick off and sent him off to get on with things for himself.

Of course, Kalanick's arrival had nothing to do with Liu Qing, even though the influence of Goldman Sachs was there behind Uber. No. However annoyed Liu Qing was, initially, at being rebuffed by Cheng Wei, she was not so angry that she would call in the American; otherwise she would not have put up her own money.

It was Cheng Wei's gift that he was very perceptive.

Even so, a shiver ran through him. Although he had the 'Grand Master of Heaven' of the Chinese travel world, Ma Huateng, behind him, Kalanick had the rest of the world behind him, and that included many big-name capitalists. He, Cheng Wei, had to cling on to one thread of opportunity, one thread of possibility, and that possibility was Liu Qing and what she had said.

Uber and Kalanick were the context behind Cheng Wei and Liu Qing's week of discussions.

They were also the context behind the trip to Tibet.

It was the context of life and death and of going to the extreme. Later on, Cheng Wei couldn't help imagining what things might have been like if Liu Qing hadn't come on board. Especially because it was Liu Qing who had talked round Ma Yun, that giant helping hand, that Primeval Lord of Heaven, and when you added Ma Huateng and Liu Qing herself into the mix, there was no way Kalanick's arrival could be viewed as comparable to the arrival of the foreign powers in 1840.

It is interesting, however, that Uber not only had American capital, it also had some Chinese investment from sources that included HNA[3] Group, CITIC Securities, China Life Insurance, Vanke, Minsheng Bank and others. Meanwhile, DiDi had Apple's huge investment (at US$1 billion,

4. SHARING OR ENJOYING TOGETHER

this served not only to replenish DiDi's initial round of financing, it also carried a powerful symbolism), and Ma Huateng's capital came from something of a foreign context. Sorting through both sides' financing history, it is easy to see that there were several figures in the background common to both: for example, China Life Insurance, Tiger Global Management and Hillhouse Capital all invested in both companies simultaneously. Although Kalanick had the attitude of 1840, there was no going back to that time as the process of globalisation meant that it was no longer a case of either one thing or the other, but rather that each was now inextricably a part of the other. On the other hand, Cheng Wei's rejection of the 1840 attitude was just as much an attitude belonging to past history, and both sides' affairs were inextricably intertwined in terms of capital, ideology, personal style and many other aspects. This new age could absolutely not be controlled from one individual viewpoint; there is nothing more complex than reality, and reality's greatest enemy is simplicity.

The great war began like this: Uber brought US$2 billion of complex finance into the Chinese marketplace and DiDi prepared not just a similar riposte but an even more ample one. Cheng Wei took the opportunity at Davos to announce that DiDi had obtained US$3 billion in financing, including the US$1 billion from Apple, mainly thanks to Liu Qing's amazing efforts. Both sides had plenty of firepower and, in 2015, after Uber launched 'People's Uber' which offered subsidies to both drivers and passengers, Uber's orders increased dramatically. In the first half of 2015, they burned through US$1.5 billion in China. DiDi spent the same amount and more, and some people compared this 'cash-burning war' to a nuclear conflict.

Uber made smooth progress to begin with, and quickly established coverage in 21 cities in China. Their cut-price private-hire service 'People's Uber' became their principle strategic tool for seizing the Chinese market. The woman in charge of Uber's China campaign, Liu Zhen, told the media at the outset that Uber's carpooling product 'People's Uber+' was perfectly suited to the Chinese way of doing things and that the volume of business it was doing in five Chinese cities already surpassed its equivalent in San Francisco. Through the carpooling system, their product was demonstrating the perfect combination of economic efficiency and social benefit. They had increased the product's efficiency through a process of reduction so that from two cars being needed to fulfil two people's travel transport requirements, it had been simplified down to one car being able to take one extra passenger. This both increased efficiency and reduced costs. Starting from its foundations in taxi hire, DiDi at the same time had already developed seven product lines including taxis, private hire, express hire, free rides, substitute drivers, coaches and test drives. Altogether this constituted a multi-dimensional counterattack which covered more than 400 cities across China.

Cheng Wei not only continued to fight hand-to-hand on his home ground, sword blades clashing, he also joined up with international 'partners' to build a fortified wall encompassing the worldwide industry (how different from 1840!): he made successive investments in South East Asia's taxi hire service GrabTaxi, America's Lyft, and India's Ola – these three companies were Uber's biggest competitors in each area and he pumped US$480 million of investment into them. By forming a strategic partnership with Lyft, whenever Chinese travellers were in America, they could go directly through DiDi to access Lyft's American rental service, and American travellers in China could do the same in reverse going through Lyft to access DiDi's services.

Kalanick oversaw operations from Beijing, announcing that he was going to apply for Chinese citizenship. Cheng Wei, in turn, went to America, and installed his top executives there. He took several groups to Silicon Valley to study a string of internet companies so that as many of them as possible could get to understand their organisational set-up and composition, what their fundamental thinking was and what talents their personnel had. DiDi had rapidly changed from a guerrilla band into a regular standing army. They had plenty of firepower, more than their opponents, so they were not to be outdone by them in their marketing campaigns, and the same was beginning to be true of their capitalisation. Of course, this was not how they saw it, and Cheng Wei discovered that the enemy's greatest strength was their talent pool and their philosophy. Talent was DiDi's greatest pinch-point, as China did not have big reserves of technicians in the fields of big data and computing. Moreover, 20% of the personnel in a string of companies in Silicon Valley, like Uber and Facebook, were actually Chinese. Liu Cheng left behind his CTO and a team of company representatives to invite these Chinese engineers to meet up with them, and they ended up bringing several dozen major talents back with them.

This encircling campaign, using the company's capital in a major outflanking, pincer movement to recruit new talent, was pretty successful as it not only left Kalanick up to his ears in work in Beijing, it also induced severe misgivings about the security of his rear. When he was interviewed by *Caijing* magazine, he said openly, "DiDi's existence makes me lose two hours sleep every night as I consider how to combat them." Finding himself hard put to it to shake DiDi, Kalanick was in a gloomy mood, so much so that he changed his whole line of thought, reckoning that DiDi's scope of operations was bigger than Uber's, its order numbers were greater, and it was able to burn even more money in every comparable round of subsidies. However, he had done his sums, and if Uber devoted US$4 to subsidise its one million daily orders, it would need a total subsidy over the period of US$1.46 billion. However, DiDi's order numbers and deficit would be even greater, and this brought him some consolation.

Of course, it is not the case that in these circumstances all your backers are going to grit their teeth and let you burn up all your capital and, moreover, DiDi and Uber shared many of the same investors and it would really have been a bit strange for shared investors to wage a 'cash-burning war'. Naturally, they were not going to be willing to tolerate such a bizarre waste of money for any length of time. As Uber's field of operations grew steadily bigger, Kalanick realised that the subsidy would be very difficult to maintain and it couldn't go on indefinitely. However, even though Apple and Uber were actually partners in a different marketplace, Apple had given Cheng Wei an enormous investment of US$1 billion, putting themselves firmly in DiDi's camp which, at the very least, showed that they were not very optimistic about Uber's future in China. With DiDi's infiltration of Uber's business, it was being said that Apple's move had effectively squashed Uber's hopes of continuing the fight. If you analysed the reasons, it showed that Uber placed prime importance on linking up driver and customer, but the Chinese marketplace was not particularly mature yet, and the customers valued the subsidy much more highly than the level of service. Uber's so-called 'settled long-term tactic' could not compete with the way a direct subsidy fed the voracious maw of the market and, at the same time, DiDi instituted an even simpler and more direct method of breaking into new markets. You could say that from the time Uber entered the Chinese marketplace it was already at odds with the rules of the local market. In applying its experience of the mature worldwide market to an immature market, and expecting that market to accept 'better', more advanced, methods is an empirical mistake made by many companies that try to make the move into transnational business. In the world of the internet, the cost of this mistake can be very great indeed. In the later stages of this period, Uber went on to follow the completely opposite path, introducing even crazier subsidies than its opposition, as if it was trying to make a 'localising' adjustment while, in fact, revealing Kalanick's 'secret plan'. He wanted to put short-term pressure on DiDi to gain a bargaining chip, but he had already taken his eye off the necessary changes to the product and its associated services.

Rumours of peace talks between DiDi and Uber emerged in May 2016. On 28 July, the Chinese Ministry of Transport and seven other ministries and commissions announced the first national-level app-based taxi legislation anywhere in the world: *Interim Measures for the Administration of Online Taxi Booking*, thereby establishing the legality of app-based taxis. On 1 August news of DiDi and Uber's merger arrived as it unfurled over the course of one day with conjecture followed by denial followed by ultimate confirmation. Cheng Wei announced the news on Weibo that day (although it did not amount to an announcement of a final end to hostilities), saying that DiDi would buy out the Uber brand in China and its business, databases and all its property would be absorbed into the Chinese operation. DiDi would make an investment of US$1 billion in Uber, and Uber would take a 20% shareholding in the new company. After the merger, the valuation of the new company would be as high as US$35 billion. Consequently, the competition between Uber and DiDi would no longer be a question of the ultimate survival of one over the other, of who could destroy whom, but would be one of sharing and mutual prosperity.

Once the smoke had cleared and the scene could be surveyed properly, this innovative regularisation of the internet taxi business, the first in the world, put Chinese business management right at the international cutting edge. The internet taxi business had developed in America two years earlier than in China, and now it was being legislated continent by continent. But across Europe, with the exception of London, the vast majority of cities were prohibiting it as a highly dangerous phenomenon and, as a whole, the continent was effectively closing its borders to the advance of the internet age. Of course this was not a level playing field, nor is such a thing necessarily desirable. There needs to be an element of chance and competition as that is what finds balance in complexity.

DIARY NOTE 19: ENTREPRENEURSHIP AND INNOVATION UNSTOPPABLE

In the two months between 29 July and 8 October 2016, the fate of internet taxis enjoyed a roller-coaster ride. With the appearance of the Ministry of Transport's *Interim Measures for the Administration of Online Taxi Booking*, in terms of legalisation, the internet taxi business, until then suspended in a kind of limbo, was given a chance to draw breath.

In Beijing, Shanghai, Guangzhou, Shenzhen and other cities, their *Draft Appeal for Opinions on the Management of Internet-Based Taxi Hire* left the future of restrictions on drivers, cars and license plate registration hanging in the balance.

At the time of writing, nothing definite had yet been decided, including the fate of DiDi DaChe. But this is Zhongguancun we are talking about: Zhongguancun the pathfinder, Zhongguancun the experimenter, Zhongguancun the cutting edge. DiDi emerged from Zhongguancun, its office building is situated in the Digital Valley of Zhongguancun's Science and Technology Park and whatever its fate, the roads it has travelled are all illustrations of the spirit of Zhongguancun: entrepreneurial, innovative, indomitable, dauntless and always moving forward. This is why DiDi's story of innovation will always be of interest, no matter how it ends, and why it is a profoundly meaningful reflection of our times.

In the face of the most severe challenge, DiDi's heroism does not falter; it remains steady and rational, as if to reassure people of its future. On 21 October, at the well-established American magazine *Vanity Fair's* '2016 New Year Achievements Award Ceremony', DiDi's president, Liu Qing, Alibaba's chairman, Michael Evans, and Bloomberg News anchor, Emily Chang, held a 'conversation', and in the segment called *Shorting China*, Liu Qing responded that "from its seat in the front row, the world should properly understand the real power of China's growth".

According to a *China News Service* report, during the conversation, Liu Qing expressed the view that scientific and technological innovation had already become the engine of Chinese economic growth, and the new economy and the sharing economy provide China with an important cushion during China's transformation. She quoted some research by McKinsey which said that internet innovation was contributing between 7% and 25% to China's GDP, and this had already formed part of a systematic top-down policy. Not only are the contributions of the internet and the sharing economy growing very fast indeed, they are also beginning to transform the very core of traditional business. The ever-increasing growth of the internet industry has become the cutting edge of innovation not just in China but across the whole world. Liu Qing explained how Tencent and Alibaba had fallen over themselves in their rush to be involved in the 'internet+ government services and how DiDi also promotes the same initiative countrywide. For example, recently, at the 'China App-based Taxi Hire Sharing

Centre' in Guiyang, they have been promoting cooperative use of big data, exploring management of internet taxi apps and so on. In the course of the conversation, Liu Qing mentioned how, not long ago, she had met one of DiDi's star drivers. This man had once been a worker at China's biggest steel company, Wuhan Iron and Steel Corporation, and was now able to keep his household comfortably solvent through his new profession. Liu Qing said that she believed that this was an illustration of the real China.

She also responded to the recently published new regulations covering internet taxi hire across China. In her view, the most recent enactments by central government served to confer legitimacy on the principle of shared transport at a national level, and this was a part of an even bigger strategy to support innovation. She went on to say that although the pace of development was very rapid, transport sharing across the world was still in the germination stage. "We understand that administrators everywhere have to confront the challenges of urban management and also the challenges of adapting their responses. We are also proactive in our direct contacts with government, and we are very confident that policymakers will direct their policies in the best interests of society and the people." You can see the moderation and good faith in what Liu Qing said, and that is representative of the worth of Zhongguancun.

---

1 November 2016
Chenguang – Taiyang City

AFTERWORD

Two years have passed almost without my noticing between the time I started reading about Zhongguancun, undertook fieldwork and began writing, to my completion of this work. As I said in the preface, this was a new departure for me, a change in direction. The person I knew as myself at the outset became a stranger: the person who wove his way through the office blocks of Zhongguancun, who met all these different people, who wrote words he had never written before, seemed to be someone else. Non-fiction is a particular literary genre, and in contrast with all the forms I was already familiar with, every instant of every day I knew exactly what I should be doing. It was more like a form of manual labour: very seldom was there anything I didn't already know, anywhere I had to let my imagination run free, anything showy and superficial, or any scope for free-wheeling. I found this very tiring. But this fatigue was worthwhile, not to say necessary, because the rewards have been so great: not only have I changed completely and emerged with a new type of literature, it is also as though my future 'fiction bag' is stuffed with new material.

It goes without saying that I could not have completed the fieldwork and writing involved without all manner of help. My profound thanks are due to the Chinese Academy of Sciences, the Beijing Municipal Party Committee Publicity Department, the Zhongguancun Management Committee and the Beijing Publishing Group's Beijing October Literature and Art Publishing House; and also to Wu Jian, Hu Xiaodong, Hou Jianmei, Zheng Junbin, Liu Hang, Dong Changqing, Song Yingying, Cong Zhongxiao, Han Jingqun and Han Xiaozheng. I would also like to thank the authors of all the related books I read, all the people I interviewed, and everyone else who generously gave me their time.

APPENDIX

CHRONOLOGY OF MAJOR EVENTS IN ZHONGGUANCUN

1980

On 23 October, Chen Chunxian, researcher at the Physics Institute of the Chinese Academy of Sciences and other scientific and technical staff founded the first privately-owned advanced technology service department in the science and technology establishment named after the Beijing Plasma Institute. In his three last trips to America between 1978 and 1980, Mr Chen Chunxian visited Silicon Valley and Highway 128 where the light dawned on him, and his subsequent establishment of the above-mentioned service department makes him deserving of the title 'The First Man of Zhongguancun'.

1981

On 16 April, the Central Committee of the Communist Party of China and the State Council promulgates the party leadership of the State Committee for Science and Technology's *Synopsis of the Report on National Policy on Scientific and Technological Development (Publication of the State Council of the Central Committee of the Communist Party of China [1981] document No. 14)*, raising for the first time the subject of the paid transfer of ownership of the results of scientific and technological achievement, also the need for the formulation of preferential taxation policy and pricing reform measures to encourage the transfer of such results.

On 8 July the first prototype laser photo-typesetting system (Huaguang Model 1), achieved through research presided over by Peking University's Wang Xuan, undergoes appraisal by a combined committee of the Central Office of the State Computer Industry Administration and the Ministry of Education.

1982

On 22 December, Wang Hongde resigns from his government post at the Chinese Academy of Sciences Computer Institute and sets up on his own in Zhongguancun, along with seven technical staff, founding the Beijing Shanghai Computer Machine Room Technology Development Company (known for short as the JingHai Company). The JingHai Company undertakes research, engineering projects, skills marketing and product manufacturing combined with mechanisms for 'self-funding, voluntary cooperation, independent operation and financial autonomy'.

In the same month, the Xinhua News Agency's Beijing branch details a reporter to write an article entitled *Researcher Chen Chunxian Sees the Initial Results of his Experiment in the Promulgation of Technology*, which is subsequently included in the *Xinhua Agency Confidential Internal Report*, making clear to the leadership of the Central Committee "the circumstances surrounding the activities, achievements and even the social upheaval caused by the Beijing Plasma Institute's Service Department's Advanced Technology Service Department."

1983

On 7 January, Fang Yi, vice-premier of the State Council, comments on the report about Chen Chunxian in the *Xinhua News Agency Confidential Internal Report*: "Comrade Chen Chunxian's work methods are entirely correct and deserve to be encouraged."

On 8 January, Hu Qili, committee member of the Politburo of the Central Committee comments, "Comrade Chen Chunxian is taking the lead in opening up an innovative situation and may well be travelling a completely new path. On the one hand he is swiftly turning scientific research into worthwhile productivity and on the other hand he is adding a new channel for scientists and technicians to make a contribution to the Four Modernisations. It is certainly true that some of these people will become rich in breaking the iron rice bowl and the communal rice pot. Of course, we must also study essential management techniques and regulatory policies, and these matters can be entrusted to the enthusiastic support of the scientific community. Yaobang is requested to make the decision on how these matters are handled."

On the same day, Hu Yaobang , the general secretary of the Central Committee comments, "We may request the Science and Technology Leading Small Group (LSG) to work out policy guidelines on this matter."

On January 13, Zhao Dongwan, the director of the office of the Science and Technology LSG of the State Council comments, "When we are formulating systems and policies, we may follow Comrade Hu Yaobang's comments in conscientiously considering Comrade Chen Chunxian's ideas." On 25 January, China National Radio reports the gist of the Central Committee leadership's comments on Chen Chunxian, clearly indicating that Chen Chunxian's lead in the promulgation of technology and the overall direction of his service department are entirely correct and should be supported.

On 4 May, the Chinese Academy of Sciences' New Technology Joint Development Centre (known as the Kehai Company, or Scientific Haidian Company, for short) is established in the Sijiqing Commune in the Haidian District of Bejing, with Chen Qingzhen in charge of its development. The Kehai Company is run on the principles of "the public institution, business management, independent accounting and financial autonomy". The deputy director of the Chinese Academy of Sciences, Ye Duzheng, secretary of the Haidian District Committee, Jia Chunwang and other dignitaries attend its foundation celebration.

In May, Wang Yongmin's 'five-stroke' Chinese character input encoding system passes evaluation. This system later becomes the one most used by specialist programmers.

1984

On 4 January, the Zhongguancun Planning Development Office publishes its draft *Zhongguancun Science and Technology Education and Emerging Technology Development Zone Outline Plan*. This 'outline plan' proposes to make Zhongguancun the centre of Haidian District, allocating an area of 80 sq km and establishing the Zhongguancun Science and Technology Education and Emerging Technology Development Zone.

In October, the Chinese Academy of Sciences Computer Technology Research Institute invests Rmb200,000 in the launch of Liu Chuanzhi's and 11 other scientific and technical personnel's Chinese Academy of Sciences Computer Technology Research Institute's New Technology Development Company (the forerunner of Lenovo).

1985

On 13 March, the Central Committee publishes its *Decision on the Reform of Science and Technology Organisation*. The decision states, "It is required to select a number of areas with concentrated high intelligence resources across the whole country." "Currently, the most important components of the reform of science and technology organisation are operational mechanisms, organisational structures and human resource systems." "The essential aims of the reform of science and technology organisation are to speedily put the results of scientific and technical research into practical widespread production, to maximise the development of the work of scientific and technical personnel, to widely liberate scientific and technological production capability and to promote economic and social development."

In December, the finished computerised laser Chinese character phototypesetting system of Wang Xuan and others from Peking University is chosen as one of the top 10 scientific and technological achievements of the year on the inaugural occasion of the awards in 1985.

1986

On 10 May, the Haidian District Government decides to establish the Beijing Stone Group Company as a district-department-level enterprise under the direct leadership of the district government, supervised by the relevant local economic planning committee and positioned economically as a large city-level collective enterprise.

In November, with the approval of the Haidian Technology Committee, the Beijing Haidian Electricity Generation Technology Research Institute is established as the first independent technology company on Electronics Avenue.

1987

On 24 March, Stone Group and the Japanese Mitsui & Co's joint venture, Beijing Stone Office Automation Equipment Co Ltd, is given permission to establish itself as the first Sino-foreign joint venture technology company on Electronics Avenue.

In October, Taiji Computer Company's NCI-2780 and the Taiji 2200 microcomputer and hyper-small computer go into mass production. These machines, which are technologically advanced and characterised by their wide range of applications, enjoy a very high profile on Electronics Avenue.

1988

On 1 July, the Tsinghua University Technology Development Parent Company is officially established with the deputy vice chancellor of the university, Xiao Wen, presiding over the parent company's first directors' board meeting.

On 6 December, Wang Wenjing's YonYou financial software services agency is established. It is an independent computer software development company (later it becomes the privately-owned science and technology company, YonYou Financial Technology Co Ltd)

1989

From 2 to 6 February, the Beijing City Experimental Industrial Development Zone participates in the Beijing City New Technology and New Product Symposium in Hong Kong. Twenty-one companies with a total of 23 exhibition stands participate in the symposium and US$3 million-worth of contracts are signed. This symposium is a first step for the experimental zone into the field of export-oriented business development.

On 16 July, the Beijing Haidian District Committee of the Communist Party of China's Beijing City Experimental Industrial Development Zone's Enterprise Working Committee is established.

1990

On 4 May, in Haidian District's Yongfeng Township, Deputy Mayor of Beijing Lu Yucheng convenes the Beijing City Industrial Development Zone Yongfeng Township Base of Operations Construction Planning Meeting. The meeting is overseen by the Office of Capital Planning and Construction Committee and attended by the director of the Municipal Science and Technology Commission and others. The meeting considers that high-tech industry is vital to Beijing's economic development and establishes a base for new high-tech development to act as the country's biggest knowledge zone – the Zhongguancun district's extension and radiation is essential, and the meeting agrees to plan and construct the headquarters for the experimental zone in Yongfeng Township.

On 29 December, the Beijing City Experimental Industrial Development Zone's Foreign Business Investment Enterprise Association is established.

1991

On 17 January, Beijing City's acting deputy mayor, Zhang Baifa and deputy mayor, Lu Yucheng, call an on-the-spot management meeting of the 26 relevant work units at Shangdi in Haidian District's Dongbeiwangxiang, where they decide to establish the Shangdi Information Industry Headquarters of the Beijing City Experimental Industrial Development Zone.

On 21 October, the First National Information Industry Headquarters Experimental Zone, which followed the ground-breaking Shangdi Information Industry Headquarters, is situated in Shangdi in Dongbeiwangxiang, comprising an area of 1.8 sq km.

1992

On 28 May, the experimental zone holds a working meeting on a pilot scheme for reform of the company shares regulatory system as a curtain-raiser to highlight the experimental zone's shares regulation.

From 4 to 6 November, Lenovo's first Chinese microcomputer, the 586, is officially launched at the 16th technology conference.

On 11 December, the first restructuring of the joint-venture company share system is completed and the establishment of the Beijing Longyuan

Joint-Stock Limited Company is announced. In the course of this year, the income from skills-based companies in the experimental zone breaks through the Rmb10 billion barrier, reaching its target a year ahead of schedule.

1993

On 18 February, the 'Founding General Meeting of the Beijing Founder Group as the Peking University Founder Group Company' is held at the Shangri-La Hotel in Beijing. Vice-premier of the State Council Zhu Rongji, Central Politburo committee member Li Tieying and others send congratulatory letters and telegrams.

On 13 July, the founding general meeting of the Tsinghua Ziguang Group is held. This company is formed from the restructuring of the Tsinghua University Science and Technology Development Company head office, and integrates technology, industry and trade under one roof, using science and technology development as its base. It takes the information, environmental protection and pharmaceutical industries as the mainstays of its diversification in developing into a new high-tech business conglomerate. Zhang Benzheng takes up the post of president of the company.

On 18 October, the Beijing Huaqi Information Digital Technology Co Ltd is established. This is a high-tech company that combines many different areas including computer peripherals, portable computer memory storage, digital entertainment, data security, electronic education and other emerging fields. Its director is Feng Jun.

On 31 December, a Lenovo board meeting decides to award bonuses to be enacted in 1995 according to the shareholding split of 20% to the Chinese Academy of Sciences, 45% to the Computer Institute and 35% to Lenovo staff. According to this, Lenovo staff have a 35% dividend right and a corresponding shareholding.

1994

On 4 January, Beijing Founder holds a press conference to announce the new success of the Founder Electronic Colour Publishing System and to mark the practical application of this new high-quality product.

On 17 January, the Beijing Experimental Zone and the American law firm Hayes Kelly jointly hold the 'International China Science and Technology Enterprise Overseas Financing Work Conference' to raise the curtain on the experimental zone's overseas financing.

On 24 February, Lenovo Group's Lenovo (Hong Kong) Company is successfully floated in Hong Kong.

1995

On 4 January, the Beijing Peking University Qingniao Communications Technology Llc is successfully registered with a capitalisation of Rmb10 million. Wang Yangyuan is chairman of the board.

On 22 December, Zhongguancun Customs officially opens for operation on Zhongguancun's Zhichun Road. This is the first National Customs point to open in a high-tech development zone and is ratified by both the National Science and Technology Commission and the General Customs Administration.

1996

On 9 January, Vice-premier of the State Council, Li Lanqing, accompanied by the director of the Chinese Academy of Science, Zhou Guangzhao, inspect the Lenovo Group. Wu Yi, head of the Ministry of Foreign Trade and Economic Cooperation, Liu Jianfeng, acting deputy head of the Ministry of Electronics Industry, Hu Qiheng, deputy director of the Chinese Academy of Sciences, Hu Zhaoguang, deputy mayor of Beijing and others also join the inspection.

In August, returned overseas student Zhang Chaoyang founds ITC (Internet Technologies China) which later becomes Sohu. The company is founded with venture capital from MIT Media Lab director Nicholas Negroponte and venture capital specialist Edward B Roberts, and is the first Chinese internet company founded with venture capital funding.

1997

From 2 to 4 March, the State Council Intellectual Property Rights Bureau holds a working conference to plan a pilot scheme for the protection of work units' intellectual property rights at which Peking University, Tsinghua University, YonYou Financial Software Company, Beijing

Founder and Lenovo are identified as the five companies to form the first batch of work units to trial the intellectual property rights protection pilot.

On 25 June, Tsinghua Tong Fang Co Ltd is officially established with a capitalisation of Rmb575 million with the Tsinghua University Business Group representing the state as majority shareholder. It is focused on the electronic information, energy and environmental industries.

1998

On 29 March, Zhongguancun's first construction project, the Hailong Building, holds its groundbreaking ceremony.

From 8 to 12 May, the first Zhongguancun Computer Festival is held in Zhongguancun in Haidian District. It is held under the auspices of the Beijing Experimental New Technology Industries Development Zone's management committee, the Haidian District People's Government and the Haidian Experimental Zone's management committee. The festival's theme is: 'Zhongguancun: advancing China's informationisation'. Activities at the festival include: the opening ceremony, a public lecture on the festival theme, a software products exhibition, pop science and law consultation services.

1999

On 1 May, the second Zhongguancun Computer Festival's large-scale exhibition holds its grand opening at Beijing Silicon Valley Computer City's 'Computers and Health Hall'. At the same time, this marks the first official use of Zhongguancun's western district's first major building 'Beijing Silicon Valley Computer City'.

On 2 July, the Zhongguancun Science Park, Haidian Park and Tsinghua University sign a collaboration protocol agreeing to cooperate on the construction of a workstation in Haidian to support engineering Masters students and postgraduates, and on the construction of the Tsinghua Entrepreneurship Park.

On 16 October, Peking University holds the groundbreaking ceremony for the Peking University Biology City.

On 26 October, the Beijing City Education Committee ratifies the establishment of the Zhongguancun Innovation Research Institute in Haidian Park.

2000

On 3 January, the Zhongguancun Innovation Building unveils its nameplate. This is the first large-scale high-tech innovation 'incubator' construction project in the Haidian Innovation Base Construction Programme.

On 20 June, construction starts on the Shangdi Information Industries Base Northern Zone.

On 28 July, the Haidian Park 'Digital Park Zone' electronic government affairs system is put into operation.

On 28 December, the formal groundbreaking is held for the key engineering project of the Zhongguancun Software Park.

2001

On 22 February, a key component of 'Digital Beijing' in the 'Haidian Park Digital Park Zone Construction and Government Management Mode Transformation' project undergoes specialist evaluation. This is China's first international-standard, internet-based electronic government system.

On 10 July, China's first practical 32-bit CPU microchip with independent intellectual property rights, the ARK-1, is unveiled in Zhongguancun. It ends the period of the Chinese IT industry's reliance on assembling and installing microchips imported from abroad.

2002

On 27 July, the country's first returned overseas students' labour association is established as the Beijing City Returned Overseas Student Personnel and Haidian Innovation Park Amalgamated Labour Association.

On 13 August, the American company Honeywell invests in the establishment in Haidian Park of the Honeywell (Beijing) Experimental Research Co Ltd, to undertake research, development and production of computer software.

2003

On 10 January, the Zhongguancun Aviation Science and Technology Park opens.

On 28 February, Beijing's first property rights economics company is established in the form of the Zhonghaiyuan Property Rights Transaction Management Co Ltd.

On 23 June, the Zhongguancun Financial Centre officially starts operating.

On 9 December, the Ministry of Science and Technology officially announces the successful manufacture of the Lenovo Group's Shenteng 6800 super-computer which symbolises China's arrival at a new level of research into high-level computer systems. This represents another great success for National Project 863.

2004

On 24 February, the National Technology Department's Torch Centre selects Haidian Park as the pilot work unit for the provision of a one-stop-shop style of science and technology service.

On 30 October, the TD-CMA industry alliance is established, led by Datang Telecom Technology.

On 8 December, Lenovo Group announces its purchase of IBM's worldwide PC and notebook computer business, and forms a strategic alliance with IBM.

2005

On 2 March, the AVS101 high-definition decoder microchip is successfully developed, marking a hugely successful phase in the industrialisation of Haidian Park's AVS (Audio Video Coding Standard China Working Group).

On 6 June, 10 of Haidian's 'incubators' initiate the establishment of the 'Haidian Entrepreneurship Incubation Community' in Zhongguancun's Entrepreneurship Building. This is an entrepreneurship platform formed by the Tsinghua Incubator, the Peking University Incubator, the Beihang Entrepreneurship Park, the Haidian Entrepreneurship Centre and more than 10 other organisations.

On 3 September, the Zhongguancun 'V815' National Brand Promotion Activity is held in Hailong Electronics City. The most important of the 'V815' products promoted there are digital cameras, notebooks, scanners and software, all of which have national brands protected by independent intellectual property rights. More than 10 national brands, including Lenovo, Tsinghua Unigroup, Huaqi Information, Kaicheng HD, Zhongguancun Science and Technology Software and Yadu Science and Technology all exhibit their products there.

2006

From 2 to 3 March, at Beijing Empark Grand Hotel, the '11th Zhongguancun Project Promotion and Investment Conference' is held under the auspices of the Zhongguancun Management Committee, the Beijing branch of the Chinese Academy of Sciences and the City Science and Technology Committee.

On 7 September, the New Oriental Education & Technology Group enters the market on the New York Stock Exchange, becoming China's first vocational training company to list on a foreign market.

2007

On 23 April, Bill Gates, chairman of the board of Microsoft, announces that the general headquarters of Microsoft Asia is coming to Zhongguancun's western district with the construction of the Microsoft Building.

On 16 August, Beijing Bank and the Zhongguancun Western District Management Committee sign a 'strategic cooperation framework agreement' with the goal of 'policy guidance, financial support, exceptional service and ambition for excellence'. It aims to advance the depth of strategic cooperative financial relationships and optimise the park district's investment systems.

On 5 November, China's biggest search engine company, Baidu, based on a share price in excess of US$400, becomes the first Chinese internet company with a valuation in excess of Rmb10 billion on the NASDAQ stock exchange in the US.

2008

On 6 May, Microsoft China Research and Development Group holds the groundbreaking ceremony for the Microsoft China Research and Development Group Building in Zhongguancun Square.

On 13 May, 50 famous entrepreneurs from the Zhongguancun Science and Technology Park District, including Liu Chuanzhi, Duan Yongji, Wang Wenjing, Wang Xiaolan, Feng Jun and Yan Wangjia, launch China's first entrepreneur angel investor alliance, the Zhongguancun Entrepreneur Angel Investment Alliance.

On 3 September, Hanwang Technology launches the first model of its 'electronic book' which combines an electronic book reader, handwriting recognition and computer graphics in one device.

2009

On 13 March, the State Council published its *Official Response in Approval of the Construction of an Independent National Model Innovation Zone in the Zhongguancun Science and Technology Park District (Letter of State [2009] No. 28)*. This explicitly acknowledged Zhongguancun Science and Technology Park District's new status as an independent national model innovation zone with the aim of becoming a science and technology innovation centre with worldwide influence.

From 4 to 6 December, 'Innovation Zhongguancun 2009' themed activity is held at the Haidian Exhibition Hall. The themed activity had the two threads of 'creativity' and 'innovation', and it included the five main elements of the launch ceremony for 'Zhongguancun Innovation 2009', a Zhongguancun innovation exhibition, the launch of innovative products and technologies, the China Innovation Competition and the 12th Zhongguancun Computer Festival.

2010

On 5 January, the world-famous business periodical *Forbes Magazine Chinese Edition* announces the '2010 List of Promising Chinese Companies'. Zhongguancun has 33 entries, of which 14 are chosen for at least the second time, and Beijing Strong Biotechnologies Inc for the fifth time.

On 2 December, three intellectual property rights innovation alliances, the Cloud Computing Innovation Alliance, the Diagnostic Reagent Innovation Alliance and the High-Tech Service Industry (Steel Industry) Innovation Alliance are established in Yizhuang Park, Zhongguancun.

2011

On 22 February, *The Notification of the Essential Points of the Development Plan for the Zhongguancun Independent National Model Innovation Zone (2011-2020) (General Office of the National Development and Reform Commission [2011] No. 367)* is issued, stating that "Up to 2020, the model zone's innovation environment will be further developed, innovation activities will be significantly augmented, innovation efficiency and effectiveness will be improved, and gross income will increase to Rmb10 trillion". Also that "10 years of intensive work will create a centre with worldwide influence for scientific and technological innovation and a base for high-tech manufacturing."

On 6 May, the official establishment meeting for the Zhongguancun Service Platform is held at the Zhongguancun Software Park. At the meeting, Baidu Online Network Technology Co Ltd's 'Cloud Computing Centre' and eight other model cloud computing platforms are launched, as are Beijing Teamsun Technology Co Ltd's 'Cloud Computing Data Centre Service Platform' and 20 other of Zhongguancun's major technologically innovative products and services. The celebration is attended by the chairman of the Zhongguancun Management Committee, Guo Hong and others.

2012

On 12 April, the Industrial and Commercial Bank of China's (ICBC) Beijing office and the Zhongguancun Management Committee hold the 'Ceremony celebrating the "Credit Innovation Zhongguancun" activity in honour of the arrival in Zhongguancun of ICBC's specialised small and medium science and technology enterprise financial services'. At the ceremony, the Commercial Bank of China's Beijing office and the Zhongguancun Management Committee sign a 'strategic alliance framework agreement'.

On 7 July, Microsoft's Beijing Microsoft Asia-Pacific R&D Group announces the formal launch of China's first seed-accelerator, the 'Cloud

Accelerator'. This will offer free office space for selected projects, the Windows Azure cloud computing platform, Office software and entrepreneurial guidance, and so on.

On 15 August, the Brand Name China Industrial Alliance's '2012 Zhongguancun News Conference on the Launch of the Top 10 Series Selection Activity' is held. These include the 2012 Zhongguancun Top 10 People of the Year, the Top 10 Rising Star Overseas Returnees, the Top 10 Outstanding Brands, the Top 10 Innovation Successes, the Top 10 Innovation Standards, the Top 10 Venture Capital Activities, the Top 10 Mergers and Acquisitions, the 10 Strongest Innovative Companies, and the Top 10 News Stories of the Year.

2013

On 7 May, the Leshi Internet Information & Technology Corporation (Beijing) launches the Leshi TV X60 super-television, which is the world's first internet company's own-brand television.

On 5 September, the 'Xiaomi 2013 News Conference' is held. It is attended by more than a thousand guests and other representatives. Xiaomi Science and Technology Llc launches its third-generation cell phone and the Xiaomi television.

On 6 November, the major national research equipment project run by the Chinese Academy of Sciences known as the 'Deep-Ultraviolet Diode-Pumped Solid-State Laser (DUV-DLP) cutting edge equipment development' undergoes and passes inspection. This makes China the only country in the world with the manufacturing capability for this device.

2014

On 20 October, under the organisation of the Zhongguancun Private Ownership Entrepreneurs Association, the 'High-end Seminar On Using Collaborative Innovation To Lead Cooperative Development in Beijing, Tianjin and Hebei' is held at the Zhongguancun Model Zone Exhibition Centre. At the seminar, the chairman of the Zhongguancun Management Committee, Guo Hong, delivers the lead lecture on the topic.

On 22 October, the Zhongguancun Management Committee and the Haidian District Government jointly hold the 'General Meeting To Establish the Hardware Industry Alliance'. The alliance comprises 21 companies including the Beijing Jingdong Century Trade Co Ltd, Baidu Online Network Technology (Beijing) Co Ltd and Beijing Xiaomi Science and Technology Llc. Chairman of the Zhongguancun Management Committee, Guo Hong, and other dignitaries attend.

2015

On 7 May, President of the State Council Li Keqiang conducts an inspection visit to Zhongguancun Avenue and holds informal discussions with local entrepreneurs. He is accompanied by Vice-President of the State Council, Liu Yandong, Beijing City Committee Secretary, Guo Jinlong, Minister of Science and Technology, Wan Gang and other leadership figures. Chairman of the Zhongguancun Management Committee, Guo, attends. On the same day, the Beijing Makerspace Alliance is established.

On 5 August, the Zhongguancun Independent National Model Innovation Zone Business Finance Service Working Committee is established.

On 8 September, the Baidu Worldwide General Meeting is held in Beijing.

In November, the Zhongguancun International Makerspace Launch and Contract Signing Ceremony is held in Haidian Park.

APPENDIX
INDEX OF PEOPLE

FENG KANG (1920-1993), mathematician, was a fellow of the Chinese Academy of Sciences, founder of modern Chinese computational mathematics research, sole creator of the finite element method, the natural return method and the natural boundary integral method. He also established research into the new fields of symplectic geometry and symplectic format and made a major contribution to the development of the establishment and leadership of our China's computational mathematics strength and is a scientist who holds an important place in the history of world mathematics. Recipient of the Fields Medal and overseas fellow of the Chinese Academy of Sciences, Professor Shing-Tung Yau says in his report, *My View of The Development of Chinese Mathematics* written for Tsinghua University, "There are three main reasons that modern Chinese mathematics is able to overtake the West, or at least keep pace with it. The most important of these is because of three famous factors in the history of mathematics: one is Professor Shiing-Shen Chern's work on characteristic class; one is Hua Luogeng's work on multiple complex functions; and one is Feng Kang's work on the finite element method."

Feng Kang's ancestral home was Shaoxing in Zhejiang Province and he was born in Wuxi in 1920. He grew up in Suzhou, Jiangsu Province, and in 1939 he passed the exams to enter the department of electrical engineering at Zhongyang University where he studied physics and mathematics as joint majors. In 1945, he took up a post as a teaching assistant in Shanghai's Fudan University's mathematics and physics department. In 1946 he went to Tsinghua University as a teacher and from 1951 to 1953 he undertook advanced studies at the Steklov Mathematics Institute in the Soviet Union under the famous Soviet mathematician Lev Pontryagin. In 1954, he published his dissertation entitled *Distributions Theory* and following Professor Hua Luogeng's suggestion, he established the Mellin transform in distributions theory. In the 1950s, the Chinese Mathematics Institute was in its early stages and Feng Kang led a small team of scientists and technicians in developing Chinese mathematics' successful route from the practical to the theoretical and from the theoretical back to the practical. In 1965, the essay *Difference Scheme Based on Variational Principle* he published in *Applied Mathematics and Computational Mathematics* was an indication of China's establishment of the finite element method independently from Western systems. From 1978 to 1987 he was director of the Chinese Academy of Sciences Computer Centre, also undertaking research there, and from 1980 to 1993 he was a fellow of the Chinese Academy of Sciences. From 1985 to 1990, he was the chairman of the Chinese Computational Mathematics Society. He died in Beijing in 1993.

Chen Chunxian (1934-2004) was from Chengdu in Sichuan Province and is a famous Chinese nuclear physicist. From 1952 to 1958 he studied abroad in the Soviet Union, and from 1959 to 1966 he concentrated on theoretical physics at the Chinese Academy of Sciences Physics Institute, breaking new ground in research into the new fields of lasers, new types of semiconductor and other things. From 1970 to 1986 he undertook national research into nuclear fusion and, at the Chinese Academy of Sciences Physics Institute, he built the nation's first Tokamak Device (Number 6). Later, he established the academy's successful base of operations for nuclear fusion at Hefei which remains, right up to the present day, a jewel in the nation's crown both for its scale and its standards. In 1978 after the Cultural Revolution, he was in the first tier of exceptional promotions to lead researcher (with professorial rank) along with other people such as Chen Jingrun. He participated in the First National Science and Technology Convention. He was approved by the academic degree committee as an academic adviser to Ph.D students. Between 1978 and 1981 he visited America three times, proposed the building of a Chinese Silicon Valley at Zhongguancun and, following his own advice, he established the 'Advanced Technology Service Department', promoted the development of Zhongguancun's high-tech industry, earning the title of "Number One in Zhongguancun's privately-owned science and technology industry". In 1986 he resigned from the Chinese Academy of Sciences devoting all his efforts to the development of new high-tech production. In October 1997, he was engaged by Beijing City's Science and Technology Committee as a high-level consultant to their High-Tech Entrepreneurship Centre. In 1988, along with entrepreneurs and scientists from America's Silicon Valley, he initiated the establishment of the Jinmen Bridge Science and Technology Development Centre, and devoted all his energy in the group to promoting the development of important high-tech manufacturing projects. In 2002, he initiated the establishment of an entrepreneur advice agency, the Chen Chunxian Studio. He died early in the morning on 9 August 2004.

Wang Hongde was born in 1936. He graduated from the Harbin Electronics Institute in 1956 and entered the Chinese Academy of Sciences Computer Institute. In 1957 he was classified as a 'rightist'. In 1979 he was made team leader of the Computer Institute's No. 4 research unit's electric air-conditioning team. On 22 December 1982, the 46-year-old Wang Hongde took eight engineers with him to found the Beijing City Beijing and Shanghai Computer Development Company. One year after its founding, the JingHai Company achieved an output value of Rmb8 million. In 1986, the JingHai Company established a commercial head office, and that year had sales of more than Rmb50 million. In 1987, the JingHai Group was set up and in 1999 its annual output value reached Rmb920 million. In 2001, JingHai established Beijing's first privately owned science and technology industry incubator limited company. After three months, the incubator had produced 49 companies and the Guangyuan Building was formally named by the Beijing Municipal Government as the city's high-tech industry incubator base.

In 2003, Wang Hongde announced that he was withdrawing from the front line, choosing instead to build a small-scale commodity wholesale shopping centre in Huizhou in Guangdong Province. Within three years of its opening, the Huizhou Yiwu Small Commodities Mall occupied a site of 120,000 sqm, with 6,000 businesses selling more than 600,000 different types of commodity. Its cumulative total of foreign and domestic customers was in excess of 6 million, and it had done Rmb3 billion worth of business. In February 2009, the Ministry of Science and Technology's China Privately-Owned Science and Technology Promotion Association and the office of *Science and Technology Daily* held a big awards ceremony celebrating 30 years since the 'Opening Up and Liberation' and of Chinese privately-owned science and technology innovation development. Acting as representatives of their generation were Liu Chuanzhi, Yin Mingshan, Guo Guangchang, Ren Zhengfei, Zhang Ruimin, Duan Yongji, Wang Hongde, Shi Yuzhu, Li Denghai and Liu Yonghao who were named as "celebrated entrepreneurs in the development of the privately-owned science and technology industry".

Liu Chuanzhi was born in 1944 in Zhenjiang City, Jiangsu Province. He was chairman of the board of Legend Holdings Corporation and founder of the Lenovo Group. In 1967, he graduated from the Chinese People's Liberation Army Military Telecommunications Engineering College and founded Lenovo in 1984. In doing so he broke through the traditional thinking that kept the minds of scientific researchers in shackles and entered onto a uniquely Chinese path for high-tech manufacturing industry. He pushed through Lenovo's purchase of IBM's worldwide PC business, lifting the Lenovo Group onto the world stage and gathering precious experience for China on what it is like to make such a move. He was successively president of the Lenovo Group, chairman of the board and honorary chairman. In February 2009, he resumed the position of chairman of the board, helping the company to navigate through a very difficult period, turning the situation round completely. Under his leadership, the Lenovo Group achieved complete success against its foreign competitors and became the world's leading PC business. In November 2011, Liu Chuanzhi left the post of chairman of the board of the Lenovo Group to concentrate his energies on the brand-new parent company, Legend Holdings.

Under Liu Chuanzhi's leadership, Legend Holdings has become a large-scale integrated business, spanning commercial enterprise and investment, which has created numerous outstanding companies. In the meantime, the Lenovo Group has become the world's biggest PC company, the world's second biggest PC and tablet company and, by the fourth quarter of 2014, the world's third biggest smart phone manufacturing company. It is ranked in the world's top 500 companies. Legend Capital, Hony Capital and Lenovo have become the leading names in the Chinese investment industry.

Simultaneously, Legend Holdings' 'strategic investment + financial investment' innovative dual-engine business model has created an investment organisation that constantly grows in value. The strategic investment business is divided between the five main areas of IT, financial services, innovative consumption and services, modern agricultural industry and foodstuffs, and the chemical and energy industries. The most important financial investment services include angel investment, venture capital investment and private equity investment, covering all the stages of business growth and all devoting their energies towards creating a new tranche of successful companies in even more fields, all contributing to the Chinese economy. Liu Chuanzhi has been deputy chairman at the eighth and ninth meetings of the All-China Federation of Industry and Commerce, a member of the Advisory Board of Tsinghua University School of Economics and Management, an honorary tutor for the Executive MBA programme at the Beijing University Guanghua School of Management and was the first person on the Chinese side to be appointed as a guest tutor in the China-Europe International College of Industry and Commerce.

Wang Xuan (1937-2006) was born in Shanghai, was an expert in computerised word processing and the inventor of computerised Chinese-character laser phototypesetting. He is known as the modern-day Bi Sheng. In 1958, he graduated from Peking University's Department of Mathematics and Mechanics. In 1965, along with Chen Kunqiu and Xu Zhuoqun, he worked on the planning of the DJS21's ALGOL 60 compiling system. In 1967, the manufacturing process was completed and the system was rolled out to several dozen clients. The ALGOL 60 compiler system became one of the earliest high-level language compiler systems to receive formal promotion on the internal market. From 1969 onwards, because his health was not good, he nursed his illness at home for an extended period surviving only on his labour insurance allowance. In 1975, Wang Xuan joined 'Project 748', working on the Chinese-character word processing system project. As the person with overall responsibility for the technology, he led the projects on the Chinese-character laser phototypesetting system and later on the electronic publishing system. This system was a market leader both at home and abroad, bringing about a fundamental change to several centuries of Chinese lead-font printing. Starting in 1981, Wang Xuan concentrated his energies on the commercialisation of the results of his research, resulting in the Chinese-language laser phototypesetting system going into commercial production from 1985, receiving heavy promotion on the market.

After 1988, Wang Xuan was an important decision-maker and technical planner for the Peking University Founder Group, bringing an 'indomitable' method to high-tech industrial production, vigorously advocating the marriage of technology and commercialism, and thrusting forward along a successful path that was an amalgamation of commercialisation with academic research. In 1994, he was made a fellow of the Chinese Academy of Engineering; in 1995, he joined the Jiu San Society; in July 1995, the Peking University Computer Institute and the Peking University Founder Group jointly established the Founder Technology Institute, with Wang Xuan as its director. In the same year he became chairman of the board of Founder (Hong Kong) Co Ltd and set up an integrated system comprising middle-to-long-term research, development, production, system testing, marketing, training and after-sales service. Wang Xuan died in 2006.

Wang Yongmin was born in December 1943 into a poor farming family in the Yahe District of Nanyang City, Henan Province. After five years of research between 1978 and 1983, he invented the 'five-stroke Chinese character input system' (Wangma) described by experts at home and abroad as "no less significant than the invention of moveable type". By synthesising and building on the newest results of inter-disciplinary research, he proposed "the three principles of form, sound and meaning", created "the periodic table of Chinese character radicals" and invented the highly efficient 25-key four-code Chinese character input system, and compatible words and phrases technology. For the first time anywhere, this broke through the 100-character per minute Chinese character computer input barrier and was patented in China, America and the UK. In 1983, after 15 years of energetic promotion and popularisation, he achieved coverage of over 90% of users at home and abroad. In 1984, he was honoured with, amongst other things, the 'May 1 Labour Medal', the title of 'Supreme National Expert' and 'National Outstanding Worker in Science and Technology'. In April 1988, he became one of the 10 'National Model Workers' specially named by the State Council. After 1994 he successively invented '98 Wangma', the 'Reader and Voice Translator', the 'Business Card Organiser' and five other innovative patented technologies.

In February 1998, he invented the world-leading '98 Standard Wangma' code which was the first encoding system to conform to national language and character standards which could simultaneously handle Chinese, Japanese and Korean, the three languages that use Chinese characters. At the same time, he launched the world's first Chinese-character keyboard input 'comprehensive resolution programme' and its accompanying software, which was a milestone for China in the practical development of

Chinese-character input technology. On 26 June 2004, after five years of research, Wang Yongmin completed the development of a digital Chinese-character input method with five patented elements, starting China's character input digital revolution and fundamentally solving the problem of the difficulty of entering Chinese characters on standard cell phones, telephones and other programmable devices.

Wang Qizhi was born on 26 January 1941. He is a master engineer. His father was the famous Chinese linguist, Wang Li. In 1957 he passed the examinations to go up to Peking University's Department of Mathematics and Mechanics. He graduated in 1963 with a bachelor's degree in mathematics and mechanics. In 1980, he participated in the debugging work on the introduction of the computerised engineering control system for the Wuhan Iron and Steel Corporation's 1.7-metre rolling mill and afterwards was awarded the title of 'Technical Expert' by the project's headquarters. In 1984, he successfully invented a Chinese control system on an Australian-made microcomputer, and his paper on it was selected by the 1983 International Chinese Language News Conference. In April 1986 'the development, application and promotion of the M1570S/SC colour printer Chinese character card" was awarded the Haidian District Technology Progress Gold Medal. In October 1986, his "Chinese-English character printer' took the silver medal at the Second National Invention Exhibition. In September 1987, the 'Sitong MS-2401 Chinese-foreign language character printer' was also awarded the silver medal at the Third National Invention Exhibition. In 1988, he was awarded the honorary title of 'Outstanding Contribution Expert' by the Beijing City Government. In April 1990, his electronic printer external design was awarded a national patent. In June 1991 his 'display method for small screen word-processing equipment' was awarded a national patent. In November 1991, he was honoured with the title 'Outstanding Chinese Private-Ownership Industrialist' conferred by a combination of the National Science and Technology Committee, the All-China Federation of Industry and Commerce, the China Association for Science and Technology, the China Non-Governmental Science Technology Entrepreneurs Association and four other work units. In June 1996, he took his 'method and equipment for inputting target language into computer systems' to the National Patent Office to request a patent and was given an application number. He was a Beijing City Haidian District Member of the Standing Committee of the National People's Congress, a council member of the National Chinese News Association, a council member of the China High-Tech Industry Association, and a council member of the China Privately-Owned Industry Association.

Feng Jun was born in 1969 in Shaanxi. He was one of the first tranche of independent operators in Zhongguancun. In 1992, he graduated from the civil engineering and construction department of Tsinghua University and in 1993 he set up the Beijing Huaqi Information Digital Science & Technology Company, giving it the trade name Aigo in 1997. In 2006 he was honoured with the 'CCTV China Economic and Innovative Person of the Year Award'. He is currently president of the Huaqi Information Group, chairman of the board of the Aigo Group and chairman of the board of Aigo O2O (Beijing) Internet Technology Co Ltd. He is a member of the CPPCC National Committee, and of the China National Democratic Construction Committee, and is a Davos 'World Youth Leader'.

After Feng Jun graduated from Tsinghua University in 1992, he turned his back on a secure career in public service and set out on his dream of setting up business in Zhongguancun, starting out selling computer cases off a flat-bed trike. Thirteen years later, after experiencing many trials and tribulations, he succeeded in turning Aigo into a highly successful national IT brand. Under his leadership, Huaqi Information's turnover achieved a compound annual growth rate (CAGR) of 60% over a 10-year period. Aigo's portable memory devices, MP3 players and display monitors have reliably occupied the top three places on the Chinese market. Outside China, Huaqi Information already has more than 10 subsidiary companies and is advancing across the whole international marketplace, becoming an international brand to make the Chinese people proud! In 2006, he received the CCTV awards for being the China Economic Personality of the Year (group award) and the China Innovator of the Year (individual award). On 24 March 2008 , he was the first person representing Chinese high-tech in the Olympic torch relay, and he was part of the Olympic torch relay in Athens on the day the Beijing Olympics received the sacred flame. In 2009 he was awarded the titles 'Outstanding Contributor to New Ideas in Intellectual Property Rights' and 'Leader of the Year in the Promotion and Celebration of Chinese Brands'. In 2011, he was named in the '2011 10 Great Innovators of the Year' at the China Brand Name Innovation Conference.

. . .

Wang Jiangmin (1951-2010) was founder and president of Beijing Jiangmin Science and Technology Co Ltd (Jiangmin Antivirus Software). He was a famous antivirus expert, a national top-level engineer, a council member of the China Disabled Persons Federation, member of the Shandong Province Yantai City Political Consultative Committee and deputy director general of the Shandong Province Disabled Persons Federation.

Wang Jiangmin was born in Shanghai in 1951. As a result of contracting poliomyelitis at the age of three, he was left disabled in his legs, and life seemed to have dealt him an unplayable hand; after he left middle school, he returned to his family hometown of Yantai in Shandong Province and started work as an apprentice at a well-known neighbourhood factory. He worked hard at self-study and by the time he reached adulthood, he was an expert with more than 20 creations and inventions in the fields of machinery and photo-electric devices. In 1988, he came into contact with computers for the first time and he realised that the automation of opto-electronics was going to have to rely on computerisation. In 1989, he spent more than a thousand Rmb on buying himself a China Educational Computer, and the next year he also bought himself an 8088 PC. The first thing he did was learn BASIC programming language and he worked at developing user-control software. Unfortunately, his customers' computers were often infected with viruses and not operating properly, which made his customers think that his software was no good. It was these circumstances that motivated Wang Jiangmin to find a solution to the virus problem. First of all, he came up with the manual 'Debug' antivirus programme, and then he wrote virus-specific programmes, the first of which operated against the 1741 virus. He developed an excellent way of doing things: as soon as he had come up with a particular anti-virus, he would write an article for the press in which he published the programme. Later, he came to realise that these specific individual anti-virus programmes were a bit of a bother, so he pulled six different ones together and called the result KV6. This was followed by KV8, KV12, KV18, KV20, all the way up to KV3000. At around 10 o'clock in the morning of 4 April 2010, Wang Jiangmin suffered a sudden heart attack. Attempts at resuscitation were unsuccessful and he died at the age of 59.

Wang Zhidong was born in 1967 in Dongguan, Guangdong Province. He is the founder of Sina Corp. In May 1989, he went to work at the Peking University Computer Technology Institute led by Professor Wang Xuan. The most important project there was the 'Chinese multi-window graphics support environment', which passed departmental evaluation in December of the same year. In June 1991, he independently researched and developed the first practical Windows 3.0 Sinification system, the 'Peking University Chinese Windows System' (BDWin 3.0). This was one of Peking University Founder's seven main new products for 1991. After he left Peking University Founder, in April 1992, he founded the 'Xintiandi Electronic Information Technology Research Institute', holding the posts of both deputy general manager and chief engineer. In May 1992, he independently researched and produced the first practical Windows 3.0 Chinese language platform, 'Chinese Star 1.1', and in February of the following year he produced both an overseas version and an upgraded version, 'Chinese Star 1.2'. Chinese Star rapidly gained widespread popularity in China and speeded up practical Chinese computing.

In 1993, Wang Zhidong set up Stone Rich Sight Information Technology Co Ltd. In 1997, by attracting US$6.5 million in venture capital funding, it became the first domestic IT business to attract such funding. In December 1998, he completed a merger with the American company Sinanet to form Sina, where he was the founding executive officer and president. He led Sina to become the first Chinese internet company to be quoted on the American NASDAQ index. In July 1999, Sina climbed to the top of the website rankings announced by the China Internet Information Centre. On 3 December 2001, Wang Zhidong set up Beijing Dianji Science and Technology Co Ltd and concentrated on the three great modern technologies of compatibility software, the internet and communications, in order to develop collaborative software that offered the broad spread of informatised users a practical environment for working together.

Bao Jie was born in Taiyuan, Shanxi Province in 1983. He graduated from the chemistry department of Tsinghua University in 2006 and was awarded a Ph.D by the American Ivy League Brown University in 2010 and went on to do post-doctoral research at MIT. In 2013, he was simultaneously an assistant professor at Brown and visiting professor and chief researcher at the California Institute of Technology. In the same year, he joined the Tsinghua University Department of Electrical Engineering as a Ph.D adviser and was chosen as one of the thousand young talents in the national 'Thousand Talent Plan'. In 2012, he proposed, for the first time on the international stage, a new method for quantum dot micro-spectrometry which could achieve a reduction of several orders of magnitude in both the size and cost of currently existing spectrometers. He published this work in *Nature* magazine as its inventor, creator and promulgator. He was the subject of an eight-minute special report on CCTV's 'Live News' and also of reports in several dozen national and overseas mainstream and specialist science and technology media, including America's NBC and *Nature* magazine. So far, the honours and awards he has received include the 'Young Scientist Award' which is the Ministry of Education's highest award for outstanding school scientific research, the Rao Yutai Foundation Optical Prize, the '2015 National Top 10 Cutting-Edge Scientists and Technologists', the '2015 China Young Scientist of the Year', the 'Zhongguancun 10 Great Innovations' and many others. The company Bao Jie founded has the mission statement "to help China lead the rest of the world into a new world of spectrum informatisation" and to lead its team into the active implementation of the industrialisation of micro-spectrum technology.

Su Lan was born in May 1979 and graduated from Beijing Union University, specialising in electronic information. He is the founder of the Garage Café on Beijing's Entrepreneur Street. He joined ChinaCache in 2006, initially as a salesman. On the basis of the numerous contacts he made in the internet business and his many years' experience of the same, within three months he had signed up the big-name Roxbeam International from which followed several million Rmb of contracts. He quickly became ChinaCache's sales manager and went on to be their head of investment.

In April 2011, Su Lan set up the Garage Café on his own. It is situated on the second floor of a hotel on Haidian District's Book City pedestrian street. It specialises in entrepreneurial services, bringing together all kinds of entrepreneurial communities and services, offering use of the café's free workspaces, incubating early-phase entrepreneurial project teams, employing all three styles of "incubation": practical + theoretical + mobile. Taken altogether it forms an early-phase entrepreneurial platform. Currently, the Garage Café club has 50 'members' with projects involving e-commerce, social networking, computer games, local services and many other areas; 10 of these have already obtained financing, 10 are in the process of merging with other teams, and 50 products have gone online. The Garage Café has initiated a surge in 'coffee entrepreneurship' across the country, like spring bamboo after the rain, and Su Lan himself has received the '2013 Beijing May 5 Youth Award'. In 2015, Su Lan also set up the 'You+' international youth community. This is a community aimed at connecting the lives of modern urban youth, and its business model is to rent accommodation, renovate it and then lease it out to young people. This allows the community to provide even more early-phase entrepreneurial services and allows youngsters to raise their standard of living and their contribution to society.

Wu Gansha was born in 1976 and is from Nantong, Jiangsu Province. He is the founder and CEO of the UISEE Technology Alliance which concentrates on developing the most advanced automated driving technology in order to change the nature of travel across the world. He was formerly director of Intel Research Labs China and was also their first Chief Engineer. He joined Intel in 2000 and worked successively in the programming system laboratory and the embedded software laboratory, simultaneously holding both technology and management positions. Meanwhile, he also participated in special time-limited research projects, XScale microarchitecture, multi-core architecture, data parallel editing, and tools to exploit high productivity equipment embedded device drivers. In 2011 he was promoted to chief engineer and in the same year he published more than 10 academic papers, obtained 25 American patents (more than 10 of which became international patents) and had 14 patents going through the investigation phase.

In 2015, Wu Gansha decided to take a risk. He and four colleagues decided to resign from Intel Labs China and set up on their own in his chosen field of smart driving technology for cars. They established the self-driving car system service company, UISEE. There were two ways of developing smart cars: one was the same as BMW, holding back from anything major for a good while before making one explosive move on a given day. The other was to be like Tesla, and release a 'first edition', let the consumer try it out, then constantly monitor the feedback data to refine the technology. Wu Gansha chose the latter – UISEE would enter the enterprise market, and sell the company's black box stuffed with a huge quantity of calculations, their binocular camera and their solutions to the challenges of driverless vehicles to those driverless vehicle brands that were interested in new technology.

Cheng Wei was born in 1983 in Shangrao, Jiangxi Province. He is CEO and chairman of the board of DiDi Chuxing Technology Co. In 2012, he founded Xiaoji Technology in Zhongguancun and released the DiDi Dache cell phone taxi-hiring software. In February 2015, DiDi Dache and Kuaidi

Dache formed a strategic merger. In September 2015, DiDi DaChe (DiDi Taxi Hire) formally changed its name to DiDi Chuxing (DiDi Travel). In August 2016, DiDi Chuxing bought Uber China, and Cheng Wei joined the board of Uber Worldwide.

After four years of development, DiDi has become the leader in the field of the Chinese mobile internet and one of the most valuable technology start-up companies in the world. From a single piece of taxi-hire software, it has grown into the world's biggest one-stop-shop travel platform, offering a complete travel solution platform to 400 million users which includes services for taxis, private car hire, express cars, free rides, substitute drivers, car hire, test drives and more. The company continues to maintain its premier place in the innovation of mobile internet travel products and in the development of the market, and has been honoured at Davos for its worldwide commercial growth. In 2015, Cheng Wei was chosen to chair the Davos Worldwide Economic Forum; he was named by *Wealth* magazine as one of the 'World's 40 Young Business Heroes'; along with DiDi Chuxing's chairperson, Liu Qing, he was named one of 'China's 10 Economic Personalities of the Year'. In 2016, Cheng Wei was chosen by *Wealth* magazine as its '2016 World Commercial Personality of the Year'.

ENDNOTES

3. THE PULL OF THE FUTURE

1. American sociologist Robert K Merton, whose concept was that: "the self-fulfilling prophecy is, in the beginning, a false definition of the situation evoking a new behaviour, which makes the originally false conception come true."

4. TILTING AT WINDMILLS

1. The myth concerns a foolish 90-year-old man who lived near a pair of mountains (given in some versions as the Taihang and the Wangwu mountains in Yu Province). He was annoyed by the obstruction caused by the mountains and sought to dig through them with hoes and baskets. When questioned as to the seemingly impossible nature of his task, the foolish old man replied that while he may not finish this task in his lifetime, through the hard work of himself, his children and their children, and so on through the generations, some day the mountains would be removed, if they all persevered. The gods in heaven, impressed with his hard work and perseverance, ordered the mountains separated.
2. Jingwei is a bird in Chinese mythology, who was transformed from Yandi's daughter Nüwa. After she drowned when playing in the Eastern Sea, she metamorphosed into a bird called Jingwei. Jingwei was determined to fill up the sea so no one else could drown in it; she continuously carried a pebble or twig in her mouth and dropped it into the Eastern Sea.
3. Bei Dao is the pen name of the Chinese-American writer Zhao Zhenkai. Among the most acclaimed Chinese-language poets of his generation, he has been repeatedly nominated for the Nobel Prize in Literature. In addition to poetry, he is the author of short fiction, essays and a memoir. Known as a dissident, he is a prominent representative of a school of poetry known variously in the West as 'Misty' or 'Obscure' Poetry.

1. LENOVO CHINA (1)

1. The Gongshe Shangshu Incident was the start of a political movement in late Qing-Dynasty China, seeking reforms and expressing opposition to the Treaty of Shimonoseki in 1895. It is considered the first modern political movement in China. Leaders of the movement later became leaders of the Hundred Days' Reform.
2. Kang Youwei was a Chinese philosopher and politician of the late Qing Dynasty. Through his connections, he became close to the young Guangxu Emperor and encouraged the promotion of his friends, souring the relationship between the emperor and the Empress Dowager Cixi. His ideas inspired a reformation movement, the Hundred Days' Reform. He was forced to flee China for repeated attempts to assassinate the Empress Dowager Cixi. He was an ardent Chinese nationalist and internationalist.
3. *Tongzilou* (筒子楼), also referred to as Heluxiaofu Buildings (Khrushchovka Buildings) are a type of housing built in Beijing and in many big cities of China in the 1950s and 1960s. The typical *tongzilou* was a 3-6 story apartment building designed with shared kitchen and bathrooms; in short, the idea was to build a 'mini-commune' in the city to let the families in the building function as a big (not necessarily related) family.

4. The May 7 Cadre Schools were established in the People's Republic of China during the Cultural Revolution. Their function was to train cadres to follow the 'mass line', which was the communist equivalent of the formula, "Of the people, by the people, and for the people. " The principal method of training in these schools was hard manual labour, which had been the Chinese peasants' way of life. It was hoped that through such training, civil servants would be one with the masses.

1. FENG KANG'S PLAN (2)

1. *A Mirror for the Wise Ruler* (or *Comprehensive Mirror for Aid in Government*), is a huge (294 scrolls) chronological general history, written by Sima Guang (1019-1089) and collaborators during the Northern Song in 1084, covering the period 403 BC-959 AD.
2. A biblical reference to the passage in the Sermon on the Mount where Jesus says, "Enter through the narrow gate. For wide is the gate and broad is the road that leads to destruction, and many enter through it. But small is the gate and narrow the road that leads to life, and only a few find it."
3. A literal translation of 牛棚 (*niupeng*) which is a general term for any place where the so-called 'monsters and demons' were confined during the Cultural Revolution.
4. Refers to the violent conflicts between different factions during the Cultural Revolution.

2. MS—2401

1. The May 7th Cadre Schools were Chinese labour camps established during the Cultural Revolution that combined hard agricultural work with the study of Mao Zedong's writings in order to 're-educate' cadres and intellectuals in proper socialist thought.
2. *Guo Biao* refers to the Chinese national standards issued by the Standardisation Administration of China.
3. *Hanyu Pinyin* is the official romanisation system of the PRC.
4. A verse form consisting of 8 lines of 7 syllables, with rhymes on alternate lines.

3. THOUSAND YEARS

1. During public 'criticism' and 'struggle' sessions in the Cultural Revolution, the objects of the criticism were often made to wear paper dunce's caps with the nature of their offences written on them.
2. Bi Sheng (972–1051 CE) was a Chinese artisan and inventor of the world's first movable type technology.
3. A period of the Cultural Revolution when Red Guards took public transportation for free across the country to exchange revolutionary ideas.
4. Louis Cha Leung-yung GBM OBE, better known by his pen name Jin Yong, pronounced 'Gam Yoong' in Cantonese, was a Chinese *wuxia* novelist and essayist who co-founded the Hong Kong daily newspaper *Ming Pao* in 1959 and served as its first editor-in-chief. He was Hong Kong's most famous writer. Yang Guo and Little Dragon Maiden are the fictional protagonists of his novel *The Return of the Condor Heroes*. In the novel, Little Dragon Maiden is Yang Guo's lover and martial arts master.
5. Bi Sheng invented the world's first movable type technology (1039-1048) during the Song Dynasty to facilitate the first-ever printing machines.
6. The Sino-Soviet border conflict was a seven-month undeclared military conflict between the Soviet Union and China at the height of the Sino-Soviet split in 1969.
7. During the Cultural Revolution, the Black Five factions were landowners, the wealthy, counter-revolutionaries, bad elements and rightists.

8. Mencius wrote: "When Heaven is about to place a great responsibility on a great man, it always first frustrates his spirit and will, exhausts his muscles and bones, exposes him to starvation and poverty, and harasses him with troubles and setbacks so as to stimulate his spirit, toughen his nature and enhance his abilities.
9. This refers to one of Mao Zedong's last actions in which he attempted to stem the growing influence of Deng Xiaoping and his liberal economic policies. Mao named Deng as the country's foremost 'rightist' and ordered him to write self-criticisms.
10. See previous footnote about the Tiananmen Incident of April 1976.
11. The Jiusan Society is one of the eight legally recognised minor political parties in the PRC that follow the direction of the CPC and are members of the CPPCC.

1. LENOVO CHINA (2)

1. An area in Beijing which used to be famous for street artists, performers and street peddlers.
2. So fundamental was this 'associative connection' technology to Lenovo that these two Chinese characters – 联想 *lianxiang* – comprise Lenovo's Chinese name – 联想集团有限公司 - Lenovo Group Co Ltd.
3. Reference to a famous episode in the *Romance of Three Kingdoms* in which Liu Bei recruits Zhuge Liang to his cause by visiting him three times in the thatched cottage to which he had retired.

2. WANGMA

1. Chinese characters generally comprise two components, a radical and a phonetic. In the Simplified Character System there are 214 radicals which indicate the fundamental category of meaning of the character. The term phonetic is misleading, as they no longer give any accurate indication of sound or pronunciation, although they did in the early stages of character development.

3. FENG WUKUAI

1. Urban villages are villages that appear on both the outskirts and the downtown segments of major Chinese cities; they are commonly inhabited by the poor and transient, and as such they are associated with squalor, overcrowding and social problems. However, they are also among the liveliest areas in some cities and are notable for affording economic opportunity to newcomers to the city.

1. FENG KANG'S PLAN (3)

1. See above for Jin Yong. Gu Long (1938-85) was a Taiwanese author of *wuxia* (martial arts) novels and a screenwriter. He was heavily influenced by Western writers such as Ernest Hemingway, Jack London, John Steinbeck and Friedrich Nietzsche, whereas Jin Yong primarily incorporated elements of traditional Chinese history, literature and philosophy.
2. A character in Gu Long's Lu Xiaofeng series of novels. He appears as a cold-blooded, unfeeling and ruthless killer to others but he is willing to help Lu Xiaofeng whenever Lu asks for his assistance. He was played by Christopher Lee in a TV series based on the Lu Xiaofeng novels.
3. Xuanzang was the Tang Dynasty Buddhist monk who made a 17-year pilgrimage to India to bring back Buddhist scriptures. Along with Sun Wukong, the Monkey King, he is the central character of the famous Ming Dynasty novel *Journey to the West*. The Leiyin Temple

is situated near Dunhuang in Gansu Province and was an important stopping point on the Silk Road.
4. Ye Duzheng (1916-2013) was a meteorologist and academician at the Chinese Academy of Sciences.

1. LENOVO CHINA (3)

1. Reference to a poem by Tang Dynasty poet Du Fu: *Traveller's Rest / That temple, I've been there before / And I recognise this bridge now I cross it / The landscape seems to be expecting me: / The trees and flowers are idle bystanders / The fields glisten in a thin bright mist / And the sandy riverbank basks in late sunlight / My traveller's ennui declines / As I have found the perfect spot to spend the night.*
2. An excerpt from a poem by 20th century Chinese poet and author Lu Xun, "When we have experienced many troubles, the relationship between us still exists. At the time of meeting again, we forget the past betrayal and revenge with a laugh."
3. Mount Hua and Mount Tai are two of the five great sacred mountains of China. Mount Hua is known for the challenging steepness of its slopes and Mount Tai represents steadiness and stability.

2. KV300

1. *Qinggong* is a technique in Chinese martial arts that is visually reminiscent of parkour. The use of *qinggong* has been exaggerated in *wuxia* fiction and movies, in which martial artists have the ability to move swiftly and lightly at superhuman speed, and perform gravity-defying moves such as gliding on water surfaces, scaling high walls and mounting trees.
2. Another reference to Jin Yong's *wuxia* novel *The Legend of the Condor Heroes*.
3. Wen Rui'an, also called Woon Swee Oan, is a Hong Kong-based Malaysian Chinese poet and writer of *wuxia* novels.
4. A mythical martial arts text from another Jin Yong *wuxia* novel, *The Smiling Proud Wanderer*.

3. INTERNET

1. The Chinese family name 王 *wang* is the character for 'king'.
2. Beijing University – *Beijing Daxue* (北京大学) in Chinese – is normally shortened to *BeiDa*, hence the initials BD in BDWin.
3. Ximen Chuixue, surname Ximen (literally West Gate), first name Chuixue (literally Snow Blower), one of the characters in the *Legend of Lu Xiaofeng* series of Gulong martial arts novels , a close friend of Lu Xiaofeng, usually clad in white, his face is cold and withdrawn. Ruthless and god-like, his sword technique is not visible to the human eye.
4. China's first internet service provider. In October 1996, ZTE Corp took a stake in Yinghaiwei, increasing Yinghaiwei's registered capital to Rmb80 million. In February 1997, Yinghaiwei opened its national network with eight city branches coming on stream within three months.

2. FINGERPRINTS OF ALL CREATION

1. Black coal pits are illegal industrial enterprises run on slave labour.
2. *Thick Black Theory* is a philosophical treatise written by Li Zongwu (1879–1943), a disgruntled politician and scholar. It was published in China in 1911 when the Qing dynasty was

overthrown. Li was a scientist of political intrigue. He wrote: "When you conceal your will from others, that is Thick. When you impose your will on others, that is Black (Dark)."

3. GARAGE CAFÉ

1. The Chinese parasol tree (*Paulownia imperialis*) is said to be the only tree on which the phoenix will perch.
2. His real name is Guo Hongcai; Er Bao (二宝) means second-born (the literal meaning of Bao is treasure or precious) and is a common nickname used in China for a second-born child.
3. Cao Cao, whose courtesy name was Mengde, was a Chinese warlord, statesman and poet. He was the penultimate grand chancellor of the Eastern Han Dynasty who rose to great power in the final years of the dynasty.
4. A 1984 film directed by Xie Tian and based on a novel by Lao She. It follows the fortunes of a Beijing teahouse from the Boxer Rebellion to the founding of the PRC.

4. SHARING OR ENJOYING TOGETHER

1. Badachu, which means 'Eight Great Sites', is a complex of monasteries located on the outskirts of urban Beijing. The name refers to the eight Buddhist temples and nunneries scattered across the Shijingshan District, at the foot of Beijing's Western Hills.
2. The distinction between these two is that with 'express hire', the customer has no say in the type of vehicle whereas with 'private hire', which is more expensive, they can specify a higher-grade vehicle.
3. Hainan Airlines Group that boasts Warren Buffet as a long-term investor.

ABOUT THE AUTHOR

Ning Ken, born in Beijing in 1959, is a visiting professor at Beijing Second Foreign Language Institute. He was the executive deputy editor of *October* and is now a professional writer at the Lao She Literary Institute in Beijing. His major works include *The Collected Works of Ning Ken* (eight volumes,) including the full-length novels *Heaven-Tibet, The Masked City, Three Trios, The Ringed Mountain,* and *The Gate of Silence,* the essay collections *Beijing: The City and the Year, My Twentieth Century,* and the non-fiction *Zhongguancun Notes.* He has been nominated for the Lao She Literary Award, the first Shi Nai'an Literary Award, the seventh Lu Xun Literary Award, the 2014 Asia Weekly Top Ten Novels, the 2017 China Good Book Award, the first Hong Kong Dream of the Red Chamber Award, and the U.S. Newman Literary Award. His works have been translated into Czech, English, French, and Italian.

ABOUT THE TRANSLATOR

James Trapp has published China-related books on language, astrology, science and technology. His translation works include new versions of *The Art of War* and *The Daodejing*. He has also translated several titles with Sinoist Books including *Longevity Park, Final Witness: The Story of Song Ci China's First Crime Scene Investigator, Shadow of the Hunter, Open-Air Cinema: Reminiscences and Micro-Essays from the author of Raise the Red Lantern*, and *The Elm Tree* series. Much of his work revolves around integrating the study of Chinese language and culture, and breaking down barriers of cultural misunderstanding that still persist.